The Informed Writer

Using Sources in the Disciplines

Second Edition

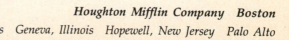

Charles Bazerman

Baruch College City University of New York

Houghton Mifflin Company   Boston

Dallas   Geneva, Illinois   Hopewell, New Jersey   Palo Alto

The following permissions acknowledgments are made to publishers and authors:

Chapter 1: Excerpts from pp. xii–xiii "Going to the field . . . makes the material come alive for me." in *A Way of Seeing* by Margaret Mead and Rhoda Metraux. Copyright © 1970 by Margaret Mead and Rhoda Metraux. By permission of William Morrow & Company.

Chapter 2: From Samuel Clemens, *Selected Mark Twain-Howells Letters* (Cambridge, Mass: Harvard University Press, 1967), pp. 130–131. Copyright © 1960, 1967 by the Mark Twain Company. Reprinted by permission. Taken from *The Annotated Mother Goose* by William S. & Ceil Baring-Gould. Copyright © 1962 by William S. & Ceil Baring-Gould. Used by permission of Clarkson N. Potter, Inc. From Cicero, *On Old Age and On Friendship* (trans. Frank O. Copley), pp. 55–56. Copyright © 1967 by the University of Michigan Press. Used by permission. Three journal entries ("June 23," "October 26," and "May 11") from *Working and Thinking on the Waterfront* by Eric Hoffer. Copyright © 1969 by Eric Hoffer. Reprinted by permission of Harper & Row, Publishers, Inc.

(continued on page 517)

Cover photograph: Skolos, Wedell, Raynor

Printed in the U.S.A.

Library of Congress Catalog Card Number: 84–82364

ISBN: 0–395–35499–4

ABCDEFGHIJ-VB-8987654

Contents

Part 2   Writing Using Reading   199

Part 3 *Writing in Disciplines*   327

To the Teacher

This is a book about reading and writing—complementary elements in the learning and use of written language. Reading provides not only a model and a provocation to write but also the very occasion and situation for most writing. Without a sense of continuity between statements, between reading and writing, students can learn only to create voices calling, and being lost, in the wilderness.

The Informed Writer deals with writing in social contexts, for every piece of writing is a form of social action, whether its purpose is to persuade holders of different views, to propose the construction of a bridge, to justify the return of a shipment of paperclips, or to lay out and order one's thoughts for personal inspection. Writing makes things happen in the social world, and much of that social world is embodied in previous pieces of writing. Writers need to be able to understand and assess the social situation and then shape writing as an effective response within that context.

Students constantly read books, reproduce the books' contents, and respond to, interpret, and evaluate the meaning of their reading. They must make the old new again, and the tasks they must perform are precisely those covered in this book: close and analytical reading, summary, synthesis, response to reading, interpretation and analysis, book reviews, reviews of literature, and research papers.

This book introduces students to writing in the various disciplines by exploring the underlying issues that make for commonalities and differences. The different methods of developing and presenting statements are portrayed as evolving attempts to carry on the particular discipline's work of creating knowledge. By understanding the purpose of the procedures and formats of writing in the different disciplines, students can approach disciplinary writing with confidence and independent creativity while still respecting the communal objectives. This approach teaches students to command the forms of disciplinary writing, rather than simply follow them.

This book encourages creativity and originality in writing. Uninformed writing is usually a derivative, unthinking reflection of cultural and social forces of which the writer is unaware. Informed writing develops the mind against the background of what others have said.

Several marked changes distinguish this edition of *The Informed Writer* from the previous one.

A new first chapter introduces students to a basic way of thinking about writing as problem solving. Procedures for analyzing writing situations and writing problems help students discover purposes and strategies. By seeing their writing as purposeful within a context, students can focus their ideas and invent means to fulfill their purposes, to solve the writing problem.

In a major substantive and structural change, a new five-chapter unit (Part 3), "Writing in the Disciplines," introduces students to the uniformities and differences of developing and presenting arguments in the range of academic disciplines. Because what appears in a disciplinary essay results to a large extent from the process of formulating ideas, designing research, and gathering and analyzing data, methodology is discussed throughout this book as a set of prewriting procedures, to be controlled and varied depending on the disciplinary setting, the questions to be investigated, and the tools available. These methodological procedures are at every step tied to the process of writing and the final form of the writing. Examples and exercises from a range of disciplines, historical to theoretical, help students see how research interests become realized during the writing process.

In a final structural change, students are introduced to the concepts and informal methods of response before they are drawn into the detailed examination of texts through paraphrase and summary. By expressing their reactions to texts immediately, students will gain a fuller sense of themselves in relation to the text; and the deeper understanding of texts achieved by means of paraphrase and summary exercises will be enlivened by the deeper responses evoked in the students. Students will find that as they understand texts more deeply, they will have more to say in response to them.

Many other changes, expansions, clarifications, and additions (such as the material on use of computer-assisted bibliographic searches) appear throughout this edition. I have changed many examples and exercises, keeping those that have worked best and adding others that I hope will work even better. Finally, the documentation instruction is in keeping with the recent change in Modern Language Association policy. The MLA parenthetic style is explained in detail and used in the sample research paper. Because the MLA still recognizes (though does not encourage) endnoting, procedures, formats, and some examples for endnotes remain, following the latest MLA revisions. American Psychological Association documentation procedures are also presented and illustrated.

With this new edition, my debts have been compounded. The wealth I have now taken from my friends is too great to account, but I would like to add the following to the roll call of the previous edition: Ed Davenport and Charles Piltch of John Jay College, Greg Myers and Les Faigley of the University of Texas at Austin, Susan Miller of the University of Utah, Don McCloskey of the University of Iowa, and Edwin Thumboo of the National University of Singapore.

For their thoughtful suggestions toward the development of this revision, I am grateful to Jay Balderson and Paul Cioe, Western Illinois University; James Crosswhite and Brooke Neilson, University of California at San Diego; Susan McLeod, San Diego State University; Nancy Moore, University of Iowa; Virginia Sullivan, SUNY at Farmingdale; Connie Sutherland, Northeast Missouri State; Carol Slade, Columbia University; Rita Sturm, Albuquerque; and Michael Vivion, University of Missouri.

Shirley Geok-lin Lim, my spouse and colleague, deserves my continuing gratitude for her patience with the domestic tedium engendered by such projects as this.

Checklist of Readings

This list notes the major readings (either substantial excerpts or full-length essays) in the text. Essays by student writers are indicated with an asterisk (*). Numerous shorter extracts are found throughout the text; they are noted in the general index that begins on page 508.

1 Writing About Reading

1 Writing

Writing involves other people. You respond to and build on other people's statements; you then write for other people to read. As a reader and a writer, you converse with others over the written page. To converse effectively you need to know what is on other people's minds, how you want to affect other people, and how you plan to achieve that effect. Thus writing well requires that you understand the writing situation, grasp the particular writing problem, and carefully plan your writing strategy.

The Writing Situation

A Writer Is Never Alone

Although a writer seems to work in private, writing communicates between minds. Without other people to share our thoughts and experiences, to be affected and influenced, we would have little reason to write. We write letters to share our lives with friends; we write business reports to influence the decisions of other managers; we write essays to convert others to our vision of the truth.

Just as we wish to touch other people's minds through writing, our own minds have been deeply influenced by the writing of others. Will Rogers's famous quip, "All I know is what I read in the newspapers," has great truth. Most of what we learn about the world—events in the distant past or in distant countries, the collisions of subatomic particles or of corporate finance, the secrets of the beginnings of the world or of another person's mind—is filtered through written communication. Even when we learn things directly, we perceive and interpret that experience through attitudes influenced by the words of others. Through language we take part in an exchange that both draws our minds together through shared ideas and defines the differences among us through disagreements.

The Written Conversation

Imagine this: your political science professor asks you to write your opinion of a disagreement between Congress and the president over a proposed new energy law. If you know the facts and have a strong opinion—you don't want energy to be squandered as in the past or you object to oil drilling that will threaten wildlife—you sit down at the typewriter and pound out the required number of words. You sit back in relief and look at your work with some pride. There it is, an original paper written entirely from your own mind. Or is it entirely from your own mind?

Of course, you had to learn the basic facts on the subject from somewhere—perhaps from newspapers or television. Persuasive editorials may have influenced you or made you react strongly against the proposed law. A bit more deeply in the background are ideas you have read or have heard about this particular president and his relations with Congress. Even further back are high school teachers and textbooks explaining the structure and history of our government. You relied on all these resources before you even began writing.

Then, as you wrote, you could not forget the professor's lectures and assigned readings. That material helped you become more informed and thoughtful; now you have a chance to present your matured, informed opinion. All semester the professor has been holding forth; now it is your turn. The professor's views may suggest specific issues you want to discuss and get a reaction to. At the very least, you probably want the professor's approval for doing competent work, so you need to keep his or her standards in mind.

When you write, your statements are your own. You choose the words and organize the thoughts. But you use those words because you share a common vocabulary with your readers. And your thoughts began elsewhere—with things you read, heard, or experienced. A social scientist might say that your statements are socially imbedded; that is, your words are surrounded and conditioned by the acts, words, and attitudes of the many people who form your social context.

This social context also establishes the specific writing situation that helps define any writing task. You sit down to write at one moment in time for particular purposes, which are usually related to the people around you. Your teacher assigns you an essay. A company advertises a job you want. An unusual experience, an encouraging teacher, or a moving poem inspires you to write your own poem.

Think of a conversation. In a spoken conversation it is essential to pay attention to what has just been said and to the person you are addressing. Even when arguing for your original ideas, you are attempting to convince people directly in front of you. To make other people feel you are talking *with* them and not *at* them, you must listen to the facts, ideas, and emotions that they express in order to know what kinds of answers they will understand and accept.

As you react to others in spoken conversation, so you do in written conversation. The more you understand and assimilate what others have said before, the more you understand the context of the "conversation" in which you are participating. If you have a sense of the people to whom you are writing, you can then decide how you wish to affect them and what you should write.

Reading and writing go hand in hand. The better you read, the better you write. In order to develop your own thoughts, you need to be able to gather information from reading; even more, you need to understand the ideas and implications of your reading so that you can respond. You have to read well enough to see what people are really discussing, what the real issues are. You need to understand what has already been written to decide intelligently what you can contribute. Otherwise, you may simply wind up only repeating what others have already written.

This book explains the skills of digging more deeply into your reading and then using that reading to develop your own original statements. The assignments in this book give you practice in gaining control over the knowledge you are acquiring in all your courses and reading, so that knowledge can help you formulate and express your own thoughts. Writing assignments will help you read more deeply and precisely, respond to and think about what you read, and analyze and evaluate it. They will help you develop your own conclusions and ideas based on research. At the end of this course, you should be better able to take part in all the written "conversations" that will come your way in school, in your career, and in other facets of your life.

Written Versus Spoken Conversation

To envision all the people who form the context of a written conversation taxes the imagination. Although the participants in a spoken conversation are limited to those in hearing distance, the participants in a written conversation include all those whose words you have read or heard on the subject and all those who are likely to pick up and read what you have written. Fortunately, the immediate conversational context for most writing is limited to a few persons. A student writing an assigned paper in a philosophy course may be responding only to a few authors she has read as part of the course and to the lectures of the professor; her readers will be that same professor and perhaps a classmate or roommate. A biochemist, although ultimately relying on all those teachers and writers of scientific works who contributed to her training, may base her immediate work on the findings of only a few colleagues, and she may address her highly technical conclusions to only a few specialists. The biochemist may feel the need to address a wider audience only if she discovers something that has broad social implications, like an insight into the growth of cancer cells. And she would need to reevaluate the basic literature of biochemistry only if her findings call into question fundamental principles she has learned earlier.

Or consider again that philosophy student, whose case is typical of most students in most disciplines: the range of sources she would have to ponder for much of her education would be limited to the books assigned or recommended by her teachers. A research paper or personal curiosity may lead her to look at other sources, but only near the end of her academic training would she regularly work with less generally familiar material. And only at that late point would the audience for her work move beyond the classroom. Thus the academic context—in which most readers of this book find themselves—readily defines the participants of most written conversations. The writers to whom we are responding are those who contributed the recognized major works of any discipline, and our readers are those who regularly help evaluate student papers—the professor, graduate assistants, and class members.

In addition to the difference in participants, there are further differences between written and spoken conversation. In writing, the words alone must carry the entire message; when you write, you cannot rely on tone of voice, pitch, pauses, facial expressions, or gestures to pick up where words leave off. Nor can you keep an eye on your audience to see if a baffled face, wandering attention, or an angry look suggests you change what you are saying. The reader cannot stop you, ask you questions, raise objections, or demand clarification. Writing must stand intelligible, complete, and convincing in itself.

Because your audience is not there to interrupt you as you write, you can think through your ideas fully, and you can find the best way to state them. When speaking, you must reply on the spot with whatever thoughts come immediately to mind. In talking, in fact, you may be more concerned with keeping the conversation going in a pleasant way than with logic, consistency, or truth; one topic leads to another with only the loosest connection, and a topic rarely remains stable for long. Because speech goes by so fast, you may get away with many careless, unconsidered, and even irrelevant comments. You may not always speak to the point—nor do you always care whether you are making a substantive point. In the process of writing, you have time to consider, develop, and sharpen every statement. When you get stuck, you can take a long pause, go out for coffee, and then pick up where you left off. If words wander, you can later edit out the digression. When revising, you can satisfy yourself that the argument is coherent and fully developed, and you can polish the words before any reader sees them. Similarly, when the reader finally does get your writing, that reader can go through it slowly, evaluating everything that is there—or is not there. The conversation committed to paper slows down, grows thoughtful, and becomes more careful.

Who Participates?

The best way to get a feel for any conversation—oral or written—is to listen in for a while before you make your own comments. In that way you come to know the participants, the issues, the level of the conversation, the typical ways of speaking, and the rules of proof and evidence being used. The more you listen, the more likely you are to have ideas you want to contribute, and the more likely you are to phrase the ideas in ways that will fit the conversation.

In the course of her long and varied life, the anthropologist Margaret Mead communicated with many different groups, from Samoan tribespeople to international political leaders. She advanced knowledge among the specialists of her field, and she shared that knowledge with the general public. Despite her reputation as a major authority, she always considered her writing as a process of interaction that improved with conversation with her readers. Only by remaining in touch with their ideas and needs could she know how best to keep up her end of the conversation. Here she tells how the interchange between herself and the readers of her magazine column motivated her to continue the discussion. Contact with the lives and concerns of real people gave life to her own writing. The following comments appeared in the preface to a collection of columns she originally wrote for *Redbook*, a popular magazine:

> Going to the field, anthropologists expect to—hope to—struggle with new questions of how to make sense of an unfamiliar mode of living. Past experience provides a framework for thinking about what is strange; but the new experience also sheds a different light on what is already familiar.
>
> Thinking about American culture as I meet with different audiences also has this kind of challenge for me. With every new question proposed to me by a particular audience, my memory takes me back to some experience in field work—to an early morning in Samoa forty years ago, to the market in a Balinese village twenty-five years ago, to Peri Village, in the Admiralty Islands, in 1928, when it seemed to me that only misery lay ahead for the proud Manus people, and to my visits to Peri in the past ten years, when Manus leaders have sat talking with me about their children's modern careers and the future of all the peoples of New Guinea.
>
> These are the experiences on which I draw, and each new audience, concerned with a different problem, refocuses my thinking about the past and the present. But the vividness of field experience also enters into my awareness of an audience. I remember very vividly my first radio broadcast. It was in Australia. As I tried to focus words flung out into a void, I suddenly visualized mothers all over the country bathing and feeding their children, hustling them into their night

clothes and tucking them into bed, while they half-listened to my talk. In order to speak to them, I found that I had to take into account all the other things the listening mothers must be doing at that hour.

I could see these mothers in my imagination, but I could not know how they responded to what I said. Today all this is changed. I can sit in New York and, using my own telephone, give a telelecture to students on seven different college campuses. At the end, each group of students can ask questions, so that we are all drawn together in our give and take. Or a lecture may be put on video tape. Then I can sit with the listening audience and participate in their responses. Over the years the audience has become far more a part of what is being said. The lecture and the monologue have become dialogues.

In much the same way these essays are a product of initiation and response. Readers send in questions, argue points, agree or explode in furious disagreements, and from all this we learn. There are also the occasions on which we have talked with a few of them as a group. Once on the anniversary of Hiroshima a group of young wives and mothers came together to discuss what they are doing and what they were telling their children about war and peace. On another occasion a group met with us to talk about their marriages and their hopes for their children's future. And as I go about the country giving lectures, there are very often young people in the audiences who identify themselves as readers by their comments on one or another of the *Redbook* columns. Later, when the next column is in the making, I remember what they have said. All this is what makes the material come alive for me.

Margaret Mead, as she describes here, writes to help individual people. To do that she must interact closely with them to understand their problems and to improve her relationship with them. Just as people must work at personal relationships to make them successful, writers must work at the relationships they establish with their readers.

Informed Writing in School

The writing relationship you probably know best is the one between you and your teachers. The teacher selects material to discuss with you, gives you books to read, and assigns writing for you to do. You in turn write papers for the teacher to read; the teacher returns those papers with corrections, comments, and grades. The comments may then lead you to write differently in the future.

As you learned more and advanced to higher grades, you were

able to write more developed papers on more complex subjects. At the same time the attitudes and expectations of the teachers became more demanding. Remember those first times you had to write by yourself in school, perhaps about a class trip to the zoo or your pet turtle. The teacher probably discussed the topic with you beforehand and then read and praised that youthful literary effort. A sympathetic teacher was encouraging you to express yourself, and proud parents were looking for early signs of ability. Almost any faltering attempt would satisfy that group of readers and lead you into the next stage of the written conversation—more complicated papers.

Now consider the last essay you wrote for one of your college teachers. How much guidance and encouragement were you given beforehand? What level of knowledge and skills was necessary to prepare the assignment? And with what attitude do you think the teacher read the essay—with willingness to accept any attempt or with a demand for a high level of performance? Although both the second-grade theme and the college essays are in the context of the teacher-student relationship, there is a whole education of difference between the two.

As your education and interests become more specialized, your writing will increasingly depend on your being informed by the knowledge of your specialized field. Your teachers and fellow students will come to expect that you are basing your statements and judgments on your ever-increasing body of knowledge, on things you have read and learned.

Informed Writing on the Job

If your career takes you into nonacademic professions and business, your decisions will still depend on wide, informed, reasoned knowledge. You will still have to argue, support, and report in writing. To be persuasive and command respect, your writing must exhibit quality of thought and effective use of the appropriate knowledge. In order to write memos, letters, and reports, business executives need to know the facts of the situation as well as the background economic, administrative, and technical information. In writing legal briefs, lawyers must discuss laws and their interpretation, judicial decisions, administrative rulings, contracts, documents entered into evidence, and the arguments of the opposition. Engineers must prepare reports relying on their technical knowledge and their knowledge of similar designs to present, argue for, and report on the progress of their plans; and they must take into account the voluminous information about each project presented in the reports of other engineers.

Even responsible involvement in community affairs requires that you first become informed. To fight the building of a shopping center behind your house, you may need to read (in addition to the local newspapers) the rulings and reports of the community planning board, the proposal of the developers, the local zoning laws, and reports of construction and environmental engineers. Only then will you be able to write effective petitions, letters, pamphlets, and speeches that might have some effect on the issue.

Throughout your life, you will be participating in increasingly informed conversations, and you will be called upon in many ways to express your informed opinion. As the old adage says, knowledge may be power—but the power will be useful only if you can harness it to serve your own purposes. This book is about learning to control that power.

Writing Assignment

Write a short essay of perhaps three hundred words, discussing either (1) your changing relationship with the readers of your school writing as you moved from first grade to college *or* (2) one particular relationship with a reader of your writing, either in school or out. In either case you should consider who the reader or readers were, what you knew about them, how you knew this information, and what you tried to do in your writing as a result of knowing your reader. You may also consider whether the readers had any favorable attitudes toward your work, what kinds of reactions the readers had to your writing, and whether you changed your approach to writing in response.

Try to support your generalizations with as many specific details as possible. Before writing the essay, try to remember details such as individual assignments and pieces of writing, and choose those details that you think will be of interest to the reader. If possible, include comments made on your earlier papers by teachers.

Consider this essay as part of a written response to this chapter. The audience will be your classmates, who have been considering the same issues, but from their own experiences and perspectives.

The Writing Problem

The Real Problem

Many think filling the blank page is the main problem of writing. If you think that, you start to solve the problem by looking for a good opening sentence. Perhaps other page fillers will continue flowing. There is a small truth to this, but only a very small truth. Such thinking misses the real problem, which is knowing why you are writing—that is, *knowing what you wish to accomplish in that particular writing situation.* Once you know the why, the how and the what will follow.

Let us step back for a minute to think about the idea of a problem. On the one hand, a problem can be something gone wrong, as in "There is a problem with my car. It won't run." Many people think of writing in just that way. "My life will be miserable until I get this paper written, but I don't know what to write. That's my problem." When you think of a problem as an obstacle or unpleasant condition, all you want to do is get rid of it quickly so life can get back to normal. On the other hand, a problem can be seen not as something wrong, but as something to do. An engineering problem is not something wrong; it is only something to think about and solve. "The problem was to design a car combining low gas consumption and low pollution with adequate power and enough luxury to keep the consumers happy." Nothing is wrong; life would go on without such a car, but solving the problem would provide us with something good that we would not otherwise have. That is really what writing is all about: making words do something for us that we would like done.

The first type of problem points to a breakdown in the current situation which needs to be repaired, whereas the second is creative, bringing something new into the world. In thinking of the first kind of problem, you do not have to think deeply about what you wish to do—only get things back to normal. Thinking about the second kind of problem, however, requires you to imagine some kind of future situation that will embody your goals. Then you can decide on the best course of action to reach those goals. *Understanding your problem will suggest a solution, because your well-defined goals will help you choose among the various tools and techniques available.*

Consider, for example, the problem of having no money. Approaching that problem in the first way may tempt you simply to rob a bank, because, as the notorious bank robber Willie Sutton said, "that's where the money is." Although a quick trip with a machine gun to the corner financial institution may temporarily end the hollow sound in your purse, the total consequences for your lifestyle may not be what you bargained for—on the lam or in the slam.

But if you think of the problem in the second way, you may start to reformulate it in the following manner: "What I want is for someone to give me some money. My parents might, except that, since I became an art major, they think I have been wasting my time and their money. So I can't just ask them straight out. I need to make them happier with me, perhaps in a letter. So now it's a writing problem. In this letter I could describe all the useful things I have been learning and how I had to drop my part-time job in order to study more. I guess I have to sound very serious and earnest. . . ." Although the student is still far from putting pen to paper, what will eventually appear in the letter is starting to emerge. Even the style and tone of the letter are dictated by the analysis of the problem. Perhaps the analysis might even suggest some research to make the letter convincing—such as the cost of studio supplies for the commercial art course that might lead to a paying job.

Analyzing Writing Problems

In analyzing a writing problem, you need to answer the following questions:

1. *What do you ultimately wish to accomplish?* Do you want to sell a product, or argue for a theory, or share an experience?

2. *Whom do you intend to address in this piece of writing?* Are you writing to a single distinct person with known expectations, interests, and criteria, such as a teacher who wants to evaluate your knowledge of a subject or a boss who wants specific information to help her make a decision? Are you writing to a larger but definable group united by shared experiences, interests, or institutional arrangements, such as members of your class or all dungeons and dragons fanatics? Or are you writing for a more open-ended audience, such as readers of a general-circulation magazine?

3. *What is your relationship to this audience?* Do you already have its confidence or must you prove your authority? Are you in a

position to lay down the law or are you lucky if anyone even reads your words? Will readers be sympathetic or critical?

4. *What effect do you intend to have on these specific readers, and what actions do you want them to take as a result of reading your writing?* Do you want the teacher to respect your thinking or to put an A on the paper? Or both? Do you want your colleague to think about a question or to accept your answer? Do you want somebody to vote for your candidate or do you want that somebody to change political philosophies?

5. *What kind of strategy is likely to lead to the desired effect in your particular audience?* In order for the boss to feel that you have helped her make a decision, should you provide many statistics, briefly present only your conclusions, or echo her own opinions? On the other hand, if you wish to dissuade her from what you consider an ill-advised policy, what kind of argument or information might be most persuasive?

Writing Assignments

1. Think of a recent situation outside of school when you wrote something: a personal letter, a short memo for your job, or even just a shopping list. In one or two paragraphs, analyze the writing problem you were responding to by using the list of problem-defining questions on pages 12–13.
2. Using the questions on pages 12–13, in one or two paragraphs analyze the writing problem posed by a recent school assignment, preferably one you are still working on.

The Writing Strategy

After you have analyzed the problem, you will have a general strategy for achieving the desired effect within the given social context. The strategy will suggest the kind of document you want finally to emerge, although the content will still need to be developed and the details of language will still need to be worked out. The actual writing then becomes a more limited task of choosing and realizing the techniques that will achieve your purpose. (In Chapter 6 you will be looking at this process from the opposite direction. There, instead of analyzing what you—the writer—want to do to a reader, you will analyze what another writer is trying to do to you—the reader.)

To turn the general strategy into a plan of action, you must decide how to find and develop the detailed substance of the paper. Will you need to read some background documents, collect statistics, or talk to some consumers in order to come to conclusions or develop supporting evidence? Will you need to analyze government economic statistics or design an experiment or think through a philosophic question? In this process of discovering ideas and information, you may learn many new things and come to new conclusions. You may even start to see your writing situation and problem in a new light and consequently need to reevaluate your strategy.

Then, when you are ready to put the ideas and information together, you must decide on the best way to organize the material, the appropriate level of language, and the tone you are going to adopt. That is, you must decide on some general questions of policy for the paper. These policy decisions may again lead you to new realizations about your material and purposes. As you start to visualize how your writing will fit together, you may see weaknesses or power in your argument that you had never imagined. By this point you have made so many decisions that a general picture of the kind of paper you want to write will emerge. You will know how you want to fill the blank page.

Repeated Situations, Cookbook Strategies, and Originality

Much of this book is devoted to suggesting specific strategies, procedures, and even patterns of organization for writing assignments. In each chapter, the purpose of each assignment, the general strategy for approaching each problem, the steps for preparing the material, and the formats for the completed assignment are all laid out in detail so you can complete the assignment—almost as though you were following the recipe in a cookbook. Such fixed analyses of specific writing problems are possible, not because writing must always follow the same pattern, but because many writing situations arise again and again. That is, many basic elements of the writing problem repeat, so similar solutions are possible. Many business situations, such as ordering parts from a supplier, are so repetitive that a single form letter can be used time after time with only a few names and numbers changed to meet the specific circumstance.

The assignments in this book probably bear some similarity to writing you may have done in previous writing courses. After all, the school situation inevitably defines much about writing in writing courses. Thus these assignments rely on much you have learned earlier, such as the importance of the thesis statement, organization, coherence, and development through the use of detail. But because the assignments here are probably more specific than you may be used to, these principles of writing are presented as parts of detailed formats rather than as general rules. Similarly, the concepts and skills of the writing process also run throughout this book, but as parts of specific instructions for specialized assignments.

The assignments and instructions in this book are based largely on the kinds of writing situations that occur in academic and other intellectual and professional contexts. The purpose of writing in such situations is generally coming to understand some subject against a background of information and ideas received through reading. The audience is usually limited to a small group of people who are interested in understanding or acting on the same subject— what might be called a research or professional community. Throughout the book, you and your classmates are writing to each other on the basis of what you have found and sharing your discoveries, understanding, perceptions, and conclusions. Specifically you want the other members of the research community, your classmates, to accept your ideas and information as valid and intelligent; the foundation for achieving this effect is careful research of the relevant information and thoughtful analysis of the evidence you discover, as is discussed in Part 2 of this book. The specifics of each assignment vary, of course, because the kind of material you are examining and the method of analysis or interpretation vary the writing task.

The fact that you are students is an additional factor in the social situation. You are not expected to have a wide background in your subjects yet; moreover, in most cases, an important reader of your papers is a teacher. The teacher usually gives grades, and most students would prefer to have good ones, so students become very adept at discovering what teachers like. Fortunately, what most teachers like is thoughtful writing that takes into account a range of evidence and background knowledge appropriate to the student's level. At the college level, most teachers see their role as introducing students to the work of their professional community, so their standards and ideals vary little from general academic and professional values.

Even though many of the basic requirements of writing in the academic situation seem fixed, one student's paper does not and should not look exactly like the others in the way business letters resemble one another. A number of factors vary, and that is where your originality comes in. The background knowledge, the reading, ideas, evidence, and thought you bring to each subject are your individual contribution and will lead to an original argument. No matter how narrowly defined your research assignment is, for example, most students in the class will be investigating slightly different subjects and will be finding different materials to think about. Even if several students research exactly the same topic, they will approach the subject with different attitudes, interests, and questions; each will discover a different range of sources and will come to different sets of conclusions, which in turn will lead them to organize their arguments differently. Even the same data may lead two different people to different interpretations. These differences are what make for intellectual excitement and debate. Every research project is a journey of personal discovery that bears the stamp of the researcher.

Expanded Opportunities, Varied Situations

As you learn the methods, materials, and limits of your subject, the opportunities for originality expand, because your purposes may no longer be limited to basic understanding of the subject. You will be in a position to argue basic issues, seek new kinds of evidence, or bring new ideas or methods of analysis to bear. Your relationship with your colleagues changes as you evolve from student to professional. All these changes in the situation will change the writing problems you confront, and you will be less able to rely on the kinds of cookbook recipes offered in your college textbooks. The more deeply you analyze your writing situation, the more flexibly you will be able to manipulate and vary the basic patterns presented here and elsewhere in your student career. The patterns provide a starting point and some sense of how useful carefully specified writing procedures and formats can be, but ultimately it is up to you to use them intelligently to meet your own professional, intellectual, and personal needs.

As you move from one community to another, you will also find various kinds of differences. Part 3 introduces you to some of the basic ways academic disciplines (that is, different subject areas or areas of investigation) try to cope with different kinds of problems and evidence. Disciplines also change over time as different kinds of evidence and analysis become available or seem more desirable. Writing in political science has changed radically, for example, during the last thirty years as researchers have come to rely heavily on statistical evidence and mathematical analysis. Cookbook recipes will not help you advance clear, forceful, and intelligent arguments during such periods of change.

In nonacademic careers, as well, specific kinds of writing serve particular needs. Understanding what these documents are supposed to do will help you use them more intelligently. Laws, legal briefs, judicial opinions, and contracts establish the rules and interpretations that keep our society organized and ordered. Reports, memos, and letters keep the wheels of business turning. In all kinds of organizations, newsletters, brochures, and pamphlets keep people in touch. In order to use these familiar forms effectively, and even innovatively, you need to be able to analyze the basic writing problems that create the need for such documents.

Some of the pleasure of writing is finding a beautiful phrase or a striking thought; yet good writing begins with understanding why you are writing and then developing an effective writing strategy to meet the situation. You must make some of the most important decisions about your writing long before you put a piece of paper in your typewriter. If you let formulas, habits, accidents, or thoughtlessness dictate those decisions, your writing will rarely hit the mark, for you won't even know which target you are aiming at. But if you try to come to understand and control those basic decisions, you can choose your target and go after it. The power and confidence of a well-aimed shot will support the graceful motions of words and thoughts.

Writing Assignments

1. Obtain the application form for your college or for a job or other organization. Discuss how far your responses are constrained by the format and printed directions and explain how much originality is open to you. Discuss then why your options are limited as they are. Explain why such a limited recipe for providing information serves the purpose of the application. Your discussion

should be no longer than three hundred words and should be directed to your classmates as part of your joint attempt to understand writing.

2. Describe a writing situation in which you felt you had much freedom to respond in original ways. Analyze the writing problem and discuss why you could develop an original strategy. You may also consider a writing problem you are currently working on. Your discussion should be no longer than three hundred words and should be directed to your classmates as part of your joint attempt to understand writing.

2 Reacting to Reading: Annotations and Journals

*W*hen you react to your reading, you start to make a link between the ideas suggested by the page and what happens in your mind—your responses. This link is essential for any kind of intellectual work. Because reactions pass so quickly, turning your responses into words will help you hold on to them. Both writing notes in the margins of your books and keeping a reading journal will help you remember and develop your thoughts about reading.

The Reader's
Active Role

Real intellectual exchange begins when we *react* to what we read. The writer's words touch our minds; soon we will have something to say in reply. The reader becomes a writer.

But if we swallow our reading whole, without thought, we will only be accepting empty phrases. We may parrot those phrases on an examination or at a cocktail party, but those memorized words will never affect our own thinking or lead us to say anything new. They will simply replace our thinking process with mimicry. We will probably soon forget these memorized lines in the same way we soon forget what we "learned" when we crammed for an exam. Unless we fit the words we read into everything else we think and know, we are only pretending to read.

The only way that your reading will affect you and stay with you is for you to react to it. Actively consider whether you agree with the ideas you read and how these ideas relate to questions you find personally important. As you read with greater care, your reactions too will develop. (The techniques of paraphrase and summary discussed in the next two chapters will increase the precision of your reading.) But whatever level you are reading at, you need to ask yourself in many different ways, "What do I think about this idea? How true is it? How important is it to me? Does it challenge anything I already believe? Does it raise questions or answer questions?"

At times the personal importance of particular books moves us with unquestionable force. We know immediately when those books speak to our condition. While he was in prison, Malcolm X began to read history books and started to grasp the process of racial oppression at work. As he writes in his *Autobiography*, these volumes provided what he was looking for: "Ten guards and the warden couldn't have torn me out of those books." Information directly applicable to our personal situation can excite our minds in ways that may have the strength of a religious conversion.

More frequently, we must make efforts to grasp the book before it will excite us as Malcolm X was excited. The initial impetus to read a particular book may be unformed and tentative; glimmers of thoughts may be forgotten as our eyes move on to the next sentence, to the next paragraph, to the next chapter. A nagging desire to get up for another cup of coffee or anxiety about an upcoming exam may prevent us from reacting fully to the words in front of us. Without conscious effort to record, sort out, and develop full responses to reading, the ideas quickly fade to the back of the mind. We soon remember the book only vaguely—as either interesting or dull.

Not paying attention to your personal reactions may lead you to feel disconnected from the communication going on—as though some other people were arguing about something that you had no interest in. Words parade past the eyes and boredom settles in the mind. You have a case of pseudo-boredom. Genuine boredom occurs when you are reading material you already know only too well; nothing new emerges to occupy the mind. Pseudo-boredom comes when you feel you just cannot be bothered to figure out what all the new information and ideas mean; the mind backs away from a real and demanding occupation. The cure for real boredom is to find a more advanced book on the subject; the only cure for pseudo-boredom is to become fully and personally involved in the book already in front of you. By recording and developing your reactions and thoughts, you can talk back to the book and consider yourself engaged in conversation with the author. Although the consecutively numbered pages of the book keep coming past you in a straight line, you can turn the thoughts expressed on them in your own direction. Once you are involved, pseudo-boredom vanishes.

Putting First Reactions into Words

The way to begin sorting your first reactions to your reading is to put them in words—either by talking or by writing. The problem is to find someone you can trust with these tangled, contradictory, half-formed thoughts. As you struggle to find words to express your dim intuitions, you should not worry about whether what you are saying is "right or wrong" or whether it is elegantly expressed. To whom can you speak or write without committing yourself permanently to your unconnected fragments of reactions and your rambling journeys to nowhere? Sometimes a friend will let you talk out your ideas without making you defend every tentative assumption, which you yourself might reject the next moment, but a friend with sufficient patience to hear out all the most trivial ramblings that occur during reading is a rare find.

Mark Twain's letters to the novelist William Dean Howells reveal

Mark Twain in his study at Quarry Farm, Elmira, New York. (Mark Twain Memorial, Hartford, CT)

such a friendship. Twain trusted Howells enough to change his opinions from one sentence to the next in the most informal manner. In the following passage, Twain sorts out his opinion about a new book by Bret Harte, explaining how he shifted his opinion of Harte's work on a second reading.

Dear Howells—

... [A publisher] sent me Harte's new book of Sketches, the other day, ("An Heiress of Red Dog," etc). I have read it twice—the first time through tears of rage over the fellow's inborn hypocrisy & snobbishness, his apprentice-art, his artificialities, his mannerisms, his pet phrases, (such as the frequent "I regret to say,"). ... he peppers in his seven little French words (you can find them in all

his sketches, for he learned them in California 14 years ago,) . . .
The struggle after the pathetic is more pathetic than the pathos
itself; if he were to write about an Orphan Princess who lost a Peanut
he would feel obliged to try to make somebody snuffle over it.

The second time I read the book I saw a most decided brightness
on every page of it—& here & there evidences of genius. I saw enough
to make me think, "Well, if this slovenly shoemaker-work is able to
command the applause of three or four nations, what *mightn't* this
ass accomplish if he would do his work honestly & with pains?" If
I ever get my tedious book finished, I mean to weed out some of my
prejudices & write an article on "Bret Harte as an Artist"—& print
it if it will not be unfair to print it without signature.

By the end of the passage, Twain has reversed his opinion about
Harte. At first Twain has only the most biting comments about
Harte's pretentiousness and overwriting, but finally he grudgingly
admits that Harte shows some "evidences of genius." Twain, however,
would make such an admission only to his close friend Howells,
for he still considers Harte too craftless to deserve even his grudging
public endorsement. If he ever does publish his ideas on Harte,
Twain does not want to sign his name to the article. Throughout
this letter Twain writes with an informal, personal candor that
he would never use in public, even though he was famous for his
comic honesty.

Marginal Annotations: A Running Account of Your Thoughts

You may not always have a friend handy to discuss all your reading
with. A more realistic practice is to confide in yourself, writing
down your thoughts, reactions, and questions as they occur to you
in the margin of your book—next to the passage that triggered the
response. Once you overcome your inhibitions about writing in
books, marginal comments flow almost naturally from the desire
to engage the writer in a dialogue. The conversation starts to come
alive. If you own the book, show that it is really yours by leaving
your thoughts in it. When you reread the book at a later date, you
will know what you liked and what you didn't, what reminded you

of a personal experience, and which ideas stimulated your interest and curiosity. Or if you weren't sure just what you thought back then, you can sort out the many directions of your earlier thoughts when you return for a second look.

Lord Macaulay, the historian, writing during the middle of the nineteenth century, was in the habit of annotating his books, as the more recent historian George Trevelyan describes:

> His favorite volumes are illustrated and enlivened by innumerable entries, of which none are prolix, pointless, or dull; while interest and admiration are expressed by lines drawn down sides of the text,—and even by double lines, for whole pages together. . . .

In a typical example, Macaulay annotated Cicero's essay *On Duty* with acid comments like "trashy Sophistry, admirably explained" and "beautifully lucid, though the system is excessively absurd."

Annotation to Clarify

With pencil in hand, ready to comment on your reading, you may find you want to make two different kinds of remarks: some to help you understand the meaning of the text more fully and others to express your own reactions, evaluations, and associations. Although annotation works best with no rules—the whole trick is to feel free to jot down whatever comes to mind—it helps to keep the two kinds of comments separated. My own practice is to put comments on the meaning in the narrower margin near the book's spine and to leave all the other margins—the wider side, top, and bottom—for reactions.

You may already use annotations for meaning as a study technique. Underlining key statements, numbering supporting arguments, defining unusual words, and paraphrasing difficult passages all help you approach the surface meaning of a text. But annotations can go more deeply to establish the connections and logic of the entire selection. In the margin you can explicitly state underlying assumptions of the text—that is, ideas only indirectly suggested by the original. Marginal comments can provide an overview of where the argument has come from and where it is going to; they can bring out the structure of the original as well as restate the obvious meaning of the words. Where the meaning of words or structure is unclear, a well-placed question mark—even better, a purposeful question—will remind you of what is puzzling.

Annotation to Evaluate

On the second level of annotation, your thoughts interact with the ideas suggested by the text. Feel free to express the most outrageous of opinions in the most informal way. For the most part no one but you will see these comments, so allow yourself freedom. Wander from the point, contradict yourself, speculate without substantive support, be irreverent, and express extreme opinions. All these are acceptable indulgences in marginal notes. Any type of phrase, mark, smudge, or sign that conveys your attitude is legitimate. With this freedom—with this pleasurable irresponsibility—you will eventually find your own topics, your own things to say. To get you started, here are some typical kinds of comments:

approval and disapproval— √,*,????, NO!, not bad, exactly, yeccch, nonsense, right

disagreements—I can't agree because . . . , no, the actual facts are . . .

exceptions—doesn't hold for the case of . . .

counterexamples—isn't case x just the opposite?

supporting examples—exactly what happens in case y

extensions—this could even apply to . . .

discoveries—this explains why . . .

possible implications—would this mean that . . . ?

personal associations—my uncle acts just like that, *or,* in student government . . .

reading associations—Z in his book argues the same thing, *or,* this fits in with what A wrote.

distinctions—but then again it's not like Z's argument because . . .

It doesn't take long to get in the spirit of annotation; once you are attuned to it, you can throw out all these suggestions and develop comments most appropriate to the way you think. In the Writing Assignments for this chapter, a passage by Cicero has been provided for you to annotate. The passage is about friendship—a subject with which everyone has had direct experience. Probably you will find much that you like and much that you do not like in it. The important thing is to react and put your reactions in writing.

First, here is an example of how one student annotated the opening lines. Cicero's opening sentence set off two lines of thought. The student was surprised first by the extremity of Cicero's claim about the importance of friendship and second by Cicero's associating love with friendship instead of romantic relationships.

isn't this too strong?

How can there be a life worth living ... unless it rest upon the mutual *not romantic love but love of friends* love of friends? What could be finer than to have someone to whom you may speak as freely as to yourself? How could you derive true joy from good fortune if you did not have someone who would rejoice in your happiness as much as you yourself?

without friends you should die?

yes — remember that all night talk with Jack

Scholarly Annotation

The annotations discussed so far in this chapter have been for personal use; making personal annotations is a way to assert oneself during the reading process. In contrast, scholarly annotations (published rather than personal notes) can serve a wider audience by presenting a perspective—interpretive, evaluative, or informational— on a major literary work or on a primary legal or Biblical text. With such formal annotation, a second writer can discuss the work of the first, with the words of both appearing on the same page. In the Hebraic tradition, for example, marginal commentary is the main method of theological debate, with as many as eight or ten different sets of marginal annotations by different writers filling up the large margins around a few short lines of the original sacred text. Each commentator presents a consistent interpretation of the holy text, but each is often at odds with the other commentators printed on the same page.

In such learned marginal commentary, we can see the seed of the footnote—another device for adding additional information, interpretation, and perspective to the original passage. Well-conceived and carefully written footnotes can be quite informative, lending whole new dimensions to the basic text. They are the place for a

second voice to speak, often adding more recent findings and interpretations to the original. The following example of scholarly annotation shows how the annotator lends wisdom to the original
text, even if that text is only a few lines of a children's rhyme.
This passage, from *The Annotated Mother Goose*, illustrates the
second opinion of footnotes.

Sing a Song of Sixpence,[6]
A bag full of Rye,[7]
Four and twenty[8]
Naughty boys,[9]
Bak'd in a Pye.[10]

6. Scholars have seen supposed references to this nursery rhyme in
Twelfth Night—*Come on, there is sixpence for you; let's have a song;*
and in Beaumont and Fletcher's *Bonduca* (1614)—*Whoa, here's a stir
now! Sing a song of sixpence!*
7. *A pocket full of rye* in most later versions. It is possible that "a
pocket full" was once a specific measurement in recipes, as "a ta-
blespoonful of sugar."
8. We shall find that "four and twenty" is one of the numbers most
frequently met with in "Mother Goose" rhymes. It is, of course, a
"double dozen" and the number 12 is rich in associations, traditions,
and superstitions.
9. Later *Four and twenty blackbirds.* Theories about this rhyme abound:
the "blackbirds" are the twenty-four hours in a day, "the king" is
the sun, and "the queen" is the moon, for example. On the other
hand, Katherine Elwes Thomas identified the king as Henry VIII,
the queen as Katherine, and the maid as Anne Boleyn; the "blackbirds"
were four and twenty manorial deeds baked in a pie—as in "Little
Jack Horner" (Rhyme 50). Still another theory holds that this song
celebrates the printing of the first English Bible—the "blackbirds"
being the letters of the alphabet set in pica type ("baked in a pie").
10. According to Iona and Peter Opie, the editors of *The Oxford
Dictionary of Nursery Rhymes*, an Italian cookbook of 1549, translated
into English in 1598, actually contains a recipe "to make pies so that
birds may be alive in them and flie out when it is cut up." They
continue: "This dish is further referred to (1723) by John Nott, cook
to the Duke of Bolton, as a practice of former days, the purpose of
the birds being to put out the candles and so cause a 'diverting
Hurley-Burley amongst the Guests in the Dark.'"

When taken to the extreme, the personality and viewpoint of
the commentary writer can become so strong that they overwhelm

the meaning of the primary text; Vladimir Nabokov parodies this heavy-handed use of scholarly notes in the novel *Pale Fire.* The novel is in the form of a scholar's footnotes to the poem of his next door neighbor. The demented scholar—who imagines himself the exiled King of Zembla—is so wrapped up in his own fate that the footnotes keep wandering away from the poem to an imagined murder plot against the scholar. But if the marginal commentator takes sufficient care to avoid an obsessive overuse of footnotes, annotation remains one of the most direct ways for readers to develop some perspective and background on a text.

Writing Assignments

1. Annotate the following passage from Cicero's *On Friendship:*

How can there be a "life worth living" . . . unless it rest upon the mutual love of friends? What could be finer than to have someone to whom you may speak as freely as to yourself? How could you derive true joy from good fortune, if you did not have someone who would rejoice in your happiness as much as you yourself? And it would be very hard to bear misfortune in the absence of anyone who would take your sufferings even harder than you. Finally, the other things on which we set our hearts have each of them a strictly limited utility: money, that we may spend it; power, that we may acquire a following; honors, that we may gain praise; pleasure, that we may enjoy it; health, that we may be free of pain and make full use of our physical endowments; friendship, on the other hand, brings with it many advantages. Wherever you turn, it is at your side; there is no place not open to it; it is never untimely, never in the way. In short, not even water and fire, as the saying goes, are as universally essential to us as friendship. And I am not now speaking of the friendships of everyday folk, or of ordinary people—although even these are a source of pleasure and profit—but of true and perfect friendship, the kind that was possessed by those few men who have gained names for themselves as friends. For when fortune smiles on us, friendship adds a luster to that smile; when she frowns, friendship absorbs her part and share of that frown, and thus makes it easier to bear.

Now friendship possesses many splendid advantages, but of course the finest thing of all about it is that it sends a ray of good hope into the future, and keeps our hearts from faltering or falling by the wayside. For the man who keeps his eye on a true friend, keeps it, so to speak, on a model of himself. For this reason, friends are together when they are separated, they are rich when they are poor, strong when they are weak, and—a thing even harder to explain—they live on after they have died, so great is the honor that follows them, so vivid the memory, so poignant the sorrow. That is why friends who have died are accounted happy, and those who survive them are deemed worthy of praise. Why, if the mutual love of friends were to be removed from the world, there is no single house, no single state that would go on existing; even agriculture would cease to be. If this seems a bit difficult to understand, we can readily see how great is the power of friendship and love by observing their opposites, enmity and ill will. For what house is so firmly established, what constitution is so unshakable, that it could not be utterly destroyed by hatred and internal division? From this we may judge how much good there is in friendship.

2. Annotate either *a* or *b*:
   a. The passage on trauma, pp. 101–103.
   b. The passage on girls and computers, pp. 119–121.

The Reading Journal

Sometimes your comments may outgrow the limits of the margin. A desire to pursue one thought at length, a need to enlarge on your perception of the reading as a whole, or a need to sort out a number of confusing issues will lead you from an inch of margin to a blank sheet of paper. The reading journal provides the space for more extended ideas—and particularly for ideas not tied to any one particular passage of the original.

A reading journal is a diary of your thought processes. After each session of reading, you simply start writing about your most dominant or curious impressions, just as in a diary you might review and comment on the day's most noteworthy events. By its nature a journal will ramble, for you may have no idea what you are going to say when you begin each entry. The act of getting words and ideas on the page will help you discover what it is you want to write about. The journal is only for your own use, so you need not worry about shifting the topic, contradicting yourself, losing sense, or being unconvincing—those weaknesses in your writing that teachers are always bringing up. Correctness of language and problems with spelling should not even cross your mind. Just put down your first reactions and explore them until you have worked them out fully.

Making It a Habit

The journal works best when it is a regular habit. If you waited for the spirit to move you before you pulled out the journal, you wouldn't use the notebook very often. Set aside fifteen minutes after every reading assignment (you may wish to limit yourself to one course or subject at the beginning) for a chance to establish the habit. Some days you may not get very far with any one idea, but on other days your thoughts will gain a momentum of their own. When you look back on what you have just written, you may be surprised to see how much you had to say. To enable you to look back in the journals at a later time, you should keep all the entries together in a notebook or file folder. You should also date the entries and identify the book and page numbers to which you are responding.

Because both journals and marginal annotations are messages written to yourself, you will get much more out of them if you read them over within a day—and then again several months later. As a short-term benefit, you will be able to find topics and ideas for assigned essays—as well as the specific supporting evidence. Notice whether you kept returning to one particularly interesting idea or whether you can spot a pattern emerging in your agreements or disagreements with a piece of reading. If you discussed one particular passage of the original at length, that discussion might be the seed of something more extended, such as a research project. Over a longer period, you will start noticing how the process of your thinking has developed. You will probably be quite surprised by the differences between your first and your most recent entries. Over a long span of time, a reading journal can become an intellectual diary—a record of the development of your ideas.

As with marginal comments, what you write in the journal is up to you; with time you will find the most appropriate ways to express your own interests. No matter what topics or modes of expression you are drawn to, it is important to pursue your line of reasoning to its natural conclusion. Although you may shift away from an uncompleted thought, try to return to it. Take your ideas seriously enough to follow where they lead. In the course of developing your ideas, a viewpoint and an attitude will emerge that are yours alone. Tentative ideas will grow in strength to become ideas that you will want to express to others in your essays.

Getting Started

Until you become comfortable with keeping a journal, you may be at a loss about how to begin the day's entry. One warm-up technique is to restate those parts of the reading that most impressed you, either positively or negatively, and then try to explain why they made that impression. You may find that, as in the following journal, one thing leads to another. Here the student, Diane Hoiland, starts commenting on a later section of Cicero's *On Friendship* but returns to think about the opening sentence. She ends by commenting on Cicero's concept as a whole.

Cicero's claim about the ideal friend sounded great, but it left me feeling uneasy. "Wherever you turn, it is at your side; there is no place not open to it; it is never untimely, never in the way. In short, not even water and fire, as the saying goes, are as universally essential to us as friendship." As I write these things down, I can feel myself get angry. Stated so totally, these things just are not true!!! In rare relationships some of these things may be true, maybe even all of them. But my experience is that friends are not always available when you need them. Friendship is quite often untimely, and if the friend is untimely, then he or she must also somehow be in the way. Time creates the idea of a friend.

I do not agree that friendship is one of the bare necessities of life. I think it is one of man's interesting developments. You will not starve without a friend. Many loners have no friends, not even many acquaintances; they avoid communication with others, but they say they are far from lonely. Before one can appreciate the company of another, there must be a realization of how beautiful it is to be alone with oneself. Yes, Cicero is cor-

rect in saying that some form of sacrifice is necessary
for friendship--but if one person gives total sacrifice
and the other accepts, they are not really friends.
Friends must give and take. So it is impossible to have
an ideal friend.

Not all comments need to express simple agreement or disagreement. Our reactions to reading are complex. An article may evoke a personal memory, strike us as an unusual way to approach an issue, or start us off on our own new line of thinking. In the following entry, reacting to an article about adolescent peer groups, Joe Spasiano does a bit of all three.

The author thinks the adolescent peer group--your gang
of friends--helps teen-agers develop interactions with
people and build general conversational skills. I find
this whole approach sort of funny--good, but funny. How
many children hear from their parents, "Where do you get
those ideas? From that crowd of yours?" Sometimes it is
even "that no-good crowd of yours." My parents couldn't
understand that I had ideas different from theirs. I was
becoming my own person, drawing my own conclusions. But
to my parents my idea, just by being different, was
wrong. I reacted by totally rejecting all my parents'
ideals and values. A kind of defense mechanism, I guess.
Only when I got a little older did I realize that two
opinions are possible and that I should give my parents'
opinions some consideration. This whole situation brings
to mind something once said by Mark Twain--something
like, "When I was 18 I was surprised at how little my
father knew, but by the time I was 21, I was surprised to
find out how much he had learned in just 3 years."

Getting Unstuck

Some readings do not seem to excite any feeling, and you may find yourself hard-pressed to write anything in your journal. Before you settle for a short, perfunctory entry, you should give your thoughts time to surface. Get your pen moving in whatever way you can. Talk about how boring you find the piece, or why you do not like the style, or even the exam that is really the thing on your mind. It is only a journal; you don't have to worry about wandering too far from the subject. Eventually you may find yourself back on the track with an interesting thought in mind. Linda Cummings at first found herself totally unable to respond to Sullivan's discussion of "The Need for Interpersonal Intimacy" on pages 133–134 below, but after she warmed her pen up for a while, her ideas began to flow.

I can't get my mind on today's reading. I didn't agree or disagree with this one. I couldn't get into it or even conjure up the desire to try. The baby was up all last night. I think I am just exhausted. Besides, Sullivan's tone turns me off completely. He writes in a very technical way, as though he were writing only for psychologists. Maybe that is what he was doing. But I found the ideas I could grasp just did not seem right to me. Especially when he says that children don't start getting close pals until about age eight. My little cousin, by the time he was four years old . . .

And she was off and running with an illuminating three-page discussion of her cousin's nursery school relationships.

A Professional Writer's Journal

Professional writers frequently keep journals. Eric Hoffer, a blue-collar worker turned social theorist, kept a journal of his readings, thoughts, and activities during one year while he was working as a longshoreman and writing another book. He later published the journal under the title *Working and Thinking on the Waterfront: June 1958—May 1959*. In it, the reader can see patterns of thoughts emerging from almost random observations—just as in the student's journal. However, the writing here has been reworked, polished, and edited for publication. In one early entry, Hoffer wanders through many items before he finally finds a topic he wants to pursue.

June 23

The kink in my back is gone. Yesterday's work did it. The world looks clean and fresh after last night's rain. I have a long list of chores to do, and I am just getting ready to clean my room. Before starting I read the last few pages of *Byzantium*. I cannot tell as yet what I got out of the book. It corrected my view of the Byzantine Empire as a stagnant body. It needs vigor to last a thousand years.

5 P.M. . . . turned to a new travel book by Lord Kinross. This is a continuation of his book on the interior of Asia Minor.

7 P.M. The second Kinross book, so far as I read, is inferior to the first. Since I am in the mood to make it easy for myself I switched to another book—a delightful one. It is a book of letters written by an American woman who lived in Jerusalem 1953–54. It is a warm, sensitive, honest book. My first reaction is: What delightful people Americans are. I ought perhaps to say fine people. And saying this I reflect that I certainly am not an American. Under similar circumstances I would have been neither delightful nor fine. Here she is among total strangers and she does not carp or criticize, or betray the least trace of bad temper. The American's capacity for fraternization is a noble feature, a true foretaste of the brotherhood of man. The book is *Letters from Jerusalem* by Mary Clawson. I shall probably sit up all night reading it.

Note how Hoffer interprets his own mood, "I am in the mood to make it easy for myself," and then presents his reactions to a "delightful" new book.

On another day, Hoffer's mood leads him to think about the spirit of an author he is reading:

October 26

I woke up with the idea that it was Monday. It cheered me somewhat to realize that it was not yet. I spent several hours downtown eating breakfast and strolling about.

I wonder how much of the feeling of well-being that I have had now and then during the past two days comes from the book I am reading—Van der Post's *The Lost World of the Kalahari*. Nothing this man ever writes could be without the excitement of life. And even as he brings to life the landscape, the plants, the animals, and the human beings he also manages to put the quality of himself in every word. You wonder what would happen if he became the absolute ruler of a primitive African state, and how little it would require to change him into an ancient lawgiver, a magician, a healer. His prose though unlabored is genuine poetry. You begin to realize that the chief function of poetry is to use words as charms to evoke life and colors and smells—a sense of joy, of awe, of compassion, and so on.

Yet all the time you know that it is the man and not his words that count. Wherever he puts his foot the earth becomes portentous. It is as if his presence has diverted the elements and forces from their routine pursuits. The whole world is addressing him, and concerning itself with his tastes and intentions.

Discovering and Testing Ideas in Journals

In exploring your ideas informally in a journal, you may discover something you want to expand into an essay. An idea just starting to emerge in rough form may show promise of fuller, more orderly expansion. Thus, before writing on a subject that you have been keeping a journal on, it is worthwhile to read your journal again. If you have a piece of writing to do, perhaps an assigned paper for your history class, you could try out your ideas in an informal journal entry, where you can just get your thoughts on paper without worrying about the form. From this kind of exploration of ideas, it is only one step more to considering the problem of writing any particular paper—the process, the difficulties, the satisfactions, the dissatisfactions. Eric Hoffer, for example, plans in his journal a piece of writing he is currently working on.

May 11

The article on man and nature which I am writing for the *Saturday Evening Post* is coming along fine. Almost every idea in the train of thought has been worked out long ago. What I have to do is dovetail them more or less smoothly. There are a few gaps to be filled. One is the idea that man's creativeness originates in the characteristics which distinguish man from other forms of life. In other words, human creativeness is basically unlike any creative process that may be found in the rest of creation. I also must have a pithy section on the role of magic (words) in human affairs. The title of the article will be "The Unnaturalness of Human Nature." I ought to have it finished and typed before the end of this month.

Dianne Pari, a student, has more difficulty with drawing together the materials for a research paper she is working on. Her problem is not only to organize her material but also to focus on a particular issue about which she can come to some original, forceful conclusions. As her research continues, she begins to discover a new, important aspect to the material. The new aspect is tempting to explore, but in the limited time remaining it is too difficult to get a handle on. Thus, in this journal entry, she has to consider both sides of the conversation: her own writing and the reading that stands behind the writing.

I am going through the final stages of organizing my paper. The topic gets more involved as I continue & I have difficulty trying to limit it. I stumbled into the constitutional issue pretty late, and it really might change my mind if I knew enough about it. But to really cover it would take a doctoral thesis, so I'm going to limit myself just to the political reasons for the gun control law being passed in '68, and I'm going to drop consideration of the merits of the law. What I'm learning about the political process there reminds me of things that keep happening every day. One group makes a lot of noise about an issue and people submit to their cries. Most will not stand up for their beliefs and will buckle in under pressure, in this case from the National Rifle Association. The NRA's pressure was partly responsible for the weakening of the bill. But that constitutional issue still bothers me because the NRA might have been right on that basis.

The hardest part is coming with the organization of the mass of materials. I feel like the facts are going to take over the paper and I won't be able to bring in my ideas clearly enough.

Kenneth Wertheim, another student, focused his thoughts successfully but had a hard time crystallizing his final idea into a thesis, or a statement of his main idea.

The thesis is driving me up the wall. I think writing it is harder than the actual paper is going to be. I know WHAT I want to say, but I don't know HOW. I spent an hour

in class today searching for the right words. Even though
I have all the research completed, I am not happy. Once I
have my thesis, maybe then it will be downhill.

On a number of the papers to be assigned in this book, you will
be asked to use your journal as part of the process of discovering
ideas and planning your essay. The journal will be especially useful
as you are gathering materials for research assignments, for it will
allow you to think through the meaning and importance of research
materials as you find them.

As you develop the journal habit you will find your mental life
growing in pleasant and surprising ways. Keeping a journal for any
course with a lot of reading helps you remember the material and
develop thoughts on it. If you prepare an entry on the reading
assignment before class, you will have prepared ideas to bring to
class dicussion. As certain ideas start to intrigue you, you may find
that seemingly disparate material from many different sources seem
to relate to a single idea. The journal can become the place where
you start to fit together the pieces in the puzzle of your education.
And the journal can become the place where you discover the
abiding intellectual questions you will carry with you for the rest
of your life. If you give yourself a chance, you will wind up discussing
the things that you find important to discuss.

Writing Assignment

Keep a reading journal for the next few weeks of this course while
you work on the next two chapters. Use the journal to explore your
responses to the passages you are paraphrasing and summarizing.
You will be reading those passages closely, so you should have a
number of detailed thoughts to explore. For your last entry, read
through the entire journal and comment on it as a whole: whether
you gained from it, whether you noticed changes in your thinking
or writing, or whether any recurrent themes, issues, or problems
kept coming up in your entries.

Your teacher may also ask you to keep the journal up for the
rest of the semester or to keep the journal for some other course
that has regular reading assignments. Even if your teacher does
not suggest this, such journals will be worthwhile for you to keep
up on your own. At the very least, you will come into each class
with comments that you have thought out beforehand.

3 Paraphrasing:
The Author's Thoughts
in Your Words

In order to respond to other people, we need to understand their thoughts, but we often read inaccurately and incompletely. Writing a careful paraphrase—that is, putting the meaning of a text into new words—makes you pay close attention to the author's ideas and thereby improves your level of understanding. In paraphrasing, you should constantly keep the meaning of the original in mind, but express the same ideas in a different way. Two tricks that will help you find new ways to express the author's meaning are substituting *synonyms* and *rearranging sentence structure*. Paraphrasing will help you communicate the meaning of a difficult passage. When you go on to make your own argument, it will allow you to refer to another writer's thoughts while you maintain control of the focus and tone of the argument.

Getting the Message

How often has someone not understood what you were saying? If you are like most of us, it happens many times a day. Sometimes people misunderstand us entirely; sometimes they don't even seem to hear us, although a few minutes later they may give us back our own words, claiming the words are their own. (Such situations provide standard jokes for television situation comedies.) More often people understand only part of what we say; they get the general idea but miss the fine points or particular thrust of our comments.

On the other hand, people who listen closely and understand what other people say make more relevant responses. The more they understand the other person's comments in detail, the more they can respond directly to the problems and issues on the other person's mind. Moreover, hearing something new may inspire new ideas in such careful listeners. The closer they get to what the speaker is saying, the more a real interchange of ideas takes place. And new thoughts are more likely to arise on *both* sides.

It is very hard to listen carefully to what another person is saying. People, including ourselves, are more likely to hear what they want to hear. We like to hear what we already know. Curiosity and desire for knowledge are strong human motives, but we also have an opposite tendency to "stick by our guns" and defend the viewpoints we have already come to believe in. We resist hearing—let alone adopting—any new viewpoint or explanation. These conserving instincts underlie our positive sense of integrity (as in *integer,* "maintaining wholeness"). But they also work to spare us the effort of dealing with too many challenges.

If we know or care little about a subject, hearing something new about it will not disturb us, but if we have made up our minds and hearts, new ideas are a serious threat to our peace of mind. C. Northcote Parkinson, the economist and observer of bureaucracies, has pointed out that the less important a decision is, the more time is devoted to discussing it.* Two hours will be spent on the new color scheme of the executive conference room—but only five minutes on the opening of a new factory. On the important issues, most everyone either has an unshakable opinion already or shrinks from the effort and responsibility involved in making a serious decision,

---

*C. Northcote Parkinson, *Parkinson's Law and Other Studies in Administration* (Boston: Houghton Mifflin Co., 1957), p. 32.

so they get the anxiety-arousing items on the agenda out of the way as quickly as possible.

Read What Is Written

We have many tricks to avoid getting the message when we read. To avoid the challenge of grasping another writer's thoughts, we may simply never pick up books that will give us a hard time (think of that textbook you just dread opening). If we do get as far as turning to page 1 and looking at the words, there are many ways we can appear to read without really reading.

Immediately assuming that the book contains nothing worthwhile allows us to focus on its faults and not think about what it is trying to tell us. If we spend the whole time arguing with the book, we may not even get a clear impression of its main message and the evidence it marshals in its own defense. Disturbing, challenging books are especially likely to make us react negatively at many intermediate points. Petty fault finding is a very effective way to avoid considering whether the book might indeed have something to tell us.

If we aren't quarreling with a challenging book, we may be assuming it says what we want it to say—and not what it actually does say. We may latch on to phrases that sound similar to ideas we subscribe to and then mindlessly skim those parts that sound unfamiliar or too complex. Just because we interpret a few words as similar to our own thoughts doesn't mean that the writer had anything like our thoughts in mind. We may even ignore a few key qualifying words, such as "not generally" or "rarely," to make the book read the way we want it to! Even if we avoid such extreme distortion, we still may smooth over more subtle differences. Given the variety of human thought, we cannot assume that any writer shares our exact perspective on all points.

Right Word, Wrong Meaning

We may even read a word, know the meaning of it, and still misunderstand the meaning the author intended. Words, particularly abstractions, can mean many different things to different people.

To a debater a *point of view* is an opinion, to an art critic it is the angle from which we view a piece of sculpture, and to a novelist it is the character through whose eyes we see the story. Certain loosely defined words like *fact, objectivity,* and *determinism* have been under dispute for centuries, and each user is likely to have a particular meaning in mind. If we want to understand a particular writer, we have to understand the word according to that writer's definition.

Other words gain such popularity so rapidly that they are used to describe many different ideas before any one meaning gets set: the kind of analysis called *structuralism* differs substantially in the fields of anthropology, sociology, religion, literature, history, and philosophy.

Even if a word is used with its most common meaning, we may misunderstand it unless we remain sensitive to the *context*. Everyone knows what the animal called a *horse* is, but that word still means very different things to a jockey, a bettor, and a ten-year-old child. In order to understand how and why any writer is using any word, we have to recognize the writer's way of thinking and his or her special interests. Although two authors may be concerned with military force, they may be concerned with very different issues and may make very different kinds of connections and arguments. In reading an author interested in the present-day uses of military force in international politics, we must be receptive to an entirely different kind of reasoning than we would find in a writer interested in the social structure of a militarized country. Each of the works might shed light on the other, but they are operating in two separate spheres.

Review for an Overview

Once a reader is receptive to the language and the spirit of a written work, the reader still has to be willing to see how the parts fit together into a coherent whole. Every book does not fit together well: the argument may ramble, or the later chapters may contradict the earlier. Sometimes a book coheres on one level, clearly presenting the chronological narrative of, say, Thomas Jefferson's life, but lacks coherence on another—not explaining the development of his character. Until we have made a serious attempt to draw the parts together in our own minds, we will have no basis for evaluating a book's overall significance. Fortunately, most books are more than collections of loosely connected statements, and we must look for the significant connections.

The remainder of this chapter discusses paraphrasing, a task that requires a close reading of a given passage and a careful rewriting. We might think of paraphrasing as a trick that forces us to get the message when we read. In recasting another writer's thoughts into our own words, we must pay close attention to the content of statements and the precise meanings of words. The task of paraphrase keeps our attention on the page. In later chapters we will return to expressing personal thoughts and reactions—and to contributing to the conversation.

Rethinking; Restating

Every school day at almost every level, many students are asked to restate in their own words information they encounter in books, lectures, and films. Teachers assign this kind of loose paraphrase to see whether students have remembered and understood the course material. For such purposes, a student needs only to reproduce a few key concepts without making gross errors. True paraphrase, however, is part of a larger process of understanding and responding to a specific written passage. Before you can use or argue with anyone's ideas, you must understand these ideas accurately. Careful paraphrase requires close attention to every nuance of meaning so that, when you later come to refer to these ideas or argue against them, you will know exactly what you are working with. Paraphrase can serve as a form of note taking, allowing you to preserve the writer's exact meaning in those terms that you understand best. Even more important, paraphrase can serve as a way of referring to other writers' thoughts in your own original essays so that you can build on and answer their ideas even while you are advancing your own.

To *paraphrase* is to restate a passage precisely in your own words and phrasing in order to clarify the meaning. The task at first does not appear difficult. However, words that are similar are not always interchangeable, and the meanings of words shift subtly with their context and their use. Further, sentences put words into exact relationships. Thus creating an accurate paraphrase forces you to consider both the exact use of words and the sense of the entire statement. In considering the word-by-word meaning of a text and in searching for possible substitutions, the paraphraser must literally come to terms with what has been written. Turning your understanding of a text into written language banishes the looseness of understanding that often remains hidden in the privacy of your silent reading.

In writing paraphrases you must attend to two things: the meaning of words as they are used in context and the relationship between words. In both you must reach for more than loose approximation. You must include all that was in the original, without adding anything new and without misrepresenting the original content.

Different Words . . .

Two techniques will help you gain a precise understanding of the original: substituting synonyms and rearranging the sentence structure. To paraphrase the opening sentence of the Gettysburg Address, for example, you might first replace the original words with other words of the same meaning. The original, as you know, reads:

> Four score and seven years ago, our fathers brought forth on this continent a new nation, conceived in liberty and dedicated to the proposition that all men are created equal.

First, replacing synonyms may lead to this first draft of the paraphrase:

> Eighty-seven years before now, our ancestors founded in North America a new country, thought of in freedom and based on the principle that all people are born with the same rights.

Then restructuring the sentence might lead to a more total paraphrase:

> Our ancestors thought of freedom when they founded a new country in North America eighty-seven years ago. They based their thinking on the principle that all people are born with the same rights.

Note that this final version breaks the original single sentence in two. The main subject (ancestors) is brought to the front, and the time period is relegated to the end of the first sentence. Moreover, the verb structure is simplified. Hence the ancestors are doing all the actions directly, instead of the actions being described as qualities of the nation (conceived, dedicated). This paraphrase is not nearly so eloquent as the famous original, but it does get the meaning across simply and directly.

In restructuring sentences, check first to see whether longer sentences might be broken into shorter units or shorter sentences might be combined into longer ones. Also consider whether a passive verb might be made into an active one or how the verb structure might otherwise be changed. Also note whether some phrases might be moved to other positions in order to make the sentence easier to follow.

A thesaurus, or dictionary of synonyms, may help you find alternative ways of expressing the meaning conveyed in the original, but be sure you use such reference books in the right way. Do not blindly choose a substitute word simply because it is listed as a synonym and sounds fancy or unusual. There are often subtle differences—shades of meaning—among the many synonyms listed. These differences can make a blindly chosen synonym silly or inappropriate in the context of a particular paraphrase. Pity the poor student who, looking for a synonym for *pickle,* wound up with a *predicament* with his sandwich. Instead, use the list of synonyms to remind you of possible alternatives, and then choose the alternative that best fits the meaning you want to convey.

For example, *Webster's Dictionary of Synonyms* includes among the synonyms for *conceive* the words *think, imagine, fancy,* and *realize.* Although in some contexts *conceive* does mean the same as *imagine* (as in the question "How could you conceive I would do that?"), in the opening of the *Gettysburg Address, imagine* is inappropriate. *Imagine* implies something that has nothing to do with reality, but Lincoln was using *conceive* to suggest a thought that leads to a reality, almost as though the idea gives birth to the reality, as a child is conceived in its mother's womb. Similarly, *fancy* is not a serious enough thought and *realize* is too sudden, too unplanned. The only word from that list that fits appropriately is *think,* a form of which was used in our paraphrase.

Sometimes the thesaurus will not provide an adequate substitute, but in thinking through why the listed synonyms are not appropriate, you may come up with a better word or phrase of your own. A thesaurus should help you think by jogging your memory, not serve as a substitute for your thinking.

"Occasionally."

(Drawing by Chas. Addams; © 1976 The New Yorker Magazine)

. . . But the Same Meaning

After substituting words and rerranging the sentence, you must ask yourself whether your paraphrase means the same as the original. For example, the phrase *created equal* might be paraphrased *made the same,* but *made the same* suggests that people look and act exactly alike—not Lincoln's meaning. The context of the phrase is political, and Lincoln refers to political equality, so *born with the same rights* is a more accurate paraphrase.

Any paraphrase that does not consider the total meaning of the original can easily become as absurd as the distortions made by a student and a teacher who were discussing the meaning of a famous line from Shakespeare's *The Merchant of Venice*. The line is "the quality of mercy is not strained," which may be accurately paraphrased as "compassionate forgiveness is given freely and easily." But the student tried substituting words without considering context; she wanted to know whether *strained* in the passage meant "strained as in rubber band or strained as in soup." The teacher, looking only at the sentence structure, answered, "Well, since it's *not* strained anyway, I don't see that it matters."

Substituting words and moving sentence parts around do not guarantee accurate paraphrase; you must always check the meaning of the paraphrase against the meaning of the original.

Paraphrase:

Selection 1

The best way to see how creating paraphrases can lead to more precise understanding is to do a few and explore the problems that arise. You will get the most from the following examples of paraphrase if you write your own paraphrases of the passages given before reading the sample paraphrases. When comparing your paraphrases to the sample paraphrases, remember that there is no absolute right and wrong—only variations on how close the paraphrase comes to the original in meaning.

The first passage to paraphrase is a discussion of the benefits of democracy from an essay by the philosopher Bertrand Russell.

Ideas That Have Helped Mankind

Democracy was invented as a device for reconciling government with liberty. It is clear that government is necessary if anything worthy to be called civilization is to exist, but all history shows that any set of men entrusted with power over another set will abuse their power if they can do so with impunity. Democracy is intended to make men's tenure of power temporary and dependent upon popular approval. In so far as it achieves this it prevents the worst abuses of power. The Second Triumvirate in Rome, when they wanted money with a view to fighting Brutus and Cassius, made a list of rich men and declared them public enemies, cut off their heads, and seized their property. This sort of procedure is not possible in America and England in the present day.

This passage discusses a topic familiar to most of us, for we have been told about the virtues of democracy and liberty all our lives. Yet Russell has a new and particular point to make. Our paraphrase, of course, should reflect Russell's viewpoint rather than our own familiar thoughts.

Sample Paraphrase

Democracy was made up by humans to allow social control at the same time as individual freedom and rights. Any ordered civil society certainly requires some form of social control. Whenever a group of people have been made guardians of social control, however, they have always perverted their authority for their own benefit, if they could get away with it without being punished. Democracy purposely limits the authority of these guardians to only a limited time period and only so long as most people support them. Democracy keeps people from perverting authority to the extent that it keeps authority limited. In ancient Rome the government identified wealthy people as criminals, beheaded them, and confiscated their wealth, when the Second Triumvirate (rule of three) desired funds to battle Brutus and Cassius. The governments of contemporary Britain and the United States cannot do this.

Comments on the Paraphrase

Although words are changed and clauses are rearranged, none of the original meaning is left out and nothing is added. In the process of finding equivalent terms for several of the words, however, specific interpretations and expansions are given. *Government* is paraphrased as *social control,* for example, and *liberty* is paraphrased as *individual freedom and rights.* These words can have many possible meanings, with subtle differences among the various definitions. Many other paraphrases could be proposed for these terms, but in the context of the particular point Russell was making, the paraphrases that have been chosen seem to make sense. These examples emphasize that one must not substitute words blindly but rather must consider the whole meaning being conveyed.

One key word—*democracy*—is *not* paraphrased because this word identifies the very concept being discussed and defined. To change this word would undermine the meaning of the passage. Similarly, the names of particular individuals and institutions remain (Brutus, Cassius, and the Second Triumvirate) because these identify unique things. Nevertheless, when exact synonyms are available, such as *Britain* for *England* and *United States* for *America,* the synonyms are used.

Writing Assignment

Paraphrase either passage A or passage B. Passage A is the continuation of the Bertrand Russell passage on democracy and liberty. Passage B, by Lewis Thomas, discusses ethical problems raised by biological research on cloning.

A. Ideas That Have Helped Mankind (continued)

We owe the fact that it is not possible not only to democracy, but also to the doctrine of personal liberty. This doctrine, in practice, consists of two parts, on the one hand that a man shall not be punished except by due process of law, and on the other hand that there shall be a sphere within which a man's actions are not to be subject to governmental control. This sphere includes free speech, free press and religious freedom. It used to include freedom of economic enterprise. All these doctrines, of course, are held in practice with certain limitations. The British formerly did not adhere to them in their dealings with India. Freedom of the press is not respected in the case of doctrines which are thought dangerously subversive. Free speech would not be held to exonerate public advocacy of assassination of an unpopular politician. But in spite of these limitations the doctrine of personal liberty has been of great value throughout the English-speaking world, as anyone who lives in it will quickly realize when he finds himself in a police state.

B. On Cloning a Human Being

Cloning is the most dismaying of prospects, mandating as it does the elimination of sex with only a metaphoric elimination of death as compensation. It is almost no comfort to know that one's cloned, identical surrogate lives on, especially when the living will very likely involve edging one's real, now aging self off to the side, sooner or later. It is hard to imagine anything like filial affection or respect for a single, unmated nucleus; harder still to think of one's new, self-generated self as anything but an absolute, desolate orphan. Not to mention the complex interpersonal relationship involved in raising one's self from infancy, teaching the language, enforcing discipline, instilling good manners, and the like. How would you feel if you became an incorrigible juvenile delinquent by proxy, at the age of fifty-five?

The public questions are obvious. Who is to be selected, and on what qualifications? How to handle the risks of misused technology, such as self-determined cloning by the rich and powerful but socially objectionable, or the cloning by governments of dumb, docile masses for the world's work? What will be the effect on all the uncloned rest of us of human sameness? After all, we've accustomed ourselves through hundreds of millennia to the continual exhilaration of uniqueness; each of us is totally different, in a fundamental sense, from all the other four billion. Selfness is an essential fact of life. The thought of human nonselfness, precise sameness, is terrifying, when you think about it.

Well, don't think about it, because it isn't a probable possibility, not even as a long shot for the distant future, in my opinion. I agree that you might clone some people who would look amazingly like their parental cell donors, but the odds are that they'd be almost as different as you or me, and certainly more different than any of today's identical twins.

Paraphrase:

Selection 2

The next excerpt for paraphrase appears in Alexis de Tocqueville's *Democracy in America*. De Tocqueville, a French aristocrat, visited

Alexis de Tocqueville. Photo from a lithograph by Chasseriau. (The Bettmann Archive)

the United States in 1831 and commented on what he saw. This passage requires you to consider an aspect of American life you might not have thought about before. Furthermore, it asks you to compare democracy to the less familiar system of aristocracy. By suggesting that democracy might in some ways not be as effective as aristocracy, the passage may contradict ideas you hold firmly. In order to understand the author's viewpoint, you have to think yourself back to a time when people with more traditional forms of government were trying to figure out the strange experiment of democracy going on in a new country called the United States.

It is not necessary that you wind up agreeing with de Tocqueville, but you must entertain his argument long enough to find out exactly what he is saying in order to paraphrase accurately.

Of the Use Which Americans Make of Public Associations in Civil Life

Aristocratic communities always contain, amongst a multitude of persons who by themselves are powerless, a small number of powerful and wealthy citizens, each of whom can achieve great undertakings single-handed. In aristocratic societies, men do not need to combine in order to act, because they are strongly held together. Every wealthy and powerful citizen constitutes the head of a permanent and compulsory association, composed of all those who are dependent upon him, or whom he makes subservient to the execution of his designs.

Amongst democratic nations, on the contrary, all the citizens are independent and feeble; they can do hardly anything by themselves, and none of them can oblige his fellow-men to lend him their assistance. They all, therefore, become powerless, if they do not learn voluntarily to help each other. If men living in democratic countries had no right and no inclination to associate for political purposes, their independence would be in great jeopardy; but they might long preserve their wealth and their cultivation; whereas, if they never acquired the habit of forming associations in ordinary life, civilization itself would be endangered. A people amongst whom individuals should lose the power of achieving great things single-handed, without acquiring the means of producing them by united exertions, would soon relapse into barbarism.

Unhappily, the same social condition which renders associations so necessary to democratic nations, renders their formation more difficult amongst those nations than amongst all other. When several members of an aristocracy agree to combine, they easily succeed in doing so: as each of them brings great strength to the partnership, the number of its members may be very limited; and when the members of an association are limited in number, they may easily become mutually acquainted, understand each other, and establish fixed regulations. The same opportunities do not occur amongst democratic nations, where the associated members must always be very numerous for their associations to have any power.

In order to understand this passage fully, one must conceive of life in an aristocracy where a few rich and powerful members of the nobility control the means to act on their own decisions. The opinions of most people do not matter, for they must do what the nobility tells them. Their livelihoods and their whole way of life depend on the desires of the powerful aristocrats.

To complete the comparison, one must conceive of how people take action in a democracy, where no one individual has the power of a king or duke to make unilateral decisions. Citizens must group together in political parties, pressure groups, or other organizations to pool their resources and have the power of large numbers. After picturing these two different situations and comparing them, one needs to imagine how easy or difficult it is to form such groupings. Only after assimilating all these ideas can the reader hope to paraphrase the meaning of this passage accurately.

Sample Paraphrase

Where people living together are ruled by a small, privileged class of people considered to be better than others, a few individuals have much financial and political strength, in the middle of a much larger group of common people with little control over their own lives. Each of these few, mighty aristocrats can on his own carry out very large and important projects. Under such government, the forceful ties that bind individuals together into a community mean that citizens do not have to come together consciously and voluntarily to carry through decisions. Each financially and politically strong member of the aristocracy is already, by nature of the social structure, in charge of a stable and lasting involuntary group, made up of the people who rely on the aristocrat and those people whom the aristocrat places under his control in order to carry out his plans.

On the other hand, where countries are controlled by the mass of people, each individual is separate and weak. People who belong to a democracy cannot force their fellow citizens to help them carry out plans, nor can they accomplish very much individually. Consequently, if citizens in a democracy do not find out how to cooperate in mutual aid, no one has any significant control over his life. Without the privilege or desire to join together to affect governmental actions, although they might easily lose their individual freedoms, they still could possibly keep their property and social advancement for a substantial time. On the other hand, without the regular practice of joining together to carry out everyday activities, organized and advanced society might not last. Savagery would not be long in taking over a community where single citizens can no longer accomplish significant actions on their own and do not develop a way of accomplishing significant actions by working together.

Unfortunately, this very situation of communal organization, requiring cooperative groups in countries ruled by the mass of people, makes it that much harder to create such groups. A few members of the nobility in an aristocratic country can easily join together if they want to. Very few aristocrats are needed to make a very strong organization, because each individual aristocrat has much power to add to the group. Moreover, when the group is small, the individuals can come to know each other with little difficulty, find out what all the members have in mind, and agree to rules and procedures for carrying out the group's action. In democracies, however, these favorable conditions for forming groups do not exist, because the number of individual citizens joining a group must be extremely large if the group is to be strong enough to carry out its plans.

Comments on the Paraphrase

Because this excerpt compares forms of social organization in democracy and aristocracy, all the political and social organizational terms are crucial. Often simple synonyms do not adequately bring out de Tocqueville's meaning. Instead, phrases several words long have to be used. Thus *aristocratic* is paraphrased as *ruled by a small, privileged class of people,* and *democratic* is paraphrased as *ruled by the mass of people* in order to convey de Tocqueville's fundamental distinction between the few and powerful rulers versus the many and weak rulers. The terms *power, wealth, association, independence, social condition,* and several others require similar care.

In paying close attention to the words of the original, I discovered that de Tocqueville used the word *community* to identify the political unit in aristocracies and the word *nation* for the political unit in democracies. In doing so, de Tocqueville contrasts the social cohesiveness of aristocracy with the governmental distance of democracy, so I tried to preserve that distinction in the substitute terms, *people living together* and *country.*

This distinction between the social cohesion of aristocracies and the isolation and consequent weakness of democracies builds from one paragraph to the next. In writing the paraphrase, I became aware of how much of de Tocqueville's argument depended on his vision of how orderly aristocracies worked. With all individuals having a fixed and stable place in the hierarchy, everyone naturally pulled together to do great things. He sees that world as simple and strong because only a few people need to make decisions. All the rest just obey their superiors.

De Tocqueville starts off by presenting an attractive vision of the powerful aristocrat. He then contrasts this with the more complicated situation in democracies, where one has to go to the trouble of gaining the cooperation of others rather than acting by direct coercion. Still democracy seems to come off acceptably, able to accomplish things through the praiseworthy activity of cooperation. Only in the last paragraph does de Tocqueville find real difficulty in democracy by comparing the ease of organizing effective associations in aristocracies to the difficulty of doing so in democracies.

As I began to understand the true direction of de Tocqueville's reasoning, I noticed that he does not mention any of the negative effects of the aristocratic coercion of the lower classes. Moreover, he seems to assume that the upper classes will always have the active cooperation of the lower classes. Nor does he mention the motivating factor in democracies that each person is working for his or her own interests and so might work that much harder to achieve effective cooperation. Yet de Tocqueville's argument also reminded me of how difficult it is to achieve effective cooperation, and I remembered numerous occasions when something positive did not happen because people did not act together.

The more deeply I looked at de Tocqueville's precise meaning and reasoning, the more deeply I could react to it. Only by looking closely at the passage to paraphrase it could I observe those details and shades of meaning that led to my analysis and reaction. Similarly, as you learn to read more deeply through paraphrase, the comments in your journal (see Chapter 2) should be gaining subtlety and relevance to the texts you are discussing. By making you confront another person's argument fully, paraphrase leads to a carefully thought-out answer, full of discoveries and new ideas. Close interaction with the text you are reading makes sparks fly.

You probably paraphrased the Russell and de Tocqueville passages differently than the samples here, pointing out other aspects of the originals. In some instances, your versions may even be closer to the meaning of the originals. Comparing paraphrases and explaining the differences among them will help you better understand the shades of meaning conveyed by different word choices.

Writing Assignment

Paraphrase either passage A or passage B. Passage A is the continuation of the passage from de Tocqueville, looking further at the consequences of the difficulties of cooperation and of individual weakness in democracies. Passage B, by two eminent biologists,

P. B. and J. S. Medawar, discusses common misunderstandings about the evolutionary principle of natural selection.

A. Of the Use Which Americans Make of Public Associations in Civil Life (continued)

I am aware that many of my countrymen are not in the least embarrassed by this difficulty. They contend, that, the more enfeebled and incompetent the citizens become, the more able and active the government ought to be rendered, in order that society at large may execute what individuals can no longer accomplish. They believe this answers the whole difficulty, but I think they are mistaken.

A government might perform the part of some of the largest American companies; and several States, members of the Union, have already attempted it; but what political power could ever carry on the vast multitude of lesser undertakings which the American citizens perform every day, with the assistance of the principle of association? It is easy to foresee that the time is drawing near when man will be less and less able to produce, of himself alone, the commonest necessaries of life. The task of the governing power will therefore perpetually increase, and its very efforts will extend it every day. The more it stands in the place of associations, the more will individuals, losing the notion of combining together, require its assistance: these are causes and effects which unceasingly create each other.

B. The Biological Principles of Population Control

It is an historical accident that the principle of natural selection is most often introduced to young students by means of a syllogism that runs as follows:
1. Organisms produce offspring in numbers vastly in excess of their requirements.
2. Only a small minority of these survive to the age of reproduction.
3. Natural selection must act in such a way as to preserve the organisms best fitted to survive.

The first proposition in this argument embodies a grave fallacy. Organisms do *not* produce offspring in numbers vastly in excess of their requirements. Whenever an exact study has been made of the correlation between fertility and mortality, it has turned out that organisms produce just about the right number of offspring to ensure their survival. The most thorough of these studies is that of David

Lack on nesting birds. Nesting birds lay a characteristic number—a 'clutch'—of eggs, and there is every reason to suppose that this number is under the control of natural selection: a smaller number would prejudice the chances of survival, and a larger number of nestlings would put a physiological strain upon the mother which she might be unable to meet. Any particular clutch size probably represents a compromise between these two factors. To envisage an unlimited growth of population as in premise 1 above is therefore to combine a real rate of fertility with a quite imaginary rate of mortality. All real populations are limited in size by density-dependent factors. In human populations a special anxiety is, of course, that these density-dependent factors will include major sources of human distress, such as death from starvation and infectious disease. It is therefore imperative to restrain the growth of human populations so that they do not become prey to any such disasters. The present situation, as is well known, is that mortality is in decline, without any proportionate reduction of fertility, so that the very situation envisaged by the Malthusian syllogism outlined above is being realized. Although the principal obstacles to the adoption of birth control procedures are educational and administrative, there are biological obstacles as well: these may be summarized by saying that there is a physiological conspiracy against the adoption of effective birth control procedures. No behaviour has deeper evolutionary roots than reproductive behaviour and the biological 'forces' that do so much to promote fertility and reproduction cannot be easily annulled; nevertheless, the problem is a soluble one and fortunately none of the many scientists trying to solve it are deterred by the foolish accusation that their work might be said to betray an enmity to nature.

Knowing When
to Paraphrase

If you were to paraphrase all your reading, you would get to read very little, although you would know that little reading very well. Obviously, paraphrasing for your own purposes should be saved for extremely difficult passages that must be worked through word by word to wring out all the meaning.

Paraphrasing can also serve you in your own writing: you can use the paraphrase to restate a passage in terms your reader will understand more clearly. You can also use paraphrase to interpret difficult concepts and to make explicit facts and ideas that are implicit in the original. You will need to paraphrase when you want to take precise notes of your reading and when you wish to mention another writer's exact ideas in your own research papers.

To Explain Simply

When somone who is not as knowledgeable as you is having difficulty understanding some assigned reading, the best way you can help is through paraphrase. If, for example, a younger member of your family is having problems with the reading for her ninth-grade class in social studies, she may ask your help in explaining the preamble to the Constitution:

> We the People of the United States, in Order to form a more perfect Union, establish Justice, insure domestic Tranquility, provide for the common defence, promote the general Welfare, and secure the Blessings of Liberty to ourselves and our Posterity, do ordain and establish this Constitution for the United States of America.

You might help out by paraphrasing the original something like this:

> All the citizens of the United States are setting up and agreeing to this set of basic rules for our government. We are doing this for several reasons. We desire a better government with fewer problems than we had before. We want to guarantee everyone is treated fairly. We want to make sure that we have peace within the country and that we can protect ourselves from outside attack. We want to help all of us live better. And we want to enjoy freedom not just for ourselves but for all the people who come after us.

Notice how the paraphrase makes the passage easier to understand. A long, complex sentence is broken down into several shorter ones, and the parts are rearranged so that only one idea is discussed at a time. The unfamiliar terms, such as *domestic tranquility,* are replaced by more common words, such as *peace within the country.* Finally, abstractions such as *general welfare* are made more concrete, as in *all of us live better.*

In many technical and scientific areas, paraphrasing basic principles helps explain the complexities of a subject to the reader. Textbooks and popularizations of science often rely heavily on simplifying paraphrases of more complex writing.

To Interpret the Text

In addition to helping the student, the paraphrase can aid professionals in coming to agreement over the meaning of important pieces of writing. In literature, philosophy, and religion, experts often disagree on their interpretations of significant books. Only by paraphrase can they make their readings explicit enough to compare and discuss.

Another area where it is essential for professionals to develop a shared understanding of important texts is the law. Many legal books attempt to clarify exactly what particular laws say and, consequently, how they should be applied in particular circumstances. If there were not some agreement over the meaning of laws, our system of government would collapse.

However, laws as originally phrased frequently have ambiguous or unspecific meanings, which leave unclear how they should be applied to a particular case. In all legal arguments, the courts must interpret the exact meaning of laws; thus many parts of legal decisions are a kind of extended paraphrase, clarifying the meaning and function of the laws. Legal texts, in turn, make use of these decisions and other legal precedents in order to restate the laws in terms of current legal practice.

Consider, for example, the Eighth Amendment to the Constitution. This part of the Bill of Rights outlaws "cruel and unusual punishments." You can see that the exact meaning of the phrase *cruel and unusual punishments* is open to various interpretations. What makes one punishment cruel and another acceptable? If it weren't unpleasant, it wouldn't be a punishment. The only way to clarify the meaning is to include much legal background in the paraphrase, as Corwin and Peltason do in *Understanding the Constitution:*

> The historic punishments banned are burning at the stake, crucifixion, breaking on the wheel, the rack and thumbscrew, and in some circumstances, solitary confinement. Capital punishment inflicted by hanging, electrocution, lethal gas, or a firing squad are permissible. And the Supreme Court has ruled that there was no constitutional inhibition against electrocuting a prisoner after a first attempt failed because of a power breakdown.
>
> Punishment may be cruel and unusual if it is out of all proportion to the offense as, for example, capital punishment for a petty crime. The Supreme Court declared unconstitutional a California statute that made the mere act of being addicted to drugs a crime because it inflicted punishment simply for being ill. Chief Justice Warren,

speaking for the Court in an opinion supported by only three other justices, ruled that Congress violated the Eighth Amendment when it attempted to make loss of citizenship part of the punishment for members of the armed forces who had been convicted and dishonorably discharged for desertion during time of war.

This passage aims at a nonprofessional audience; legal points are, of course, explored in much greater detail in books for practicing lawyers.

To Restate the Case

Works like the United States Constitution and the Bible express laws and ideas on which people build their lives. Thus paraphrases that expand on their full meaning are valuable in themselves. More often, writers use paraphrases of specific passages as passing references or as background material. If a philosopher wants to take issue with the ideas of a previous thinker, the philosopher must first restate the point he is arguing against. If a historian of science wants to show how one idea grew out of another, she must restate both ideas before she can demonstrate the connection. If a lawyer wants to cite an earlier judicial interpretation that strengthens his case, he must restate the important points of that judicial interpretation. In each instance, a precise paraphrase is often the method used to restate a passage. The other methods of restating a text passage are by quoting directly or by summarizing the major points. Each method has its advantages for different situations. The comparative advantages and appropriate times to use each are discussed in detail in Chapter 17.

The paraphrase allows you to make your point complete, just as a quotation does, but it is more flexible in allowing you to fit the original material in with the flow of your argument. Through the paraphrase you can bring out your interpretation, and you can emphasize those points that are most crucial to your argument. Moreover, you can write the paraphrased sentences to fit in smoothly with the surrounding material of your argument. Your argument does not have to stop short as another voice takes over; with paraphrase, the voice always remains your own.

You must always clearly identify the source (both author and text) of the ideas you paraphrase. This documentation allows the reader to distinguish between your own ideas and the ideas you derived from your source. (See Chapter 17 for a full description of documentation.)

James Madison, for example, paraphrased parts of the Constitution effectively in *Federalist Paper Number 62*. Before the Constitution was approved, Alexander Hamilton, James Madison, and John Jay wrote a series of newspaper articles in support of the proposed government. In one of these articles, Madison discussed the proposed composition of the Senate. In order to argue in behalf of various provisions of Article I, Section 3 of the Constitution, he first provided paraphrases of those provisions. However, because he is paraphrasing instead of quoting, he can also bring in material from an earlier section of the Constitution, which describes the composition of the House of Representatives. Thus, paraphrase gives Madison the flexibility to compare the provisions of two sections within a single sentence. Once he has set up his comparisons through paraphrase, he can then argue in favor of the provisions.

> The qualifications proposed for senators, as distinguished from those of representatives, consist in a more advanced age and a longer period of citizenship. A senator must be thirty years of age at least; as a representative must be twenty-five. And the former must have been a citizen nine years; as seven years are required for the latter. The propriety of these distinctions is explained by the nature of the senatorial trust, which, requiring greater extent of information and stability of character, requires at the same time that the senator should have reached a period of life most likely to supply these advantages; and which, participating immediately in transactions with foreign nations, ought to be exercised by none who are not thoroughly weaned from the prepossessions and habits incident to foreign birth and education. The term of nine years appears to be a prudent mediocrity between a total exclusion of adopted citizens, whose merits and talents may claim a share in the public confidence, and an indiscriminate and hasty admission of them, which might create a channel for foreign influence on the national councils.

For Discussion: A Student Example

Frequently in your college courses you will be asked to discuss ideas and information presented in the books you are studying. In such discussions, as in your journal, you must identify the specific thoughts you are responding to, so the reader will know exactly what you are writing about. Paraphrase allows you to present in a precise way the thoughts you have gleaned from your reading. You can emphasize those aspects of the passage you will discuss while interpreting the original. In short, paraphrase allows you to set up the basic terms of your discussion.

The following is the beginning of a student paper written for a political philosophy course. It discusses some of the underlying concepts of a passage from Aristotle's *Politics* that reads: "The man who is isolated—who is unable to share in the benefits of political association, or has no need to share because he is already self-sufficient—is no part of the polis, and must therefore be either a beast or a god." Notice how the student, Chris Silver, uses the opening paraphrase to interpret and expand on a few of the key terms from Aristotle: the "god or beast" distinction and the underlying concept of humanity in the middle. Silver then discusses Aristotle's political and social definition of being human, leading right into the student's main point: the difference between this view and the moral definition of humanity that the student himself was brought up with.

In Chapter 1 of *The Politics*, Aristotle identifies the individual who lives by himself apart from the Greek city-state as either subhuman ("a beast") or superhuman ("a god"). That isolated individual is either below politics (not able to take advantage of all the civilizing effects it offers) or above politics (no longer needing those benefits because he already contains these things within himself). By excluding the extremes, this definition of being human suggests that human beings are thoroughly social creatures, separated from the life of animals only by their ability to establish political communities. Without the kinds of benefits the city offers, we would be reduced to a life of bare subsistence without art, culture, order, or even companionship. On the other hand, these benefits are not simply luxuries; they are basic needs of human beings. Only gods can satisfy their needs on their own.

This social definition of being human goes against much I have learned. My upbringing has emphasized faith,

morality, and integrity as what makes me better than an
animal. A hermit to me can be truly human if he is adher-
ing to his beliefs, but a city-dweller can be a beast if
he has no morality or beliefs. Being human has nothing to
do with political law in my view, but rather with a
higher law, a divine law if you will.

My belief, based on a religious view of life, differs
from Aristotle's. From what we have studied of Greek religion, it seems their gods set out no higher law for humans to follow, unlike the God of the Bible, both the Old
and New Testaments, who not only set out commandments,
but had many other spiritual teachings.

Writing Assignments

1. Paraphrase the opening lines of the Declaration of Independence
   in order to explain the meaning fully and clearly to a ninth-
   grade student:

   When in the Course of human events, it becomes necessary for
   one people to dissolve the political bands, which have connected
   them with another, and to assume among the powers of the earth,
   the separate and equal station to which the Laws of Nature and of
   Nature's God entitle them, a decent respect to the opinions of mankind
   requires that they should declare the causes which impel them to
   the separation.—We hold these truths to be self-evident, that all
   men are created equal, that they are endowed by their Creator with
   certain unalienable Rights, that among these are Life, Liberty and
   the pursuit of Happiness.—That to secure these rights, Governments
   are instituted among Men, deriving their just powers from the consent
   of the governed,—That whenever any Form of Government becomes
   destructive of these ends, it is the Right of the People to alter or to
   abolish it, and to institute new Government, laying its foundation
   on such principles and organizing its powers in such form, as to
   them shall seem most likely to effect their Safety and Happiness.

2. Compare your paraphrase of the opening lines of the Declaration
   of Independence with H. L. Mencken's version of the same lines.
   By his paraphrase, H. L. Mencken was commenting on the level

at which most Americans discuss politics. By having fun with a certain style of language, Mencken seems to be criticizing a way of thinking. In a short essay, discuss how Mencken's version changes the original and what exact point you think Mencken was making.

The Declaration of Independence in American

When things get so balled up that the people of a country got to cut loose from some other country, and go it on their own hook, without asking no permission from nobody, excepting maybe God Almighty, then they ought to let everybody know why they done it, so that everybody can see they are not trying to put nothing over on nobody.

All we got to say on this proposition is this: first, me and you is as good as anybody else, and maybe a damn sight better; second, nobody ain't got no right to take away none of our rights; third, every man has got a right to live, to come and go as he pleases, and to have a good time whichever way he likes, so long as he don't interfere with nobody else. That any government that don't give a man them rights ain't worth a damn; also, people ought to choose the kind of government they want themselves, and nobody else ought to have no say in the matter. That whenever any government don't do this, then the people have got a right to give it the bum's rush and put in one that will take care of their interests. Of course, that don't mean having a revolution every day like them South American yellow-bellies, or every time some jobholder goes to work and does something he ain't got no business to do. It is better to stand a little graft, etc., than to have revolutions all the time, like them coons, and any man that wasn't a anarchist or one of them I.W.W.'s would say the same. But when things get so bad that a man ain't hardly got no rights at all no more, but you might almost call him a slave, then everybody ought to get together and throw the grafters out, and put in new ones who won't carry on so high and steal so much, and then watch them.

3. Paraphrase the following excerpt from "Culture and Freedom" by E. M. Forster. The British novelist published this during the Second World War as part of a book of essays *Two Cheers for Democracy*. Through paraphrase, show your interpretation of the full meaning of the passage to your instructor in order to demonstrate your understanding of Forster's argument.

As a writer, I have three reasons for believing in freedom.
Firstly the writer himself must feel free, or he may find it difficult

to fall into the creative mood and do good work. If he feels free, sure of himself, unafraid, easy inside, he is in a favourable condition for the act of creation.

The second reason also concerns the writer—and indeed the artist generally. It is not enough to feel free; that is only the start. To feel free may be enough for the mystic, who can function alone and concentrate even in a concentration camp. The writer, the artist, needs something more—namely freedom to tell other people what he is feeling. Otherwise, he is bottled up and what is inside him may go bad ... He is not like the mystic; he cannot function in a vacuum, he cannot spin tales in his head or paint pictures in the air, or hum tunes under his breath. He must have an audience, he must express his feelings, and if he knows he may be forbidden to express himself, he becomes afraid to feel. Officials, even when they are well-meaning, do not realise this. Their make-up is so different. They assume that when a book is censored only the book in question is affected. They do not realise that they may have impaired the creative machinery of the writer's mind, and prevented him from writing good books in the future.

So here are two of my reasons for believing that freedom is necessary for culture. The third reason concerns the general public. The public, on its side, must be free to read, to listen, to look. If it is prevented from receiving the communications which the artist sends it, it becomes inhibited, like him, though in a different way: it remains immature. And immaturity is a great characteristic of the public in Nazi Germany. If you look at a photograph of our enemies they may strike you as able and brave and formidable, even heroic. But they will not strike you as grown up. The have not been allowed to hear, to listen, or to look. Only people who have been allowed to practise freedom can have the grown-up look in their eyes.

I do not want to exaggerate the claims of freedom. It does not guarantee the production of masterpieces, and masterpieces have been produced under conditions far from free—the *Aeneid*, for instance, or the plays of Racine. Freedom is only a favourable step—or, let us say, three little steps. When writers (and artists generally) feel easy, when they can express themselves openly, when their public is allowed to receive their communications, there is a chance of the general level of civilisation rising.

4. Paraphrase the following discussion of the interaction between biology and intellect in human evolution by the winner of the Nobel Prize in biology, S. E. Luria. Consider your paraphrase an attempt to bring out all the meaning of the passage as preparation for a seminar on the subject.

Mind

In the species *Homo sapiens* a new way of adaptation had arisen, much faster than slow-working natural selection. Intelligence could accumulate knowledge and thereby provide fitness of a new kind, permitting man to alter his environment rather than simply being selected by it. Coupled with the stupendous evolution of the human hand, that most exquisitely delicate of all tools, the development of intelligence made it possible for the species of man to spread over the earth, from the tropics to the polar regions, making the whole globe its domain.

The biological basis of the process that made the human mind what it is was the explosive development of the human brain, presumably brought about by selection for greater and greater skills. In weight, but above all in complexity, the brain of man is unique. A few million years ago, more than a hundred thousand generations, and after a much longer period of relative stability, the hominoid brain started to grow to the enormous proportions it has today, about one-fortieth the weight of the body. This growth has involved mainly those parts of the brain concerned with the higher functions of cognition and coordination—the cortex. The idea that some sort of directional process must have taken place seems inescapable. Biologically speaking, this means that once certain mutations started to produce a more powerful brain system, this system proved so valuable for differential reproduction that any new gene combinations that perfected it further were powerfully favored. One might almost say that in the recent evolution of man practically everything else was neglected in favor of increased brain power. Man lost the protective fur of the apes, their early sexual maturity, and many other adaptations useful to lower mammals. In exchange he won the brain and with it the faculty of language, speech, thought, and consciousness.

The central role of speech and language in the development of thought-power and in the success of man as a species suggests that a major part of the evolution of the human brain from that of man's ape-like ancestors must have been a continuous perfecting of the speech centers, which are located on the left side of the brain. The location of some of these centers is known from the symptoms observed in individuals who either from strokes or from accidents have received localized brain injuries. These injuries result in various kinds of speech trouble; the so-called aphasias, their nature depending on the exact site of the damage.

5. Imagine that your college newspaper has a regular opinion column called "What I Learned in School Today," where each week a different student comments on something controversial or in-

teresting from class lectures, assigned readings, or personal reading. This week it is your turn to write the column. Begin your column of two to three hundred words with a paraphrase of the material you will discuss.

6. Imagine that you are taking a course in political science (or biology) and your teacher asks you to comment in a short essay on any appropriate excerpt from this chapter. Write a two-hundred-word essay (similar to the example on pages 61–62). Be sure to identify the source of the idea you are discussing, and begin with a paraphrase of the relevant passage.

4 Summarizing:
The Author's Main Ideas

Summary, like paraphrase, allows you to reproduce another writer's thoughts—but in shortened form. In writing a summary, you focus on the most important statements of the original passage and eliminate the less important material. Four techniques—deleting, selecting, note taking, and miniaturizing—can help you shorten the material. As you become more adept at summarizing, you will devise your own combination of these techniques for each occasion. But in all cases, the summary must be written in readable prose that reflects the essential meaning of the original text. Like paraphrase, summary can be used for many purposes: to help you understand the main points and structure of an author's argument, to convey that understanding to others, to present background information quickly, or to refer to another writer's ideas in the course of making your own original statement.

The Essence
of the Matter

The word-by-word attention required for a good paraphrase will lead you across all the contours of another writer's thought. You will follow the main trail of meaning, the ridges of fine distinctions, the cutbacks of qualifications, and the waysides of association. As the patient hiker on such a slow trek, you must mentally pull together all the major events of the journey in order to feel some sense of the total experience. Writing a summary, on the other hand, allows you to review the entire journey as a whole.

To highlight the essentials of another writer's idea—rather than to provide a complete and detailed restatement—is the purpose of summary writing. A summary will help you understand the major direction, the main points, and the overall shape of the more detailed original. A summary restates the essence of the original in as few words as possible, *but not necessarily in different words*. Unlike the paraphrase writer, who must discover new ways to restate the meaning, the summarizer looks for the most compact restatement. Of course, you must give adequate credit to the original by techniques described fully in Chapter 17.

Writing Summaries

To rewrite a longer piece in short form, you must first understand the piece you are working with. Begin by reading the piece carefully, making sure you absorb the full meaning. If there are words you do not know, look them up. If some sentences are confusing, paraphrase them. Identify the main ideas and determine how the less important material relates to those main ideas. In short, read.

Once you understand the piece you are summarizing, you must decide which parts you are going to include in the summary and which you are going to leave out. Of course, how much material you select depends on how long you want the summary to be and for what purpose you are going to use the summary. (We will discuss these issues in the latter part of this chapter.) However, unless you have a more specific ratio in mind, you should generally try to create a summary about one-fifth to one-quarter the length of the original.

This chapter presents four methods for choosing the material to include in a summary: deleting, selecting, note taking, and miniaturizing. The methods overlap somewhat. By deleting, for example, you in effect select the material that remains, and miniaturizing is only a structurally focused version of note taking. A good summary takes into account all four methods, and in practice people switch back and forth among them. Because each of these methods emphasizes slightly different skills, however, we will discuss them separately. Through the somewhat artificial separation and isolated practice of these skills, you will master the art of making concise and exact summaries. After you gain control of all the methods, you will be able to combine them as you see fit. Before we discuss these methods, however, let us briefly examine the subsequent steps in writing a summary.

Informative and Descriptive Summaries

Having selected the material to include in your summary, you must then decide whether your summary will be informative or descriptive. *Informative summaries* adopt the tone of the original full text, simply presenting the information it contains in shorter form. *Descriptive summaries* adopt a more distant perspective, describing the original text rather than directly presenting the information it contains. An informative summary of the Declaration of Independence might begin as follows:

> When people declare themselves independent of their political ties, they should give reasons. Governments are formed to protect equality and rights, including life, liberty, and the pursuit of happiness. If government does not do this, people can change the government.

A descriptive summary of the same passage might begin:

> Jefferson opens the Declaration of Independence by stating that a country declaring independence needs to give its reasons. He goes on to discuss the purposes of government in protecting individual rights and the legitimacy of change if government does not live up to its obligations.

Note that the informative summary does not mention the author or title of the piece but rather gets right down to the content. Thus it can present more information more compactly and more precisely. *For most purposes, informative summaries are preferable to descriptive summaries.* (All the summaries in this chapter are informative.) In addition, when research material is simply reported for its factual content, as in the paper of synthesis on pages 266–270, the informative summary is used.

On the other hand, descriptive summaries give a more nearly complete picture of the structure of the original. Descriptive summaries also establish a certain distance between the writer of the summary and the writer of the original piece. This sense of objectivity is useful whenever the summarized material is to be analyzed, evaluated, or otherwise discussed. Hence descriptive summaries should be used in book reviews (see Chapter 7), in essays of analysis (see, for example, pages 213–216), and in other essays discussing a text (see, for example, pages 248–251).

The Summary as Writing

The key to writing an effective summary is combining the material you choose to include into concise, coherent sentences and paragraphs. If your sentences are carelessly formed, not only will the summary be unreadable but you will also lose the connection among the pieces of information in the summary. You could simply wind up with tossed word salad. On the other hand, carefully written sentences can help show how the separate facts and ideas fit together to build the meaning of the whole. Thoughtful word choice and sentence structure can help you reduce a summary by half with no loss of information, ideas, or clarity. (Chapter 16 offers suggestions for sharpening your phrasing.) Incidentally, because the summary form places such a premium on conciseness and clarity, writing summaries provides excellent practice for the improvement of your general writing style.

Because you are taking information from many parts of the original text, you could easily lose sight of the logical structure of the whole piece. You need to pay close attention to the new transitions and paragraph structure of the summary. Rather than running all the information together in a series of seemingly unrelated sentences, you can use transitions to show the connection between sentences, and you can create new paragraphs to reflect large divisions in the original material.

Finally, in your finished draft of the summary, be sure you identify the source of the original material in a heading, an introductory phrase, or a footnote. When summaries stand by themselves, the source usually appears in the heading. When summaries are worked into the course of longer arguments, you can cite the source of your material in an introductory phrase or a footnote without interrupting the flow of your argument.

Steps in Writing a Summary—A Review

1. Read the original carefully.
2. Choose material for the summary.
3. Decide whether your summary will be informative or descriptive.
4. Rewrite the material in concise, coherent sentences and paragraphs.
5. Identify the source of the original text.

Methods of Choosing
Summary Material

Method 1: Deleting Less Important Material

Because a summary moves quickly through the main points of the original, you should omit all the less important information. As you go through the original text, cross out all unnecessary words, all repetitions, all digressions, and all minor supporting details. This should leave only the most important ideas and information.

This method often works well where clearly stated major points are immediately followed by extensive discussion, details, or examples. Once you have read the main point, it is easy to cross out all the secondary information that follows.

The following example is taken from an essay by Lawrence Lichty. This discussion of the influence of television on news illustrates the deletion method of summary writing. First the passage is given in its original form; then the passage is shown with all the secondary and superfluous material crossed out; finally, one possible rewrite of the summary is presented. You will gain more from the example and the discussion after it if you first choose the material *you* would retain (by deleting all superfluous material) and write your own summary of the original passage before going further. You will then be able to compare your results with the sample and comments that follow.

The News Media: Video Versus Print

Unsure of the future, a dozen newspaper managements, from the *New York Times* to Times-Mirror, Knight-Ridder, and Copley, are starting or testing "teletext" or home "videotex" services in New Jersey, Florida, California, and elsewhere. (Such electronic services use cable or telephone lines to send textual matter and graphics to a TV screen at the viewer's behest.) The *Washington Post* in early 1982 disclosed plans to provide local news and advertising programming for all cable TV system operators in the metropolitan Washington area. And publishers lobbied vigorously in Washington against moves to permit AT&T to send news via telephone lines into homes.

Yet a 1982 study of videotex usage in Britain found that most customers were usually seeking specific pieces of data (e.g., 60 percent regularly looked up classified listings; nearly half looked up stock exchange information at least every other day). "News" was not the main attraction. Indeed, as a Canadian operator observed, with videotex, information is "the tail not the dog. The dog is [electronic] shopping and banking."

The biggest expansion in news has come in television. TV news is the child of radio news, and of the Paramount newsreels of the 1930s and '40s; it is not the child, or, in its basic attitudes even a very near relative, of the newspapers. In their rivalry for audiences (ratings) which govern TV advertising revenues, the producers of the evening news shows—local or national—can never relax; when Walter Cronkite retired as an anchorman in 1981, the question for CBS was: Could his successor, Dan Rather, officiate over the news as well, i.e., draw the most viewers? The answer was yes, but all three networks were changing their style and on-camera personalities in late 1981 and early 1982.

The spread of cable television (to one-third of all U.S. television households) prompted Ted Turner last January to start Cable News Network 2, a 24-hour Atlanta-based TV news service, in a direct challenge to the networks. The networks responded by announcing plans to present news from 2 A.M. to 7 A.M.—when 4.9 million TV sets are in use.

This impending surge in broadcast news seems only to confirm the ascendancy of video. Already, the TV viewer in a medium-to-large-sized city faces no shortage of "news." In Washington, D.C., for example, the city-dweller has only one full-fledged local daily, the *Washington Post,* but he can watch "news" for nine and one-half hours each weekday, including two stretches of three hours (6 A.M. to 9 A.M., 5 P.M. to 8 P.M.). Another five and one-half hours of news is available via Cable News Network 2 from Baltimore's station WMAR-TV.

All told, in the Washington area, there are more than 14 hours of programming—network, syndicated, and local—on three network stations, two independent stations, and PBS's station. If one includes such programs as the PBS *Nightly Business Report,* as well as the lighter *Phil Donahue* and *Hour Magazine,* the total comes to 24 hours.

Here is the same passage with all minor information deleted.

~~Unsure of the future, a dozen~~ newspaper managements, ~~from the New York Times to Times-Mirror, Knight-Ridder, and Copley~~, are starting ~~or testing~~ "teletext" ~~or home "videotex" services in New Jersey, Florida, California, and elsewhere~~. (~~Such electronic services use cable or telephone lines to~~ send textual matter and graphics to a TV screen at the viewer's behest.) ~~The *Washington Post* in early 1982 disclosed plans to provide local news and advertising programming for all cable TV system operators in the metropolitan Washington area. And publishers lobbied vigorously in Washington against moves to permit AT&T to send news via telephone lines into homes~~.

~~Yet a 1982 study of videotex usage in Britain found that~~ most customers ~~were usually~~ seeking specific pieces of data ~~(e.g., 60 percent regularly looked up classified listings; nearly half looked up stock exchange information at least every other day)~~. "News" was not the main attraction. ~~Indeed, as a Canadian operator observed, with videotex, information is "the tail not the dog. The dog is [electronic] shopping and banking."~~

The biggest expansion in news has come in television. ~~TV news is the child of radio news, and of the Paramount newsreels of the 1930s and '40s; it is not the child, or, in its basic attitudes even a very near relative, of the newspapers. In their rivalry for audiences (ratings) which govern TV advertising revenues, the producers of the evening news shows—local or national—can never relax; when Walter Cronkite retired as an anchorman in 1981, the question for CBS was: Could his successor, Dan Rather, officiate over the news as well, i.e., draw the most viewers? The answer was yes,~~ but all three networks were changing their style and on-camera personalities in late 1981 and early 1982.

~~The spread of cable television (to one-third of all U.S. television households) prompted Ted Turner last January to start~~ Cable News Network 2, ~~a 24-hour Atlanta-based TV news service, in a direct challenge to the networks~~. The networks ~~responded by~~ announcing plans to present news from 2 A.M. to 7 A.M. ~~when 4.9 million TV sets are in use.~~

~~This impending surge in broadcast news seems only to confirm the~~ ascendancy of video. ~~Already~~, the TV viewer in a medium-to-large-sized city faces no shortage of "news." In Washington, D.C., for example, ~~the city-dweller has only~~ one full-fledged local daily, ~~the *Washington Post,* but he can watch "news" for nine and one-half hours each weekday, including two stretches of three hours (6 A.M. to 9 A.M., 5 P.M. to 8 P.M.). Another five and one-half hours of news is available via Cable News Network 2 from Baltimore's station WMAR-TV.~~

~~All told, in the Washington area, there are more than~~ 14 hours of programming ~~network, syndicated, and local—on three network stations, two independent stations, and PBS's station. If one includes such programs as the PBS *Nightly Business Report,* as well as the lighter *Phil Donahue* and *Hour Magazine,* the total comes to 24 hours~~.

Sample Summary

Newspaper managements are starting "teletext" services, sending textual matter and graphics to a TV screen at the viewer's request. Most customers, however, seek specific pieces of practical information, not news. The biggest expansion of news has come in television. All three networks were changing their style and on-camera personalities in late 1981 and early 1982. Cable News Network 2, a 24-hour news service, led the networks to announce plans for all-night news. The TV viewer in a medium-to-large city faces no shortage of "news." Even though, for example, Washington, D.C., has only one daily newspaper, it has more than 14 hours of television news programming. Video news is on the rise.

Comments on the Summary

Much of the original presents specific details backing up or explaining the main ideas, which are usually contained in only a single sentence or two of each paragraph. Even these key sentences in each paragraph contain many more specific details than are necessary for understanding the basic points being presented. That is why it was possible to cross out so much.

In addition to leaving out secondary details, I was able to shorten the summary by collecting information given in several sentences in a single sentence. Combining points in this way also helped emphasize the relationships among the key ideas. For example, the opening sentence of the summary combines the fact that teletext programs have been started with a definition of the service. The next to last sentence of the summary is particularly effective in showing the connections among many pieces of information presented in the last two paragraphs of the original. The closing sentence of the summary comes from a bit earlier in the original, but I put it at the end because it effectively and compactly sums up the whole point of the excerpt.

Writing Assignment

Using the method of deleting nonessential information, summarize the following continuation of Lichty's article discussing video news.

What is striking, of course, is how thin and how much the same all this video news is. On the three network evening news shows, for example, there is about 50 percent duplication of major stories, far more duplication than exists on, say, the front pages of the San Francisco *Chronicle* and the *St. Louis Post-Dispatch,* leaving aside strictly local items.

The half-hour evening news show has room for 17 or 18 items in 22 minutes (commercials eat up eight minutes). Eight or nine of these items are film snippets lasting from a few seconds to one and a half minutes; the rest are the anchorman's brief reports written by anonymous network writers from the news dispatches coming in over the studio teletype from Associated Press (AP) and United Press International (UPI). In Washington or the Mideast, the TV correspondent, as NBC's Douglas Kiker put it, is "making little movies," directing a camera crew, scribbling the words he will utter to give significance to the film. he is no "reporter," in the sense that reporters for AP, UPI, and newspapers are. He has little time for fact-finding, and little time on the air to present any facts he does find.

The requirements of TV news do not, therefore, impel ABC, CBS, and NBC to deploy large numbers of information-seekers—although the logistics and technology require a sizable supporting staff. In Washington, locale of 40 percent of CBS News's stories and (not coincidentally) site of its largest bureau, there are 200 CBS News employees. Of these, only 25 are reporters, for both radio and TV—versus 35 Washington reporters for the *New York Times* and 100 for the AP. In Manhattan, station WCBS-TV, like its local rivals, has no such creature as a City Hall reporter, wise in the ways of Mayor

Koch and the Board of Estimate; the station usually sends a reporter and camera crew to City Hall only when the AP ticker indicates in advance the probability of "good film."

Overseas, CBS has only 23 full-time correspondents, versus 32 for the *New York Times,* 36 for *Time,* eight for the Baltimore *Sun,* 19 for the Knight-Ridder papers—and about 300 for the AP, whose operatives and those of rival UPI supply most of the news that, without attribution, Dan Rather (like his ABC and NBC counterparts) reads off a teleprompter every weekday evening.

Television, as *Newsweek* columnist Jane Bryant Quinn observed, gives us "the faces," the voices, the scenery—albeit in highly selective bits and pieces. Its infrequent documentaries draw relatively small audiences but occasionally strike political sparks. At its best, TV provides us with a live view of the great spectacles: a space shot, a presidential inaugural, the national political conventions, the 1973–74 Watergate hearings (when the cameras were allowed to run without interruption), the World Series.

Thus, the further expansion of "video," even as it promises greater diffusion of the same news, does not add greatly to the array of information available to the public. Yet "electronic home delivery" has persuaded many analysts that the "news" in print, as it has evolved over the past 150 years in America, is all but dead. (Rare is the major publisher who has not invested in TV or cable, or both.) Predicts James Martin, author of *Future Trends in Telecommunications* (1977): By the early 1990s, there may be only a "minor intellectual press, a few picture newspapers for low-IQ readers, and some local newspapers," along with a few news magazines. Citing television's pre-eminence at the Dupont Awards ceremony this year, NBC's anchorman Tom Brokaw spoke of the young people who "have come to rely on us as their primary and only source of news."

Method 2: Selecting More Important Information

Highlighting the central facts and ideas can help you see how the main parts fit together. Underline only the key words: those that express substantial information or make major statements. Ask yourself, "What is central here? What is the author's specific point? What statements draw the whole piece together?" Where an underlying idea is expressed only indirectly or implicitly, write a direct or explicit statement of the idea.

This method is often useful when the original is very wordy, digresses often, does not state its main ideas clearly, or otherwise makes the main idea difficult to follow. Such situations sometimes arise when generalizations do not balance details; either the piece confuses many generalizations or presents many details without stating their overall meaning. Then you have to hunt carefully for those few words that signal the underlying ideas and logic of the piece.

The following excerpt, by Mort Rosenblum, discusses the problems of reporting international news. You will benefit more from it if you try selecting material and writing your own summary before reading the sample and comments that follow.

Censorship and Government Pressures

We are pleased to announce, the Nigerian government was pleased to announce, that we are lifting censorship.

Does that mean, asked a correspondent, that we can send a story saying so?

No, replied the officer, because it was never announced that there was censorship.

The measures contrived by authorities to influence news about their countries go far beyond the old-fashioned censor with a pot of black ink and pinking shears. Direct and indirect pressures in scores of countries make it impossible for casual readers and viewers in the West to have a balanced view of world events. Not only are correspondents often prevented from reporting vital information, but also they frequently cannot—or do not—warn their readers that they are providing only a partial picture. Some correspondents practice self-censorship without even realizing it; others are artfully conned by official propaganda and managed news.

In the most extreme case, Cambodia, not a single reporter or traveler was allowed inside the country for a long time after the Khmer Rouge took power, and the few diplomats in Phnom Penh were under severe restrictions. The world's knowledge of Cambodia was limited to official radio broadcasts and accounts of embittered refugees who could speak only of the small areas in which they had lived. Background stories were based on the thinnest of details. In 1977, the French press discussed at length the relative importance of two Cambodian leaders, until someone realized the two leaders were the same person; he just had a long name. North Korea, Albania and several other authoritarian countries allow journalists in only on the rarest of occasions and then under careful surveillance. All but a few countries in the world make at least some effort to convince correspondents to report things in a favorable light—or to prevent them from reporting anything at all.

Some direct measures are casual enough to be circumvented easily. In the late 1960s, when Congolese authorities decreed that all news dispatches had to be sent in French, reporters simply cabled things like, "Les mercenaires sont holed up en Bukavu avec beaucoup recoilless rifles, anti-aircraft guns et Scotch whisky." One British journalist in Nigeria dictated a coup d'état story in Welsh to his wife back home. From Sri Lanka—then Ceylon—reporters covering a rebellion chatted from hotel telephones about the weather and the local curry until the censor hung up, bored with what he considered to be tourist prattle.

But sometimes action against correspondents is brutally direct. Reporters have been beaten bloody; some have been found dead in mysterious circumstances. Many reporters have spent at least a few nights in jails, military barracks or confined to their hotel rooms. Expulsions are almost routine.

The situation is worsened by the general imbalances of the system. One such problem is that some countries are reported more sympathetically than others, despite news organizations' efforts to be evenhanded. If a country has a favorable image in the United States, and its authorities are hospitable and helpful to correspondents, it is usually given the benefit of any doubt. This was illustrated when Lebanon imposed censorship on outgoing dispatches in 1976. When the measure was announced, agencies and newspapers carried long stories about the harsh new restrictions. Most dispatches from Beirut carried editors' notes warning that the contents had been censored. But for years the same organizations have accepted without comment a more subtle but equally effective censorship by Israel. Under the Israeli system, correspondents must submit to the censor all dispatches on specific subjects, including military, oil and nuclear matters. Censors sometimes hit the "garble button" which obliterates outgoing dispatches on sensitive issues. As a result, reporters avoid certain forbidden stories. For a long time, for example, they could not say Israel imported oil from Iran. Until the mid-1970s, news organizations could not even say that a story had been altered by censors. Few correspondents protest, since the censors are usually reasonable and sometimes can be persuaded to change their minds. But readers are often not given the full picture, and they are seldom warned about it.

Here is the same passage with the key words underlined.

We are pleased to announce, the Nigerian government was pleased to announce, that we are lifting censorship.

Does that mean, asked a correspondent, that we can send a story saying so?

No, replied the officer, because it was never announced that there was censorship.

The measures contrived by authorities to <u>influence news</u> about their <u>countries</u> go far beyond the old-fashioned censor with a pot of black ink and pinking shears. <u>Direct</u> and <u>indirect pressures</u> in scores of countries make it <u>impossible</u> for casual <u>readers</u> and <u>viewers</u> in the <u>West</u> to have a <u>balanced view of world events</u>. Not only are correspondents often prevented from reporting vital information, but also they frequently <u>cannot</u>—or do not—<u>warn</u> their <u>readers</u> that they are providing only a partial picture. Some correspondents practice <u>self-censorship</u> without even realizing it; others are artfully <u>conned</u> by <u>official propaganda</u> and managed news.

In the most extreme case, <u>Cambodia</u>, not a single reporter or traveler was allowed inside the country for a long time after the Khmer Rouge took power, and the few diplomats in Phnom Penh were under severe restrictions. The world's knowledge of Cambodia was limited to <u>official radio broadcasts</u> and accounts of embittered <u>refugees</u> who could speak only of the <u>small areas</u> in which they had lived. Background stories were based on the thinnest of details. In 1977, the French press discussed at length the relative importance of two Cambodian leaders, until someone realized the two leaders were the same person; he just had a long name. North Korea, Albania and several other authoritarian countries allow journalists in only on the rarest of occasions and then under careful surveillance. <u>All but</u> a few countries in the world <u>make</u> at least <u>some effort</u> to convince correspondents to <u>report</u> things in a <u>favorable light</u>—or to prevent them from reporting anything at all.

<u>Some direct measures</u> are casual enough to be <u>circumvented easily</u>. In the late 1960s, when Congolese authorities decreed that all news dispatches had to be sent in French, reporters simply cabled things like, "Les mercenaires sont holed up en Bukavu avec beaucoup recoilless rifles, anti-aircraft guns et Scotch whisky." One British journalist in Nigeria dictated a coup d'état story in Welsh to his wife back home. From Sri Lanka—then Ceylon—reporters covering a rebellion chatted from hotel telephones about the weather and the local curry until the censor hung up, bored with what he considered to be tourist prattle.

But <u>sometimes action</u> against correspondents is <u>brutally direct</u>. <u>Reporters</u> have been <u>beaten bloody</u>; some have been found <u>dead</u> in mysterious circumstances. Many reporters have spent at least a few nights in jails, military barracks or confined to their hotel rooms. Expulsions are almost routine.

The situation is worsened by the general imbalances of the system. One such problem is that <u>some countries</u> are <u>reported more sympathetically</u> than others, despite news organizations' efforts to be evenhanded. If a country has a <u>favorable image</u> in the United States, and its authorities are <u>hospitable</u> and <u>helpful</u> to correspondents, it is usually given the benefit of any doubt. This was illustrated when <u>Lebanon</u> imposed <u>censorship</u> on outgoing dispatches in 1976. When the measure was announced, agencies and newspapers carried long stories about the harsh new restrictions. Most dispatches from Beirut carried editors' notes warning that the contents had been censored. But for years the same organizations have accepted without comment a more subtle but equally effective censorship by <u>Israel</u>. Under the Israeli system, correspondents must submit to the censor all dispatches on specific subjects, including military, oil and nuclear matters. Censors sometimes hit the "garble button" which obliterates outgoing dispatches on sensitive issues. As a result, reporters avoid certain forbidden stories. For a long time, for example, they could not say Israel imported oil from Iran. Until the mid-1970s, news organizations could not even say that a story had been altered by censors. Few correspondents protest, since the censors are usually reasonable and sometimes can be persuaded to change their minds. But readers are often not given the full picture, and they are seldom warned about it.

Sample Summary

Countries attempt to influence news by exerting direct and indirect pressures, making a balanced view of world events impossible for Western readers and viewers. Reporters often cannot warn readers. Sometimes they unconsciously censor themselves or are conned by official propaganda. In the extreme case of Cambodia, news came only from official broadcasts and refugees, who knew what was happening in only a small area.

   Most countries make some effort to have events reported in a favorable light, if at all. Some direct measures are easily circumvented, but sometimes action is brutally direct: reporters beaten bloody and killed. If countries have a favorable image and are hospitable and helpful to reporters, they are reported more sympathetically than others, as in the reporting of censorship in Lebanon versus the lack of mention of it in stories from Israel.

Comments on the Summary

The original moves forward through the telling of anecdotes and examples, each of which conveys an important point. The important meaning behind each of the interesting stories has to be brought out by identifying certain key words and concepts. The important material, which I underlined, is almost randomly spaced out over the whole selection—a few words here and a few words there.

Each of the rewritten sentences draws together information from a number of sentences and helps bring out the underlying structure of the piece. For example, the next to last sentence of the summary draws together the contrasting concepts of two paragraphs, and the last sentence of the summary brings out the unified concept of the whole last paragraph of the original.

The summary is also broken into two paragraphs to reflect the structure of the original, which in the first half raises the problem of government interference in the news and in the second half begins to discuss specific types. By bringing out the underlying argument of the piece, the summary has lost some of the dramatic quality of the original, with its exciting journalists' stories, but the basic meaning does come across compactly.

Writing Assignment

Using the method of selecting the most important information, summarize the following continuation of Rosenblum's discussion of governmental interference in international reporting.

News organizations respond differently when direct measures are imposed. When former Indian prime minister Indira Gandhi insisted that Western reporters sign a list of guidelines for coverage, there were three reactions. Some refused to sign and left the country in a blaze of integrity; some signed and respected the restrictions; and others signed and paid no attention to them. Correspondents who stayed and ignored the guidelines say they pulled no punches. But some editors who followed events closely said they detected a slightly tempered tone.

The imposition of self-censorship can be more damaging than direct measures. Many authorities will let correspondents file whatever they want, but they react harshly if they are unhappy with what is reported. This was called the "File now, die later" policy in Chile after the 1973 coup. Faced with undefined threats, reporters may inadvertently withhold sensitive information by convincing themselves that their perfectly reliable sources are not good enough. And the more timid deliberately omit material that might well have gotten by an official censor.

A number of foreign editors tell their correspondents to ignore pressures and report frankly. Should they get thrown out, they will be reassigned somewhere else. But other editors prefer that their correspondents do not risk getting thrown out except on the biggest of stories. An expulsion is not necessarily a badge of honor. Often authorities will not allow news organizations to replace ejected correspondents. News agencies can be particularly sensitive if they sell their news and photos to local papers in the country. AP and UPI policy is to report the news, whatever the consequences, but local bureau chiefs and correspondents are sometimes reluctant to jeopardize agency income by risking having their offices closed down. Regardless of an organization's policy, correspondents know that if they provoke the wrath of hard-line rulers, they could suffer a fate worse than expulsion.

When borders are sealed, the usual result is either that the country is ignored completely or that it is reported almost totally in the negative with scant mention of any possible saving graces. The level of international concern about a particular country determines whether reporters will go through the time-consuming process of finding alternate sources of information outside of its closed borders. In either case, the reader is left ill-informed.

Idi Amin Dada of Uganda and Francisco Macias Nguema of Equatorial Guinea are both absolute despots responsible for mass murders, torture and whimsically imposed prison terms. Macias' record is far worse than Amin's. He has killed a larger percentage of his population, and he has imposed virtual slavery on a wide sector of his tiny nation. And yet, while almost everyone in the United States knows about Amin, hardly anyone has heard of Macias. Because of the vagaries of the system, Amin and Uganda are "good stories"; Macias and Equatorial Guinea are not. Amin decided for his own reasons that he wanted publicity, and he learned how to get it. His antics attracted attention among the most casual readers, and editors knew it. The slightest reference to Amin got into newspapers around the country. Also, by geographical coincidence, Uganda is next to Kenya, where many correspondents are based. The official radio can be monitored in Nairobi, and telephone calls are often easy. Since Uganda has "news value," reporters seek out refugees, churchmen and defectors for accounts of depredations. Under Amin, newsmen could not move freely in Uganda to report on whether the regime accomplished anything positive, so the picture which emerged for an eager audience was one of unbridled bloodshed. By contrast, Macias has shunned publicity, withdrawing behind his tightly sealed borders. No demand has been created for news about him. A number of exiles live in the Cameroun and in Gabon, but those countries are off the normal itinerary for reporters in Africa. When correspondents do write about Equatorial Guinea, the name rings no bell of recognition, and the stories are soon forgotten.

Some countries become inadvertent victims of their own openness to reporters. One good example is the Philippines under Ferdinand Marcos. The government violates human rights on a grand scale, but it also allows correspondents in to travel with relative freedom to write about what is happening. Reporters can interview victims and conscience-stricken security officers. Marcos himself is accessible to reporters, who can ask do-you-still-beat-your-wife questions. As a result, correspondents are able to write detailed accounts of government abuses, rich in quotes and color. Other governments commit more flagrant violations of basic rights, but they escape public censure by closing their borders to reporters. If they are not of sufficient interest to merit intensive coverage from the outside, they are hardly mentioned at all. This results in the lasting impression that countries like the Philippines are the worst of a bad bunch.

Even if there were no restrictions or pressures on correspondents, some countries would still get more attention than others. But, ideally, correspondents would be able to apply some standard yardstick so that readers could evaluate the actions and the conditions of one government in light of others. The present system, however, gives the reader only scattered fragments of the whole picture.

Method 3: Note Taking

Taking notes on the key ideas for each of the sections of the original reveals the logic of ideas in the whole piece and the connections among them. As you write down the key idea for each paragraph or so of the original, you will be concerned more with large chunks of meaning than with specific details. As you look over your notes, you may notice that each paragraph has its own meaning, which is related to the meaning of the paragraph before or after it. You will become aware of the whole piece as a series of ideas, one following another.

This method may be useful when summarizing a piece that clearly develops an idea in each paragraph but seems to change from paragraph to paragraph, as a more complex idea builds from each of the parts or a large idea breaks into many subsections. The notes then become an outline of the flow of the author's thought. Try working through the following passage (an excerpt from Daniel Boorstin's *The Image*), which discusses "pseudo-events" or what are now called "media events," on your own before reading the sample and comments.

News-Making: The Pseudo-Event

The new kind of synthetic novelty which has flooded our experience I will call "pseudo-events." The common prefix "pseudo" comes from the Greek word meaning false, or intended to deceive. Before I recall the historical forces which have made these pseudo-events possible, have increased the supply of them and the demand for them, I will give a commonplace example.

The owners of a hotel, in an illustration offered by Edward L. Bernays in his pioneer *Crystallizing Public Opinion,* consult a public relations counsel. They ask how to increase their hotel's prestige and so improve their business. In less sophisticated times, the answer might have been to hire a new chef, to improve the plumbing, to paint the rooms, or to install a crystal chandelier in the lobby. The public relations counsel's technique is more indirect. He proposes that the management stage a celebration of the hotel's thirtieth anniversary. A committee is formed, including a prominent banker, a leading society matron, a well-known lawyer, an influential preacher, and an "event" is planned (say a banquet) to call attention to the distinguished service the hotel has been rendering the community. The celebration is held, photographs are taken, the occasion is widely reported, and the object is accomplished. Now this occasion is a pseudo-event, and will illustrate all the essential features of pseudo-events.

This celebration, we can see at the outset, is somewhat—but not entirely—misleading. Presumably the public relations counsel would not have been able to form his committee of prominent citizens if the hotel had not actually been rendering service to the community. On the other hand, if the hotel's services had been all that important, instigation by public relations counsel might not have been necessary. Once the celebration has been held, the celebration itself becomes evidence that the hotel really is a distinguished institution. The occasion actually gives the hotel the prestige to which it is pretending.

It is obvious, too, that the value of such a celebration to the owners depends on its being photographed and reported in newspapers, magazines, newsreels, on radio, and over television. It is the report that gives the event its force in the minds of potential customers. The power to make a reportable event is thus the power to make experience. One is reminded of Napoleon's apocryphal reply to his general, who objected that circumstances were unfavorable to a proposed campaign: "Bah, I make circumstances!" The modern public relations counsel—and he is, of course, only one of many twentieth-century creators of pseudo-events—has come close to fulfilling Napoleon's idle boast. "The counsel on public relations," Mr. Bernays explains, "not only knows what news value is, but knowing it, he is in a position to *make news happen.* He is a creator of events."

The intriguing feature of the modern situation, however, comes precisely from the fact that the modern news-makers are not God. The news they make happen, the events they create, are somehow not quite real. There remains a tantalizing difference between man-made and God-made events.

A pseudo-event, then, is a happening that possesses the following characteristics. (1) It is not spontaneous, but comes about because someone has planned, planted, or incited it. Typically, it is not a train wreck or an earthquake, but an interview. (2) It is planted primarily (not always exclusively) for the immediate purpose of being reported or reproduced. Therefore, its occurrence is arranged for the convenience of the reporting or reproducing media. Its success is measured by how widely it is reported. Time relations in it are commonly fictitious or factitious; the announcement is given out in advance "for future release" and written as if the event had occurred in the past. The question, "Is it real?" is less important than, "Is it newsworthy?" (3) Its relation to the underlying reality of the situation is ambiguous. Its interest arises largely from this very ambiguity. Concerning a pseudo-event the question, "What does it mean?" has a new dimension. While the news interest in a train wreck is in *what* happened and in the real consequences, the interest in an interview is always, in a sense, in *whether* it really happened and in what might have been the motives. Did the statement really mean what it said? Without some of this ambiguity a pseudo-event cannot be very interesting. (4) Usually it is intended to be a self-fulfilling prophecy. The hotel's thirtieth-anniversary celebration, by saying that the hotel is a distinguished institution, actually makes it one.

Notes on the Passage

Pseudo-events, or false events, are flooding our experience.

Example: Hotel wants to increase prestige and business. Instead of improving facilities, it stages anniversary celebration, with prominent people and press coverage.

Event itself makes it appear that the hotel is distinguished. Report of event in news media makes an impression on potential customers. Making event makes experience.

But event is not quite real.

Characteristics of pseudo-events:
1. Planned, planted, or incited
2. Scheduled for media convenience
3. Ambiguous relationship to reality
4. Self-fulfilling prophecy

Sample Summary

The hotel that, in order to boost its prestige and business, stages an anniversary celebration instead of improving its facilities exemplifies the pseudo-event, or false event, which now floods our experience.

The news reports of the event, involving prominent citizens, make the hotel appear distinguished and impresses potential customers. Making the event makes an experience, but the event is not quite real. Pseudo-events like this one have four characteristics: they are planned, planted, or incited; they are scheduled for media convenience; their relationship to reality is ambiguous; and they are self-fulfilling prophecies.

Comments on the Summary

This excerpt develops a definition of the pseudo-event through the discussion of one main example. By developing a set of notes, I discovered how the more general opening and closing paragraphs led into and out of the specific case. In the first sentence of the summary, I was able to show that connection by directly tying the example to the general topic. In the last sentence I was again able to clarify the link to the example with the phrase "like this one."

The excerpt itself proceeds from a direct description to an analysis to more general conclusions. Again the notes help trace the flow of thought, which I can then recapture in the written summary. Some important details, first described and then analyzed (such as the news reporting and the participation of prominent people), could be combined with the analysis. The contrast of ideas in the next to last sentence of the summary reflects the two levels of analysis in the fourth and fifth paragraphs of the original. Note also that the summary, like the outline, preserves the list structure for presenting the four characteristics of pseudo-events.

Writing Assignment

Using the method of note taking, summarize the next section of Boorstin's discussion of pseudo-events. It probes the historical causes of the rise of these media fictions.

From News-Gathering to News-Making

In the last half century a larger and larger proportion of our experience, of what we read and see and hear, has come to consist of pseudo-events. We expect more of them and we are given more of them.

They flood our consciousness. Their multiplication has gone on in the United States at a faster rate than elsewhere. Even the rate of increase is increasing every day. This is true of the world of education, of consumption, and of personal relations. It is especially true of the world of public affairs which I describe in this chapter.

A full explanation of the origin and rise of pseudo-events would be nothing less than a history of modern America. For our present purposes it is enough to recall a few of the more revolutionary recent developments.

The great modern increase in the supply and the demand for news began in the early nineteenth century. Until then newspapers tended to fill out their columns with lackadaisical secondhand accounts or stale reprints of items first published elsewhere at home and abroad. The laws of plagiarism and of copyright were undeveloped. Most newspapers were little more than excuses for espousing a political position, for listing the arrival and departure of ships, for familiar essays and useful advice, or for commercial or legal announcements.

Less than a century and a half ago did newspapers begin to disseminate up-to-date reports of matters of public interest written by eyewitnesses or professional reporters near the scene. The telegraph was perfected and applied to news reporting in the 1830's and 1840's. Two newspapermen, William M. Swain of the *Philadelphia Public Ledger* and Amos Kendall of Frankfort, Kentucky, were founders of the national telegraphic network. Polk's presidential message in 1846 was the first to be transmitted by wire. When the Associated Press was founded in 1848, news began to be a salable commodity. Then appeared the rotary press, which could print on a continuous sheet and on both sides of the paper at the same time. The *New York Tribune*'s high-speed press, installed in the 1870's, could turn out 18,000 papers per hour. The Civil War, and later the Spanish-American War, offered raw materials and incentive for vivid up-to-the-minute, on-the-spot reporting. The competitive daring of giants like James Gordon Bennett, Joseph Pulitzer, and William Randolph Hearst intensified the race for news and widened newspaper circulation.

These events were part of a great, but little-noticed, revolution— what I would call the Graphic Revolution. Man's ability to make, preserve, transmit, and disseminate precise images—images of print, of men and landscapes and events, of the voices of men and mobs— now grew at a fantastic pace. The increased speed of printing was itself revolutionary. Still more revolutionary were the new techniques for making direct images of nature. Photography was destined soon to give printed matter itself a secondary role. By a giant leap Americans crossed the gulf from the daguerreotype to color television in less than a century. Dry-plate photography came in 1873; Bell patented the telephone in 1876; the phonograph was invented in 1877; the roll film appeared in 1884; Eastman's Kodak No. 1 was produced in 1888; Edison's patent on the radio came in 1891; motion pictures came in and voice was first transmitted by radio around 1900; the first national political convention widely broadcast by radio was that of 1928; television became commercially important in 1941, and color television even more recently.

Verisimilitude took on a new meaning. Not only was it now possible to give the actual voice and gestures of Franklin Delano Roosevelt unprecedented reality and intimacy for a whole nation. Vivid image came to overshadow pale reality. Sound motion pictures in color led a whole generation of pioneering American movie-goers to think of Benjamin Disraeli as an earlier imitation of George Arliss, just as television has led a later generation of television watchers to see the western cowboy as an inferior replica of John Wayne. The Grand Canyon itself became a disappointing reproduction of the Kodachrome original.

The new power to report and portray what had happened was a new temptation leading newsmen to make probable images or to prepare reports in advance of what was expected to happen. As so often, men came to mistake their power for their necessities. Readers and viewers would soon prefer the vividness of the account, the "candidness" of the photograph, to the spontaneity of what was recounted.

Then came round-the-clock media. The news gap soon became so narrow that in order to have additional "news" for each new edition or each new broadcast it was necessary to plan in advance the stages by which any available news would be unveiled. After the weekly and the daily came the "extras" and the numerous regular editions. The *Philadelphia Evening Bulletin* soon had seven editions a day. No rest for the newsman. With more space to fill, he had to fill it ever more quickly. In order to justify the numerous editions, it was increasingly necessary that the news constantly change or at least seem to change. With radio on the air continuously during waking hours, the reporters' problems became still more acute. News every hour on the hour, and sometimes on the half hour. Programs interrupted any time for special bulletins. How to avoid deadly repetition, the appearance that nothing was happening, that news-gatherers were asleep, or that competitors were more alert? As the costs of printing and then of broadcasting increased, it became financially necessary to keep the presses always at work and the TV screen always busy. Pressures toward the making of pseudo-events became ever stronger. News-gathering turned into news-making.

Method 4: Miniaturizing

As you read through the original, pay attention to the various parts of the structure: the order of ideas, their relative lengths, and their relationships. Think of a large photograph reduced to wallet size. In a relative sense all the parts remain the same; only the scale has changed. Notice the shape, flow, and overall impression of the original passage so you can create a miniature version of it in your summary. As in the note-taking method, you should jot down the main ideas and key statements of the original, but you should also try to keep the size of your notes in rough proportion to the size of the original. Follow the logic of one idea flowing from another, and recreate the transitions and structure of the original.

Where the arrangement, logical development, and balance of parts of the original are important, miniaturizing will help you retain the overall meaning and impression. Generally this method is most appropriate for more complex and subtly argued originals, where the parts of the argument fit together in unusual ways or in ways that are difficult to follow. Attempt your own version of the following passage by Michael Schudson before reading the sample and comments.

The Politics of Narrative Form: The Emergence of News Conventions in Print and Television

Generally speaking, people do not see news as it happens; rather, they hear or read about it. Parents do not experience their child's day at school directly, but learn of it as it is narrated, turned into a story by the child. Children learn that the accounts of their experiences, like the stories and legends they are told, must have certain formal qualities. A child I know told his older sister the following story: "Once upon a time there was a small boy who went out into the forest. He heard a sound. A lion jumped at him and ate him but he tore out the lion's stomach, killed the lion, and dragged it home. The end." Then he told the story again: "Once upon a time, a small boy went into the forest and a lion tried to eat him, but he killed the lion. The end." Then once more: "Once upon a time a boy killed a lion in the forest. The end." And at last he said: "Once upon a time. The end."

The child had learned something important about form. Journalists know something similar. They do not offer boys, forests, and lions raw, but cook them into story forms. News is not fictional, but it is conventional. Conventions help make messages readable. They do so in ways that "fit" the social world of readers and writers, for the conventions of one society or time are not those of another. Some of the most familiar news conventions of our day, so obvious they seem timeless, are recent innovations. Like others, these conventions help

make culturally consonant messages readable and culturally dissonant
messages unsayable. Their function is less to increase or decrease
the truth value of the messages they convey than to shape and narrow
the range of what kinds of truths can be told. They reinforce certain
assumptions about the political world.

I want to examine in detail the emergence of a few of these
conventions:

1. That a summary lead and inverted pyramid structure are superior
   to a chronological account of an event
2. That a president is the most important actor in any event in
   which he takes part
3. That a news story should focus on a single event rather than
   a continuous or repeated happening, or that, if the action is
   repeated, attention should center on novelty, not on pattern
4. That a news story covering an important speech or document
   should quote or state its highlights
5. That a news story covering a political event should convey the
   meaning of the political acts in a time frame larger than that
   of the acts themselves

All are unquestioned and generally unstated conventions of twentieth
century American journalism; none were elements in journalism of
the mid-nineteenth century, nor would any have been familiar to
Horace Greeley, James Gordon Bennett, or Henry Raymond. Unlike
reporters today, the nineteenth century reporter was not obliged to
summarize highlights in a lead, to recognize the president as chief
actor on the American political stage, to seek novelty, to quote speeches
he reported, or to identify the political significance of events he
covered. How, then, did the convention emerge, and why?

A study of reports of the State of the Union message demonstrates
that these conventions, among others, incorporate into the structure
of the news story vital assumptions about the nature of politics and
the role of the press. They make it plain that American journalists
regard themselves, not as partisans of political causes, but as expert
analysts of the political world. They make it equally clear that,
although as journalists they hold to principles of objective reporting,
they nevertheless view their role as involving some fundamental
translation and interpretation of political acts to a public ill-equipped
to sort out for itself the meaning of events. Further, these conventions
institutionalize the journalists' view that meaning is to be found, not
in the character of established political institutions, but in the political
aims of actors within them. The journalist's responsibility, as they
see it, is to discover in the conscious plans of political actors the
intentions that create political meaning.

The Constitution of the United States provides that the president
shall report to Congress "from time to time" regarding the "state of
the Union," and every American president, following the custom
inaugurated by Washington, has delivered a message on this subject
at the beginning of each winter's congressional session. While the

event itself—the way in which the annual message is presented—has changed in some significant respects in the past two centuries, it still provides a reasonably good basis for a comparison of news reporting, having remained more or less constant over the years. Changes in the way the message is reported, therefore, cannot be attributed simply to changes in the event itself, but must be linked to changing precepts in journalism about the nature of politics and what a news story should be.

Notes on the Passage

INTRODUCTION—Anecdote; news generally second-hand through stories "Once upon a time, the end."

Stories have set forms—news conventions help make stories readable, but make other stories untellable.

BODY—Conventions to be examined:
1. Summary lead and inverted pyramid
2. President chief actor
3. Single event, novelty
4. Quotation or highlights of speech or document
5. Background time frame

These conventions not around a century ago.

Conventions assume journalists are nonpartisan, expert analysts, interpreting political aims to public.

TRANSITION—Changes in news reports of the annual State of Union speech help reveal journalistic changes.

Sample Summary

People usually receive news secondhand through stories that have set forms; the child who summarized a story by saying, "Once upon a time. The end," understood forms. In news reporting, these set forms or conventions help make stories readable, but they make some stories impossible to tell.

Modern news conventions, not used a century ago in America, include:
1. Summary lead and inverted pyramid structure
2. The chief role of the president
3. News story focusing on a single event or novelty
4. Quoting or highlighting of speeches and documents
5. Background time frame given for political events

These conventions assume that journalists are nonpartisan, expert analysts, whose role is to interpret to the public the political aims of the main political actors.

A study of changes in news reporting of the annual presidential State of the Union speech reveals how these conventions came about.

Comments on the Summary

The original passage breaks down into three sections: introduction of the concepts of form and convention, presentation of current conventions and underlying assumptions, and a lead-in to historical material that appears to follow. In the summary, I tried to preserve these three sections in my paragraphing. I also tried to preserve the relative proportions of the parts—except for the central list, which, because of its prominence visually and structurally, received a larger proportion of space. The visual impact of the list was also preserved.

Because ideas in the original are frequently developed over an entire paragraph, the notes and the summary sentences combine widely separated material and often develop new wording to achieve the combination. Yet the sequence, flow, and structure of the ideas remain fixed.

Writing Assignment

Use the method of miniaturizing to summarize the continuation of Schudson's analysis of news conventions. The following excerpt presents some of the historical development of these conventions.

Reports of the State of the Union message have taken three basic forms: the stenographic record of congressional business, from 1790 to about 1850; a chronology and commentary on congressional ritual, from 1850 to 1900; and the report of the message, with an increasing emphasis on its content and its long-range political implications, from 1900 on. Despite journalism's vaunted objectivity, the reporting of the presidential message in each successive period became more interpretative, more divorced from what an ordinary observer could safely assert the message said or that Congress itself heard. This has not made reporting less truthful, but has widened the scope for the journalist's discretion—indicating that, over time, the journalistic function has served rather different intentions.

Early newspaper reports of the message printed it in its entirety, framed as part of congressional proceedings. The report of Washington's 1791 message by the weekly *Boston Gazette,* for instance, appeared on page two under the heading, "Columbia. Congress of the United States. (First Session—Second Congress). House of Representatives. Monday, October 24." The item notes that a joint committee of the Congress waited on the president, who agreed to meet with the Congress the next day in the Senate. Then, in the same column, under the heading, "Tuesday, October 25," there is a one-sentence account of the president's arrival in the Senate Chamber. The reader is then referred to the paper's last page for the full message, and the account moves on to proceedings in the House of Wednesday, October 26. The *Gazette* followed this pattern for all of Washington's messages, although in most years, the speech followed under the first heading. But in no case was there any commentary on the speech.

The most significant change in the message as an actual event was initiated by Thomas Jefferson, who felt that for the president to address Congress in person was too imperial a gesture, and so chose to give his State of the Union message in written form. It remained so until Woodrow Wilson reverted to the Federalist precedent of a personal appearance. Depite Jefferson's change, the message continued to be printed in full, either without any reported context or as part of a briefly sketched list of the day's proceedings in Congress. Any commentary on the message was confined entirely to the editorial column, where from the early 1800s on, the message was discussed at length, and the president's statements praised or castigated from an engaged and partisan stance.

By midcentury, and especially after the Civil War, the news report of the president's message was set in a much fuller discussion of Congress. The frame for the message continued to be provided by the congressional ritual of appointing a committee to wait on the president, announcing its readiness to hear a written communication from him read by a clerk. But two additional elements became standard. The first was the coverage devoted to the "spectacle" of the opening of Congress, which typically provided the beginning of the news story. As early as 1852 we read in the *New York Times:* "It is a bright and beautiful day, and the galleries of the House are crowded with ladies and gentlemen; all is gaiety." In 1870 the *Times* story began, "A beautiful Indian summer sun, a balmy atmosphere, and crowded galleries, resplendent and brilliant hues of gay toilettes, greeted the return of Congress to its chambers." The press noted, sometimes in great detail, the cordial greetings across party lines as Congressmen reassembled. Reports described the lavish bouquets of flowers on the desks of Senators and Representatives, gifts from loyal supporters.

The second change, which became standard from 1870 on, and which was more notable in the long run, was the attention given to congressional reaction to the president's message—several decades before reporters took it upon themselves actually to *report* what the message said. Where at first only the general response to the message was noted on House and Senate floors, in 1870 the *Times* reported that two or three Democratic Senators "appeared to go to sleep" when the portion dealing with foreign relations was read. In the 1870s, reporters typically confined themselves to observations of Congressmen's behavior on the floor, though they sometimes attempted a general characterization of the congressional response, as in the *Times* in 1874: "It may be said there is little fault found with the President's message as a whole, though some of its views find strong and special opposition." Occasionally, notable Congressmen were singled out. A *Times* reporter observed in 1870 that when the message discussed revenue reform, many people looked at Carl Schurz, "whose consciousness of the fact caused a faint smile to play over his face." In 1878 the *Times* reported that the message's mention of investigating people who disfranchise Southern voters "gave encouragement to the Republicans while the Democrats exhibited unmistakable signs of disapprobation" and caused a "scowl . . . to overspread the faces on the Democratic side."

In the late 1870s and the 1880s, journalists interviewed individual Congressmen. Reporters on the *Chicago Tribune* and *Washington Post,* for example, did interviews at the reading of the message in 1878, as these papers and others began to publish separate news stories on congressional responses to the message. The *Post's* story in 1886 began: " 'Didn't hear a word of it. Must wait until I see it in print.' That was the general response made by Congressmen to any question asked about the President's message, after it had been read in both houses." This was typical. Rarely did the Congressmen in these accounts regard the interview as an opportunity for publicity; rather, they seemed irritated that they had been asked questions.

Stories of congressional response to the message grew more elaborate in the 1880s and 1890s. Occasionally there were stories of the response of other bodies, particularly editorial comments in foreign newspapers. But by the end of the century, the attention given to the splendor of the opening of Congress, so prominent in the 1860s and 1870s, seemed to wear on the press. The *Washington Post* drily observed in its December 3, 1878, report that the public showed curiosity at the opening of Congress, "as if it were a new thing." The *Chicago Tribune* teased in its headline of December 4, 1894, "Toil of the Solons / Makers of Laws Resume Business at Washington." Evidently bored, the Washington *Evening Star* announced in its 1890 story, "Here We Go Again."

Thus, at the same time that the press took Congress as its beat, and regarded the opinions of individual Congressmen more and more seriously, its respect for the ritual and spectacle of office declined, and it began to delight in the lampooning of congressional affairs. The change taking place in the relation of journalists to officials was part of the new view that journalists took of their own purpose. They began to strain at the tradition of reporting normal occurrences and everyday proceedings. No longer the uncritical reporters of congressional ritual surrounding the reading of the message, they became increasingly uneasy about writing of something that happens again and again, year after year. The uneasiness came out in humor or in self-conscious commentary about how everything is the same as ever but people get involved nonetheless. The notion that the journalist should report original events and not record ongoing institutions grew stronger as the journalists of the 1880s and 1890s found themselves torn between two modes of activity, one might even say two forms of consciousness.

By 1900 the news story had been partially transformed, as the strictly chronological account of the reopening of congressional proceedings gave way to a descriptive account of the reopening of Congress, with a summary lead focusing on the spectacle of Congress, and some affectionate, jocular remarks about the reassembly of the group. The president's message remained buried within the story on Congress, though always printed in full on another page. The account, beyond the descriptive overview in the lead, tended to be chronological, but it was not as dry and formal as it had been in the early part of the century.

With the establishment of the summary lead as newspaper convention, it becomes clear that journalists began to move from being stenographers, or recorders, to interpreters. Still, in 1900 there was no mention of the content of the president's message in the news story, nor was the president mentioned by name, but referred to simply as "the president." Although he was the author of the message, attention in newspaper reports continued to focus on Congress. Journalists stayed in the here-and-now, reporting on congressional reactions on the floor, and turning to interviews only to supplement the central work of observing the event itself.

After 1900 all of this changed: the president's message, not congressional response to it, became the subject of the lead paragraph, and the president became the chief actor. The highlights of the address were summarized before noting congressional response to the address, as reporters increasingly took it as their prerogative to assert something about the larger political meaning of the message. Although these changes did not happen in all papers simultaneously, or with utter consistency, the trend is unmistakable.

Varying Summaries

Summary Length

The sample summaries in this chapter are about one-quarter the length of the full versions; however, the relative length of any summary is not a fixed proportion. The compactness of the style of the original, the compactness of the summary writer's style, and the purpose of the summary all help determine how short the summary will be.

If the original is densely written (that is, much information is presented in few words), then making the summary too short may destroy the integrity of the ideas communicated. If the original contains subtle relationships, complex sentences, difficult concepts, and relatively few details and examples, it is very hard to eliminate many words and still maintain the sense of the original. On the other hand, if an author introduces only one idea to a page, repeats that idea in different ways, gives many similar examples, and relies on simple sentences that present only one or two bits of information, the summary can eliminate much without distortion or over-simplification.

The second factor, the tightness of the language in the summary, depends on your skill with sentences and words (this skill is discussed on pages 70–71 and in Chapter 16). In writing more concisely, however, be sure to keep the meaning and sentence structure clear. Abstract and conceptual language, in particular, may become confusing in densely written passages. Compactness in writing should therefore be practiced in moderation; it is important not to jeopardize ease of reading. A clear, simple statement is often most compact.

Summaries That Serve Different Purposes

How you will eventually use the summary determines what is important to include and what is unimportant. The relative distinction between major and minor pieces of information depends very much on the interests of those who you anticipate will read your summary.

If the purpose of the summary is to give only a general idea of what is in the original—so that the reader can decide whether or not to read the full version—the summary can be quite spare, even less than 1 percent of the original. Some professional journals are simply collections of short abstracts of work published in other specialized journals. Journals such as *Research in Education, Biological Abstracts,* and *Economic Abstracts* help keep professionals aware of new work in their fields. But to obtain substantive information, the researcher must turn to the original. A typical professional abstract might contain bibliographical information, the major thesis or findings, and a suggestion of the method or the argument, as in the following example from *Sociological Abstracts,* which indicates that Soviet sociologists suspect that television presents some of the same problems for Russian youth as for American.

> Resenchuk, M. S., Podrostok u televizora (Teenagers and Television) *Sotsiologicheskie Issledovaniya,* 1980, 7,4, Oct-Dec, 109–112.
>
> The explosive development of the mass information media has posed significant problems for the upbringing of the younger generation. A survey is presented of the TV viewing habits of 2,500 students aged 11–12 & 15–16 from Arkhangelsk, Orel, & Moscow, USSR. Russian children were found to watch television less than their European counterparts. Although 69.3% of subjects usually watch TV with their families, it was determined that most young people do not adequately discuss program content with their parents. As teenagers grow older & develop a more active social life, they are less likely to watch TV. (© 1984 by SA, reprinted by permission.)

The other extreme is the summary that is so detailed that the reader can get all necessary information without referring to the original. In government and business, higher level officials who have too many responsibilities and too little time may make important decisions on the basis of summaries of reports and background documents. Subordinates who sift through the volumes of original material to prepare such summaries must select all the information that a manager might find useful in making the decision. The informative summary is, in fact, a set part of official reports so that readers can get to the essential findings without having to wade through all the evidence.

On the more popular level, such condensations of best sellers as those published by *Reader's Digest* provide readers who lack the patience to read full books a short version of the originals—although subtlety, style, characterization, and other literary qualities frequently suffer.

In the middle length are summaries created for various reference purposes. A book tracing the development of economic thought might devote a few pages to summarizing Adam Smith's *Wealth of Nations* in order to introduce the reader to that economist's ideas. Books like *Masterplots,* which summarize the plots of famous plays and novels, serve to refresh readers' memories about books they read long ago as well as to help new readers through the more difficult original. The various kinds of study guides and pamphlets you may be familiar with also serve this last function. They are useful to help you through the original but cannot stand in place of the full work.

When to Summarize

The most frequent and most important use of summary is to refer to another writer's work in the course of a new and original essay. Summary has the advantage over paraphrase in that it allows the writer to pick out and focus on only those aspects of the original that are most relevant to the new points being made. The flexibility of wording in a summary also allows the writer to fit it in smoothly with his or her original, ongoing statements.

When you are incorporating a summary into your own statement, it is important to remember that you should summarize only as much of the original text as is necessary to advance your own argument; do not let the summary overwhelm the direction of your own writing. A fuller discussion of the relative merits and appropriateness of each form of reference—summary, paraphrase, quotation, and name—can be found in Chapter 17.

Many of the writing assignments that appear later in this book rely on summary to introduce material for discussion. In the next chapter, for example, the first paragraph of the sample essay comparing reading and experience presents a summary of a psychologist's discussion of friendship. The rest of the essay compares the ideas in that summary to the student's actual experiences.

A Famous Use of Summary

The following quotation from Sigmund Freud's *The Interpretation of Dreams* presents one of the most prominent summaries of the past century. It demonstrates how a summary can be used to advance a new idea and how, at the same time, the summary is shaped by the new writer's specific interests. In the chapter "The Material and Sources of Dreams," Freud explores the conflicts that give rise to typical dreams. In discussing dreams about the death of a much-loved relative, Freud considers how infantile attraction to the parent of the opposite sex leads to competition with the same-sex parent and a desire to replace that same-sex parent. If not resolved, the tension created by the attraction and competition may lead to adult

Sigmund Freud. (Brown Brothers)

neurosis and may become the material of dreams. Finding these same tensions expressed in the Greek myth of Oedipus, Freud then summarizes the story as it appears in Sophocles' play *Oedipus Rex*.

Oedipus, son of Laïus, King of Thebes, and of Jocasta, was exposed as an infant because an oracle had warned Laïus that the still unborn child would be his father's murderer. The child was rescued, and grew up as a prince in an alien court, until, in doubts as to his origin, he too questioned the oracle and was warned to avoid his home since he was destined to murder his father and take his mother in marriage. On the road leading away from what he believed was his home, he

met King Laïus and slew him in a sudden quarrel. He came next to
Thebes and solved the riddle set him by the Sphinx who barred his
way. Out of gratitude the Thebans made him their king and gave
him Jocasta's hand in marriage. He reigned long in peace and honour,
and she who, unknown to him, was his mother bore him two sons
and two daughters. Then at last a plague broke out and the Thebans
made enquiry once more of the oracle. It is at this point that Sophocles'
tragedy opens. The messengers bring back the reply that the plague
will cease when the murderer of Laïus has been driven from the
land.

But he, where is he? Where shall now be read
The fading record of this ancient guilt?

The action of the play consists in nothing other than the process of
revealing, with cunning delays and ever-mounting excitement—a
process that can be likened to the work of a psycho-analysis—that
Oedipus himself is the murderer of Laïus, but further that he is the
son of the murdered man and of Jocasta. Appalled at the abomination
which he has unwittingly perpetrated, Oedipus blinds himself and
forsakes his home. The oracle has been fulfilled.

The summary is followed by a detailed analysis of the themes
of the play, as Freud sees them, and leads to the first formulation
of the now-famous *Oedipus complex.* Although the story he summarized eventually gave its name to a major concept, the summary
was originally just a tool, a way of providing an example to be
analyzed, buried among other examples and other ideas.

Freud's summary of the play does cover all the major actions
and adds nothing; however, the psychologist's interests—as defined
by the surrounding chapter—cause him to concentrate on certain
aspects of the play: "ancient guilt," parentage, good intentions,
unavoidable destiny, and the sense of abomination. Other critical
commentators, moved by different concerns, claim Freud distorted
the play. They emphasize other aspects—such as the role of kingship,
Oedipus's pride in thinking he could avoid fate, or Sophocles' de-
tective-style unraveling of the plot. These dimensions are also in
the play and are considered more significant by those interested
in political philosophy, Greek ethics, and dramatic craftsmanship,
respectively. Freud's actual purpose was to present underlying
causes for dream stories, and that is why he summarized the story
as he did.

Notice that in introducing the quotation from Freud, I used a
brief summary of his surrounding chapter to give background material

and to explain how Freud integrates *his* summary into his discussion. My summary of Freud's chapter was, of course, shaped by the point I was making about the use of summary.

Writing Assignments

1. Using any method or combination of methods for selecting material, write a summary of either of the two following passages. The summary should be about one-quarter the length of the original and should convey to the reader all the significant information contained in the original. Then write a very short summary (about fifty words) of the same passage for the same purpose. The first passage is by Donald Trunky, the second by Ernest Hartmann.

Trauma

Trauma is the medical term for a personal injury or wound. Including both accidental and intentional injuries, physical trauma is the principal cause of death among Americans between the ages of one and 38. In 1982 there were about 165,000 deaths from trauma in the U.S., and for each death there were at least two cases of permanent disability. Statistics compiled by the Department of Health and Human Services indicate that for Americans between the ages of 15 and 24 the combined death rate from motor-vehicle accidents, homicides and suicides has risen by 50 percent since 1976. Among young whites motor-vehicle accidents are the leading cause of death, accounting for about 40 percent, whereas among young blacks homicide is the leading cause of death, accounting for approximately the same percentage. In large cities black males have a one-in-20 chance of being murdered before the age of 30. Increased urban violence has been a major contributor to the rise in the national homicide rate: from 8,464 in 1960 to more than 26,000 in 1982. Overall the death rate for American teenagers and young adults is 50 percent higher than it is for their contemporaries in other industrialized societies.

Because trauma primarily affects people at or near the beginning of their most productive work years, its cost measured in lost productivity from both death and disability is high: more than $63 million per day in lost wages from accidental trauma alone, according to a recent estimate by the National Safety Council. The total annual cost of accidental trauma, including lost wages, medical expenses and indirect work losses, comes to about $50 billion.

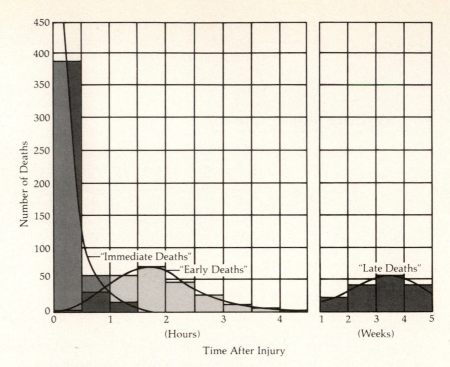

Trimodal distribution of trauma deaths is observed when the death rate for a large enough sample of such deaths is plotted as a function of time after injury. The first peak (*"Immediate deaths"*) corresponds to people who die very soon after an injury; the deaths in this category are typically caused by lacerations of the brain, the brain stem, the upper spinal cord, the heart or one of the major blood vessels. The second peak (*"Early deaths"*) corresponds to people who die within the first few hours after an injury; most of these deaths are attributable to major internal hemorrhages or to multiple lesser injuries resulting in severe blood loss. The third peak (*"Late deaths"*) corresponds to people who die days or weeks after an injury; these deaths are usually due to infection or multiple organ failure. The graph is based on a sample of 862 trauma deaths recorded over a two-year period by the author's group at San Francisco General Hospital.

Trauma patients currently take up a total of about 19 million hospital days per year in the U.S., more than the number needed by all heart-disease patients and four times the number needed by all cancer patients. In the past decade the death rate from heart disease and stroke has fallen by 22 and 32 percent respectively. In contrast the death rate from accidents has risen by about 1 percent per year since 1977. Trauma is clearly a major medical and social problem in the U.S. To a large extent, however, it is being neglected by physicians, hospital administrators, government officials and the general public.

Data from several parts of the country show that death from trauma has a trimodal distribution: when the death rate is plotted as a function of time after injury, three peaks appear in the resulting graph [*see illustration above*]. The first peak, characterized as "immediate deaths," represents people who die very soon after an injury. Invariably these deaths are caused by lacerations of the brain, the brain stem, the spinal cord, the heart or one of the major blood vessels. Only a fraction of the patients in this category could in principle be saved, even under the most favorable medical conditions.

The second peak, characterized as "early deaths," represents people who die within the first few hours after an injury. These deaths are usually caused by major internal hemorrhages of the head, the respiratory system or the abdominal organs, or by multiple lesser injuries resulting in severe blood loss. Almost all injuries of this type are considered treatable by currently available medical procedures. The interval between injury and definitive treatment, however, is critical to the probability of recovery.

The third peak, characterized as "late deaths," represents people who die days or weeks after an injury. In almost 80 percent of these cases the cause of death is either infection or multiple organ failure. Here time is less of a factor than the quality of medical care and the extent of medical knowledge.

The Psychology of Tiredness

We have already discussed sleep deprivation, and this has taught us something about the functions of sleep; but sleep deprivation is an artificial, stressful condition, occurring in a complex social-experimental setting. In many human sleep-deprivation situations the subject has a desire to perform well; especially if he is in a group, there is an ésprit de corps that can produce good performance in spite of sleep deprivation. This is particularly true in laboratory sleep-deprivation experiments, where the subject is challenged, mobilizes his defenses, and has a "set" to perform well. When sleep deprivation is used in a different setting, for instance as part of a "marathon" group dynamics session, the set is rather to regress and to become more "open"; here very different results are found. All behavioral sleep-deprivation results are thus heavily influenced by the setting and expectations.

I will now turn to a related situation which is closer to our everyday experience—simple tiredness. By tiredness I do not mean the fatigue after exercise, from which one recovers merely by lying down without sleeping, but the tiredness at the end of a day, apparently reversible only by sleep. One approach to the functions of sleep is to examine carefully the state of tiredness and to determine what characteristics or structures of the mind appear to wear out during the day and to need restoration by sleep. A study of what happens during a day as one becomes increasingly tired suffers from none of the above problems connected with experimental sleep deprivation; on the other hand, tiredness might be expected to produce less marked or obvious changes than prolonged sleep deprivation.

It is surprising how little has been written that can be useful to us here. Although a number of books and articles exist apparently dealing with tiredness or fatigue, they usually consider the muscular aspects and say almost nothing about the psychology of tiredness. Nonetheless, it is perfectly obvious both from our own subjective experience and from observation of other persons, especially children, that considerable changes in psychological functioning are produced by tiredness, and these are what we shall examine here.

This chapter necessarily will be clinical and somewhat impressionistic, and findings will be conceptualized in psychiatric and psychoanalytic terms. What I will discuss here is based on experience with patients in psychotherapy and psychoanalysis, several hundred interviews with normal and abnormal sleepers in various sleep studies, observation of children, and introspection. The chief problem lies in attempting to extricate constant themes from the changing, variegated clinical material, for the effects of tiredness clearly depend to a great extent on the background mental characteristics of the person, as well as on his social and physical environment.

Nonetheless, it appears to me that two patterns or "syndromes" of tiredness can be identified. They are seldom present in pure form, and not everyone reports both types, but a large number of individuals, when they stop to think about it, can pick out these two very different characteristic sorts of tiredness in themselves. One is the tiredness that comes after a day of purely physical activity, such as a day of skiing or physical work. This could be called physical tiredness or simple tiredness and is associated usually with a relaxed feeling in the musculature, including the facial and head muscles, and very seldom with any tightness or headaches. It is usually described affectively as either pleasant or neutral and is not associated with any characteristic psychic changes: people find it difficult to say that their mental functioning was altered in this kind of tiredness. In children my impression is that this physical tiredness is associated with relaxation and with rapid sleep onset without fuss or bother.

The second kind of tiredness, which we might call mental tiredness, is reported more frequently after a long day of intellectual or emotional and intellectual work. This tiredness, with which most of us are all too familiar, is often accompanied by tension or tightness of the muscles, especially muscles of the face and head; and it is usually described with a negative tone—it is unpleasant or at best neutral.

It sometimes has the paradoxical effect of making it hard to fall asleep. Associated with this sort of tiredness is an obvious lack of energy or unwillingness to try anything new; irritability and anger are also prominent. One feels uncomfortable and on edge in social interactions and wants to be left alone in an undemanding situation. One tends to read easy material and to lapse into wish-fulfilling daydreams.

The following are some of the words and phrases people have used in describing themselves, their friends, or their children at times when I believe they are discussing this second kind of tiredness: "cranky, impatient, selfish, dissatisfied, feel cuddly, want support, think loosely, sensuous, crying, stubborn, loss of energy, quick to anger, depressed, unaccepting, less sense of power, less self-confidence, more babyish, hate to be disturbed, don't want to think, can't think in a concentrated fashion, want to read easy material, I want what I want when I want it, want to be patted, less superego, less idealistic, more grabby, more selfish, very aggressive, hard to control, perseverates, repeats the same phrases or actions, temper tantrums, refuses to get to sleep although very tired, unwilling to act, less feeling of freedom, poor social functioning, poor adaptation, more denial of painful reality, distractible, hard to keep attention centered, hard to stick to one subject for long, unable to change mind, a little paranoid, less need to achieve, less control, less integration."

The above are very general effects of this sort of tiredness. The exact effects obviously vary with the individual's personality structure. In some persons with a tendency toward depression, increasing depression is characteristic of tiredness, and they may even go to sleep to avoid depression. For others (especially certain patients with sleep-onset insomnia) the great problem in becoming tired is the feeling of losing control, losing one's normal ways of dealing with sexual and especially aggressive impulses.

2. Write short summaries (roughly twenty-five words each) of three papers you have written for previous courses. The abstracts are to inform other members of the class of the kinds of interests and ideas you have.

3. Imagine that one of your teachers has announced a quiz on a five-page section from the textbook for the next day. That evening you receive a phone call from a close friend and classmate who is out of town playing with a rock band. You tell your friend about the test, but he has left the textbook home and will not be returning until fifteen minutes before the next class. As a good friend, you offer to meet him before class with a summary. Using a five-page section of any textbook from one of your current courses, prepare such a summary.

4. For an appropriate college course, rewrite the children's story "The Three Little Pigs" in summary form so that the summary might serve as an example of one of the following themes:

   a. In times of need, one should rely on family members to provide shelter and help.

   b. An obsessive desire for security is an appropriate response to a threatening world.

   c. The destructive alienation of the villain-type of personality only leads to further isolation, frustration, and hatred for the world.

   If you wish, you may substitute any other children's story with which you are familiar for this assignment. Be sure, however, to identify a theme or idea for which the summary is to serve as an example.

5. To share with your classmates your reactions to a selection you have already summarized for this chapter, write a short essay (one hundred to two hundred words) presenting your thoughts. Begin the discussion with a brief summary of the ideas to which you are reacting.

5 Developing Responses:
Essays

To discover how your reading re-
lates to your own patterns of thinking or your image of the world, you must develop
your responses into extended, coherent statements. The argumentative essay establishes
your position either agreeing or disagreeing with some idea you have read. The essay
comparing reading and experience allows you to explore how your reading relates
to those experiences that have helped shape your thinking; on the basis of your
experience you can begin to evaluate the validity of what you read. Both these forms
of essays prepare you for the kind of thoughtful choice and advocacy of positions
that you will need in any profession.

The Argumentative
Essay

The privacy of making annotations and keeping a reading journal allows you to explore your reactions without committing yourself to any public statement, but sometimes you must take a stand on what you read. On a philosophy exam, in responding to a business report, or in a late-night bull session, you will be cornered into agreeing or disagreeing with something you have read. It starts in school, when you are asked to agree or disagree with some statement or other in an exam question. Lawyers argue against the opposing lawyers' briefs; the judge agrees with one side or the other. Managers must argue for or against proposals affecting corporate decisions. Technical experts must give their opinions about projects. Political life is a constant debate.

The more important and public the situation is, the more focused, developed, and organized your argument must be. A random catalog of your top-of-the-head opinions—as expressed in annotations and journal entries—will not form a coherent, well-developed response. Your thinking must go through several stages of development before it can lead to an argumentative essay.

The purpose of the argumentative essay is to present and support a direct opinion about some idea, position, or piece of information you have encountered in your reading. You need not list all your ideas, associations, and reactions to the entire piece; you need only locate one specific thought or theme to comment on. You might agree or disagree with *anything* in the reading—from how a word is spelled to the truth of the main idea—but obviously, the more important the aspect you choose to discuss, the more forceful and significant your own comment is likely to be.

Whether you agree or disagree with what you read depends, for the most part, with how well it fits with what is already in your mind, or what Kenneth Boulding calls your "image of the world." That is, everything you have heard, read, thought, said, done, or experienced has been combined in your mind to create your own picture of the way the world is. Some readings are consistent with that picture, and you are likely to say that those readings sound right, that you agree with those readings. Other readings clash with parts of your image of the world, so you will disagree. (We will discuss in Parts 2 and 3 those special cases wherein you withhold judgment until you go out and gain some more information, adding to your world view through new primary experience, reading, or other forms of research.)

Because your world view is deeply ingrained, you may not always be fully aware of why you agree or disagree with what you are reading. You will have to work hard to discover your reasons. You need well-developed reasons to make your essay convincing, to show that you are giving more than a glib comeback. Without well-supported reasons, the reader has only your word to go on. No doubt, you are an honest and trustworthy person, but that alone will hardly convince readers who do not even know you.

The human mind being what it is, you can often come up with strong reasons for disagreement more easily than you can think of reasons for agreement. Disagreement creates friction. The mind objects to something and comes up with counterarguments: "But doesn't that stupid writer see . . ." What you are seeing (that the writer does not) is the source (or underlying reason) of your opinion in the first place. Explaining your reasons fully, giving examples, citing experiences, and referring to other things that you have read or simply know will help you develop a convincing argument.

Agreement is harder, because when you agree you are at peace with the reading. You can easily nod your head yes and read on. Unless you push your reasons for agreement very hard, you are likely to come up with little more than a summary of the original with occasional declarations of agreement: "Another true thing this author says is . . ." In order to create a well-developed statement of agreement, you must either (1) recall those experiences, ideas, or pieces of information that first led you to the same conclusions or (2) take the idea in the reading further to show how well it conforms to other aspects of your knowledge.

Developing the Essay

To develop an argumentative essay, you should first *read over your annotations and journal entries* on the text you are going to discuss. See which comments seem the most significant in retrospect, and determine whether several comments may be related to a common theme of agreement or disagreement.

Second, *decide which of your comments will become the basis for your essay*. A single comment may be the source of your essay, or you may develop a single consistent theme out of several comments that seem to point in the same direction. Try to pick a theme that raises a significant issue in the reading and that you will be able to support and develop convincingly. Commenting on an idea central to the original article or essential to a fundamental criticism or having application to other broader issues will add to the interest of your essay and keep you from petty nit-picking on side issues.

You may find that some of your comments agree with certain aspects of the article while other comments disagree. Remember, you need not cover every aspect of the article, so try to pick an aspect on which you have a consistent, clear position. If you find that you have mixed feelings on every significant issue, part in agreement and part in disagreement, you can write your paper partly agreeing and partly disagreeing. But if you do this, make sure the paper remains focused on the single issue you choose and develops the complexity of your reaction fully. Let the reader know how your agreements and disagreements balance each other. Sometimes the complexity of reaction may even be connected to a single source, as when the daring of a political proposal seems to cut right to the core of a problem, but such boldness seems unrealistic, given the difficulties of the political process. However you organize your complex position, do not let the paper deteriorate into a checklist of statements you like and do not like.

Third, you should *formulate your agreement or disagreement into a main conclusion,* or thesis, that will guide the overall direction of your paper. The essay should provide a single strong reaction stemming from one issue suggested by the original text.

Fourth, you should *list and develop all the arguments that support your disagreement or agreement.* Look deeply into why you feel the way you do, and convey to the reader in concrete and substantial detail the good reasons you have.

Fifth, *reread the original text and your previous comments* to consider two things. First, by rereading the original, you should make sure your reaction is substantial and clearly justified. Sometimes the original will say something different from your memory of it. A strong reaction to an idea can lead your memory to oversimplify the original to make the idea more clearly agreeable or objectionable. After having written out your own feelings, you may be in a better position to read the original more dispassionately and accurately. Second, rereading the original and your first reactions may also enable you to advance your ideas further and may suggest more key passages, details, and examples that you can use to develop your discussion. Now that you have focused on a topic, you will know much better exactly what details you need to support your argument.

Sixth, after you have gathered, selected, focused, and developed your ideas, you need to *plan how this material will fit together.* Although there are many ways to organize an argumentative essay, often a very straightforward pattern is all that is necessary. The opening should include (1) the book or article that evoked your response, (2) the particular item, idea, or theme to which you are responding, and (3) a clear statement of whether you agree, disagree, or take a more complex, mixed position. The opening section should also include whatever background is necessary to understand either the idea you are responding to or your response. But do not feel you need to summarize all the original text or tell your whole life story as background. Just tell enough to make your discussion intelligible.

The substance of your agreement or disagreement should form the main body of the essay. If you have several separate points to make in support of your position, you might simply build a paragraph around each of these points. Carefully consider, however, the order in which you should place the paragraphs so that the argument will get stronger instead of sliding downhill. If you wish to make a series of logically related points, again you might devote one paragraph to each point, but you should arrange the paragraphs to bring out the logic of their connection. Finally, if you are making only one, extended point, break that single, large reason down into a series of stages or aspects to be developed in several paragraphs. That will make your reasoning easier to follow and your point more memorable.

No matter how you organize your essay, the reader should be able to follow the organization and ideas readily and fully. Carefully chosen examples will help the reader grasp your complete idea. Using appropriate transitions between ideas and constantly tying each point to the main idea will help the reader see how your whole essay fits together. The ending should offer a sense of completion by linking your ideas effectively in some strong statement of your position. Because this essay is responding to a text, the conclusion might recall the original idea to which you are responding, reminding the reader exactly what you are agreeing or disagreeing with.

An Example: George Orwell Disagrees with G. K. Chesterton

During the 1940s George Orwell, the British political commentator and novelist who wrote *1984* and *Animal Farm*, wrote a weekly newspaper column, frequently taking his themes from his recent reading. On one occasion he took exception to a statement made by G. K. Chesterton, another essayist and novelist. The statement appeared in the course of Chesterton's introduction to a Dickens novel, but Orwell does not tackle the major argument of the introduction; in fact, we never find out what the introduction is really all about. Rather Orwell finds a significant theme in a passing comment, "there is nothing new under the sun," that reveals one of Chesterton's basic beliefs—a belief with which Orwell distinctly disagrees. By arguing with that passing comment, Orwell is able to define major differences between himself and Chesterton and to raise issues of great sweep. As Orwell moves from Chesterton's specific statement to the larger philosophical and political issues lurking behind it, he reveals how radically opposed the two views are. In response to Chesterton, Orwell winds up defining his own position. Yet he never wanders far from the original statement that prompted the disagreement: "there are no new ideas." Each paragraph examines that position in a different light. The first examines its history to show that it is a stock idea; the second looks at the unworthy fear behind it; and the last argues directly against the idea by a politically significant counterexample. Each paragraph opens with a direct reference to the idea, and the closing sentence reminds us of Orwell's disagreement and drives home his deeper point about the connection between new ideas and progress. There is also an underlying critique of Chesterton's religious-political position, out of which his passing comment grew.

Looking through Chesterton's Introduction to *Hard Times* in the Everyman Edition (incidentally, Chesterton's Introductions to Dickens are about the best thing he ever wrote), I note the typically sweeping statement: "There are no new ideas." Chesterton is here claiming that the ideas which animated the French Revolution were not new ones but simply a revival of doctrines which had flourished earlier and then been abandoned. But the claim that "there is nothing new under the sun" is one of the stock arguments of intelligent reactionaries. Catholic apologists, in particular, use it almost automatically. Everything that you can say or think has been said or thought before. Every political theory from Liberalism to Trotskyism can be shown to be a development of some heresy in the early Church. Every system of philosophy springs ultimately from the Greeks. Every scientific theory (if we are to believe the popular Catholic press) was anticipated by Roger Bacon and others in the thirteenth century. Some Hindu thinkers go even further and claim that not merely the scientific theories, but the products of applied science as well, aeroplanes, radio and the whole bag of tricks, were known to the ancient Hindus, who afterwards dropped them as being unworthy of their attention.

It is not very difficult to see that this idea is rooted in the fear of progress. If there is nothing new under the sun, if the past in some shape or another always returns, then the future when it comes will be something familiar. At any rate what will never come—since it has never come before—is that hated, dreaded thing, a world of free and equal human beings. Particularly comforting to reactionary thinkers is the idea of a cyclical universe, in which the same chain of events happens over and over again. In such a universe every seeming advance towards democracy simply means that the coming age of tyranny and privilege is a bit nearer. This belief, obviously superstitious though it is, is widely held nowadays, and is common among Fascists and near-Fascists.

In fact, there *are* new ideas. The idea that an advanced civilisation need not rest on slavery is a relatively new idea, for instance: it is a good deal younger than the Christian religion. But even if Chesterton's dictum were true, it would only be true in the sense that a statue is contained in every block of stone. Ideas may not change, but emphasis shifts constantly. It could be claimed, for example, that the most important part of Marx's theory is contained in the saying: "Where your treasure is, there will your heart be also." But before Marx developed it, what force had that saying had? Who had paid any attention to it? Who had inferred from it—what it certainly implies—that laws, religions and moral codes are all a superstructure built over existing property relations? It was Christ, according to the Gospel, who uttered the text, but it was Marx who brought it to life. And ever since he did so the motives of politicians, priests, judges, moralists and millionaires have been under the deepest suspicion—which, of course, is why they hate him so much.

Much reading has, of course, gone into Orwell's thinking expressed here. The essay is informed by the Bible and Marx's works, as well as a general knowledge of the history of Europe and Asia. The issue of whether or not there are any new ideas may have occurred to Orwell earlier—perhaps in response to another statement similar to Chesterton's. The more you read, the more knowledge and insight you bring to bear in responding to the author's point. In this case, Chesterton's comments did act as a catalyst to bring together Orwell's complex thoughts on the subject—all that was stored in his mind to help him make sense of the written page.

Though he wanders through many levels of ideas to explore the issue, he never loses contact with the starting point—the original issue that aroused his response. In the last paragraph, Orwell rejects Chesterton's idea and returns to the fundamental issue of conservatives versus progressives—those who favor the old ways and the old privileges versus those who see change as adding to life's possibilities. The last sentence, though it seems to raise entirely new issues, is only a return to the fundamental argument of the essay.

Sample Essay: A Complex Position

After reading the section of Dale Carnegie's book *How to Win Friends and Influence People* that is reprinted on pages 117–118, Carolyn Ross, a student, finds herself agreeing that Carnegie's methods work but rejecting the kind of friendship that results. In writing her response, Ross identifies clearly in what way she agrees and in what way she disagrees. She also makes clear how her agreement and disagreement are closely connected, two sides of the same coin, for just those methods she agrees work lead to just that kind of friendship she rejects.

                    What Kind of Friendship?

Each writer has a personal definition of friendship. Whenever you read about friendship, you have to figure out exactly what the author means by that term before you can judge whether what the author says is right or wrong. In his own terms Dale Carnegie makes a valid point when he says, "You can make more friends in two months by be- coming interested in other people than you can in two years by trying to get other people interested in you." People are genuinely egotistical, are always interested in themselves, and usually are suckers for flattery. If you want to be accepted by them and to be their friend, all you have to do is stroke their egos by showing an in- terest in them. But you then must ask yourself what kind of friendship Dale Carnegie is teaching you. On that level I find Carnegie's concept of friendship not only misguided, but actually repellent.

Friendship, of course, usually means some kind of sac- rifice, for a relationship implies that each person

"They're friends—leftovers from the old Dale Carnegie days."

(Drawing by George Price; © 1938, 1966 The New Yorker, Inc.)

gives and gets something. But Dale Carnegie takes this idea to an unpleasant extreme, for he asks you to sacrifice entirely your own ego, because the other person is too egotistical to recognize you. It is no accident Carnegie chooses the dog as the model of the ideal friendship, a dog so slobberingly hungry for love that he will do anything his master desires. A master—slave relationship—that is exactly what Carnegie is recommending, with you as the slave. If you offer to be somebody's slave, by showering your "friend" with attention and affection and asking nothing in return, it is not surprising that you can make a lot of "friends." As the title of the section says, "Do this and you will be welcome anywhere."

But what will you get in return? If you request nothing and the other person is so filled with ego that he or she will not think of your identity, how will your needs and desires be met? Is that "friend" so wonderful that you are willing to sacrifice your entire being, just to be in his or her presence? Or are you that desperately lonely?

I must admit that at certain points in my life, I have been that unsure of myself and that lonely. I simply gave my mind and identity over to someone who seemed so certain of herself, so together, that I was sure she would handle all our problems, because she was my "friend." I soon discovered that she only used me for her purposes. I listened day and night to her plans, her problems, her needs. Together we decided which was the dreamiest boy in the class for her to go after, we planned her strategy, even planned her next day's wardrobe and makeup. When he did not seem to notice her, I listened to Gloria's woes and then took her shopping to buy some new perfume, to absolutely trap her desired hunk. And when she finally did catch him, did she help me with my own man-hunt? Not at all. She forgot I existed, because she was too busy being taken around by the guy I helped her catch. Now I pity the poor guy. I am sure she just took and took and took, and never thought about him either.

If that is what Carnegie has in mind, he can keep it. Of course you have to be interested in your friend and have to be willing to make some sacrifices. But neither should you expect that your friend will be nothing more than an ego monster ready to swallow you. You have to expect, even demand, something in return. Otherwise, in my book, what you have is not a friendship, no matter what Carnegie calls it.

In her essay, Carolyn raises the question of the proper definition of friendship even before she begins to discuss Carnegie's ideas.

Then she introduces the specific idea she wants to discuss and identifies the levels on which she agrees and disagrees. The second paragraph explores the definition of friendship implied in Carnegie's advice and, in particular, criticizes Carnegie's ideal of "man's best friend." The third paragraph looks at the consequences of that kind of friendship through some sharply put questions and some unpleasant personal memories. The final paragraph clinches the rejection of Carnegie's kind of friendship by proposing a more satisfactory kind of relationship. The essay never wanders from a discussion of Carnegie's concept of friendship, and each paragraph advances the logic of each previous one by taking it one step further.

In both George Orwell's and Carolyn Ross's essays, a well-developed response to reading helps to formulate the writer's thinking. Reacting to reading means finding out and clarifying what is in your own mind. When you read, you must decide whether you accept or reject what the author tells you. You can hardly do that if you do not know your own mind.

Writing Assignments

1. Write an essay either agreeing or disagreeing with some aspect or issue of either the selection from Cicero's essay *On Friendship* on pages 28–29 or the selection from Dale Carnegie's book *How to Win Friends and Influence People* reprinted below. The essay should be directed to your classmates and designed to communicate your concept of friendship.

Do This and You'll Be Welcome Anywhere

Why read this book to find out how to win friends? Why not study the technique of the greatest winner of friends the world has ever known? Who is he? You may meet him tomorrow coming down the street. When you get within ten feet of him, he will begin to wag his tail. If you stop and pat him, he will almost jump out of his skin to show you how much he likes you. And you know that behind this show of affection on his part, there are no ulterior motives: he doesn't want to sell you any real estate, and he doesn't want to marry you.

Did you ever stop to think that a dog is the only animal that doesn't have to work for a living? A hen has to lay eggs; a cow has to give milk; and a canary has to sing. But a dog makes his living by giving you nothing but love.

When I was five years old, my father bought a little yellow-haired pup for fifty cents. He was the light and joy of my childhood. Every afternoon about four-thirty, he would sit in the front yard with his beautiful eyes staring steadfastly at the path, and as soon as he heard my voice or saw me swinging my dinner pail through the buck brush, he was off like a shot, racing breathlessly up the hill to greet me with leaps of joy and barks of sheer ecstasy.

Tippy was my constant companion for five years. Then one tragic night—I shall never forget it—he was killed within ten feet of my head, killed by lightning. Tippy's death was the tragedy of my boyhood.

You never read a book on psychology, Tippy. You didn't need to. You knew by some divine instinct that one can make more friends in two months by becoming genuinely interested in other people than one can in two years by trying to get other people interested in him. Let me repeat that. *You can make more friends in two months by becoming interested in other people than you can in two years by trying to get other people interested in you.*

Yet I know and you know people who blunder through life trying to wigwag other people into becoming interested in them.

Of course, it doesn't work. People are not interested in you. They are not interested in me. They are interested in themselves—morning, noon, and after dinner.

The New York Telephone Company made a detailed study of telephone conversations to find out which word is the most frequently used. You have guessed it: it is personal pronoun "I." "I." "I." It was used 3,990 times in 500 telephone conversations. "I." "I." "I." "I." "I."

When you see a group photograph that you are in, whose picture do you look for first?

If you think people are interested in you, answer this question: If you died tonight, how many people would come to your funeral?

If we merely try to impress people and get people interested in us, we will never have many true, sincere friends. Friends, real friends, are not made that way.

Napoleon tried it, and in his last meeting with Josephine he said: "Josephine, I have been as fortunate as any man ever was on this earth; and yet, at this hour, you are the only person in the world on whom I can rely." And historians doubt whether he could rely even on her.

The late Alfred Adler, the famous Viennese psychologist, wrote a book entitled *What Life Should Mean to You.* In that book he says: "It is the individual who is not interested in his fellow men who has the greatest difficulties in life and provides the greatest injury to others. It is from among such individuals that all human failures spring."

2. For a special supplement to your school newspaper on either computer education or feminism, write an argumentative essay responding to the following article on the sexist biases of computer culture.

Second-Class Citizens?

Little girls, it is said, are made of sugar and spice and everything nice. These days, however, "everything nice" includes the ability to operate and, in general, feel comfortable with the computer. We believe that little girls possess this ability, but the so-called computing culture places obstacles before them. These obstacles, while not insurmountable, present genuine problems. Unless they are removed, the girls of today may find themselves second-class citizens in the computer-intensive world of tomorrow.

Consider the video arcade. Peer inside and, save for the electronic bells and whistles, you will see the poolroom of yesterday. Like the poolroom, it is largely a male preserve, a place where boys and young men gather. For many, it provides the first taste of the computer and, as such, serves as a doorway into a culture that is rapidly transforming the fabric of work. Closing that doorway to girls may inadvertently stack the deck against women in the electronic work place.

Within a few years, according to some industry estimates, computers will be the primary tools in 25 percent of all jobs. Increasingly, computer literacy is becoming an essential skill in the marketplace. One computer ad, for example, shows a young job applicant sinking lower and lower in his chair as he is forced to admit that he does not know how to program.

Children who are exposed to computers early on are most likely to develop "computer efficacy," learn procedural thinking and programming, and develop the sense of mastery that will encourage them to tackle more complex computer tasks.

The culture of computing is overwhelmingly male. With few exceptions, men design the video games, write the software, sell the machines, and teach the courses. Most games, according to Dan Gutman, editor of *Video Games Player,* are "designed by boys for other boys." Until recently, boys outnumbered girls in programming courses and in computer camps by as much as eight to one. (In recent years, however, according to officials at several computer camps, the enrollment ratio has dropped to about three to one.) If this bias leads to an equivalent gap in competence and confidence, the girls of today will undoubtedly become second-class citizens.

At first, computing is a strange and potentially humiliating activity,

"Please, Daddy. I don't want to learn to use a computer.
I want to learn to play the violin."

(Drawing by Weber. Copyright © 1984 by The New Yorker Magazine, Inc.)

and girls need to be encouraged to take the initial plunge. The stylized nature of computing, and its arbitrary conventions, can be threatening. But those boys and girls who do acquire some proficiency usually advance rapidly. They learn discriminating attitudes toward games, machines, software, and programming styles. They learn to work their way through the complexities of computing syntax, devices, and programs. And they learn the language and values of "hackers"— those who spend most of their free time "fooling around" with computers.

Most children receive their initiation into the world of computers by playing video games in the arcades, at home, or at their local computing center. One study of children who had home computers found that 67 percent of those over 12, and 88 percent under 12, used them to play games, along with other activities.

The video arcade is a den of teenage male culture, a place where teenage boys gather with their buddies. Occasionally they bring their girlfriends, whose main role is to admire the performance of their boyfriends, not to play themselves. In an informal survey we made on several busy Saturdays in a suburban Pittsburgh shopping mall, we found the video arcade populated overwhelmingly by boys. Of the roughly 175 people we counted, only 30 were girls. We saw several groups of girls playing the games; all the other girls were with boys. Not once did we see a girl playing alone.

The software sold for home computers offers an array of land battles, space wars, and other forms of destruction, as well as typically male sports. This bias is reflected on the colorful covers of the game packages. On the rack in one store, for example, we found such games as Olympic Decathalon (four male athletes on the cover), Cannonball Blitz (five men in battle), and Swashbuckler (seven pirates). In all, there were 28 men and only four women depicted on the game packages that we saw on this rack. This bias is unlikely to attract girls to such games.

In the arcades, however, things are beginning to change. For example, Pac-Man, and a dolled-up version called Ms. Pac-Man, seem to appeal especially to girls. This year, each of these arcade games produced record sales of nearly 100,000 machines. Industry executives, trying to take advantage of the still largely untapped market of female players, are turning out an increasing number of nonmacho video games designed with enough whimsy to appeal to girls.

Computer stores are also an alien environment for most girls and women by virtue of the very products they stock. Most women are not familiar with electronics equipment, wires, and related accessories. This comes as no surprise, since the first customers for these stores were mostly male electronics hobbyists of the sort who used to build their own stereos. Computer stores are, in fact, electronics stores. The operators and sales people are mainly male, usually young, and often fervent advocates—to male customers—of computing as a way of life.

Even the educational software designed for children bespeaks a young, male culture. As Mark Lepper, a Stanford psychologist, points out, "One sees . . . a variety of presumably educational games that involve the same themes of war and violence that are so prevalent in video-arcade games, and another large class of programs that involve largely male sports—baseball, basketball, and football. In the game of Spelling Baseball, for instance, the child's reward for superior performance is the opportunity to see one's own baseball team outscore the computer's team. When one watches children exposed to these games, it is hard to avoid the conclusion that these choices are not optimal for interesting girls in the world of computers."

The Essay Comparing Reading and Experience

Whenever you read, you understand what the writer writes only because you are already in part familiar with the objects and concepts the writer symbolizes in the form of language. If the writer uses words you do not know to describe objects you have never seen, you might as well be reading gibberish. An advanced physics textbook or a specialist's book on horse racing would mean little if you were ignorant of either subject.

Even when you recognize all the words, if the writer puts them together in a way that contradicts your knowledge, you will reject the statement as nonsense—contrary to sense. You are not likely to accept a writer's construction of reality if he claims that "babies are found under cabbage leaves."

However, just because statements make sense to you—you understand them and they fit your perceptions of the world—does not guarantee that they are absolutely true. Your knowledge can grow by the conflict between what you have already accepted as sense and new claims that at first seem to be contrary to sense. To Europeans in 1492, Columbus's claim that he would sail around the globe violated both their sense of possibility and their sense of specific fact. Only when other navigators, following Columbus, sailed entirely around the world and returned alive did new possibilities and new facts replace the old. Evidence for a curved earth had been noticed by Greek astronomers two thousand years before Columbus; Eratosthenes could even calculate the earth's diameter. But the same evidence, easily observable without special equipment, was ignored by the astronomers of Columbus's time. They "knew" the world was flat, so they had no motivation to look for evidence of roundness. Human beings tend to observe only what they already believe is there. Such examples point to a difficult situation: we must rely on what we know to understand and judge what other people say, yet we must keep in mind that what we know may be eventually proved wrong. (Chapter 8 will explore the process by which we learn new things from our reading.)

If we are to be thoughtful and critical as readers, we must rely on what we know to identify and judge the ideas presented by the reading. Yet reliance on previous knowledge stands in the way of learning and accepting new ideas. There is no way to escape this dilemma. But by keeping it in mind and trying to accept a book *on its own terms* before judging it on ours, we can be both critical and open to new ideas. By being attentive to a writer's claims, by doing our best to see what that writer wants us to see—even though the writer's claims go against our prior knowledge—we may discover new ideas we can accept as part of our own view of the world. Finally, no matter how sympathetic a reading we give to any piece of writing, we must return to the question of whether it makes sense. The remainder of this chapter will be devoted to judging any piece of reading by using common sense and experience in a more careful, less biased way.

In sociology, psychology, political science, and other social science courses, you are often called on to relate the concepts presented in the course to your personal experience. Making such comparisons helps you understand what the concepts mean and how they work in the real world. You may even be assigned an essay comparing reading and experience, as described later in this chapter.

Out of school, when you try to persuade people to accept your ideas, evidence drawn from your own experience will help convince your readers that your ideas are more than nice-sounding abstractions. Opinion essays in newspapers and magazines often advance ideas based on the essayist's experience. The essay comparing reading and experience is also the first step toward the more disciplined use of evidence that you will learn in your academic and professional specialties, as discussed in Part 3.

Experience, Memory, and Common Sense

To see both the value and the problems of that grab bag of personal experience and random knowledge we bring to any particular reading, let us look at the case of George Washington Plunkitt, the Tammany Hall politician. In the late nineteenth century, the government of New York City was run by a group of politicians known collectively as *Tammany Hall*. Under the leadership of Boss Tweed, they took advantage of the power they held for their own profit and the profit of their friends. Eventually a number of journalists, including Lincoln Steffens, exposed the Tammany Hall politicians as crooks; since then Tammany Hall has become the symbol for political corruption. However, from George Washington Plunkitt's inside view as a member of the Tammany organization, the situation didn't look nearly as bad as it appeared to the reforming journalists on the outside.

"What are you laughing at? To the victor belong the spoils." Cover of *Harper's Weekly*, November 25, 1871. (Courtesy of The Newberry Library, Chicago)

When Plunkitt came to read Lincoln Steffens's exposé, *The Shame of the Cities,* he reacted by presenting his own insider's viewpoint. He expresses his down-to-earth thinking in down-to-earth language.

On *The Shame of the Cities*

I've been readin' a book by Lincoln Steffens on *The Shame of the Cities.* Steffens means well but, like all reformers, he don't know how to make distinctions. He can't see no difference between honest graft and dishonest graft and, consequent, he gets things all mixed up. There's the biggest kind of a difference between political looters and politicians who make a fortune out of politics by keepin' their eyes wide open. The looter goes in for himself alone without considerin' his organization or his city. The politician looks after his own interests, the organization's interests, and the city's interests all at the same time. See the distinction? For instance, I ain't no looter. The looter hogs it. I never hogged. I made my pile in politics, but, at the same time, I served the organization and got more big improvements for New York City than any other livin' man. And I never monkeyed with the penal code.

The difference between a looter and a practical politician is the difference between the Philadelphia Republican gang and Tammany Hall. Steffens seems to think they're both about the same; but he's all wrong. The Philadelphia crowd runs up against the penal code. Tammany don't. The Philadelphians ain't satisfied with robbin' the bank of all its gold and paper money. They stay to pick up the nickels and pennies and the cop comes and nabs them. Tammany ain't no such fool. Why, I remember, about fifteen or twenty years ago, a Republican superintendent of the Philadelphia almshouse stole the zinc roof off the buildin' and sold it for junk. That was carryin' things to excess. There's a limit to everything, and the Philadelphia Republicans go beyond the limit. It seems like they can't be cool and moderate like real politicians. It ain't fair, therefore, to class Tammany men with the Philadelphia gang. Any man who undertakes to write political books should never for a moment lose sight of the distinction between honest graft and dishonest graft, which I explained in full in another talk. If he puts all kinds of graft on the same level, he'll make the fatal mistake that Steffens made and spoil his book.

A big city like New York or Philadelphia or Chicago might be compared to a sort of Garden of Eden, from a political point of view. It's an orchard full of beautiful apple trees. One of them has got a big sign on it, marked: "Penal Code Tree—Poison." The other trees have lots of apples on them for all. Yet the fools go to the Penal Code Tree. Why? For the reason, I guess, that a cranky child refuses to eat good food and chews up a box of matches with relish. I never had any temptation to touch the Penal Code Tree. The other apples are good enough for me, and O Lord! how many of them there are in a big city!

Steffens made one good point in his book. He said he found that Philadelphia, ruled almost entirely by Americans, was more corrupt than New York, where the Irish do almost all the governin'. I could have told him that before he did any investigatin' if he had come to me. The Irish was born to rule, and they're the honestest people in the world. Show me the Irishman who would steal a roof off an almhouse! He don't exist. Of course, if an Irishman had the political pull and the roof was much worn, he might get the city authorities to put on a new one and get the contract for it himself, and buy the old roof at a bargain—but that's honest graft. It's goin' about the thing like a gentleman, and there's more money in it than in tearin' down an old roof and cartin' it to the junkman's—more money and no penal code.

Plunkitt's candid first-hand observations reveal some everyday facts about the political world of his time. His distinction between honest and dishonest graft amuses us because both types are crooked enough by our standards—particularly since we now have more stringent conflict-of-interest laws—but apparently he believed the distinction existed in his world. From his insider's view we also get a sympathetic portrait of the human desire to profit from situations. Plunkitt presents a working system that makes civic improvements by spreading the money around to friends. He even has some firsthand observations on ethnic and moral differences between New York and its rival in corruption, Philadelphia. If Plunkitt doesn't disprove Steffens's accusation that he and his friends are crooks, at least he lets us know the human workings of the corrupt system.

On the other hand, Plunkitt's comments are bigoted, self-interested, and narrow-minded. The whole point of the distinction between honest and dishonest graft is to show that he and his cronies are honest fellows, much better than those rascals in Philadelphia. To make his own crowd look better, he flatters his own ethnic group and insults another. Since his whole life has been committed to the Tammany system, what he knows and thinks are mostly Tammany rationalizations and self-defense. For intellectual, emotional, and legal reasons, George Washington Plunkitt cannot step outside the Tammany viewpoint in order to consider the criticisms of reformers like Lincoln Steffens. He finds some sense in Steffens only when he can bend the reformer's statements to prove what he already believes—that Philadelphia is more corrupt than New York.

In Plunkitt's case the stakes are unusually high. To accept Steffens's book as making sense, the Tammany Hall politician would have to admit that he and his friends were dishonest. Very few people have that much intellectual honesty. Even under less extreme conditions, we tend to defend our existing opinions and commitments. We would rather not pay much attention to ideas that might upset our personal apple carts.

Yet a stubborn defense of our personal opinions is not simply narrowness; those apple carts we have constructed in the course of our experience are the sum of all we have come to know. We usually work to make sense of our past experiences, so that our generalizations—those structures of thought that form our common sense—are worth taking very seriously and should not be given up simply because a writer comes along with an opposite viewpoint.

Writing an essay in which we compare our experiences to the claims of an author allows us to develop in explicit form our knowledge about the accuracy of the writer's claims. With all the issues out in the open, we can see how much we agree or disagree, and we can begin to judge where the better sense lies. Intellectual honesty enters if we are able to rearrange or even add to our apple carts on the basis of some new and convincing ideas we have read.

Developing the Essay Comparing Reading and Experience

The *essay comparing reading and experience* is simply a paper in which you compare the ideas described in your reading to personal experiences that the text reminds you of. As you carry out the early steps of reading, annotating, and journal writing, keep in mind two key questions: "What experiences does this reading bring to mind?" and "How do the generalizations in this passage compare to what I have learned from personal experience?" In your marginal comments and journal, list as many related examples from your own life as you can.

When you read through your first responses and marginal comments, think about them in two ways. First, see whether your personal experiences generally agree with or contradict the ideas of the passage. Second, see which of these personal associations presents your general train of thought most accurately. Follow through all the implications of your chosen comments—those that are most promising and forceful. Analyze in detail how your examples and ideas support or diverge from the statements in the reading. You can develop your thoughts through extended reading notes, journal entries, preliminary outlines, or even sketchy first drafts. Remember that you can always revise these first attempts to cut out digressions and tighten up the organization and logic.

In the early part of your essay, you should identify both the specific passage and the specific experiences or personal beliefs that you are comparing to that passage. Further, you should set up the general pattern of agreement, disagreement, or qualified agreement that will ultimately emerge from your comparison.

The main body of the essay will, of course, be comparative in structure. Because the reading stands independently of your essay—and can be referred to by the reader—you will probably devote more space to your personal experiences than to the reading. However, you need to summarize or paraphrase the passage with enough precision to enable your reader to know exactly what you are comparing from the original passage. Decide whether a short quotation, tight paraphrase, or compact summary will be most effective in acquainting your reader with the original. Exactly how much of the original you repeat will depend, to some extent, on how familiar your readers are with it; further guidance on methods of referring to the original appears in Chapter 17. In any case, the body of your paper should be devoted to those experiences that bear favorably or unfavorably on the reading. Always make sure that your experience is discussed in relation to the ideas from the reading; do not allow the narrative of your experiences to become an end in itself. The purpose of the essay is to illuminate and to evaluate, through your experience, the ideas contained in the reading.

Four Frameworks for Making Comparisons

Your comparison may be organized in one of several ways. The first method is to use your personal experiences to explain and develop one or more of the important ideas in the original passage. If you use this method, your introduction will consist of a concise statement of the major ideas of the original. In the body of the essay, you will explore these ideas by examining carefully chosen, effective examples taken from your own life and experiences. In the conclusion, you will reassert the general truths of the ideas as confirmed by your personal understanding of them. You may be familiar with this organization under the name of *exemplification,* or illustration.

A second organization is the *traditional comparison,* where ideas are compared on a point-by-point basis. The first point from the reading is discussed with your first related experience; the second point, with your second related experience; and so on. For the conclusion of this essay, you sum up all the smaller insights that you reached by the point-by-point comparisons.

A third method—still *another form of comparison*—is useful when the reading presents a consistent point of view that directly contradicts a consistent point of view suggested by your experience. In the first part of the essay, you draw together all the points from the reading to show the consistent pattern; then you draw together all the observations from your own experience to show the opposite pattern. In the conclusion, you discuss the specific differences between your point of view and the point of view of the original writer. The trick of this method is to maintain the comparative tension between the two points of view, even though you discuss them separately; otherwise, the essay may simply fall into two unrelated parts. You can avoid this pitfall and keep your reader aware of the two opposing viewpoints (1) by making clear cross-references and explicit comparisons between the two parts, (2) by repeating key phrases, and (3) by maintaining parallel order of points between the two parts.

Finally, if the reading and your experience agree, you may use the reading to *explain the experience.* Then the essay will punctuate a personal narrative by references to the reading to show the full meaning of the experience. You may then focus the conclusion directly on the usefulness of the ideas you derived from the reading. This last method is particularly good for demonstrating how compelling ideas, presented persuasively by a writer, can reveal to the reader the order behind the apparently haphazard events of day-to-day life.

Sample Essay

The following essay illustrates the first method of organization, exemplification. The student, Steve Slipka, uses his memories of a childhood friendship as an example of the preadolescent intimacy that Harry Stack Sullivan discusses in the selection reprinted on pages 132–134. The student's essay begins with a summary of key features of preadolescent friendship identified by Sullivan. In the following paragraphs, the student reveals details of his friendship, exemplifying those features that he summarized in his opening paragraph. The student concludes his essay with the ways his friendship did not totally live up to Sullivan's ideal, but he relates even these limitations to Sullivan's model of social development.

My Friendship with Jesse

The psychiatrist Harry Stack Sullivan in his discussion of the "Need for Interpersonal Intimacy" describes the close friendship that develops in preadolescence between youths of the same sex. The friendship, or intimacy

as Sullivan calls it, is nonsexual, but it is marked by
love. Mutual sensitivity and concern for each other's
feelings lead the two friends to know each other well.
They come to respect each other's opinions and to rely on
each other for approval and validation of their personal
worth. Even more, they begin to collaborate in developing mutual satisfactions, and they share in each other's
successes. Each comes to consider the other as important
as the self. When stated in such abstract terms, Sullivan's concept of friendship sounds too perfect, too
pure--not at all like the rough-and-tumble world of late
childhood. Yet when I think back on my childhood friendships, Sullivan's description reminds me of my friendship with Jesse Hunt. The details that I remember of our
friendship help make Sullivan's idea of friendship more
plausible and familiar.

Jesse and I were, I guess, a bit slow in developing our
friendship because we did not start to get close until we
were twelve, even though Sullivan says such friendships
can begin as early as the age of eight and one-half. Once
we were friends, however, we stayed close for almost five
years. Together we discovered books, girls, and the
world around us. Together we developed attitudes and
values that have lasted even though Jesse and I have lost
contact over the past two years.

Although Jesse and I had been neighbors and classmates
since we were nine years old, we did not get to know each
other well until we went off to junior high school. Every
day we walked the mile and one-half home together; we
talked about the teachers and the other students and what
stupid things we had to put up with. We communicated by
nasty jokes, making fun of the authority figures at
school who were trying to turn us into well-behaved,
well-rounded, and thoroughly boring young citizens. We
satirized our classmates as phonies and straight arrows.

We exchanged schemes about how to get over, around, and through the seemingly crazy requirements of school and the even crazier requirements of the social world in which we found ourselves. As puberty started to overtake us, we also began plotting--alas, unsuccessfully-- against the virtue of the unsuspecting girls in our classes.

We built up a stock of private jokes, which we thought were funny but which earned us reputations as cynics and pessimists among our classmates. As our critical atti- tudes developed and became public, the school authori- ties began to consider us potential troublemakers. We liked our reputations because then we had a special iden- tity. Our rejection of the phony world around us was the sign of our intelligence and sensitivity. Even if others did not understand or approve, we knew we were right. We looked to our shared reading to validate our socially critical point of view. In the eighth grade we read J. D. Salinger's <u>Catcher in the Rye</u>; the main character, Hol- den Caulfield--a boy our age who was disgusted by the "phoniness" around him--became our hero. The next year we thought that Sinclair Lewis's <u>Elmer Gantry</u>, with its portrait of a hypocritical gospel preacher corrupted by lust and money, was the truth to end all truths. From our reading, our jokes, and our shared troubles with the school administration, we built up a shared image of our- selves that gave us mutual respect and a sense of self- worth, despite our being considered outsiders by most of our peers.

Out of our shared respect for each other, we developed a shared concern. Actually this concern was only ex- pressed in small ways because the crises that affected us were small. If one of us had an argument with a teacher, the other would carry on the argument in the next class. If a girl turned one of us down for a date, the other would slyly insult her later. Our behavior may have been childish, but it showed us that we were aware of each other's feelings.

As time went on, we began to collaborate on more positive projects: we made some social studies presentations together and then went on to become partners on the school debate team. After we realized that the way to a girl's heart was not through plots or insults, we double-dated together.

There were, however, limits to our friendship. We were so immature that we were embarrassed to express our feelings directly. Instead Jesse would make jokes about my hair, which he called a "rusty Brillo pad," and I would make jokes about his laziness. I was in fact upset by the way Jesse would let projects slide, but I did not know how to help him, so I just made jokes. I could also never understand his strong feelings for his younger brother and sister; he never talked about them. On my side, I never talked about the difficulties I was having with my family because I thought he would not understand.

I realized these limitations only after I moved on to other relationships. By the middle of our junior year in high school, we both had steady girlfriends and started to lose contact. Without that first intimate friendship with Jesse, I would not have been as well prepared to form relationships with girls when the time for that came. As Sullivan suggests, the preadolescent friendship is an important stage in learning how to love other people.

Writing Assignments

1. Write an essay comparing your own experience of close friendship with the psychiatrist Harry Stack Sullivan's discussion (from

his book *The Interpersonal Theory of Psychiatry*) of the formation of close friendships during the preadolescent years. Consider the audience to be your classmates in a psychology class, where you all are trying to come to understand the practical meaning of the concepts presented in the course.

Need For Interpersonal Intimacy

Just as the juvenile era was marked by a significant change—the development of the need for compeers, for playmates rather like oneself—the beginning of preadolescence is equally spectacularly marked, in my scheme of development, by the appearance of a new type of interest in another person. These changes are the result of maturation and development, or experience. This new interest in the preadolescent era is not as general as the use of language toward others was in childhood, or the need of similar people as playmates was in the juvenile era. Instead, it is a specific new type of interest in a *particular* member of the same sex who becomes a chum or a close friend. This change represents the beginning of something very like full-blown, psychiatrically defined *love*. In other words, the other fellow takes on a perfectly novel relationship with the person concerned: he becomes of practically equal importance in all fields of value. Nothing remotely like that has ever appeared before. All of you who have children are sure that your children love you; when you say that, you are expressing a pleasant illusion. But if you will look very closely at one of your children when he finally finds a chum—somewhere between eight-and-a-half and ten—you will discover something very different in the relationship—namely, that your child begins to develop a real sensitivity to what matters to another person. And this is not in the sense of "what should I do to get what I want," but instead "what should I do to contribute to the happiness or to support the prestige and feeling of worth-whileness of my chum." So far as I have ever been able to discover, nothing remotely like this appears before the age of, say, eight-and-a-half, and sometimes it appears decidedly later.

Thus the developmental epoch of preadolescence is marked by the coming of the integrating tendencies which, when they are completely developed, we call love, or, to say it another way, by the manifestation of the need for interpersonal intimacy. Now even at this late stage in my formulation of these ideas, I still find that some people imagine that intimacy is only a matter of approximating genitals one to another. And so I trust that you will finally and forever grasp that interpersonal intimacy can really consist of a great many things without genital contact; that intimacy in this sense means, just as it always has meant, closeness, without specifying that which is close other than the persons. Intimacy is that type of situation involving two people which permits validation of all components of personal worth. Validation of personal worth requires a type of relationship which I call collaboration, by which I mean clearly formulated adjustments of one's behavior to the expressed needs of the other person in the pursuit of increasingly identical—that is, more and more nearly mutual—satisfactions, and in the maintenance of increasingly similar security operations. Now this preadolescent collaboration is distinctly different from the acquisition, in the juvenile era, of habits of competition, cooperation, and compromise. In preadolescence not only do people occupy themselves in moving toward a common, more-or-less impersonal objective, such as the success of "our team," or the discomfiture of "our teacher," as they might have done in the juvenile era, but they also, specifically and increasingly, move toward supplying each other with satisfactions and taking on each other's successes in the maintenance of prestige, status, and all the things which represent freedom from anxiety, or the diminution of anxiety.

2. Write an essay comparing the following article on the effects of television watching on children's concepts of relationships to your own experience as you grew up and the experience of people you know. Consider your audience to be a group of parents concerned about the influence of television on their children. Your experiences may serve either to calm their fears or to make them more likely to take some kind of action.

The Effects of Television on Children's Social Relations

TV presents the child with a distorted definition of reality. The child in the affluent suburb or the small midwestern town exists within his own limited reality. His experience with social problems or people of different races, religions, or nationalities is probably somewhat limited. To the extent that television exposes him to diversity of people and ideas it surely expands the boundaries of his reality. It is precisely because he now relies so heavily on TV to define other realities for him that we must examine so carefully what those images are. If they are distorted, inaccurate, or unfair, then television's reality is potentially harmful.

TV distorts reality by selecting certain kinds of images and omitting others and by portraying people in a stereotyped way. It portrays some categories of people with beauty, power, and importance and renders others weak, helpless, or invisible. So serious is the relative invisibility of some groups on TV that Dr. George Gerbner of the Annenberg School of Communications contends, "If you're not on

TV, you don't exist." Yet how often do you see yourself on TV? Or a Hispanic child? The physically handicapped? An intact Black family? The Jewish holidays?

The TV camera selects certain images to be examples, sometimes functioning like a magnifying glass held up to the worst in civilization instead of the best. When TV producers focus on violent ugliness, they lift it out and hold it up for all to see, making it impressively larger than life. A fistfight that occurs outside my window and is witnessed by only five people may be videotaped, broadcast, and "witnessed" vicariously by millions of people, thus multiplying the example set by the fistfighters. In the United States, most people have not witnessed murder, yet because of television most children have seen hundreds of thousands of violent deaths and therefore believe that the world is more violent than it actually is.

"For many people the relatively passive acceptance of TV fare defines what is typical, what is desirable, what is probable, and what is possible," says Dr. Chester Pierce, psychiatrist at Harvard University. "In fact, lower-income people, minorities and children may be more likely to believe that what they see on TV represents reality."

TV says, in effect: This is the way the world works. These are the rules. The images presented on TV tend to be exaggerated or glorified, and so believed and accepted as models to be *copied*. One demonstration of such TV power to influence behavior became apparent during Evel Knievel's heavily promoted attempt to "fly" his motorcycle over the Snake River. Many children imitated his stunts with their bicycles on homemade ramps. And many landed in hospitals. "The kids are really caught up in the Evel fervor," said one doctor. "The television carried a special on Saturday night just before he made his big jump, showing him jumping over 10 garbage trucks or whatever he does, and this is what the kids are trying to imitate." Even the children who did not see Evel Knievel took up the bike jumping because they, in turn, caught the idea from friends who had been watching the Knievel TV promotion.

TV affects human relationships as well as behavior by influencing our feelings about ourselves and our expectations for ourselves and others. Too frequently stereotypes provide us with instant definitions. The stereotype assigns to an individual characteristics associated with a group that may or may not be accurate. We tend to note a single feature of a person and fill in the details from a storehouse of stereotypes.

Psychologist Joyce Sprafkin says of stereotypes: "Overall TV appears to be a somewhat dramatized, but accurate representation of the non-TV world. However, like the funhouse mirror, television actually reflects characteristics which are unquestionably ours, but with distortions which may not be entirely laughable."

Via TV's stereotypes we see men as strong and active, women pretty and at home. All too frequently, minorities are cast in exaggerated portrayals and stereotyped roles, more as white male producers perceive them than the way minority persons perceive themselves.

Exposure to stereotyped presentations can easily influence viewers' behavior toward unfamiliar people. Viewers use what they learn from these TV images to establish norms for how they will act in certain situations. These images, in fact, teach values and behaviors, especially to children who have little firsthand knowledge of the real world. To the extent that children are exposed to certain character portrayals and behaviors on TV, they may acquire or learn those behaviors and roles and eventually accept them as models for their own attitudes and actions.

Perhaps most serious are the effects of information distortions on the child's self-image. At some level we begin to judge our own meaning, dignity, and worth in comparison with the TV characters who portray people like us. How accurate or fair is this barrage of portrayals that we are exposed to each day? What are the portrayals teaching about racial minorities, family relationships, sexuality?

According to TV, how does the world in fact work?

6 Analyzing the Author's Purpose and Technique

The writer's overall purpose determines the techniques he or she uses. The writer's purpose—the reasons for writing a particular article or book—may be manipulative, as in propaganda and advertising, or may be more straightforward, as in informative writing. In either case, understanding the writer's underlying purpose will help you interpret the context of the writing. It will also help you see why writers make the decisions they do—from the largest decisions about what information to present to the smallest details of what word to use. The chapter concludes with instructions on how to write an analysis of purpose and technique. This kind of rhetorical analysis will provide the perspective required to keep you from being pushed by words in directions you don't want to go.

The Writer's Purpose

Insofar as people know what they are doing, they plan their actions to achieve their purposes. Someone who selects the purpose of being rich will design and carry out a set of actions, legal or illegal, to gain the desired wealth. A person who wants to gain great wisdom will design an entirely different life course. Writers, whether they want most to be wealthy or wise, have specific purposes they hope to achieve by any piece of work. If they are skilled writers—that is, in control of what they write—they design each aspect of what they are writing to achieve their purpose.

Being aware of the writer's purpose when you read helps you evaluate how well the writer has achieved the purpose and decide whether you want to follow where the writer is trying to lead you. The active reader reads more than the words and more than even the ideas: *the active reader reads what the writer is doing.* The active reader reconstructs the overall design, both the writer's purpose and the techniques used to realize that purpose.

In this chapter, we first consider the various purposes a writer may have and the ways in which a reader can discern that purpose. Next we discuss the various techniques available to writers and examine a case study including several examples of how technique is related to purpose. The chapter ends with specific instructions on how to write an *essay analyzing purpose and technique.*

The Ad Writer's Purpose

Living as we do in a merchandising culture, we are all sensitive to the designs of advertising. We know the purpose of most advertisements is to open up our wallets. We are also aware of most of the techniques, even though we may not be immune to them: emotionally charged language, vivid art, attractive models, appeals to our fantasies and our fears. American Telephone and Telegraph, for example, has for many years used advertising campaigns to encourage the public to make more telephone calls. How can advertising make us use the phone more? By making us *feel* like using the phone—by causing us to associate the telephone with pleasant emotions of communication. This is, of course, not sinister; it is good to talk to loved ones. Nevertheless, telephone companies profit every time we do.

One particular AT&T advertising campaign, built around the slogan "Reach out and touch someone," attempted to call forth in readers the warm feelings of human contact, and then to create an association between these warm feelings and using the telephone. The slogan made readers feel not simply that they were talking to someone on the phone, but that they were getting almost close enough to "touch someone." Of course, the reader had to *do* something to experience this feeling: "reach out" and pick up the telephone. But the slogan added incentive, implying as it did that one was helping others, doing a good deed by reaching out to touch someone.

A typical advertisement in this series pictured an excruciatingly cute child with a mischievous smile, glowing cheeks, and twinkling eyes talking on the telephone. The little boy's words, bannered across the top of the page, invited "Uncle Bill" to come to his birthday party and then sleep out in the garage with the children at the party. Those words also invited readers to take on the role of Uncle Bill and become part of a warm family group, filled with the simple, happy pleasure of a children's party. Uncle Bill could feel like a happy child just by talking to his adorable nephew — and he wouldn't have to endure indigestion and the cold, windy night above the drafty old garage. It is more convenient and more comfortable to touch someone over the telephone than in the flesh.

The ads in this campaign were so suggestive of pleasant emotions that they didn't need to provide a direct sell. The word *telephone* never appeared in them, although of course the telephone was visually prominent. The company name and logo appeared in small letters. Over many years of similar advertisements most readers knew what the ad was about; the phone company needed only to reach out and nudge them. If they then telephoned a cute nephew or long-lost friend, the designers of the advertising campaign, through evocative words and art, had achieved their purpose.

Federal regulations outlaw advertising claims that are outright deceptions; and some advertisements are designed to be simply informative, just letting us know that a product with specific features is available on the market. Nonetheless, even the plainest advertisements emphasize certain of the consumer's needs and attitudes at the expense of others. Most advertisements try to distract us from a simple, rational consideration of what we need and what we actually receive in return for our money. Even the techniques of amusement — if we laugh at the advertisement, we will remember the product and buy it — lead us away from thinking about the value purchased for our money.

Paige Rense.
Her magazines say a great deal about her.
Her watch speaks for itself.

The magazines she heads are as varied a combination as you'll find under one editor in chief: *Architectural Digest, Bon Appetit, GEO.* Yet people in publishing say that the "Paige Rense stamp" is unmistakable on each of them. And that's meant success.

After she assumed its editorship, *Architectural Digest* won the prestigious National Magazine Award for Visual Excellence. She added warmth and style to the recipes in *Bon Appetit* and made it the best-selling epicurean publication in the country. And although her appointment to *GEO* is too recent to draw any conclusions, the changes she's made thus far show she's well on her way to another triumph.

She laughs. "'The Paige Rense stamp?' Yes, I suppose there is a lot of me in my magazines. I guess that's because I love what I do. The subject matter is fascinating. But you don't produce good magazines without first having good people. And I believe the people I work with are the best in the business.

"Personally, I have only one rule for good editing: I put myself in the reader's place. And our readers have very high standards. So if I'm hard on my people, if I'm hard on myself, it's because I know how demanding our readers can be. I have to assume they're going to read every single word, and if I don't keep my standards equally high, I'm not doing my job."

High standards. You'll find them in the magazines she edits. And in the watch she wears. The Rolex Lady-Datejust Perpetual Chronometer in hand-crafted 18kt. gold.

Rolex. Because someone who accepts only the best from every word expects the same from every minute.

ROLEX

The Rolex Lady-Datejust Chronometer. Available in 18kt. gold, with matching bracelet.

Rolex watch advertisement. (Courtesy of Rolex Watch, U.S.A.)

For Class Discussion

Discuss how the writer of the ad on the facing page has designed both words and art to make you want to purchase the product. Find further examples of magazine or newspaper advertisements for discussion.

The Propagandist's Purpose

Propaganda, like advertising, aims to make us forget reason. Propaganda may serve to further political ambitions, to drum up support for questionable governmental policies, or to confuse political discussions by deflecting attention away from the real issues.

In the early 1950s, Senator Joseph McCarthy relied heavily on propaganda to advance his own career and to create extreme anticommunist fear and hysteria. The following is an excerpt of a speech McCarthy delivered in the Senate on July 6, 1950, shortly after President Truman announced that the United States would provide troops to carry out a United Nations action in Korea. Notice how McCarthy turns his apparent support of the president's decision into an attack on members of the president's administration and on other Americans.

Mr. President, at this very moment GI's are consecrating the hills and the valleys of Korea with American blood. But all that blood is not staining the Korean hills and valleys. Some of it is deeply and permanently staining the hands of Washington politicians.

Some men of little minds and less morals are today using the Korean war as a profitable political diversion, a vehicle by which to build up battered reputations because of incompetence and worse.

The American people have long condemned war profiteers who promptly crowd the landscape the moment their Nation is at war. Today, Mr. President, war profiteers of a new and infinitely more debased type are cluttering the landscape in Washington. They are political war profiteers. Today they are going all-out in an effort to sell the American people the idea that in order to successfully fight communism abroad, we must give Communists and traitors at home complete unmolested freedom of action. They are hiding behind the word "unity," using it without meaning, but as a mere catch phrase to center the attention of the American people solely on the fighting front. They argue that if we expose Communists, fellow travelers, and traitors in our Government, that somehow this will injure our war effort. Actually, anyone who can add two and two must realize that if our war effort is to be successful, we must redouble our efforts to get rid of those who, either because of incompetence or because of loyalty to the Communist philosophy, have laid the groundwork and paved the way for disaster.

The pattern will become clearer as the casualty lists mount. Anyone who criticizes the murderous incompetence of those who are responsible for this disaster, anyone who places the finger upon dupes and traitors in Washington, because of whose acts young men are already dying, will be guilty of creating disunity.

Already this cry has reached fantastic pinnacles of moronic thinking. Take, for example the local *Daily Worker,* that is, the *Washington Post.* The other day this newspaper ran an editorial in effect accusing the University of California of injuring the war effort by discharging 137 teachers and other employees who refused to certify that they were not members of the Communist International conspiracy. This, Mr. President, would be laughable if it came merely from the Communist Party's mouthpiece, the *New York Daily Worker,* and its mockingbirds like the *Washington Post.* Unfortunately, a few of the Nation's respectable but misguided writers are being sold this same bill of goods, namely, that to have unity in our military effort the truth about Communists at home must be suppressed.

McCarthy begins by *flag waving,* that is, by playing on strong national feeling. By praising American soldiers, he makes himself appear patriotic with only the interests of his country at heart. He also arouses in his listeners patriotic feeling in support of the self-sacrificing GIs. But in the second sentence, he turns this patriotic feeling against Washington politicians. McCarthy starts *name calling,* which he continues throughout the speech. With no detailed evidence or other support, he labels certain unidentified members of the government as incompetents, communists, dupes, and traitors. He repeats these labels throughout his attack, but he never becomes specific about who these traitors are, what their exact crimes are, and what his evidence is. Thus he makes only *blanket accusations* that cannot be pinpointed and therefore cannot be proved or disproved.

Guilt by Association   As part of his labeling, McCarthy employs *guilt by association:* he associates members of the government with war profiteers who had been the object of public hatred for many years. Similarly, he associates the *Washington Post,* a respected independent newspaper, with the *Daily Worker,* the official newspaper of the Communist party.

Finally, the whole excerpt relies on *scapegoating,* putting the blame on those who are not truly responsible. If American soldiers are dying and if casualty lists are mounting, McCarthy wants to make it appear that the fault belongs to our government officials and newspapers—especially those that McCarthy does not like. Rather than saying it is the North Korean army killing our soldiers, McCarthy puts bloodstains on "the hands of Washington politicians."

Unfortunately, propaganda is sometimes very effective, particularly at times of crisis when emotions run high. Playing on the Korean War and Russian expansion in Eastern Europe, McCarthy temporarily gained substantial power and created a climate of terror in this country, a climate that took many years to dispel.

Doublespeak   In the novel *1984,* George Orwell describes another kind of manipulation called *doublespeak.* In that novel a totalitarian government uses confusing language to obscure important issues and ideas. Through such slogans as *War Is Peace, Freedom Is Slavery,* and *Ignorance Is Strength,* the government in *1984* keeps its citizens from understanding what is happening to them.

Today we also experience such dissociation of events from their meaning when bureaucratic language is used—when *death* is called *negative termination of patient care* and *embezzlement* is called *temporary readjustment of asset localization.* The purpose of such language is to make us not think about what is actually happening.

The National Council of the Teachers of English has found the doublespeak problem so serious in today's public world that it has established an annual award for "the most conspicuous use of deceptive language." The 1979 award, for example, went to the nuclear power industry for phrases designed to obscure the danger of nuclear accidents: *energetic disassembly* for *explosions, rapid oxidation* for *fire,* and a whole series of terms for *accident,* ranging from *event* to *normal aberration* and *plant transient.* Other recent winners include a secretary of state, the Pentagon, and a cigarette manufacturer.

Straightforward Purposes

When advertisers or propagandists try to manipulate our opinions and actions, we may become suspicious about the truthfulness of their statements. Fortunately, only a small fraction of writing is deliberately manipulative. More often the writer's purposes are more honest, and the techniques used are not aimed at distorting our judgment. A novelist may wish to amuse us. A reporter may wish to inform us as objectively as possible. A political commentator may want us to think seriously about a matter of public concern. Still, we should know their larger designs, not to guard ourselves— as we do against propaganda and misleading advertising—but to understand the legitimate uses we can make of their statements.

If you are not aware of the larger design of a book, you may be misled about its meaning. Perhaps when you stop by the local bookstore, you pick up a paperback and start reading in the middle:

> Mario stood in the doorway, a strange light flashing from his eyes. His lips barely moved, "Carmen, I am here."
> "But Mario, I thought, . . ." her voice quivered.
> "No. There was one thing I had to do first." His deliberate steps matched the pounding of her heart. His eyes, flashing fire, fixed on her. He stopped in front of her, his lips slightly opened as if he had something to say, but couldn't say it. He reached for her.

True passion? You love romances and are about to buy it. But wait. You turn to the cover. *Compelled to Murder*. You do not enjoy thrillers so you put it back on the rack. The overall design of the work helps define the purpose and technique of each small part: the same words that bring expectation and a melting heart in a romantic fantasy bring fear and dread in a murder plot.

The message that words convey depends on the purpose of the words within the context of a larger communication. For example, when the following words appear in a dictionary, they simply provide a definition, one piece of information among many other similar pieces of information.

> affective: adj. 1. *Psychology.* Pertaining to or resulting from emotions or feelings rather than from thought.*

The dictionary tells you that *affective* is one word in the English language with a specific spelling and meaning, used particularly in the field of psychology. If, however, that same definition appears with a dozen other terms on a ditto sheet handed out by your psychology professor on the first day of class, the message is that you had better learn that word, for it is part of the basic vocabulary for the course. If your English professor writes the definition in

* © 1978 Houghton Mifflin Co. Reprinted by permission from *The American Heritage Dictionary of the English Language*.

the margin of your paper—after circling the word you wrote and changing the *a* to an *e*—the message is that you confused *affective* with the more common word *effective*. In each of these cases, your knowledge of the larger context helps you see the purpose of the words and receive the message intended.

A Catalogue of the
Purposes of Writing

The following list of some of the more common purposes of writing may help you identify the purposes of pieces of writing you may come across. Whenever you read a piece of writing, ask yourself what its purpose is and whether it fits in any of these categories. For example, the list of stock market prices in this morning's newspaper clearly belongs in the category "the conduct of business" and in the subcategory "to report information needed for making decisions." An editorial in the same paper might be considered "instigation of public thought and action," specifically "to criticize the actions" of a particular public official. The cartoons would be "entertainment," perhaps in any of the three subcategories. Textbooks, including this one, are for the "transmission of knowledge to a wider audience" either "to provide an introduction to an area of knowledge" or "to instruct rigorously."

As you try to categorize actual pieces of writing that you have read, you may find that one piece of writing may serve several purposes; an amusing parody of a political candidate aims to influence your vote even as it entertains you. You may also find that you need to add categories or subcategories to fit the special text you are examining.

Entertainment
To amuse and to delight
To arouse emotions and sympathies
To appeal to fantasy and imagination

Instigation of Public Thought and Action
To raise questions
To criticize the actions of others; to reprimand

To weaken the support of opponents

To persuade to act, vote, donate, etc.

To inform of issues of concern

The Support of a Community of Common Beliefs

To state one's beliefs; to take a stand

To repeat the accepted beliefs of a group; to encourage and reinforce these beliefs

To share recent developments and events that are of mutual concern

To gain tolerance for one's beliefs in the wider community

To persuade others of the correctness of certain views; to gain approval

To recruit active support; to proselytize

The Conduct of Business and Government

To promulgate laws, regulations, guidelines

To report information needed for making new decisions, laws, policies

To argue for certain lines of action

To request funds or propose an activity to be funded

To keep track of funds, projects, activities; to report on accomplishments and failures; to evaluate activities

To sell, advertise

Transmission of Knowledge to a Wider Audience

To satisfy curiosity

To provide practical information for everyday use

To provide an introduction into an area of knowledge

To instruct rigorously, passing on the most recent knowledge, skill, or technique

Scholarly Inquiry

To present new findings, recent information, the results of experiments

To present new interpretations, speculations, thoughts

To gather together all that is currently known on a subject to see how it fits together and to reach some conclusions

To show the relationship of two areas of study and to show the light one sheds on the other

To determine the truth of some matter and to prove that truth to other researchers

Clues to the Author's Purpose

We cannot read the minds of authors to find out what their true purposes were, but externally available clues reveal much about their purposes.

Overt Statements   Pieces of writing that begin or end with commands like "vote for Paulsen" or "donate to this worthy cause today" make no secret of their intentions. Obviously, titles can clearly indicate purpose, such as *How to Be a Big Winner on the Stock Market, The Encyclopedia of Sports, A Report on the Status of Mine Inspection Procedures, The Case for National Health Insurance,* and *Spanish Self-Taught.* Often in scholarly or professional books, and sometimes in more popular works, the introduction or preface specifically states the purpose and outlines the issues that gave rise to the book.

In the following preface to *Philosophical Investigations,* Ludwig Wittgenstein explains the curious kind of book he has produced and cites the special reasons and motives that led to it. He begins by explaining the kinds of problems that have kept him from writing a more conventional book, which develops a continuous line of thinking, and have forced him to write this disjointed set of remarks. Wittgenstein then discusses the underlying personal motives that made him persist in presenting his thoughts despite the difficulties: he was upset because people were misunderstanding his ideas, and he wanted to correct some errors he had previously published. Finally, he presents the most basic purpose: "to stimulate someone to thoughts of his own."

Preface

The thoughts which I publish in what follows are the precipitate of philosophical investigations which have occupied me for the last sixteen years. They concern many subjects: the concepts of meaning, of understanding, of a proposition, of logic, the foundations of mathematics, states of consciousness, and other things. I have written down all these thoughts as *remarks,* short paragraphs, of which there is sometimes a fairly long chain about the same subject, while I sometimes make a sudden change, jumping from one topic to another.— It was my intention at first to bring all this together in a book whose form I pictured differently at different times. But the essential thing was that the thoughts should proceed from one subject to another in a natural order and without breaks.

After several unsuccessful attempts to weld my results together into such a whole, I realized that I should never succeed. The best that I could write would never be more than philosophical remarks; my thoughts were soon crippled if I tried to force them on in any single direction against their natural inclination.——And this was, of course, connected with the very nature of the investigation. For this compels us to travel over a wide field of thought crisis-cross in every direction.—The philosophical remarks in this book are, as it were, a number of sketches of landscapes which were made in the course of these long and involved journeyings.

The same or almost the same points were always being approached afresh from different directions, and new sketches made. Very many of these were badly drawn or uncharacteristic, marked by all the defects of a weak draughtsman. And when they were rejected a number of tolerable ones were left, which now had to be arranged and sometimes cut down, so that if you looked at them you could get a picture of the landscape. Thus this book is really only an album.

Up to a short time ago I had really given up the idea of publishing my work in my lifetime. It used, indeed, to be revived from time to time: mainly because I was obliged to learn that my results (which I had communicated in lectures, typescripts and discussions), variously misunderstood, more or less mangled or watered down, were in cir-culation. This stung my vanity and I had difficulty in quieting it.

Four years ago I had occasion to re-read my first book (the *Tractatus Logico-Philosophicus*) and to explain its ideas to someone. It suddenly seemed to me that I should publish those old thoughts and the new ones together: that the latter could be seen in the right light only by contrast with and against the background of my old way of thinking.

For since beginning to occupy myself with philosophy again, sixteen years ago, I have been forced to recognize grave mistakes in what I wrote in that first book. I was helped to realize these mistakes—to a degree which I myself am hardly able to estimate—by the criticism which my ideas encountered from Frank Ramsey, with whom I dis-cussed them in innumerable conversations during the last two years of his life. Even more than to this—always certain and forcible— criticism I am indebted to that which a teacher of this university, Mr. P. Sraffa, for many years unceasingly practised on my thoughts. I am indebted to *this* stimulus for the most consequential ideas of this book.

For more than one reason what I publish here will have points of contact with what other people are writing to-day.—If my remarks do not bear a stamp which marks them as mine,—I do not wish to lay any further claim to them as my property.

I make them public with doubtful feelings. It is not impossible that it should fall to the lot of this work, in its poverty and in the darkness of this time, to bring light into one brain or another—but, of course, it is not likely.

I should not like my writing to spare other people the trouble of thinking. But, if possible, to stimulate someone to thoughts of his own.

I should have liked to produce a good book. This has not come about, but the time is past in which I could improve it.

Cambridge,
January 1945.

Knowledge About Publication   Even if the author does not state the purpose of a piece of writing directly, where an article appears reveals much. An article appearing in a professional journal like *Journal of the History of Ideas, Harvard Theological Review,* or *Journal of Geology* is most likely to present new information or research and to evaluate current knowledge with a scholarly intent. An article in a general-circulation magazine devoted to one field, like *Scientific American, Psychology Today,* or *High Fidelity,* is more likely to present existing knowledge in a way understandable and useful to the nonspecialist, rather than presenting scholarly research. An article in a magazine brought out by a corporation or some other special-interest group, such as *Ford World, Teamster International,* or *Gun and Rifle,* would tend to convey a favorable impression of the organization's interests. Thus the stated and unstated editorial policy of the magazine helps define the purposes of all articles that appear in it.

With books, attention to the publisher, the place of publication, and the date will give first approximations of purpose. A book from a reputable academic press, such as University of Pennsylvania Press or Stanford University Press, will usually have a scholarly purpose aimed at the advancement of knowledge. Commercial publishers range from well-established houses—such as W. W. Norton, Houghton Mifflin, and Random House, which, among other material, publish nonfiction books of some seriousness of purpose for a general market—to sensationalist houses more concerned with playing on prejudices or exploiting current popular topics than with providing substantive knowledge. In addition, special-interest publishers press the causes or beliefs of specific groups: many religious publishing houses, for example, are currently thriving. The more you know about the publisher, the more you will know about the purposes of its books.

The date and place of publication also may be a clue to understanding the purpose of the book. A book about Vietnam published in the United States in 1967 will probably be either highly critical or strongly supportive of American participation in the Vietnam War, and a reader would be wise to look out for partisanship. A book published a dozen years later by the same publisher on the same topic may be inquiring into what happened or how Americans now view the morality of that war. Books on the same topics published in both years by the Foreign Languages Press in Beijing, China, will have obviously different purposes. Everything you know about the history of the issues will help you place the purpose of each book involved. If you become engaged in research touching on some controversy, you will become especially aware of such factors.

Knowledge About the Author In much the same way, knowledge of a particular author will give you some sense of the purposes of his or her books, but beware of oversimplification, for the same person may write different types of books. Nevertheless, if an author is known primarily as a supporter of some cause, a book by that person is likely to reflect that cause. Although often the work of ghost writers, books by entertainment and sports celebrities frequently will play on popular ideas of a celebrity's life, either by glorification or by exposé of scandalous behavior. In this type of autobiography, even the "just plain folks" style currently in vogue is concerned with image building. You can assume, however, that the works of reputed scholars writing in their fields of expertise are serious attempts to get at the truth of some matter—just as you can assume that the next book by an evangelical preacher known for his spiritually uplifting works will be aimed at inspiring faith.

Analysis of the Text The most substantial way of determining purpose—and the way against which all these other methods must be checked—is by close reading and analysis of what actually appears in the book or article. The remainder of this chapter is devoted to this type of analysis. *What the writer includes is the best guide to what that writer is trying to do.* The use of many personal anecdotes might suggest that the writer is seeking your emotional response or sympathetic involvement in the material, just as the heavy use of statistics suggests that the writer's major interest is in providing documentation and proof.

Investigation of Apparent Cross-purposes   In any book, a discrepancy between the purposes suggested by any of the foregoing clues and what the writer actually accomplishes should make us wonder. The discrepancy may be favorably explained, as in the case of a statesman who rises above the temporary conflicts and his own political ambitions to provide a dispassionate analysis. Sometimes marketing strategy or political pressure may cause a book to be given a misleading title or introduction that is not at all indicative of the real substance. A serious sociological study of close relationships among adolescents would have a misleading title if it were called *Sex and the New Teen-agers.*

Sometimes, however, the discrepancy can be a serious weakness, particularly if an author does not achieve what he or she sets out to do. The author of an *Easy Guide to Preventive Medicine* may use language only an expert would understand. Most of all, a discrepancy may signal a desire to mislead: an interest group may attempt to lend credibility to its case by surrounding it with the trappings— but not the substance—of scholarship.

The possibility of cross-purposes should make us wary as readers, but the mere possibility does not warrant our drawing premature conclusions. If a conservationist with a well-known interest in the preservation of natural woodlands were to write a history of the lumber industry, we as readers should be most careful in evaluating the evidence. Even if the book contained much scholarly apparatus— with substantiated detail, statistics, footnotes, and other documentation—we still might want to check the facts it cites against other sources and consider whether all the writer's contentions were supported elsewhere. The writer's interest in condemning the lumber industry might be stronger than his interest in the truth. Yet we should not reject the book out of hand. The writer may have produced an accurate, scholarly work that correctly describes the lumber industry. If the facts are on the conservationist's side, the author's best strategy is indeed to present the whole case as objectively as possible.

Exercises

1. Categorize and discuss the purposes of each of the following excerpts printed earlier in this book.
   a. From Dale Carnegie, "Do This and You Will Be Welcome Anywhere," pages 117–118.
   b. From the Declaration of Independence, page 62.
   c. From Eric Hoffer's journal, pages 34–35.
   d. From George Orwell's essay, pages 112–113.
   e. From Daniel Boorstin's discussion of pseudo-events, pages 83–85.
2. Find examples of published pieces of writing, including books, magazine articles, newspaper articles, and college bulletins or handbooks. Categorize and discuss the purposes of each.
3. Find examples of unpublished writing, such as business letters, memos, college papers, and personal writing. Categorize and discuss the purposes of each.
4. Choose a book from your major field or any other field of particular interest to you. List everything you can determine about the book's purpose from the preface, the facts and context of the book's publication, the author's life and interests, and a quick examination of the text itself.

The Writer's

Technique

Because the writer's purpose is realized through the specifics of words in combination, the writer's technique is present in every sentence and in every word—as well as in the larger groupings of paragraphs. Technique is present in every choice made by the writer at every stage of creation. Thus, to observe the technique of any writer, you must use everything you know about reading and writing, about how people present themselves through words, and about how thoughts are shaped by the form in which they are put. Much in this book should help you directly and indirectly in the task of observing technique, but you must also call on everything you have learned before about your own writing and about the interpretation of other writers' works.

The only way to understand technique is through analysis of individual cases: you should attempt to analyze how a given writer goes about the task in front of him or her. However, the following check list covers some of the things you might look for and some of the more obvious questions to ask yourself. It will provide a starting place from which to begin your observation and evaluation of technique. In time, the individual character of a piece of writing should suggest to you appropriate questions for your analysis, because each piece of writing operates in its own way.

Check List of Techniques

Relationship Between the Writer and the Reader

Does the writer ask or expect the reader to do anything?

Does the writer address the reader as an expert speaking to other experts? or to the general reader?

Does the writer make sure that the reader follows the discussion?

Does the writer interest the reader through humor, drama, or unusual examples?

Is the writer hesitant or assertive?

How much knowledge does the writer assume the reader has?

Overall Structure

What holds the writing together as a whole?

How does one paragraph, one chapter, one part lead to the next?

Is the progress by a chronological narration? by a grouping of related topics? through the steps of a logical argument? by comparison? association? repetition? by accumulation of detail? by analysis? by the breaking down of the subject into parts?

Content Choices

What parts of the subject are discussed in great detail? What parts are summarized?

What statements does the writer assume as given (and therefore not back up by proof)?

What relevant topics are ignored?

What topics could have been discussed but were not?

Expansion of Topics

In what ways are individual topics developed? Are arguments given? Are anecdotes told?

Is the reader asked to believe certain ideas or to take certain actions? Is the reader asked to imagine consequences?

Does the expansion of statements prove the statements? help the reader understand? keep the reader interested or amused? obscure the issues? develop implications?

Choice of Evidence

What types of information are used to support main statements: statistics, anecdotes, quotations, original observations, scientific theories, legal or philosophical principles, definitions, appeals to emotion, to the imagination, to common sense?

Uses of Reference

How extensively does the writer rely on other sources? (Are there frequent mentions of other books or articles?) Do you notice any indirect reference to the work of others?

What methods are used to refer to other works: reference by name only, paraphrase, summary, or direct quotation?

How complete is the documentation? the bibliography?

What kinds of material does the writer cite: contemporary newspaper accounts, private diaries, government documents, specialized scholarly studies, theoretical works, best-selling nonfiction books, statistical reports, literary works?

What purpose does the reference serve in the writing: Does the reference provide specific evidence? provide the actual words of a person being discussed? provide an assertion by an authority? present an example for analysis? explain a point? present the background of a new idea? distinguish between conflicting ideas? place current work in the context of previous work? present an idea to be argued against?

Level of Precision

Is the subject simplified or presented in all its complexity?

Are all important distinctions brought out?

Are many supporting details given or are only broad principles stated?

Are potential difficulties in the argument discussed?

Sentence Structure

Are the sentences short or long? simple or complex?

Are the sentences declarative statements? Do they set up a complex condition (*if . . . then . . .*)?

Do the sentences have qualifiers (*even though . . .*)?

Do the sentences describe actions (*Sandra runs;* or *Gear c transmits the power to drive wheel d.*)? Do they describe physical qualities (*Sandra has a pulse at rest of 63;* or *Gear b and gear c are in a reduction ratio of 12 : 1.*)? Do they relate actual events to abstract ideas (*The disagreement of the leaders over the terms of the treaty marked the beginning of new tensions between the two countries.*)? Do they discuss only abstractions (*International organizations are formed in part to resolve disputes between countries without resort to war.*)?

Word Choice

Are the words short or long? common or unusual? general or technical? emotionally charged or scientifically objective?

Evaluating the Effectiveness of Technique

Having observed a writer's technique, you will be able to determine whether that technique is appropriate and successful for the writer's purpose—stated or implied. You will begin to notice how the successful comic writer makes you laugh by piling up absurd details. You will notice how carefully a historian has gathered together materials, has weighed alternatives, and has moved to a well-argued conclusion. You will notice how the philosopher uses a precise vocabulary in an attempt to minimize confusion about abstract meaning.

In certain instances you may notice a discrepancy between the stated purpose of a book or article and what is actually achieved on paper. A book that claims to present new findings may, on closer inspection, rely heavily on previously discovered evidence put together in a familiar pattern. The comic writer may not pace his jokes correctly or may be too predictable. A detective story may unfold so tediously that no one would want to spend leisure hours reading it. An author's evidence might prove only part of his or her thesis. Writers may fail in their purposes in an infinity of ways, and even the best of books have weaknesses. However, weakness is relative: a book that does not live up to a grand purpose might tell you more than one that fully achieves an extremely small goal.

Misjudgment, lack of skill, or an attempt to do too much may explain these unintentional differences between a writer's intended purpose and actual accomplishment.

Other times an author *sets out* to mislead us, and we must understand the deception to understand the true design. Beneath a pile of evidence may lie a prejudiced assumption: when a report advises against building a community college in a poor neighborhood because that community has not previously produced many college graduates, the writer's prejudices may have translated lack of opportunity into an assumption that the people of that community cannot succeed. Thus the reporter's recommendation to deny opportunity may be made to sound respectable and evenhanded while still delivering its unjust message.

The outright lie, the partial lie, and the partial truth will continue to appear in print. Deception can be achieved in many ways, and it helps to be aware not just of the deception but also of the motive behind the author's deception.

The Camel on the Pack: A Case Study

An analysis of some of the voluminous writing on the tobacco industry will give you a specific sense of how a writer's purpose is realized through every detail of the writer's technique. Although you might first imagine—as I did before I looked carefully at these articles—that most recent writing on tobacco would center on the health issue and would therefore have persuasive, or polemical, purposes, the writers I sampled had quite varied purposes in writing about the industry. These varied purposes result in substantial differences among their writings—even though these authors are, on the surface, dealing with very similar topics.

The Company Camel

The first item I pulled off the library shelf was a pamphlet entitled *Our 100th Anniversary,* put out by R. J. Reynolds Industries, Inc., one of the major cigarette manufacturers. Handsome, multicolored photographs of cigarettes, packs of cigarettes, machinery, factories, advertisements, and members of the corporate family were arranged in an eye-appealing layout. The photographs reinforced the impression that the company's main purposes were self-celebration and cultivation of a good public image. The author, sympathetic to the corporate position, writes a chronological narrative of growth— Joshua Reynolds's one-man peddling business transformed into a large and diversified multinational corporation. Since the purpose of the pamphlet is to develop a good public image, we obviously do not hear of corporate wheeling and dealing or tedious details of corporate statistics and financing. Most of the history is made up of amusing anecdotes to personify Reynolds Industries as humane and good-natured, not a cold, calculating industrial giant. Business manipulations are presented only in the attractive form of the clever hero getting past a stupidly obstinate opponent; competition is mentioned only when it has been soundly defeated. Success comes to the corporation managers because they are so humanly charming; nostalgia makes corporate history warm and touching. The following description of the appearance of the new Camel brand typifies this anecdotal, nostalgic technique. Business, production, and even tobacco get short shrift as most of the text is devoted to the familiar symbol on the pack.

> In Richmond the lithographers prepared two labels, "Kamel" and "Camel" with the latter winning out. A great deal of attention was paid to the wording, especially to the famous inscription advising purchasers: "Don't look for premiums or coupons, as the cost of the tobaccos blended in Camel Cigarettes prohibits the use of them." The label's background of temples, minarets, an oasis, and pyramids was much like it is today, but the camel in the foregound was a pathetic, one-humped beast with short, pointed ears, two-pronged hoofs and a drooping neck.
>
> Is this a camel? the Reynolds people asked each other. Consulting the "Encyclopedia Britannica," they learned that a one-humped dromedary could indeed be called a camel, although no one was too pleased with the creature's looks. Luckily, Barnum & Bailey came to town, Monday, September 29, 1913, and Roy C. Haberkern, Reynolds' young secretary, went to investigate. With a photographer, he visited the circus menagerie and found not only a dromedary, but a two-humped camel as well. When the animal boss refused permission to photograph them, Haberkern pointed out that Reynolds had always closed offices and factories for the circus, a practice that could easily be discontinued. The trainer relented, but demanded a written release from the company.
>
> Haberkern raced back to the closed office building, climbed through a window, wrote the agreement, and signed Reynolds' name to it.

Old Joe, the original Camel pack camel. (Courtesy of R. J. Reynolds Tobacco Company)

Back at the fairgrounds the circus man conceded and brought out the two animals. The camel posed willingly, but Old Joe, the dromedary, wouldn't hold still. The trainer gave him a slap on the nose. Old Joe raised his tail, threw back his ears and closed his eyes as the shutter snapped. From that photograph an improved label was designed and Old Joe became the most famous dromedary in the world.

The language is simple and direct; the author uses a familiar vocabulary and avoids complicated sentence patterns. This easily understood section forms a little self-contained narrative with a problem, some complications, a crisis, a clever solution by the young hero, and a happy ending. The details create an image of company employees as friendly and fallible. With good intentions, they first illustrate a pathetic animal, but they are eager to improve and willing to laugh at themselves. They succeed by willingness to negotiate, by well-timed bending of the rules in a good cause, and by general good will. The author hopes that this amusing circus story and the pleasant image it conveys of the company will make us feel more kindly toward the corporate giant.

The Camel Reconsidered

The immortalized camel reappears—but in a different way—in Susan Wagner's book *Cigarette Country: Tobacco in American History and Politics.* The book's appearance reveals a popular commercial venture intended for a general audience: about 250 pages, medium-size print, catchy chapter titles—and no footnotes, bibliography, or index. The author is not linked with either antismoking forces or the cigarette companies; in the preface she states her motivation to be purely curiosity.

> This is not a book with a cause. It is not an antismoking tract nor a how-to-stop-smoking book. I found myself drawn into the subject quite by chance. My interest developed out of another project, my book *The Federal Trade Commission,* published by Praeger earlier this year. As I researched a chapter on cigarette advertising for that book, the entire subject of tobacco began to interest me as a sociopolitical phenomenon. Smoking *is* a strange habit to have become so much a part of American life and mythology.
>
> The more I delved into the history of tobacco the more it intrigued me. It is a history filled with a freaky variety of anecdotes and ironies, beginning with an irony—namely, that, without realizing it, Columbus, when he discovered tobacco, discovered a source of far greater riches than all the gold carried away from the New World by the Spanish conquistadors. I was fascinated, too, to learn that from the earliest times tobacco had been simultaneously hailed as a cure-for-whatever-ails-you and as a foul habit harmful to health.

Wagner is a professional writer, unearthing a story that she hopes book buyers will find as intriguing as she does. For her, an interesting part of the "sociopolitical phenomenon" of smoking is the increasing role of advertising in the cigarette industry. As part of the discussion of advertising, she brings in Old Joe, the dromedary.

At first, Reynolds didn't realize what he had in Camels and continued to push his Reyno brand, as well as Osman, a new blend of flue-cured and Turkish. The first real sales campaign for Camels was launched in Cleveland, Ohio, where pictures and coupons and other sales gimmicks were dispensed with as an excuse to price Camels at the low rate of 10 cents for a pack of twenty cigarettes. When the trials proved successful, Reynolds decided to concentrate on one brand and push it hard. It was easier for Reynolds than the other firms that already had heavy investments in their established cigarette brands to do such a thing. All the Reynolds brands were new. In its national campaign of 1914, Reynolds adopted "teaser" advertisements, such as "Camels! Tomorrow there will be more Camels in this town than in all Asia and Africa combined!" Then came the picture on the package, clearly a concession to the early taste for Turkish leaf. Its brand image and package design were inspired by "Old Joe," a Barnum & Bailey dromedary. Reynolds spent nearly $1.5 million on advertising Camels during the brand's springboard year, and sales began to climb steadily.

Susan Wagner mentions the dromedary as an advertising theme of exotic character—one detail among many about the extent and type of advertising for the brand. Her candid judgment about the lack of coupons, the reasons for Reynolds's flexibility (that it had no established brand), and the businesslike attitude toward advertising are parts of a truth that the author of the company pamphlet had no interest in bringing out. This passage describes a shrewd business process rather than a humorous, narrative episode. Like that of the company pamphlet, the style here is simple, direct, and aimed at a general audience. However, this narrative provides more factual, general information and fewer personal incidents, vivid actions, and character confrontations. Wagner's verbs, for example, indicate general actions in a nondramatic fashion—*realize, was, proved, decided, came, spent, began.* Compare these to the vivid, energized verbs in the company anecdote—*raced, climbed, refused, pointed out, relented, demanded, conceded, threw, snapped.*

The Fighting Camel

Old Joe takes yet another bow in *Trust in Tobacco: The Anglo-American Struggle for Power* by Maurice Corina. This book is a bit thicker than the previous one, with smaller print and much scholarly apparatus (footnotes, bibliography, index, statistical charts, and several extensive statistical appendices). Although this writer deals with the same historical material as the other two, his interests are narrower and more serious: he intends to examine the growth, struggles, and structure of the giant tobacco corporations. In his introduction, the author states that he hopes the narrative "will contribute to public understanding and knowledge at a time when interest in the great corporations has never been so strong and before the big tobacco companies, now fast diversifying their interests, submerge into other industries." The author clearly believes that knowledge of the tobacco companies is important so that they can be watched and controlled if necessary.

Old Joe lumbers into view in a chapter entitled "Unlawful Conspiracy and Realignment." In this chapter, the author discusses competition among the large companies after the Federal Trade Commission had broken the monopolistic American Tobacco, owned by Buck Duke.

That new and fiercely competitive forces had been unleashed in the United States market in the period between dissolution of Duke's Trust and his death was very evident to every American smoker. The Reynolds, Liggett & Myers, Lorillard, and American Tobacco enterprises were locked in a marketing battle of national dimensions, a struggle which finally established cigarettes as the first choice of American smokers. Holding good his promise to "give Buck Duke hell," Richard Joshua Reynolds had launched several cigarette brands, such as Reyno and Osman. They included one offered in 1913 in the Cleveland sales territory featuring the motif of Old Joe, a dromedary owned by the Barnum and Bailey circus. The brand, a blend of fine cured Bright, sweet Burley and some Turkish leaf, was called Camel, priced at 10 cents for twenty. Soon the nation's tobacco stores were queuing for stocks as smokers saw local advertisements heralding the new brand: *"Camels! Tomorrow there will be more Camels in this town than in all Asia and Africa combined."*

Duke had outlived Reynolds by seven years. But that was time enough for him to see the dramatic change in cigarette marketing which flowed from Reynolds' Camel brand. It gave Reynolds no less than 40 per cent of the nation's cigarette consumption by the end of the Great War. Camels were firm, well-blended machine-made cigarettes. They were well named, for smokers seemed to prefer exotic names, even if some Turkish cigarettes were sham, oval-shaped blends selling alongside the genuine mixtures of Oriental and Turkish leaf. There was such a proliferation of names—at least fifty brands— that Camels, easy to say and remember, enjoyed an immediate acceptance. Reynolds had set out to establish Camels as a national favourite, taking on American Tobacco's Omar, Lorillard's Zubelda, and Liggett & Myers' pioneering paper cup–packeted Fatimas. Camels stood out amid the Deities, Moguls, Murads, Helmars, Meccas and

Hassans. The Cairo, Zira, Oasis, Muriel and Condax brands were others to feel the competitive challenge. Turkish-type cigarettes had continued to sell well in spite of such bright Virginian brands as Sweet Caporals, Piedmont, Home Run and Picayune, among others.

This passage is an analysis of competitive forces. In almost every sentence, Reynolds Tobacco is compared to other companies and fit into the larger pattern of market trends. Within individual sentences, the competition between companies is established: four companies are "locked in a marketing battle"; a personal rivalry exists between Reynolds and Duke; Duke watches the changes wrought by Reynolds; and the Camels win out over many other brand names. The word choice reinforces the competitive fervor: *fiercely competitive, unleashed, locked in, battles, give hell, outlived, dramatic, taking on.* Such vocabulary, not always supported by evidence, may make us wonder if the author is trying to make the case seem stronger than it actually is through verbal exaggeration. Despite the scholarly appearance of the book, detailed analysis shows limits to its scholarly objectivity. Nonetheless, the interpretation of events comes across sharply. Within such a context, Old Joe seems part of the cavalry, and the slogan about the invasion of camels becomes a corporate battle cry.

The Camel Vanishes

Another book on the industry, *Tobacco: The Ants and the Elephants,* doesn't contain a single camel or dromedary—and for good reason: this book is concerned with the economics of tobacco growing, the plight of the farmers, and proposals for government support. The author, Charles Mann, received his doctorate in economics from Harvard and is on the staff of the Rockefeller Foundation. Like Corina's, the book is fully documented—packed with charts, statistics, and equations. But because Mann's purpose is to show the human meaning of economic facts and government policy, he also includes the personal testimony of many farmers and their individual stories. He argues that, unless government policy changes, many farmers will be hurt; only by personal stories can he make that hurt visible. Since his concern is current and future policy, the past serves only as background for the current difficulties. He discusses the early years of this century—when Old Joe was posing for pictures—in only one paragraph, in a chapter entitled "The Geography and Politics of Tobacco."

The twin influences of surging tobacco demand and falling cotton demand had major impact on tobacco production. By 1920 there were more than six hundred thousand acres under tobacco in North Carolina, about half of it in the coastal plain or new belt. In the North and South Carolina border belt as well, tobacco replaced cotton, with South Carolina's tobacco acreage rising from 25,000 acres in 1910 to 98,000 in 1920. Georgia, producer of particularly high-quality cotton, shifted to tobacco only when the cotton crop was decimated by the boll weevil. Georgia's tobacco acreage rose abruptly from 7,100 acres in 1918 to 25,000 in 1919. As cigarette demand climbed during the 1920s, flue-cured production grew more rapidly in the new areas than in the old, reflecting the newer's greater comparative advantage.

The writer organizes this entire paragraph around the principle that production follows demand. The claim of the opening sentence is proved, in the sentences that follow, by three sets of comparative, before-and-after statistics. Each case is more striking in the rapidness of change than the previous one. The final sentence extends the comparison in general terms into a later period and comments on even more rapid expansion into newer areas. Thus the opening general statement of ratio is repeated four times, each time with different statistics. Always the focus is on production of tobacco and its spread, for Mann is here concerned only with the economics of tobacco.

Interestingly, none of the material we have just looked at touches on the health controversy. Although the relationship of smoking and disease is an important issue, the writers of these pieces had other purposes in mind. The issues raised in each, the overall organization, the manner of development, the kind of evidence, the word choice, and even the sentence patterns are determined by the particular purpose of each writer.

The Essay Analyzing Purpose and Technique

Perhaps in literature classes you have already written a literary analysis discussing how certain aspects of a story, such as character development or the use of irony, contribute to the overall meaning of the story. The task of literary analysis is similar to an *analysis of purpose and technique,* except that your subject is a piece of nonfiction prose rather than a poem or short story. In this type of analysis, sometimes called *rhetorical analysis,* you show how the details of technique contribute to the larger purposes of the writer.

Journalists and other political commentators often analyze politicians' rhetoric, or purposeful use of words, to reveal exactly what the politicians are trying to do. Sometimes intellectual arguments, as well, depend on rhetorical analysis rather than points of fact. Whenever you need to understand how other people's words are pushing you in certain directions, analyzing the writer's purpose and technique will give you the necessary perspective and understanding.

In most situations, the need to understand a text deeply suggests that you must analyze the text's rhetoric. When you are assigned an essay of analysis as part of your course work, however, your first task will be to select a text to analyze. First, if you choose a selection in an area about which you have some knowledge, you will already have a sense of the typical purposes and techniques of writing in that area. If, for example, you have followed a presidential campaign closely and are familiar with the issues, you already have the background against which to consider any single campaign speech. Second, if you pick a selection related to a larger project that you are engaged in, such as a term paper, you may have additional motivation for doing the analysis. The sample essay at the end of this chapter, for example, was written in the course of research for a paper on the 1968 gun control law, which was mentioned earlier in our student's reading journal. This short analysis helped the student clarify something of the emotional and political climate leading up to the passage of the law. Finally, you should choose a short passage with striking features of purpose and technique so that you can focus your paper easily and can cover all the details in a relatively short paper. As you become more adept at this type of analysis, you may wish to tackle more subtle or more extensive texts. At first, however, analyzing simple short passages will be difficult enough.

Your next task is a thorough reading and understanding of the selection. In order to analyze a text, you must know the text in detail, paying attention to every word.

Once you understand both the complete meaning and the organizational structure of the text, you should focus on identifying the details of technique. Marginal annotation is especially useful here—to help you remember details you spot as you are reading. In the margin, you can number the steps of an argument and comment on the relationship of one point to the next. You can comment on the type of evidence, on the sentence structure, on unusual word choices—or on any hunches you have about the writer's purpose. These initial marginal reactions may lead you to further thoughts and observations. Particularly useful is questioning anything that seems unusual: "Doesn't this example contradict an earlier example?" or "Why does the author linger on this point?" One clue may start you noticing a recurrent element or a general pattern.

After noting the various techniques of the selection, you should sit back and think what overall purpose the author may have had in mind—what purpose all the details serve. A journal may help you work out the connections among the separate elements you have noticed.

You should begin to think about writing your essay only when you have some consistent idea about how the selection achieves its purpose. Then you must decide on a main *analytical statement*— that is, a central idea controlling the essay, much like a thesis statement. You must decide whether you will limit yourself to one element of the overall design or will consider all the related elements in one selection. Then you must select your supporting statements and major evidence. Again use journal entries and random jottings to sort out your thoughts.

Before you begin actually writing the essay, reread the selection one more time with the following tasks in mind:

- Check to see if your analytical statement fits all the evidence of the selection or explains only a small part.
- Figure out how you will assemble all your own ideas and evidence to be an accurate representation of the original's design; let the design of your own paper crystallize by making a final survey of the selection to be analyzed.
- Fill in details of evidence that you missed in previous readings or that have become more important in light of your analytical statement.

Only with your thoughts beginning to take shape and your evidence assembled are you ready to write. If you skip over any of the steps just described, you may run into problems. Without accurate understanding of the text, your analysis will be misguided. Without calling attention to specific details of technique, your discussion will slide back into summary or generalizations. Without thought about the order in which the parts of your analysis fit together, the essay will be a disorganized jumble. Finally, without verifying your analysis against the text, you may miss important evidence or may make misleading claims. Writing a complex essay, such as an analysis of a writer's purpose, requires you to do many different kinds of preparatory tasks in order to develop your ideas fully. Only when you have completed all the preliminary tasks are you ready to communicate your findings to your readers.

The Structure of the Analytical Essay

The main purpose of your analytical essay is to present a major insight into the overall design of a selected passage of writing. That insight is the *analytical statement* of the essay, similar to a thesis statement or topic sentence. To flesh out the analytical statement, you must explain what you think the writer's purpose was and must give specific examples of writing techniques employed in the original text. In other words, your task is to show your readers the *pattern* of purpose and technique that you have discovered in a given selection.

Because this analytical task is such a specific one, you must take care that you do not gradually slide into a different task, such as a summary or argument. If your essay begins to sound like a paraphrased or summarized repetition of the original selection, you should stop and rethink what you are doing. In the course of your analysis, you may need to summarize or paraphrase a small part of the original as evidence for some claim you make, but such repetition of the original must be limited and have a clear purpose. Similarly, if you find yourself responding more to the content of the piece than to its design, you need to stop and think. Any personal reaction or response that you discuss should be directly related to the overall design. In this kind of essay, you do develop your own thoughts and opinions, but these thoughts and opinions must concern the writer's purpose and technique.

The introduction of your analytic essay should first identify the passage you are analyzing by stating the title of the book or article and the author. Include a copy if possible; otherwise give exact page and line references. Next, the analytical statement should clearly identify the major purpose and the major techniques of the original. This analytical statement will control all that follows in the paper.

The body of your essay should elaborate the separate elements that make up the larger design. Here you enumerate all the techniques you have discovered and you support them by specific examples, using quotation, paraphrase, summary, or description. You must relate each technique to the overall analytical statement so that the reader sees how each detail is tied in to the larger design. Transitional statements at the beginning of each paragraph (such as "Once again the author misleads the reader when he implies . . ." or "The emotional anecdote discussed at length prepares the reader for the direct appeal for sympathy in the last paragraph") help to tie the parts of the paper together.

Also useful are extended discussions of the relationship of each technique to the overall purpose, as in the following example: "This particular use of statistics focuses the reader's attention on the issue of economic growth, while it excludes consideration of the effect on individual lives, which the author earlier stated was not accurately measurable. By admitting only statistical evidence and limiting the way it may be interpreted, the author can offer clear-cut—but one-sided—evidence for continuation of the current policy." The connections you make between the details of technique and the analytical statement are what will give your essay its direction and strength.

Each individual paragraph of the body of your essay either may be organized around one specific technique used throughout the passage or may focus on the variety of techniques appearing in a small part of the passage. In the first method your cumulative paragraphs establish all the relevant techniques—one after the other. You should plan carefully the order in which you present the examples of techniques. In one analysis, for example, an early examination of a writer's attempts to slander through word choice may establish the ideas necessary to expose the disguised strategies of organization. In another analysis, the smaller details of technique may fall in place only after the larger organization is first examined.

The second method, covering all the techniques in each small section at one time, results in going through the original selection in chronological order. This method is particularly useful if the text goes through several distinct stages. The chronological method explores how the writer builds one stage on the previous ones by adding new elements, by shifting gears, or by establishing emotional momentum. This second method is used in the sample essay that follows.

The danger of the chronological method, however, is that you may slip into summary by just repeating the arguments in the original order. Beware of transitions like "the next point the author makes is . . . backed by the next point that . . ." Such transitions indicate that you are forgetting your analysis and are slipping into a repetition of the original argument. A way to avoid this problem is to show how the character of the writer's argument shifts and develops by stages. Always keep your eye on *purposes* and *technique*. Thus the weak transition cited above might be improved in the following way: "At this point the author initiates a new stage of her argument. Up to here she has been arguing smaller separate points, but now she brings them all together as part of a broader conclusion." Make sure you are not carried away by your example. Tell only enough to support your statement; otherwise, the ever-present temptation to summarize may overcome you. If you find the temptation to slip into summary too strong, you should avoid chronology altogether and organize your paper around specific techniques. This safer method forces you to rearrange and rethink the material.

In the conclusion of your analysis, you should do more than simply repeat your main points. You should drive home your analytical statement in a striking way that grows out of all you have said previously. After having shown the reader all your ideas and specific evidence, you should be able to come to a more penetrating observation than you could at the beginning—before you laid out the evidence. If you have additional moral, ethical, or intellectual reactions to the selection, the conclusion is the place to express such reactions. Since there is no single, all-purpose way of concluding, you should feel free to experiment. The only important point to remember is that the conclusion should grow out of and reinforce the analysis.

The article below from *Newsweek* is immediately followed by an analysis by student writer Dianne Pari. Try to analyze the purpose and technique of the article before reading Pari's essay.

Guns: Like Buying Cigarettes

By now the weapons have become inexorably linked with the victims. It was a 6.5-mm. Mannlicher-Carcano carbine that cut down John F. Kennedy. It was a .30-'06 Enfield rifle that killed Medgar Evers. It was a .30-'06 Remington pump rifle that felled Martin Luther King. And it was a snub-nosed .22-caliber Iver Johnson revolver that snuffed out the life of Robert F. Kennedy. Though the guns vary in size, shape and ballistic characteristics, all of them share one thing in common—they are, as President Johnson angrily pointed out last week, as easy to get as "baskets of fruit or cartons of cigarettes."

Indeed, the very availability of firearms in the United States amounts in one breath to a national tradition and a national tragedy. No one knows exactly how many guns are in private hands in the country; estimates range from a conservative 50 million up to an astounding 200 million. What this fantastic arsenal produces, however, is eminently measurable. In 1966, for instance, guns of one kind or another accounted for 6,500 murders in the U.S., 10,000 suicides and 2,600 accidental deaths. Since the turn of the century, three quarters of a million Americans have been killed by privately owned guns in the United States—more Americans than have died in battle in all the wars fought by the U.S.

Passage: Last week, the weight of these grim statistics combined with the outrage at the assassination of Robert Kennedy and the recent emphasis on fighting crime in the streets to push the first piece of gun-control legislation through Congress in more than 30 years. The gun-control provisions, part of an omnibus anticrime bill overwhelmingly approved by the House of Representatives and sent on to the President, makes it illegal for a person to purchase a handgun in a state other than his own, either by mail order or directly over the counter. In addition, it prohibits felons, mental incompetents and veterans who received less than honorable discharges from possessing any kind of firearms at all.

Some members of Congress were quick to claim that the gun-control legislation was an extraordinary achievement. "This bill is far, far tougher than anyone realizes," said Sen. Thomas Dodd of Connecticut, who has been fighting for gun control for years. Considering that the bill was passed over the objections of one of the most formidable lobbies in Washington, the 900,000-member National Rifle Association, which has argued long and hard that there is no connection between the availability of firearms and the spiraling crime rate, Dodd's optimism was at least understandable. Judged against the strict gun-control standards in most other civilized countries of the world, however, the legislation—and, for that matter, the NRA's argument about availability—seemed glaringly weak.

Loophole: The public apparently shares this view. The day Senator Kennedy was shot, a nationwide Gallup survey showed that most people in the U.S. favored the registration of all firearms in the country. The President also had reservations about the legislation. No sooner had the gun-control measure cleared the House last week than Mr. Johnson made a nationwide television address. The President said that strict curbs on who can own guns had had a profound effect on crime in other countries. "Each year in this country, guns are involved in more than 6,500 murders," he said. "This compares with 30 in England, 99 in Canada, 68 in West Germany and 37 in Japan." Growing more emotional, Mr. Johnson denounced the bill before him as a "halfway measure. It covers adequately only transactions involving handguns. It leaves the deadly commerce in lethal shotguns and rifles without effective control." Later, Mr. Johnson indicated that he would try to plug what he described as "the brutal loophole" in the law by trying to extend the bill's provisions to the interstate sale of rifles and shotguns as well as handguns.

Responsibility: But similar amendments proposed by Sen. Edward Kennedy last month were defeated, and it seemed likely that the President's proposals would find the going just as rough. Still, there was little doubt that for the moment, at least, Congress would have to look hard to discover a more appropriate memorial to Robert Kennedy. It was just two years ago that Bobby told his colleagues: "We have a responsibility to the victims of crime and violence. For too long, we have dealt with deadly weapons as if they were harmless toys. Yet their very presence, the ease of their acquisition and the familiarity of their appearance have led to thousands of deaths each year and countless other crimes of violence as well. It is time that we wipe this stain of violence from our land."

Sample Essay

Analysis of Purpose and Technique
in "Guns: Like Buying Cigarettes"

The unsigned article "Guns: Like Buying Cigarettes," appearing in Newsweek on June 17, 1968, turns an apparent report of events into an outraged call for action by a number of techniques aimed at crystallizing the reader's anger. Although this article appeared in the news section of the magazine, known primarily for reporting events, this piece goes beyond reporting to attempt to create support for gun legislation.

Even before the reader gets to the article, a mood is prepared by a ten-page story on the recent assassination of Senator Robert F. Kennedy. The story includes a dramatic picture of the senator being lifted from a pool of blood. Distress at these events becomes anger when the reader turns to the article on guns and sees the accompanying photograph captioned, "The Gun That Killed Robert Kennedy." The emotionally aroused reader will then have his or her emotions confirmed and focused by this article. Anger against the assassin is turned to anger against guns.

The title of the essay makes a link to another killer, cigarettes. The comparison emphasizes that objects like guns and cigarettes are to blame rather than people. The comparison creates further emotion by what it leaves unstated, that guns are obviously more threatening. The reader feels, "How can such terrible things as guns be sold over the counter, virtually unregulated? If a youngster can get a pack of cigarettes, can he also get a gun as easily?"

In the opening paragraph, the author re-emphasizes the gun as the villain, by linking guns to their victims and leaving out the murderers who pulled the triggers. The long catalogue of weapons sounds like a frightening arsenal. The language reflects that threatening atmosphere and reminds one of a gangster movie: <u>cut down</u>, <u>felled</u>, <u>snub-nosed</u>, <u>snuffed out the life</u>.

The next paragraph defines the problem in larger terms, providing statistics on the effects of guns. The writer moves from the dramatic specificity of the first paragraph to the staggeringly large numbers of the second paragraph and again points the finger at guns rather than people as the villain. The characterization of the general problem as a "national tragedy" also involves an interesting shift. Usually the term "national tragedy" refers to some specific event like a single assassination, a war, an earthquake, but this author wants to link such events with a more general condition. Notice that the topic is not even the <u>use</u> of guns; the author is talking about the <u>availability</u> of guns. The link between all the guns available and the particular guns described so vividly in the first paragraph is brought out by the term "fantastic arsenal." The comparison to war deaths also makes the link between guns and real deaths.

The writer continues to stir up our emotions in later paragraphs by using such words as <u>grim statistics</u>, <u>outrage</u>, <u>overwhelmingly approved</u>, <u>extraordinary achievement</u>, and <u>glaringly weak</u>. Readers are never in doubt about which side of the legislative struggle they should support. When the opposing view is introduced, the views of the National Rifle Association (NRA) are given only four lines after the whole article has been stirring up feelings in the opposite direction. The NRA's position is immediately buried under all the laws of other nations.

The writer buttresses the case against guns with surveys, a presidential address, and more statistics. After readers are overwhelmed with the gravity of the situation and are thoroughly enraged by the easy availability of guns, the emotions are turned to sadness as the writer remembers Robert Kennedy's speech on his proposed gun law. The reader is left feeling that the law should be passed, if only in Kennedy's memory.

Throughout the article, emotional language plays upon the vulnerable feelings of Americans who have just experienced a string of shocking assassinations. The writer whips up the emotions, turns them against the object of guns, and finally offers a way to get rid of the menace through legislation. This article and others like it must have been to some degree successful in capitalizing on the nation's mood for legislative action, because a major gun law was passed later that year.

Writing Assignments

1. Analyze the purpose and technique of a short article you have come across as part of your research for a major research project. The audience for your analysis will be someone who shares your research interest.

2. In an essay of five hundred words, analyze the purpose and technique of a chapter in an elementary textbook on a subject you know well. Consider how effectively the chapter introduces the subject to a beginning student. The reader of your analysis will be a teacher who must decide whether to use the textbook in a course next semester.

3. In an essay of five hundred words, analyze the purpose and technique of *one* of the following passages on friendship. The readers of your analysis will be your classmates. Later, compare the different designs of the three selections as analyzed by different members of the class.

   a. From Cicero's philosophic essay "On Friendship" on pages 28–29 of this text.

   b. From Dale Carnegie's self-help book *How to Win Friends and Influence People* on pages 117–118.

   c. From Harry Stack Sullivan's chapter on preadolescence in *The Interpersonal Theory of Psychiatry* on pages 132–134.

7 Evaluating the Book as a Whole: The Book Review

A book review tells not only what is in a book but also what a book attempts to achieve and how it can be used. To discuss the uses of a book, you must explore your own reactions, for these reactions reveal how you have responded to the book. Thus, in writing a review, you combine the skills of describing what is on the page, analyzing how the book tries to achieve its purpose, and expressing your own reactions. The nature and length of the review depend on the book, the purpose of the review, and the anticipated audience. The shorter the review, the more succinctly you must present your judgments. By writing reviews, you will develop your critical skills as a reader and researcher, and you will be mastering evaluative writing, which you will find useful in many situations beyond the book review itself.

The Use of Tools

Every month *Popular Mechanics* reviews tools, informing its readers about the uses of new gadgets on the market. Here is one example, a review of a thumb wheel ratchet.

Thumb Wheel Ratchet

I found S-K Tools' new quarter-inch thumb wheel ratchet terrific for reaching into cramped spaces. It gives good leverage and maneuvers in the tightest places you'll encounter under your hood. Thumb wheel set comes in an 8-piece pouch—six sockets plus the ratchet and a short extension. All are compatible with your present quarter-inch tools. We have seen S-K Set No. 4908–78 in auto parts stores for $12. Or order from S-K Tool Group, Dresser Industries, 3201 North Wolf Rd., Franklin Park, Ill. 60131.—*M.L.*

No matter how beautiful, ingenious, or well made the tool is, no one will spend any money for it unless it works. The new tool must help the user accomplish a task more easily than before. Thus a review of a tool must take into account not just what a tool is but also what the needs and experiences of the user may be. If the writer of the foregoing review had never been frustrated in working a full-sized ratchet into a tight place, he would not have been so happy to discover a thumb wheel ratchet and would not have endorsed it so highly. From the recommendation of leverage and maneuverability, the reader knows that M.L. has spent happy moments under the hood of his own car with this wonderful new invention.

A review of tools may even—strangely enough—report on the emotional response of the dirt-under-the-fingernails reviewer; as any reader of *Popular Mechanics* knows, there is a sensual pleasure in working with good tools and a personal relationship between the working person and his or her tools. The following review of a synthetic chamois tells us as much about the emotions of the reviewer B. H. as about the product: the frustration over confusing labeling, the grudging admission of the product's quality, and the supreme romanticism in praising the smell and feel of the natural product.

Synthetic Chamois

"Okay, what's in the tube?" ask friends who see the product container labeled "Fireman's Friend." There's no way to know that it's a synthetic chamois. It got its name because its first users were firemen, say the distributors. (Well, you've never seen a dirty fire engine, have you?) This high-quality plastic-sponge "skin" or "total towel" as it's variously called by its makers, is 17 by 27 inches and costs $9—cheaper than a real chamois skin. Yes, it works almost as well, is tough and durable, doesn't dry out in time like an animal skin, doesn't rot, is grease resistant and is conveniently stored wet in its own case. But, no, it doesn't feel and smell like the real thing and I'm enough of a sensualist to stick with chamois. Fireman's Friend, Inc., Box 64, Elmhurst, Ill. 60126.—*B.H.*

Books as Tools

If reviewers of ratchets and plastic cloths find it necessary to mingle personal experience and pleasures with concrete descriptions of the products, how much more does a book reviewer need to mingle personal thoughts and strong reactions with a description of the content in order to give readers a fair estimate of a book? A book is a tool for communication between two minds; learning how a reviewer reacts helps you judge how well the writer communicated.

This text has thus far kept methods of developing your subjective responses separate from methods of gaining objective knowledge of a text. Marginal annotations, journals, and the response essay have encouraged you to look into yourself for personal reactions, which you have then developed. On the other hand, paraphrase, summary, and analysis of purpose have sharpened your vision for exactly what appears on the page—outside of yourself. Actually, the division of labor isn't that simple. The more deeply you understand what is on the page, the more you will react. Conversely, the more engaged you are in a subject, the more you will want to understand what others have written. An animated conversation is a two-way affair.

In the evaluative book review, these two streams—an accurate reading and a strong response—come together, for the reviewer should indicate what is in the book and what the contents might mean to a reader. The reviewer's own reaction reveals to the book buyer the potential of what may be gained from reading it. If the reviewer does not go beyond a summary of the original, this dull restatement gives the reader no clear direction to follow. If, however, the reviewer indicates the kind of communication that passed between two minds via the printed page, the reader can decide whether the book offers the kind of mental interaction he or she wants.

Because writing a review makes you consider not just what a book says and how it is put together but also what thoughts it evokes in you and what personal use you can put it to, writing a book review forces you to come to terms with a book. You evaluate the entire transaction between the author and yourself. For just this reason, teachers in a number of disciplines (including history, sociology, and management) assign book reviews as part of the course work for their students. In whatever career you enter, you are likely to be called upon to evaluate the importance or usefulness of various documents. If you stay in the academic world, for example, reviewing your colleagues' books will be one of your regular tasks. Even if you never write formal book reviews, you may be evaluating business reports, project proposals, legal briefs, reorganization plans, and investment prospectuses. And frequently you may have to write evaluation reports, which are a kind of book review.

Books to Make Us Think

Consider the following review by Anatole Broyard of the *New York Times*. Broyard succinctly presents the contents of the book *Death as a Fact of Life*—the task of summary—and also paraphrases some of the more impressive moments of the book. As he might reveal in a journal or in marginal notes, Broyard indicates at length how the book affects him as an individual and discusses the personally important questions the book raises. In essence, he gives the sum of his own thoughts and experience on the subject. We see Broyard, excited and concerned, speculating about what he has read and engaging author David Hendin in conversation. Even the analysis of Hendin's technique is closely related to the reviewer's reactions as a reader.

The Obstetrics of the Soul

"I don't understand what I'm supposed to do," Tolstoy said on his deathbed—and neither do most of us. The conspiracy of silence with which we surround the subject of dying led Geoffrey Gorer, the British anthropologist, to coin the phrase "the pornography of death." But a "good death" is an indispensable end to a good life—so crucial, in fact, that a German writer called it the "obstetrics of the soul." To die with dignity is important not only to the dying person, but also to his or her survivors, who will always be able to remember the one they loved in this light.

According to David Hendin in his *Death as a Fact of Life,* dying today is often rendered obscene by technology. Many patients are kept alive when they are no longer human beings, but simple circulatory systems, breathing but otherwise unresponsive tissue. Under these circumstances, life may sometimes be more terrifying than death. The dying person's relatives and friends are elbowed away from him by machines. And since these machines interfere with the natural course of decline, no one knows exactly when death will come and the patient often expires with only technology for company. In this connection, the author quotes Theodore Fox's famous remark: "We shall have to learn to refrain from doing things merely because we know how to do them."

Mr. Hendin quotes surveys to show that most dying people would prefer to talk about it, and are greatly relieved when the silence is broken. I know that as I read his book, I felt my own anxieties about death first articulated, then partially assuaged. It *is* therapeutic to bring that immemorial enemy of ours out into the light. As the author points out, for some of us the threat of death can have an integrative rather than a disruptive function. It can make us see our life as a coherent whole and give us an opportunity to sum it up emotionally and intellectually—to deny the fashionable charge of "meaninglessness or absurdity."

Accepting death is not necessarily a form of resignation, of giving up: it may be a positive reorientation. We can look *back* over our life as well as forward to its end. We can congratulate ourselves on what we have done and reverse the old saw that "you can't take it with you." By renouncing the terrible duty of pretending, Mr. Hendin says, we can take the bandages off our fears and our feelings and die with love instead of lies as the last thing we hear.

The author has done a brilliant and highly sensitive job of bringing together the literature of death—from the need for revising our legal, medical and psychological criteria to the fact that the dead are forcing the living into an ever-decreasing space. He discusses the science of cryonics, or freezing the body in the hope of future resuscitation (cost, $20,000); the case for and against euthanasia; the need to train doctors to *face* death as well as to fight it; the "hospices" being built for dying people, so that they can spend their last days in as homelike an atmosphere as their medical needs permit; the advantages of cremation and its relative unpopularity in the United States, and much more.

I found the chapter "Children and Death" especially moving. Mr. Hendin knows how to evoke a feeling as well as most novelists and he is never, as far as I can remember, guilty of mere sentimentality in dealing with the most highly charged subject in our emotional repertory. Warning us against feeding inane euphemisms to children, he cites the case of a little boy who was told that his dead mother "went up into the sky." Shortly afterwards, the boy was taken on a visit by airplane and was very sad and disappointed because he had looked on every cloud but had not seen his mother. Informed that his infant brother had been picked up by God and taken to heaven, another child kept his windows locked, refused to cross open spaces and played only in the shade of trees for fear the same thing would happen to him.

Unacknowledged death haunts us far more effectively than the ghosts of our childhood. The author feels that the more fully it is faced, the sooner we are likely to recover from the shock of someone's death. If we do not make peace with them and separate ourselves from the dead through appropriate periods of mourning and grief, we may find it difficult to attach ourselves to anyone who might help replace them afterwards.

Though there is not a superfluous page in *Death as a Fact of Life,* I found myself—emotionally, not morbidly—drawn to those passages dealing with the dying person. When Mr. Hendin speaks of the indignity of deterioration, I remember the humiliation I saw in my own father's face when he was a Rube Goldberg tangle of tubes and life-coercing machines. His difficulties were increased by his "stiff upper lip" philosophy that locked both of us in the anguish of all that we wanted to, and could not say. A terrible loneliness lurked in his eyes, but it was too late for him to learn or to change.

What the author does not say because it may be beyond the scope of his intent is that our entire life is a preparation for our death, and we may expect to die well or badly depending on how we have lived. Freud told a story of visiting William James at a time when the American psychologist and philosopher had a brush with death in the form of a heart attack. He could not refrain from asking James afterward how he had felt about the prospect. James replied that he had lived his life and done his work. Death held no terrors for him. Edmund Bergler, the psychiatrist, remarks in one of his many books that, after a satisfying sexual experience with someone we love, it is natural to feel sleepy. I mention these two remarks because I feel that, somewhere between them, we may find the answer to one of life's most intimidating questions.

Broyard's personal reflections are always in contact with Hendin's themes and questions. We gain a clear impression of the main theme of the book—that the dying and the surviving do better to face death—and the various subtopics explored under that theme, ranging from present-day attitudes to the possibilities of cryonics. We also observe how each of these topics affects the reviewer and inspires his personal meditations. When the reviewer contemplates his own understanding of death and his attempts to come to terms with it, he is doing precisely what the book has urged him to do: he is facing death as a fact of life. The more deeply he reads the book, the more deeply he goes into himself. This personal journey lets readers of Broyard's review know what it might be like to read the book themselves, to consider the same questions, to face similar memories, and to experience troublesome feelings.

Fortunately for the sake of our good spirits, not all books ask us to look so deeply into ourselves. Most of the books we read do, however, remind us of our previous experiences, knowledge, thoughts, or emotions. The reviewer, though not always soul-searching, does need to seek out that part of the self touched by the book. Just as the reviewer of the thumb wheel ratchet describes his triumph in getting at difficult corners, and just as the reviewer of an artificial chamois considers the sensual pleasures of the real thing, so must the book reviewer find the appropriate kinds of response for each book.

Books to Offer Practical Advice

A specialized interest may be shared by only a limited group of people, but writers who appeal to that interest try to provide what these individuals are looking for. Flower growing, for example, is not a hobby shared by everyone, but to those who do share it the experience and knowledge involved are quite real and concrete. The following review from *Horticulture,* a magazine on gardening, reveals what information the book contains and how that information may appeal to the interested reader. Through the experience and feelings of the reviewer, we glimpse the realms of practical action, background knowledge, nostalgia, and aesthetic pleasure.

The Complete Book of Bulbs
by F. F. Rockwell and Esther Grayson.
Revised by Marjorie J. Dietz.
New York: J. B. Lippincott. $10.00.

Reviewed by Jean S. Kennedy

The gift of a dozen Red Emperor tulip bulbs and no idea of how to plant them led me to the purchase of my first book on gardening. This was many years ago and the book was one of the first editions of Rockwell and Grayson's *Complete Book of Bulbs.* It remains, for me at least, one of the best books on the subject for the amateur.

Now there is a new edition, carefully revised by Marjorie Dietz. The list of pesticides has been brought up to date along with a discussion of federal and state controls, controls which didn't exist at the time of the book's first publication. Hopefully it may never be necessary to use any of the treatments but the references are there if needed. Excellent planting guides inside the front and back covers show the actual bulbs and the depths at which to plant. The life cycles of some of the more common bulbs are presented in interesting circular diagrams easy to understand and of great help to the novice.

In the *Gardeners' Bulb Selector,* a very useful list in the back, many new varieties of tulips have been added, while the names of the species have been inexplicably omitted. The species are a delightful group—the perfect bulbs for a sunny rock garden. I miss, also, some photographs of bulbs which flowered at Gray Rock—home of the authors—but perhaps they were no longer available. These are minor criticisms, however, and I am glad to see one of my old favorites brought out in a new edition for a whole new generation of gardeners.

In almost every sentence the reviewer, Jean Kennedy, mentions a different use she makes of the book. From her recollections of an earlier edition, she can personally testify that the book is useful for beginners and remains an old and trusty reference. Even more, she immediately puts in focus the aim of the book—the pleasure of flowers. The final sentence of the first paragraph ties all these uses together.

With the mention of technical advances and of basic unchanging information, she points to the practical aspects of maintaining a garden—digging around in the soil and spraying noxious chemicals. Besides commending the technical information, the reviewer lets us know the usefulness of the information on the life cycle of bulbs presented in the book. Thus she appreciates armchair theory as well as actual practice. Throughout, she reassures the reader that all the types of information are presented in a manner appropriate to the beginner's experience and knowledge.

The final paragraph returns to the particular pleasures of flowers: she mentions an expanded list of bulbs and a discussion of the photographs included in previous editions, but unfortunately missing from this one. She ends the review with her sense of delight in sharing one of her favorite books with new gardeners.

This review does its job well, even though its subject is of limited appeal and the prose seems quite ordinary. The review does convey all the levels on which the book operates: the book's content, the response it evokes, and the uses readers might make of it.

Books to Help Solve a Public Problem

Some books, such as *Death as a Fact of Life,* are tools for mental activity; other books are tools for practical activity and pleasure; still other books are aimed at aiding public action. The basic criterion for judging such a book is whether that book will actually help people to take the steps it advocates. But to get people to take action is not an easy task. People must first be convinced that there is a problem, that the problem is serious enough to require action, and that there are effective actions they can take. Moreover, for public action to be successful, people must know exactly what they are doing. Thus the problem must be defined, the causes and mechanisms of difficulty identified, points of attack planned, necessary information provided, and specific solutions offered. The following review from the *Amicus Journal,* a magazine concerned with ecological protection, finds that the book *Hazardous Waste in America* does all these things.

Hazardous Waste in America
by Samuel S. Epstein, Lester O. Brown, and Carl Pope.
Sierra Club Books. 569 pp. $27.50.

Reviewed by James Lewis

Since Love Canal brought hazardous waste to national attention, Americans have been overwhelmed with countless stories about contaminated water and indiscriminate dumping. Yet, in all of this coverage, people have been given very little information about the root causes and long term solutions for the hazardous waste problem. *Hazardous Waste in America,* by Samuel Epstein, Lester O. Brown and Carl Pope, is an impressive effort to remedy the situation.

Written for citizens who want to know where the hazardous waste problem began and what we are doing—and not doing—to end it, this is a virtual encyclopedia on hazardous waste, pulling together valuable but scattered resources. A 200-page appendix includes a list of the 8,000 known hazardous waste dump sites, the 115 sites scheduled for Superfund cleanup, the toxicological effects of certain chemicals, the states and industries which generate the most hazardous waste, congressional committees working on the problem, and environmental organizations which can provide further information.

The book's major focus is on the laws, regulations, and strategies governing hazardous waste. The reader is warned about regulatory loopholes large enough to drive a tanker truck through and given suggestions as to how they might be closed. The authors go on to explain, however, that the hazardous waste problem "is not capable of a purely regulatory solution." Regulations can be "complemented by a wide range of additional approaches including common law litigation, compensatory remedies, economic incentives, and other forms of government influence." The authors also critique current hazardous waste disposal technology, outline methods for encouraging reduction in hazardous waste production, and provide bibliographies of waste exchange technologies. And finally, there is a timely look at how Reagan's EPA has circumvented its mandate to protect health and the environment.

One should expect no less from these authors. For each, this book is a simple extension of work they have done individually during the past decade. Dr. Epstein, known for his work with organized labor and the public interest movement and for his testimony before congressional committees and federal agencies, has helped create a superb companion volume to his 1978 book *The Politics of Cancer*. Now a professor of occupational and environmental medicine at the University of Illinois, Dr. Epstein demonstrates in *Hazardous Waste in America* that his commitment to science which serves and protects the public is as strong as ever.

This commitment is obviously shared by Dr. Epstein's coauthors, who bring their own distinct perspectives to the book. Lester Brown has served since 1975 as a staff member with several congressional committees, providing extensive investigation of such issues as Agent Orange, PBB contamination in Michigan, and carbon tetrachloride spills in the Ohio River. His detailed knowledge of these and related toxics issues, as well as his first hand observation of legislative procedures and problems, is in evidence throughout the book.

As associate conservation director of the Sierra Club, Carl Pope coordinates national office work on pollution and environmental health and is responsible for his organization's efforts on state environmental issues in California. It is clear that this book's suggestions about citizen action are not projections of what might work, but the product of what has worked.

It is also clear that the authors are thoroughly versed on the hazardous waste issue. They have omitted few resources, and while the book suffers some problems of organization and repetition, it more than compensates by being so very comprehensive. There is no better book for citizens who want to understand the legal, political, economic, and technological conditions which have gotten us into this hazardous waste mess—conditions which must change if we are to get out.

The opening lines of the review offer background information that explains the need for the book and the authors' purpose, to help citizens resolve the hazardous waste problem that they have been hearing about every night on the news but about which they have little useful knowledge. At the end of the first paragraph the reviewer, James Lewis, lets us know that he believes the book fulfills its purpose impressively.

The first half of the body of the review describes the content of the book to indicate how it provides the facts that will help people understand the nature and extent of the problem and begin to fight back. The summary lets the reader know the book gives detailed information about waste dump sites, the effects of different toxic wastes, the industries involved, the laws and regulations pertaining to waste dumping, the political interests involved, and alternative solutions. Although this part of the review only describes the book, it is clear that the reviewer approves of all this information being included and believes that this is just what people need to know to carry out effective action.

The last half of the review outlines the professional biographies of the authors, not only to emphasize the expertise of the authors in environmental ecology and to show their commitment to environmental protection, but to indicate that the book reflects the practical experience of people who have been fighting this problem for some time. The reviewer mentions several places where the authors' practical experience is directly reflected in the book.

The closing paragraph acknowledges and forgives some organizational problems, while praising again the thoroughness of the book—a quality necessary for intelligent action. The last sentence drives home the action orientation of the book by calling for the kinds of change that the ecological movement is fighting for. The reviewer clearly sees this book as the best of battle manuals.

Books to Establish Truth

Scholarly books, while they may aim at changing people's minds on important subjects, do not usually attempt to create political activity. Scholarly books try to say true things about their subjects— to expand or correct what we know. Reviews of scholarly books, therefore, usually try to evaluate what kind of truth the book is getting at, how much and what kind of evidence the author uses to support the claims, and ultimately how true the book seems. In short, the criterion for evaluating a scholarly book is how much of a contribution to knowledge it makes. Sometimes the contribution can be narrow and specific, such as the uncovering of a single important fact. Sometimes, however, the contribution can be broad, tying together much information to show large patterns of connection. The following review from *Isis,* a major scholarly journal in the history of science, finds that the book *Human Nature in American Thought: A History* reveals relationships and the broad sweep of events, even though the reviewer finds the book weak in some of its details.

Human Nature in American Thought: A History
By Merle Curti.
Madison: University of Wisconsin Press, 1980.
xvii + 453 pp., bibl., index. $25.

Reviewed by David E. Leary

After more than forty years of careful research, Merle Curti has delivered a work which promises to be of unusual interest to historians of the social and behavioral sciences. Curti's goal is not modest. He sets out to survey the entire extent of American thought on human nature, from the time of the first European settlers to the present moment, with the hope of relating this thought to its broader social and cultural context. As if this were not enough, he imposes no arbitrary, narrow definition on his subject matter. Instead he allows the protagonists of his story to define human nature as they will. As a result, Curti's treatise displays a catholicity of purview that is truly unique. Although some readers will find the treatise a bit intractable on this account, others (including myself) will consider its breadth of vision to be one of its major strengths.

Curti's theme, insofar as he proposes one, is that ideas are produced within, and bear the imprint of, certain social circumstances, and furthermore that ideas about human nature have made a difference in American life. Throughout his long excursion Curti shows over and over again how Americans have dealt with the abstract issue of human nature in the process of struggling with very tangible realities— matters pertaining to racial and sexual relations, problems emerging from political conflicts, crises begotten by the apposition of traditional values and practical developments, and on and on. In almost every case (with a notable exception discussed below) he attempts to relate the growth of thought both to previous thinking and to contemporary circumstances, and time after time he traces the concrete applications of new convictions in the development of political, legal, educational, technological, scientific, social, and even literary practices. All in all, he has drawn a broad picture of the relationship between social context and thought without pushing causal inference beyond the bounds of available knowledge. In doing so he has prepared the way for further analysis.

This is a rich book. It will be a rare person who does not find something new and worthwhile in it, no matter what his or her own area of interest and expertise. Psychology, philosophy, sociology, economics, anthropology, psychoanalysis, physiology, genetics, literature— the developments in all these disciplines and more are judiciously placed side by side and situated within the broader context of American cultural history. This inevitably enlightens our view of the whole as it adds to our knowledge of the parts.

Breadth of coverage, however, inevitably militates against depth. Although every reader will be instructed about areas previously beyond his or her ken, few readers will be satisfied with the discussions that touch precisely upon the areas of his or her own expertise. It is not that Curti has shirked his homework; but given the size of the canvas he cannot possibly pay sufficient attention to each aspect of his portrait. As a result, few discussions will go far enough, or be completely satisfactory, for those whose research and interest have led them over the same paths before. But for the uninitiated Curti will be a very helpful guide, never leading too far astray, and always covering a wide and varied terrain with a surety of gait that is enviable in this age of specialization.

It should not be surprising that having said this, I disagree with some of the emphases, directions of thought, interpretations, omissions, and even statements of fact in this book. But perhaps most disappointing is the fact that in the last four substantive chapters, which deal with the twentieth-century view of human nature, serious discussion of the social context gradually disappears as progressively more space is devoted to chronological reviews of major research traditions and debates of mostly professional interest (such as the debate over the method of introspection in psychology). This shift in emphasis accurately reflects the popular conception of the increasing autonomy and independence of the various intellectual (and now largely academic) traditions. Unfortunately, this conception is misleading. With the increasing institutionalization and subsidization of intellectual life, the social context of twentieth-century American thought is at least as important, and probably more important, than the contexts of prior modes of thought. Yet Curti does not address the crucial issues raised by this fact in any satisfactory way. This is due in part, no doubt, to the fact that historical research on this topic is just now beginning. Nonetheless the resulting gap in Curti's analysis leaves his treatise flat in the end, for it is precisely the relationship between thought and culture that he wants to trace.

If some of these criticisms are injurious, they are offered along with the conviction that this is a good book—a book that deserves critical scrutiny. Whatever its weaknesses, it must be commended again for the way it avoids, by and large, the typical narrowness of disciplinary histories. It gives us a rich and relatively integrated synthesis of a variety of perspectives on human nature in American thought, together with some of the antecedents and consequences of these perspectives. If the book does not provide a definitive map of the territory it proposes to cover, it does provide the first really useful guide.

In the opening paragraph, reviewer Leary sets the scope of author Curti's project against the background of Curti's long work and his potential audience. Not only is the subject broad, the reviewer points out, but by not imposing a narrow definition Curti has made the subject broader. This discussion leads right into the major issue of the review—the issue of breadth. Leary then passes his main judgment: he likes the book's breadth, even though it might not be to all scholars' tastes.

The second paragraph of the review summarizes the book's main theme and describes how the author has developed it. This paragraph gives a good picture of the book's contents and direction, ending with a major judgment about the value, quality, and use of the book. In creating a broad but careful picture, the book has, according to the reviewer, set the stage for further analysis by other scholars. Scholars build on one another's work; therefore, if a book lays the groundwork for further studies, it can make a significant contribution though it does not provide definitive answers. Others will finish what this author has started.

Leary's approval of the book's breadth of coverage leads directly into praise of its richness, not only in the number of areas covered, but also in the kind of insight gained from the many parts being placed next to one another. The fourth paragraph, however, presents the less fortunate side of such breadth. Because it covers so much, the book cannot go into as much detail on any single subject as narrower studies can. Nonetheless, Leary praises Curti for the trustworthiness and solidity with which he handles these many areas.

The evaluation turns more sharply critical in the fifth paragraph, where Leary differs with Curti on some details and finds fault with the entire approach of the later chapters of the book, which deal with the twentieth century. The reviewer presents an alternative interpretation of the period and suggests that Curti does not discuss the very issues that he claims lie at the core of his book. Leary accuses the author of forgetting his main theme by adopting, in the closing chapters, a simplistic point of view and an organization that avoids the crucial issues of relationships. The reviewer attributes

Curti's failure partly to the lack of work done by others, upon which Curti could have built, but he does hold Curti accountable for deflating his own thesis.

The closing paragraph, nonetheless, reasserts the value of the book in raising larger issues and integrating many branches of knowledge. Leary considers it a book worth careful attention and thought, a book that is part of a conversation that will gradually lead closer to the truth. "If the book does not provide a definitive map of the territory it proposes to cover, it does provide the first really useful guide."

Writing a Book Review

In order for you to make the fullest and most considered response to a book, your reading and thinking must go through several stages. The more questions of interest the book poses, the more time you should devote to developing your ideas before actually writing the review. When first reading the book for meaning, pay special attention to the preface or foreword and to any other information that will give a clue to the book's overall purpose and its general context. As you reread the book, annotate it with comments on the writer's technique and your own reactions. After having developed some thoughts through journal entries, look through the book one more time. Then clarify your thoughts by writing down answers to the following questions:

- What seems to be the author's main purpose or point?
- Is this purpose aimed at any particular group of readers?
- What information or knowledge does the book convey?
- What personal or practical meaning does the book have for you?
- What are the most appropriate terms by which to evaluate the book?
- Based on the criteria you have just selected, how successful do you think the author was in carrying out the overall purposes of the book?

Once you know your reactions to what the book is and what it does, you are ready to outline and write the first draft of your review.

The Shape of Your Review

Beyond a few items that must appear in a review, what you include and how you organize it is up to you. Many reviews, however, do follow one general pattern that includes all the important elements of a review.

The required items are all a matter of common sense. First, the reader must know what book you are talking about, so at the top of the review give a *bibliographic entry.* Include not just author, title, and publication information but also the number of pages and the price of the book, because readers like to know what commitment of time and money it takes to read the book. The format of this entry, used throughout this chapter, is:

Title. Author. Place of publication: publisher, date of publication. Number of pages. Price.

Sometimes, for the convenience of librarians, the International Standard Book Number (ISBN) or Library of Congress (LC) code is listed. The first time you mention the book in the review you should repeat the author and title so that the reader does not have to jump back to the bibliographic entry.

The body of the review must give a clear overview of the contents of the book, the special purposes of an audience for the book, and the reviewer's reaction and evaluation. Though reviews show a wide variety of form and organization, a typical way of opening is with a *direct statement of the kind of book and its main topic*—followed by a few words of the reviewer's evaluations. If the book raises any special problem that the review will explore later, this may be briefly mentioned here. Thus, in the first few sentences, the reader learns where both the book and the review are headed.

The next paragraph or section often includes *background that helps place the book in context,* either by describing the general problem the book addresses or by mentioning earlier books by this or another author. This section is also an appropriate place to discuss the criteria by which to judge the book, for the context helps define what the book attempts to do.

Next, a *summary of the main points of the book*—highlighted by paraphrase and quotation—gives an overview of the actual content of the book. The reviewer's reactions may be included with the ongoing summary of the contents, or all the comments may be saved for the end. Even where a personal reaction is withheld, the re-viewer's manner of describing the contents often gives a clear impression of what he or she thinks. In any case, it is important to distinguish between the ideas of the author and those of the reviewer. Careful labeling (*George Orwell continues . . . ; This reviewer believes . . .*) keeps the reviewer's ideas separate from the author's ideas. Confusion between the two weakens the value of the review.

In the final part of the review, the reviewer is free to carry on the *discussion in a variety of ways,* evaluating how well the book has achieved its goal, musing over the possibilities suggested by the book, arguing with specific points, discussing matters the book has left out, even exploring a personal experience related to the subject. No matter how far afield the comments stray, they usually return in the last few lines to a more *direct comment on the book* and tie together the issues raised in the review. Although some trick endings are clichés, a final statement that leaves the reader with a sense of completion—as with a musical cadence—lends a desirable grace to the review. That grace is important, for we should consider the evaluation of another person's work not as a cold measurement but as a civilized act of human society.

Sample Review

In the following review, Colleen Mitchell, a business student, considers the usefulness of the book *Black Life in Corporate America* in thinking about her future as a black business woman. She finds that the book gives a very concrete picture of what life is like for black managers and how they react to that life. On the basis of other things she has heard about corporate life and her own experience of prejudice, however, she finds the book less successful in letting her know exactly how much and what kind of prejudice she is likely to encounter. The book prepares her in some ways and makes her think about her future. But in other ways it leaves her confused.

Black Life in Corporate America
by George Davis and Glegg Watson.
Anchor Press/Doubleday, 204 pp., $14.95.
ISBN 0-385-14701-5
Reviewed by Colleen Mitchell

With Black Life in Corporate America George Davis and Glegg Watson have given all of us entering business,

black and white, a glimpse of the tough world we are getting ourselves into. The experiences of the black managers they recount are in a way the struggles of all who
are trying to climb the corporate ladder to success.
Their lives are just complicated a bit more by the problem of race, but all executives must learn to cope with
the problems of team playing, power games, office politics, dirty tricks, and maintaining individuality and a
private life--in short, with all the problems of surviving in corporate America. Each executive Davis and Watson interviewed had his or her own strategy for getting
on or just hanging on, but they all made me wonder what
strategy I will adopt once I get out in the real world.

The book consists mostly of interviews with over one
hundred sixty people in the business world. The executives, both male and female, discuss their problems,
fears, plans, and styles of life. The authors quote extensively and give vivid descriptions of the inter-
viewees' behavior, appearance, and surroundings, so that
the reader gets a good picture of who these people are
and how they have adjusted their personalities and lives
to fit with their place in the corporate structure.

The most striking example of this portrait painting is
the character they call Willis Thornton (names have been
changed to preserve anonymity). Willis, as he was growing up a mean, tough, near drop-out, was given the name
Nightmare. However, he got excited by the civil rights
movement in the sixties and read every black book he
could lay his hands on. Through political contacts he
went to college, eventually even the Harvard Business
School, although he still was not excited much by school
learning. Now a corporate manager of marketing for a very
large company, he sees company life as just a game, which
he is going to win. He is slick, with all the advantages
of a fat salary and an upper-class life, including psy-

chotherapy, but he really is just street-smart, grown a few years older.

Davis and Watson arrange these interviews according to categories and themes in order to show the variety of problems, coping strategies, and generational differences among the black executives. Chapters describe the first generation of black executives (the tokens of the fifties and early sixties), the more self-assertive blacks who entered the corporate world as a result of the civil rights movement, and the more self-concerned executives of the seventies who had to cope with the backlash against integration. A chapter also discusses the special problems of black women, who suffer from double discrimination. The authors distinguish among those who are floaters——just getting by without ambitious plans; those who are splashers——getting noticed and demanding their rights; those who are doggy-strokers——giving a lot of effort to get a little advancement; and the true swimmers——those devoted to really getting ahead in the corporate world. The last is what I think I would like to be, but after reading about how hard it is, and how many sacrifices the real swimmers have to make, I am not sure I have it in me. I may turn out to be a floater, just doing my job——a good job.

Although the book presents the thoughts and feelings of the black executives very well and backs up the interviews with wide sociological and historical research (the bibliography is nine pages long), I am still not sure how much of a role discrimination really plays in the careers of the black executives. The isolation and problems of socializing with fellow workers and bosses (including the fear of accusations of sexual harassment or sexual favoritism) are exactly the same kinds of complaints I've heard and read about concerning white managers. The authors give enough examples of blacks who have overcome discrimination to make the problems seem surmountable. Also the problem of maintaining individual differences within the "company way" is something I've also heard whites complain about, but I suppose that there are larger cultural differences between blacks and whites than among different white groups. But even here I find the authors somewhat confused, sometimes portraying corporate blacks as socially and educationally very similar to their white co-workers (for example, much is made of their coming from the same middle-class neighborhoods and going to the same schools), but at other times portraying blacks as really different, "brothers and sisters," who have a lot to teach the whites. The only substantial kind of discrimination they seem to come up with concerns the way blacks are promoted or not promoted: not only are they promoted more slowly, but they are put into the less important, more dead-end positions. Discrimination, I know from my own experience, can often be subtle, almost invisible and impossible to pin down, but for that very reason I wish these authors had presented this issue more carefully.

Despite these shortcomings, leaving me uncertain about exactly what the authors are trying to prove about the current state of racial discrimination in the modern American corporation, I feel this book has helped prepare me emotionally for the struggles of the business world and has reminded me how I had better prepare myself educationally. I am warned once again that I am going to have to face prejudice, but even more I am warned that I am going to have to face myself in deciding how to respond to all these pressures. This book lets me know that whatever strategy I adopt to survive and swim in the corporate world will affect my whole life, the very person I will become.

Short Versus Long Reviews

The middle-length review of five hundred to a thousand words, which we have been considering, is the most common in newspapers and magazines. It allows the reviewer room to present contents and reactions with substantial supporting examples and discussion. In any less space, the reviewer must get right to the core of the book's argument and to his or her reaction. Without space for lengthy support or involved explanations, the short review must rely on straightforward statements; precisely phrased judgments can be backed with only a few well-chosen examples. When the book is found wanting, the bluntness of a short review may produce a comic shock, as in the following capsule review from *Kirkus Reviews,* a semimonthly guide to the new trade books for librarians and others in the book world.

Rainbow: Finding the Better Person Inside You
By Dee Burton.
Macmillan $7.95.
SBN: 02–075740–9

Thirty-two banal prescriptions to improve your life, from "Engage in Altruistic Behavior on a Regular Basis" to "Make It a Point Always to Distinguish Between Low-Probability and Zero-Probability Events." No attempt is made to explain why these specific commandments are handed down, beyond the fact that they are "significant principles" for the author, or to synthesize them into any kind of coherent system; and their effect is uniformly assumed to be of a character-strengthening nature. However, the individual directives vary widely in potential merit: most would agree that we can all do with less rationalizing and stereotyping, for example, but few would be prepared to endorse some of the author's wild schemes to "Increase Your Psychological Risk-Taking"—as in "Tell your boss exactly what you think of him" or "Have an affair with a member of the sex to which you are not accustomed." The question is, why?

A few negative adjectives like *banal* and *wild* quickly convey the reviewer's negative opinion. The reviewer selects a few telling examples to make the point obvious and characterizes the book's lack of explanation and coherence in a single sentence. The final withering question "Why?" suggests that the book isn't worth serious attention. And many books aren't.

Another Capsule Review   Books worthy of serious consideration can be characterized well enough in a capsule review to give the reader a sense of the content and value of the book. The following review from *Choice,* a book review journal for academic libraries, in a short space announces the book's merits and impact, presents the main findings, and gives a sense of the range of evidence employed. Within about two hundred words, the reviewer has painted a substantial picture of a complex, detailed book and made a solid recommendation.

Trading with the Enemy: An Exposé of the Nazi-American Money Plot, 1933–1949
by Charles Higham.
Delacorte, 1983. 277 pp. ill. bibl. index, 82–14959. $15.95 ISBN 0–440–09064–4. CIP

Readers may be surprised and shocked at these revelations concerning the financial and economic aid given Hitler and Nazi Germany by American bankers and business leaders during the period 1933–49. After careful research among the thousands of documents released under the Freedom of Information Act, Higham has put together a very convincing account of how corporate executives such as Sosthenes Behn of ITT, Winthrop Aldrich of Chase National Bank, Edsel Ford, and many others collaborated with the Nazis. It was "business as usual" for the Paris branch of the Chase National Bank and for the Ford factories in Occupied France which supplied Hitler's army with money and trucks, presumably with the knowledge and approval of their respective American headquarters. There is evidence that ITT furnished much of the Nazi communication system and that Standard Oil of New Jersey shipped fuel to the enemy through neutral countries. Documents exist indicating that these activities were condoned by the public sector and that officials highly placed in the Roosevelt administration sometimes took an active part by suppressing information and stifling opposition. Written in an easy-to-read popular style, the work is scholarly in its copious documentation and the meticulous effort to separate surmise from fact. In the appendixes Higham has included photocopies of incriminating documents, lists of document sources, and a substantial list of published titles. Recommended to both public and academic libraries. It will have strong appeal to political historians and to economists, particularly those specializing in international banking and operations of multinational corporations.

Writing capsule reviews will develop your ability to react to and place a book. You will learn to get to the core of your reaction in a few words, for otherwise the review will be finished before you get to your evaluation. Learning to characterize books succinctly and to make pointed estimates of their value will enable you to find your way more easily among the variety of books available when you come to gather materials for your research paper. Even very short reviews—fifty or fewer words—will further sharpen your instincts about books and prepare you for placing books in relation to each other, a skill needed for preparing *a review of the literature* (see Chapter 10), as well as an *annotated bibliography* (see Chapter 17).

The Full Review   At the other extreme, the long review allows full discussion of all aspects of a book and the reviewer's estimate of it. Not every book warrants detailed comment, but where the book raises interesting, complex questions or where the argument needs careful weighing, the long review permits all issues to be explored to their logical conclusion. To write an extended review that looks deeply into the issues of a book, the reviewer usually needs to have substantial knowledge of the subject, of the other books in the field, and of the previous work by the same author. The more deeply one looks into any book, the more important it is to understand how the book fits into earlier "conversations." One can find examples of full reviews in many scholarly journals and in book review journals such as the *New York Review of Books*.

Writing Assignments

1. Select a book that you remember enjoying as a child. Reread it and write a 500-word review directed toward parents who are choosing books for their children.
2. For your college newspaper, write a 300-word review of a book you have read recently that was useful, amusing, or thought provoking.
3. Write a 150-word review for your classmates about the worst book that you have read in the past few years. Make it clear why readers should stay away from this book.
4. Write a 500-word review of a book you are using for a research project for either this or another course. Direct the review to the teacher and your fellow students to let them know how valuable and reliable a source the book is.
5. Choose three books from a research project you have worked on or from an area of special interest for you. Write a short, 50-word review of each to let people who are just becoming interested in the area know what books are worth reading.

6. Choose a course you have taken that had several books on the required reading list. For each title assigned in the course, write a short, 50-word review to help your instructor decide whether to assign the same books in future semesters.
7. Write a review of the first part of this textbook to let the author know to what extent this book is useful to you and where it might be improved. Mail the review to me: Charles Bazerman, c/o College Division, Houghton Mifflin Company, One Beacon Street, Boston, MA 02108.

2 Writing
Using
Reading

8 Learning from Reading

What we read points us to the world we observe around us. To understand and accept what we read, we need to recognize what in this real world the reading refers to. Reading can help us make sense of our world and can even help us come to original conclusions (as we will see in the case of Charles Darwin). The critical analysis of observation *provides a fresh look at the world through the concepts presented in reading.*

Trying Ideas on for Size: An Expanded View of the World

When we take a book into ourselves and see what the writer is talking about, we notice more of the world and therefore experience reality from a new perspective. If the writer makes sense and we absorb that sense, our personal view of the world becomes enlarged. On the other hand, if we observe the world looking for those things the writer describes but do not find what the writer says we will find, we may doubt the writer's claims—and we certainly do not accept these questionable ideas into our view of the world. The next few pages will present examples—from the simple and concrete to the complex and abstract—of how to evaluate and learn from a writer's ideas.

Discovering New Parts of the World

Most simply, a writer may call your attention to something that you may never have known. If you enjoy stargazing, for example, the following comments in *Astronomy* by Robert Baker may lead you to plan a stargazing session.

> *Some Noteworthy Meteor Showers.* The Perseids furnish the most conspicuous and dependable of the annual showers. Their trails are visible through 2 or 3 weeks, with the greatest display about August 11.

On a clear night in the second week of August, you can drive away from the city lights, lie back in an open field, and watch the shooting stars. The book has made you aware of a part of reality that you have not observed before. However, if you go out for three clear nights in a row but see no meteor showers, you may get frustrated with the book for not providing more accurate information. Certainly you would check other sources before you wasted any more gas or sleepless nights.

Reading for Advice

In addition to calling your attention to parts of reality, books offer advice: general statements about how to do specific tasks or the best ways to act in particular situations. A recipe may promise a delicious Dutch crumb apple pie if you use the proper ingredients and follow directions carefully. The evaluation of the advice, however, comes in the eating. If the recipe is good—and everyone asks for seconds and thirds—you keep the recipe in your file for future use. On the other hand, if the leftovers grow moldy in the refrigerator, you'll file the recipe in the garbage can with the leftover pie. That is, after testing the advice, you decide whether to incorporate that advice into your permanent repertoire. According to the same criterion of whether the advice works, you can judge books on how to improve your tennis swing or your writing skills or your social life. Advice accepted becomes part of your life; advice rejected vanishes.

Making Order of the World

Even more significantly, reading can point out *patterns, relationships,* and *explanations* that can help you organize your thinking and notice various kinds of order in the world. The major ideas from your reading are frequently such statements of pattern, relationship, or explanation. One way to decide whether to accept or reject an idea is to test it against new observations to see whether the idea points to patterns that really exist. For example, the elementary economic principle of supply and demand can be understood as a general relationship: if demand increases while supply decreases, prices will rise. After reading about supply and demand in your economics textbook, you might start noticing price patterns of clothing at the local stores. You notice how popular styles are priced much higher than more traditional clothes with the same amount of material and workmanship. Six months later, you notice that the stores are oversupplied with last season's fashion, and the price drops below that of more traditional clothes. Thanks to your grasp of the principle of supply and demand, prices in your local stores make economic sense to you. Once you understand the principle, you can select the best bargains and the best time to buy. You have assimilated economic theory into your own economic behavior. You have learned from your reading.

Reading may even start you observing whole new areas of reality. The first time students take courses in psychology they start to interpret the behavior of their friends and parents. Details of behavior that they previously ignored suddenly become very meaningful. One concept that almost always intrigues students is Freud's theory that a subconscious meaning lurks behind every slip of the tongue. Once students become acquainted with this idea, they start listening very carefully to Freudian slips in order to discover the psychological secrets of people they know. After they have accepted Freud's concept, no remark is ever again an innocent comment.

This absorption of new ideas from books into our daily perception of life is one of the deepest and most important ways our reading affects us. We build new ideas on knowledge of the old. In the following example of the work of Charles Darwin, we will explore at length how Darwin's assimilation of earlier ideas lay behind his educated observation of nature—even where his observations appeared radically original to his contemporaries. In this case study, we will see the many ways an observant individual can make use of reading, even if the individual is not always aware of the process of assimilating knowledge.

Originality Has Sources: The Case of Charles Darwin

If any major advance in science seems to be totally original, based on the observations and thoughts of one person only, Darwin's *theory of evolution* would at first glance seem to be it. As a naturalist on the ship HMS *Beagle,* Charles Darwin traveled to the far corners of the earth collecting samples and observing the varied forms of life on this planet. In 1836, after four years of travel, he settled back to a quiet life in England to make more observations and to think about the meaning of what he had seen. More than twenty years passed before he published his conclusions in *The Origin of Species by Means of Natural Selection* in 1859.

The first edition of this famous work made no mention of other writers who had worked on evolution and had come to similar conclusions; the few writers mentioned in passing were those with whom Darwin strongly disagreed. The material for the book seemed

Charles Darwin, circa 1854. (The Bettmann Archive)

to come only from his own observations and thought—and seemed to go against almost everything that was written and taught at that time.

Darwin in his *Autobiography* claimed that he learned little from books, even though he attended Cambridge University:

> During the three years which I spent at Cambridge my time was wasted, as far as the academical studies were concerned, as completely as at Edinburgh and at school.

Carolus Linnaeus in his Lapland dress. (Brown Brothers)

What most absorbed his attention during his college years was walking in the woods to collect insects.

> But no pursuit at Cambridge was followed with nearly so much eagerness or gave me so much pleasure as collecting beetles. It was the mere passion for collecting, for I did not dissect them and rarely compared their external characters with published descriptions, but got them named anyhow.

Yet when we look more deeply into the ideas developed by Darwin in *The Origin of Species,* we can see how he based his conclusions on the ideas of a number of writers who worked before and during his life—including the naturalists Linnaeus and Lamarck, the economic philosopher Malthus, the geologist Lyell, and Darwin's own grandfather Erasmus Darwin. Darwin drew on the ideas of these other thinkers to help him make sense of his own observations and point him toward new observations. Because the ideas Darwin worked with were publicly available in the books of earlier thinkers, other naturalists were also putting together similar theories of evolution. In fact, Alfred Russel Wallace presented an almost identical theory at the same scientific meeting at which Darwin presented his. The ideas were available—ready to be put together by anyone with sufficient training, intelligence, and observational sharpness.

Darwin's Sources

About a century before Darwin, Carolus Linnaeus classified plants and animals according to specific similarities and differences. Although Linnaeus himself did not express any belief in a theory of evolution, his classification system provided a framework that highlighted patterns of similarity and difference among life forms, and the system arranged plant forms from the simplest to the most complex. His classification helped Darwin to see family relationships between specific animals and to question whether more complex forms had developed from simpler ones. Linnaeus's extensive arrangement of life forms—from most simple to complex—suggested to Darwin that the most advanced of animals were linked to the most simple of plants by a series of small gradual changes rather than by great leaps to entirely new types of life. Darwin himself states in *The Origin of Species* that classification reveals "some deeper bond . . . than mere resemblance . . . and that community of descent—the one known cause of close similarity in organic beings—is the bond."

Jean Baptiste Lamarck, along with other naturalists, had developed a theory of evolution years before Charles Darwin. On the basis of his own observations, Darwin rejected many points of Lamarck's theory but kept one important aspect—the idea that certain characteristics make an animal better able to survive in a particular environment.

Darwin combined this idea of adaptation with his observations of how plant and animal breeders improved their stock. Horse breeders, for example, would mate two very fast horses to produce better race horses; that is, the breeders selected the traits that they wanted to foster. Perhaps nature also had a way, Darwin reasoned,

Thomas Malthus. Photo from an engraving by J. Linnell, 1830. (The Bettmann Archive)
Erasmus Darwin, grandfather of Charles Darwin. (Brown Brothers)

to select the traits best adapted for survival. But how could selection take place in the wild where there were no humans to choose which animals to mate?

The Source with the Solution

The economist Malthus provided Darwin with the answer. In discussing human population, Malthus pointed out that population tends to expand geometrically until the food supply runs out. Then population is limited by starvation, poverty, and natural disaster. In this struggle for existence in a crowded world, Darwin saw that only those specimens best adapted to the environment would survive. The method of natural selection, then, was survival of the best adapted.

In his *Autobiography,* Darwin describes the discovery of the final key:

> In October 1838, that is, fifteen months after I had begun my systematic enquiry, I happened to read for amusement Malthus on *Population,* and being well prepared to appreciate the struggle for existence which everywhere goes on from long-continued observation of the habits of animals and plants, it at once struck me that under these circumstances favourable variations would tend to be preserved, and unfavourable ones to be destroyed. The result of this would be the formation of a new species. Here, then, I had at last got a theory by which to work.

Such gradual selection of the characteristics of species through natural processes would require many millions of years to account for the wide variety of animals and plants that Darwin observed in his travels. And, on the basis of the Bible, most people of Darwin's time thought the world was only about six thousand years old. By studying rock formations, geologists were just beginning to find evidence that the earth had existed for much longer: in *The Principles of Geology,* Charles Lyell presented a theory of a world ancient enough to allow time for all the slow processes of selection that Darwin proposed. Lyell also presented an evolutionary theory concerning the gradual changes in rock formation.

Similar, but Changed

Darwin, aware of the major advance in knowledge he was proposing and of the shortcomings he found in previous writings, tended to emphasize his own originality and to diminish the importance of the writers who influenced his thinking. He knew that he had rejected certain ideas of the same writers from whom he accepted other ideas—or parts of ideas. All these ideas were transformed by Darwin as they were assimilated into his own new way of thinking. Even though he may have learned much from others, he knew he came to his major theories as a result of his own observations, thoughts, and evaluations. Thus he tended to undervalue the influence even of his own grandfather, Erasmus Darwin, who in 1794 had presented a theory of evolution in the book *Zoönomia.* Charles Darwin grants this work only a limited amount of influence in his *Autobiography:*

I had previously read the *Zoönomia* of my grandfather, in which similar views are maintained, but without producing any effect on me. Nevertheless it is probable that the hearing rather early in life such views maintained and praised may have favoured my upholding them under a different form in my *Origin of Species*.

The phrase *under a different form* is the key to understanding the feelings expressed in this passage. We have the perspective to see that Charles Darwin was, indeed, original, but that his originality grew from the interaction between his own observations and the observations of others.

Darwin as a Source

Just as Darwin was influenced by the thoughts of those who came before him, Darwin's observations and thoughts have, in the years since the publication of *The Origin of Species,* deeply influenced how later scientists have looked at life. The entire study of genetics, for example, grew directly out of Gregor Mendel's attempt to pinpoint the method by which evolutionary change is transmitted to offspring. Mendel read Darwin, accepted Darwin's ideas, and then designed experiments to explore the pattern of inheritance of traits. Current work with DNA and genetic structure has further specified the mechanisms of evolution.

Assimilating Ideas
from Reading

The process of assimilating new ideas—new ways of looking at reality—from our reading is a slow one. We gradually accept or reject material on the basis of how well it conforms to our observations. Sometimes we interpret experience on the basis of ideas we read so long ago that we no longer remember reading them; we think such ideas are entirely ours. At other times we may accept parts of someone's thoughts but reject other parts. Like Darwin, we may remember more clearly how much we rejected than how much we kept. At other times we read without even thinking how the implications of the ideas may affect our present beliefs. Thus it is not always easy to pinpoint the direct influence of reading on our thoughts and observations. The more conscious we become about this assimilation process, the more control we have over it. We can choose which thoughts to accept or reject based on conscious evaluation of the ideas, and we can open ourselves to ideas that might strike us at first as strange.

One technique to make us more conscious of assimilating new ideas as we read is to write a *critical analysis of observation* based on the ideas proposed in the reading. (*Analysis* means the division of something into its component parts, according to some scheme of categories. The word *critical* implies that there is a specific theory or set of ideas behind the categories.) The question behind the analysis is: "Do my own observations fall into the patterns or categories suggested by the reading?" If your observations agree with the ideas of the reading, and if the patterns from the reading help you understand your observations better, then the reading makes good sense to you and clarifies your ideas of reality. If your observations do not agree with what you have read, you might wonder whether your observations were appropriate or whether the ideas of the writer should be called into question.

Ideas Organize Experience

The process of assimilating ideas through reading might work as follows: a student who had not thought much about tiredness and had classed all forms of exhaustion in the same general category of "I'm wasted" might begin to think further after reading "The Psychology of Tiredness" from Ernest Hartmann's *The Functions of Sleep,* excerpted on pages 103–105. Hartmann, as you may remember, identifies two types of tiredness, one physical and the other mental. He attributes certain behavior patterns to each type and associates each type of tiredness with a different stage of sleep. He also states that the patterns aren't always pure but are sometimes mixed.

Amy Larsen, a sophomore, at first reacted against Hartmann's ideas: "Tired is tired, and the only way it feels is no good." But the class discussion of different types of tiredness interested her, so she decided to observe herself and others to find out whether she could spot Hartmann's categories of physical, mental, and mixed tiredness. She recorded her observations in a journal entry:

Went home this weekend . . . what a pain to drive two
hundred miles each way. Actually Cindy drove on Friday
afternoon while I collapsed from the chem exam that morning. I can't believe it--I must have been up half the
night studying!! In the car I sat there like some dumb
cow gaping away, wanting to stop at every McDonald's we
passed. I get so hungry after exams. And I want real
greasy kid's food. The rest of the time I just sat there
thinking about french fries. I bet I didn't say more than
ten words the whole trip--except about stopping for
food. Lucky Cindy didn't listen to me because otherwise I
would have had to starve myself the rest of the weekend.
Then she was playing a radio--all that dumbo punk music
she likes. And it seemed so loud; that trip was the worst.
But I'm not the grouchy type so I just asked her to turn
it down. She must have been tired too and since she was
driving she had a right to choose the music. But did the
music have to be so awful?

   Just looked over what I wrote--sounds like mental
tiredness, doesn't it? Withdrawn, not willing to talk,
childish desires--you know when I got home that night I
played the stupidest games with my kid sister. I mean I
was up half the night again, even though I thought I was
so tired. I just kept putting off going to bed. Dumb. I
knew I needed the sleep. Well, Hartmann says you do tend
to lose control. And I guess I was pretty irritable and
grouchy in the car, although I tried to hide it and be
nice. But I don't know, I was sort of cheerier than the
gloomy grouchpot Hartmann describes--especially when I
got home. I was more silly; but I'm not the type to get
depressed.

The journal helps her notice telling details about how she feels
when she is tired. She starts to wonder whether those details fit
into the patterns the psychologist suggests. Knowing about his pat-

terns, in turn, helps her become even more aware of her own behavior.

After making a number of such entries, observing her own behavior and feelings when tired—as well as the activities causing the tiredness—this student would have a specific sense of the meaning of Hartmann's categories. She would also have specific personal observations on which to evaluate Hartmann's claims. Her journal entries, in fact, became the raw material for the essay of critical analysis that follows.

The Critical Analysis of Observation

When reading the selection that you will compare to your personal experience, pay particular attention to the *categories* into which the author separates the phenomena being discussed. By noting these categories and the kinds of examples the author uses, determine what kinds of observations you need to make. Then consider the best way to make the observations and the best way to record them. For example, you might make a record of your own sensations of hunger or describe people meeting at a cocktail party or list the noises you can hear from your apartment window. Whether you make your observations over a long or a short period of time, keep an accurate record of what you find—through notes, tapes, or any other appropriate method. Don't rely on your memory; it may tend to tidy up the observations to make them fit more easily into the given categories.

After you have made all your observations, sit down with your notes, outline the analytical categories derived from the reading, and try to fit each observation into a category. Pay particular attention to those observations that don't fit into a specific category. These anomalies will help you think about the limitations of the categories. As you gain a sense of how well your observations fit the scheme, develop an overall conclusion, which you may eventually use as the topic sentence of your final essay. You will then be ready to organize your ideas and write a draft of your essay.

The introduction of the essay should identify the ideas you derived from the reading, the kind of observations you made, and how well the observations fit the ideas. The ideas should be identified by source (author and title), by summary of the main points, and by identification of the categories. Your observations should be identified by place, time, and method as well as by a general description.

Either a statement on how well the observations fit the categories or an explanation of how your observations contradict the theory may serve as a topic statement.

The body of the paper should be organized around the separate categories. Discuss your various observations under the appropriate categories. Reserve anomalies for separate discussion near the end. This organization will generally work better when the categories seem to explain the observations with some consistency. If your observations are at odds with the writer's scheme, or if each observation includes a complex of several categories, it may be better to organize the paper around the observations and to analyze each instance separately. After presenting each observation, you should discuss either the problems in categorizing it or the several categories it fits into simultaneously. The conclusion might then draw together similar patterns that occur in your separate observations.

A different organization might be useful if your observations are so opposed to the ideas of the reading that the writer's original categories are of little use in making sense of the material. You might begin by showing the kinds of difficulties that arise when applying the writer's categories to your observations and then go on to develop a new set of categories that are useful in organizing your observations. The conclusion might explore the differences between the writer's original categories and your new categories, or it might attempt to explain why the new categories fit better than the old ones.

Sample Essay

Some Kinds of Tiredness

Until I read "The Psychology of Tiredness" by Ernest Hartmann, I did not realize that there could be different kinds of tiredness. Hartmann defines two primary kinds of tiredness: physical tiredness (associated with relaxed muscles, pleasant feelings, and easy sleep) and mental tiredness (associated with muscle tension, irritability, childish desires, and difficulty in sleeping). Because Hartmann finds these patterns "seldom present in

pure form," he implies a third category of mixed tiredness, made up of parts of the two primary kinds. Despite
skepticism, I observed my own patterns of tiredness and
kept a record of my observations for three weeks in my
journal. I found in myself all three kinds of tiredness
during that period, but I also discovered a fourth kind
--related to boredom and laziness.

During the first week of the observation, mid-term
exam week, I was in a constant state of mental exhaustion, except when I got a rush of adrenalin just before
each test. Most of the time, I lacked energy and was in a
low-grade stupor, just as Hartmann described. I had to
force myself back into the books; my mind would wander or
I would doze off after only fifteen minutes of studying.
I seemed to have a constant headache and stiff neck. I
got irritated with my roommate for silly things, like
slamming the door too loudly. At night I would lie awake
worrying about the exams. When I did finally get asleep,
I was like a stone. The only break from this grinding
misery was Wednesday night, when eight of us decided to
break out for a night of modified insanity. As Hartmann
suggests, we lost all sense of responsibility.

The characteristics of mental exhaustion became even
more extreme in my collapse after the last exam. After a
morning chemistry exam, I rode back home (two hundred
miles from the college) with a friend. The whole trip I
daydreamed about greasy french fries and grumbled about
the irritating punk music on the radio. When I got home,
my mood swung to uncontrolled silliness. I was up until 3
A.M. playing children's games with my younger sister.

During the week of spring vacation I had plenty of free
time to relax and enjoy myself--a lot of sports, hiking,
dancing, hanging out with friends. After a day of doing
nothing, I recuperated from exams and had no problem
sleeping. In the mornings, I would get up after only six

or seven hours of sleep, but totally refreshed. Sometimes in the afternoon I would come back from a long hike
totally drained, barely able to walk; however, I would
stretch out on the couch for an hour and would be ready
for a night of dancing, despite a few stiff muscles.
Physical tiredness was a lot more pleasant than mental
tiredness.

During that vacation I also had an experience of mixed
tiredness. A cousin who is a carpenter promised to teach
me a few basics if I would help him on a small job. All
day long I helped him lift and hold, cut and hammer. But
the work was more than physical. I had to concentrate all
the time, taking care with all the measurements and tools
so that the job came out right. The power tools were also
frightening. They could tear you up before you realized
what happened. I was very careful and very nervous. Plus
the tools vibrated so much they seemed to shake up my
nervous system. After dinner I didn't feel like talking,
so I retreated into a TV movie. I went to sleep feeling
good about myself, but I tossed and turned all night. My
dreams were filled with tape measures, right-angle
joints, and menacing drills. I was both physically and
mentally exhausted.

When I returned to school, I had a tiredness that
didn't seem to fit any of Hartmann's categories. Although I was well rested from vacation and classes were
slow in getting started, I was tired on and off for three
days. It was a rainy Sunday afternoon when I arrived back
at the college, so I decided to get a bit ahead on my
reading, but after an hour I gave up because I had no energy. I drifted around the student center until evening,
when most of my friends started returning. My mood picked
up, but the next morning I was feeling listless again. I
took almost no notes in class and that night went to a
dull movie with some friends. I went to sleep early. On

Tuesday I spent an hour looking through my journal, gathering ideas for this paper and then avoided serious work for the rest of the day. My roommate said I looked "dragged out." Not until Wednesday, when I got down to real work on this paper, did I get back to my usual energetic self.

Hartmann based his categories of tiredness on the kind of work one does to make one tired. Physical work leads to relaxed, short-lived exhaustion; mental and emotional work leads to tension, loss of sociability and control, and long-lasting exhaustion. My experience confirms this generalization, but my experience also convinces me that the situation you are in can also make you tired in a different way. Boredom is tiring, and sleep is a way of killing time. Anticipating work that you have to do is also tiring. It took me a while to gather the energy to write this essay and face the work in all my courses for the rest of the semester. Just the thought of it all makes me tired.

Writing Assignments

1. Discuss a simple fact, a set of directions, or a piece of advice that you learned from reading and that somehow expanded the world available to you. The source of the information can range from a computer manual to a social advice column, from a cookbook to a medical guide. Let us know what the information was, cite its source, and explain the consequences of your discovery of that information. Your audience is your classmates, and your purpose is to share some of the pleasures and experiences you have gained from books.

2. Discuss an idea or generalization you read in a book that expanded or reorganized your thinking on a subject so that you were able to perceive or understand more, to solve a nagging problem, or to dispel confusion. Let us know what the idea was, cite its source, and explain the consequences of encountering that idea

for your thinking or perception. Your audience is your classmates; the purpose is to share your thinking processes. If you read through your journal, you may discover the seeds of this essay already there. Or you may wish to write a new journal entry exploring your significant reading before you begin the rough draft.

3. Basing your observations on categories derived from Ernest Hartmann's chapter on "The Psychology of Tiredness," excerpted on pages 103–105, record in your journal your own patterns of tiredness. Then write a short critical analysis—length to be specified by your instructor—directed to an audience of your classmates, who are making similar observations about their own patterns of tiredness.

4. Basing your observations on categories derived from de Tocqueville's analysis of the role and structure of organizations in American society, which appears on pages 51–55, record in your journal your observations of an organization that you belong to. Then write a short critical analysis—length to be specified by your instructor—directed to an audience of your classmates who have been similarly observing and analyzing their own organizations.

9 Comparing and Synthesizing Sources

Once you start comparing the statements of different books, you may discover many problems in fitting the sources together. Books may cover the same subject but with different foci and with different purposes. Books may disagree over facts, ideas, and basic viewpoints. Large gaps of knowledge may exist, not covered by any available source. In this chapter, we will study ways of fitting parts together and evaluating differences between writers. Two types of essays, the analytical comparison of sources *and* the synthesis of sources, will help you develop the skills of comparing and evaluating sources.

Knowledge Is Messy

A library presents an imposing vision: books neatly arranged according to reference numbers on endless rows of metal shelves. Initially, the wall-to-wall books make you feel that any fact you want to know must be in one of them and that the ideas in these books should fit together as neatly as the books fit together on the shelves. You have a comforting feeling that all knowledge in books interlocks to provide a smooth carpet of learning—everywhere even and firm under foot, no matter where you may tread.

When you actually start to look for specific information or try to find agreement between the books on a particular topic, you are more likely to feel that you have stepped into the badlands of the Dakotas or the swamps of Florida. You cannot always find what you are looking for; what you do find may be contradictory or confusing. On the positive side, you may uncover some wonderful surprises—ideas and information that you had no idea existed.

If you stop to consider why and how books are written, the unevenness of ground may not take you so much by surprise. Each person who writes a book makes a particular statement, based on individual thoughts and perceptions about a subject of personal interest. Moreover, each writer shapes his or her particular statement around particular purposes, as discussed in Chapter 6. Each writer does build on what came before—on the other books in the library— but each builds in an individual way to serve different functions and to speak to different readers. In some disciplines, particularly in science and technology, knowledge has been organized or codified. But even in fields with high degrees of codification, there are still major areas of disagreement, large gaps in knowledge, and different approaches to problem areas.

Think of a conversation involving a large number of people. Each person has a different viewpoint, different interests, and different points to make. Perhaps after much talk, the group may achieve a consensus on some limited facts, certain shared principles, and perhaps specific lines of action. More often there are disagreements, unresolved issues, misunderstandings, and only partial interest in what other people say.

Once you, as a reader, move beyond the coherent world of a single book in order to gain the wisdom of several authors on a single subject, you will have to make sense of the diversity of statements you will find. To make your own informed statement on a subject that other writers have discussed, you need to sort out agreement from disagreement, fact from opinion, and ideas you accept from those you reject. This chapter presents techniques and criteria for making choices between opposing statements. It also presents ways of bringing diverse materials together. In this chapter, you are asked to write two types of essays: the *analytical comparison* of two pieces of writing and the *synthesis of sources*. These two types of essays provide practice in the skills of intelligently drawing together material from different sources.

A first task, however, is to sort out the different levels at which books may either converge or diverge—on subjects, facts, ideas, and underlying perceptions.

Finding the Common Ground Between Two Books

The first condition for a successful conversation, whether spoken by party-goers at a college mixer or written by various scholars, each alone at a desk, is that the participants be talking about the same subject. If one person talks about unemployment and the other talks about television ratings, two separate monologues are taking place but no conversation—unless they have discovered a common ground between the two subjects, such as possible effects of economic downturns on television production. Topics must coincide, overlap, or intersect to allow meaningful discussion.

By bringing two books or articles together for comparison, you are suggesting some common ground between them—some relationship between the two statements. Perhaps one of the writers explicitly recognizes that such a relationship exists by citing and discussing the earlier writer's work. At times, writers deliberately answer each other. However, you may find many cases where two writers have not explicitly joined issue even though they are clearly writing about the same topic. In fact, you may bring together writers who may never have even heard of each other. But you perceived that their subjects are the same.

Even before you begin comparing two pieces of writing to see whether they are at peace or war over the common ground, you must locate and define that common ground. This is not always easy. At one extreme, you may find books that appear to take on the same subject and to have similar purposes. All biographies of Henry Ford attempt to present a true picture of the life of the great automobile industrialist, and most cover his entire life—from birth and childhood to death. Predictably, each of these books presents facts and statements about the major events in Ford's life: the building of his first car, the opening of his first factory, the creation of the assembly line, the introduction of the Model T, his libel suit against the *Chicago Tribune,* and his attempt to run for president of the United States in 1924. Other events, such as the patent battle with Selden, who had filed a patent application on the design of an automobile as early as 1879, are covered in only some of the biographies. In addition to varying on the events covered, the books vary greatly in the amount of interpretation, criticism, praise, and discussion of causes and effects. Thus, even when several books seem to be addressing precisely the same subject, you must be careful to identify that overlap, topic by topic.

In the middle ground, you will compare books that have substantial overlap even though they take on different overall subjects. Any history of the automobile industry would necessarily discuss many topics involving Henry Ford's life, just as any biography of him would have to discuss his role in the growth of the industry. Again you must specifically identify the exact topics and extent of overlap; parts of each book will have little to do with the other.

At the other extreme are books or articles that are not primarily concerned with the same topics but that do have some bearing on a particular topic. The life of William C. Durant, the founder of General Motors, at several points touched on Ford's life; a biography of Durant might, therefore, shed some additional light on their relationship, which was discussed only briefly in a biography of Ford. By identifying such intersection between two books, you may be making connections no one else has made. For example, by making connections between a history of advertising in the early part of the century and Ford's merchandising policies as presented in a Ford biography, you may find an explanation of Ford's great success.

Because the connections between books can be so wide ranging and different in kind, and because no two books cover exactly the same ground in exactly the same way, the more specific you are in pinpointing the precise areas of overlap and shared concern between books, the more you will gain by bringing them together. You will then know exactly what the discussion is about.

Do Books Differ

on Facts?

> In 1892 I completed my first motor car, but it was not until the spring of the following year that it ran to my satisfaction.
>
> —Henry Ford, *My Life and Work* (in collaboration with Samuel Crowther)

> The last days of May, 1896, saw the quadricycle almost completed. Ford and Bishop were working every night. "We often wondered when Henry Ford slept," remarked Charles T. Bush of the Strelinger company, "because he was putting in long hours working [at the Edison plant] and when he went home at night he was always experimenting or reading." Clara worried about his loss of sleep, but did not let him guess that she feared that his efforts might culminate in a breakdown. For the last forty-eight hours before the vehicle was ready he hardly slept at all. Finally early in the morning of June 4—between 2 and 4 A.M.—the task was finished, and the builder was ready to take his car out for a trial run.
>
> —Allan Nevins, *Ford: The Times, The Man, The Company*

Sometimes we can judge the truth of a statement of fact on the basis of our own observations. Often, however, we must rely entirely on secondhand reports. If all the written sources agree about the facts of a particular event, and if you have no other cause for suspicion, reliance on written reports should present few problems. You can generally assume that the facts were just as all the sources report them. For example, if all biographies of Henry Ford and all histories of the Ford company agree that the lowest retail price of the Model T touring car was $360 and that this was the price during 1916 and 1917, you may take these facts as true. Further, if company and dealer records, contemporary advertisements, and public announcements *all* confirm the facts, you have no reason to doubt them.

Conflicting Facts

What happens if written sources disagree about what happened? If different observers report different statements of fact, how can you tell which has the facts right? Here we are not talking about the meaning or the interpretation of events—that will be discussed

Henry Ford and his first car, the Quadricycle, 1896. (From the collections of Henry Ford Museum and Greenfield Village)

later in this chapter—but only about the directly observable phenomenon: What happened? When did it happen? Where did it happen? Who was involved? If sources disagree, you may become justifiably confused about what the actual events were. The two quotations at the beginning of this section present just such a conflict over facts. Henry Ford himself states he built his first working car in 1892; Allan Nevins, the historian, writes that Ford did not build his first working automobile (called a *quadricycle*) until 1896. Obviously Ford could build his first automobile only once, but who are we to believe about when it happened—Ford himself or a reputed scholar?

Your first reaction to such a conflict may be "What does it matter? Who cares?" That is, you believe the difference is minor and does not bear directly on the issues you are interested in. In some cases this response may be appropriate. If, for example, you were looking into Ford's career only as a background to studying the development of early assembly-line techniques, the exact date of Ford's first car might not matter. If you had to refer to the date, you could simply cite both sources and leave the dispute unresolved. Not all conflicts must be resolved, but you should notice when they do occur.

One reason you should make note of conflicts—no matter how minor they seem at first—is that they may later point to more important issues. If, in studying Ford's statements about the development of assembly lines, you find that Ford has a tendency to stretch the truth to make himself look better, this earlier conflict over dates may help you *confirm a pattern*.

For many questions about Ford's contribution, however, the date of his first car is crucial, for the difference of four years determines whether Ford was one of the leaders in auto invention and design or just made use of what others did before him. If Ford built a working car in 1892, it would have been the first in this country. There is no record of an operating car in the United States prior to that year—despite Selden's design on paper for well over a decade. The date determines whether Ford, in addition to being a business genius, was an inventive genius as well.

Resolving Conflicts

The significance of the date makes the conflict an important one to resolve, but—as anyone who has watched a courtroom drama on TV can tell you—it is not easy to determine the facts from the conflicting testimony of two witnesses. The difficulties in evaluating testimony in a courtroom stem from two major sources. First, testimony is given by people—people with fallible memories, limited or distorted perceptions, and personal interests. There are many reasons a person may not have seen clearly what happened—and even more reasons why that person might not state exactly what he or she saw. Therefore legal procedure defines who may testify about what and in what manner in order to reduce the effect of personal factors, limited memory, and self-interest and to increase specificity and accuracy.

The second difficulty is that many of the facts—often the most important ones—have not been observed by anyone who will or can testify. Nobody but the dead victim may have seen the accused pull the trigger. Thus the trial may have to depend on *secondary evidence* in order to establish the most vital facts. The victim's friend, for example, may testify that she was talking on the phone with the victim at 12:14 A.M. Suddenly the victim stopped talking, and the friend heard a scuffle, then a shot—then silence. The police testify that they found the body dead of bullet wounds at 12:30 A.M. From this evidence the jury can infer that a murder took place. The defense then calls as witness a bartender from the next city who testifies that the accused was in his bar from 10 P.M. until 2:00 A.M. Unless the prosecution can discredit the bartender's story by other testimony, the jury can only infer that someone else committed the crime. The main facts are pieced together indirectly, based on the interpretation and quality of the secondary evidence.

An Example: Ford versus Nevins

Now let us evaluate the dispute over the date of Ford's first car, using as criteria the credibility of the witnesses and the strength of the evidence. First, we must ask how good Ford and Nevins are as witnesses. In one respect, Henry Ford should be a very good witness: he was there when it happened and should have more precise information than an outsider like Nevins, who must rely on other people's reports. On the other hand, Ford is speaking from his memory, thirty years after the actual events. Over that long a period, recollection can get quite hazy, reflecting how Ford would like it to have been rather than how it actually was. Ford, moreover, has much to gain by reporting the earlier date: the 1892 date would make him a pioneer of auto invention. So we may wonder whether Ford's account is accurate and unbiased.

Allan Nevins also has some pluses and minuses as a witness. On the minus side, he wrote sixty years after the events; he was not even born when the first cars were being tested. Further, as the preface to his book states, Nevins's research on Henry Ford was funded by the Ford Foundation. Yet this funding by a potentially interested party ultimately makes Nevins's dating more credible, because the later date goes directly against the interests of the sponsor. Even more to Nevins's credit is his substantial reputation as a historical scholar, more dedicated to truth than to private bias.

Thus, although Nevins is more distant from the actual events, he is probably less biased as a witness.

It is on the question of evidence, however, that the real difference between the accounts of Ford and Nevins becomes quite apparent. Ford relies only on his recollection. He does not present the testimony of other witnesses on the scene at the same time, nor does he include any documentary support—such as bills for raw materials. We have only his word and memory to go on. Nevins, on the other hand, offers—in the pages around the quoted passages—substantial evidence in support of two claims for the later date. First, to support the claim that Ford's tinkering with engines did not lead to an operable car prior to 1895, Nevins cites the testimony of three people who discussed Ford's work with him at that time. All three agree that Ford's work was only at the beginning stages. Moreover, the dates used by these witnesses are substantiated by the dates of magazine articles that entered into their discussions with Ford. Furthermore, Nevins cites Ford's wife, who claims that, as of Christmas 1893, Ford had only a partially assembled engine and no other parts of a car. Once again, her date is correlated with the birth of a child, whose birth certificate is a matter of public record.

In support of his second claim—that Ford did complete a working car in 1896—Nevins cites the testimony of individuals close to the events. These witnesses confirm many secondary supporting circumstances: Ford's difficult financial condition because of the cost of materials and Ford's physical and mental exhaustion from working on the car while still maintaining a full-time job. The statements of one particular witness, Charles King, are particularly persuasive. King helped Ford in the last stages of building the car and had previously worked on one of his own. Thus he was both an expert—skilled enough to evaluate Ford's progress—and a firsthand witness, very close to the events. Nevins's evidence confirms that Henry Ford did build his first car in 1896.

Criteria for Evaluation

What characteristics make a good observer and what qualifies as convincing evidence vary substantially from field to field, as discussed in the previous chapter. Moreover, each particular conflict over facts brings in individual factors that must be considered. The following suggestions should be used flexibly. Keep in mind the specifics of each case and the special criteria of the disciplines involved. These criteria, nonetheless, do provide a starting point for the evaluation and resolution of conflicts over fact.

Criteria for Evaluating Sources or Witnesses

- Generally, the closer the witness was in time and place to the original events, the better. If the writer was not there, he or she may cite reliable sources who were.
- The more the writer or primary witness knows about the subject or events he or she is describing, the better he or she will know what to look for, what to report, and what to conclude.
- The fewer biases or prejudgments writers or witnesses have about the matters they are reporting on, the more likely they are to give an undistorted account.

Criteria for Evaluating Evidence

- The more *specific* and *complete* the evidence is, the more likely it is to present a clear and precise picture.
- The more *internally consistent* the evidence is, the more likely the report is to be accurate. Internal consistency means that one part of the evidence does not contradict another part and that all parts support a single interpretation. Be cautious: in some cases, evidence that is too consistent may mean oversimplification or fudging of observations.
- The more the evidence was recorded at the time of the events reported, the fewer problems with distorted memory will occur.
- The more the evidence is tied to matters of public record—such as contemporary newspaper accounts, government documents, or widely acknowledged facts—the more credible the evidence is.
- The less indication of bias, or fraudulence, or of false statements, the more reliable the evidence is.

At times you may not be able to make a clear-cut choice between two conflicting reports of fact: the witnesses and the evidence may be equally good—or equally poor—on both sides, or you may lack enough background information to judge. In such cases, all you can do is acknowledge the conflict and suggest what the *implications* of either report being true might be. Tracing the logical implications of each report may give you an indirect indication of which side is more likely to be true. At least you will learn the consequences of favoring one report over the other.

Working Out the Implications

Suppose, for example, that Ford did build a car in 1892 and that nobody but Ford and his employee Sam Huff (who later backed up the claim) knew about it. What would the implications be? One implication is that we have lost traces of the early history of the automobile—which is possible. Another implication is that Ford was able to keep the car secret from those around him, including his wife—a bit less likely. A third implication is that Ford was a pioneer of auto design as well as production. This last idea might be checked against the pattern of the rest of his life to see whether he displayed as much engineering genius as business genius. Did he tend to borrow engineering advances or did he make them himself?

On the other hand, if Nevins's date of 1896 is correct, we can see other implications: first, that Ford had a flexible, if not a fabricating, memory. We could check the accuracy of his memory against other claims that Ford made. Second, when Ford made his claim in 1926, he had reasons for wanting to date his first car as early as possible. And finally, Ford's skill was more in adapting other people's inventions than in developing his own; thus his real talents emerged only when he began the production and sale of his car.

The more you know about the 1890s, automobiles, and Ford, the better you can judge these implications against the conflicting facts. These implications move us toward the realm of ideas, interpretations, and conclusions.

Do Books Differ

on Ideas?

Ideas tell us what a writer thinks about a subject, not just what he or she is describing as facts. The writer's ideas may be about causes, effects, similarities, motivation, meaning, or any other kind of abstraction that goes beyond the immediately verifiable.

It is, for example, a matter of fact—verifiable in company records, newspaper accounts, and history books—that on January 5, 1914, Henry Ford announced a wage policy for Ford Motor Company, more than doubling the minimum wage of his workers from $.26 an hour to $5 for a full eight-hour workday. However, that policy gives rise to many questions whose answers are in the realm of ideas and open to a variety of opinions: what caused the company to increase wages so greatly? Why did the announcement receive such wide publicity? Why was it criticized? What was the effect of the increase for all American workers? Was the policy a success? The answers to these questions can be found only by *interpreting* the factual evidence—and not just by collecting more facts.

Even though ideas differ from facts, they are still highly dependent on facts because facts are the material on which you must base your thinking. You have already seen how a disagreement over facts can lead to a disagreement over conclusions: the evaluation of Ford's achievements, in part, depends on which date is correct for his first working model. Even if two writers agree on facts, they may come to opposing conclusions by choosing different facts on which to base their ideas. Finally, writers may come to different conclusions on the basis of the same facts by using different reasoning processes. Thus, to evaluate conflicting ideas, you must evaluate both the *facts* they are based on and the *reasoning* by which the writer developed ideas out of facts.

The Meeting of Ideas

Before we begin to consider ways of resolving contradictory ideas, we must identify whether the ideas in question agree or disagree— or have little to do with each other. Unlike statements of fact, which usually present contradictions in obvious ways, statements of ideas are not as easily compared. Two statements of fact either make a claim about the date of a salary increase or they do not. However, ideas interpreting that same event may take off in many different directions from the simple fact. For example, referring to the date of Ford's wage announcement, one writer says that the date was held up because Ford wanted to make sure that profits were great enough to support the increased costs of higher wages; another claims that the date was far in advance of the liberalization of wage policies of other American corporations; another notes that the date marked the beginning of a number of Ford policies concerned with worker welfare. Each of these ideas may be plausible, but they have nothing to do with one another. They explore entirely separate issues—even though they all concern the single fact of date. Each operates in a different realm.

So the first task in comparing ideas is to define the realm each idea operates in. The more common *realms of ideas* include:

Causes

Effects

Intentions of statements and actions

Implicit meanings

Relationships between facts

Statements of value

You will notice many other realms of ideas in the course of your reading. Further, the writer's idea may be limited—a discussion of only a part of the issue within a single realm. In explaining the reasons for Ford's dramatic wage increase, you may note the causes within the mind of Henry Ford, the causes within the company, and the causes in the political and social climate of the period. Statements about causes within each of these areas do not necessarily contradict statements about causes in the other areas. Only when statements exist in the same realm with the same limits can you find direct agreement or disagreement.

An Example: Nevins versus Sward

A direct conflict of ideas occurs between Keith Sward in *The Legend of Henry Ford* and Allan Nevins in *Ford: The Times, The Man, The Company* over the issues that led to the Ford company's change in wage policy. Sward cites fear of labor unrest, employee radicalization, and unionization as the main causes of the managerial decision to raise wages dramatically. Nevins directly contradicts this idea by claiming that the company's main concerns were a sense of fairness and a desire for increased quality of work—through increased morale and improved home life for the workers. Sward sees the company reasoning from fear; Nevins sees the company reasoning from good business practice and moral equity.

Nevins and Sward present ideas about the company management that are mutually exclusive, for each claims to be presenting the single most important motivation. If each claimed to be suggesting only one out of many possible motivations, then it might be possible to accept both statements; some of the company executives may have responded to fear, and others may have acted from a sense of fairness. Even one person may have mixed motives and mixed feelings. But because the two writers both claim to isolate the single most important factor, their statements are contradictory. Both motivations cannot be the most important. Further, each writer explicitly scoffs at the opposite idea: Sward states that Ford showed little regard for the welfare of workers, whereas Nevins argues that labor unrest and radical feeling were much less significant than they were later made out to be. In other words, you cannot explain what they both say without pointing out the conflict.

Mutual Compatibility

The concepts of *mutual compatibility* of ideas and its negative counterpart, *mutual exclusivity* of ideas, are the keys to finding relationships between ideas. Ideas of two authors are usually not so directly opposed that one says yes while the other says no. More often, you will have to determine whether the statements of two authors can reasonably fit together. Writers who make claims using extreme words like *only, most, primary, always*, and *never* frequently conflict with each other. Writers who make claims that concede other possibilities—through phrases such as *in part, along with, one of several*, or *sometimes*—are more apt to be mutually compatible. One writer's claim that Ford's large salary increase worked smoothly *in all its aspects* is not compatible with another writer's negative claim that the riots of job seekers outside the Ford factory after the announcement were a direct result of the false hopes raised by Ford. However, the negative evaluation pointing to the riots would be compatible with the more moderate claim that the Ford managers did their best to anticipate the effects of the wage increase. This qualified statement allows for the possibility that—despite the best efforts of the Ford planners—certain effects may have resulted from factors beyond their awareness.

Evaluating Disputes over Ideas

Once you have spotted disagreement of ideas—by either direct or indirect contradiction—you can turn to analyzing and evaluating the disagreement. Examine the causes of the disagreement. Does the disagreement stem from conflicting evidence, a different selection of evidence, or a different reasoning process? Does the conflict stem from the facts or what the writer does with the facts?

Disputes over Facts   Conflicting facts give rise to different ideas. As we noticed in the last section, the date of Ford's first car has many consequences for evaluating his contribution to the development of the automobile—and even for evaluating his personality. If you can resolve the conflict of facts, you can usually resolve the conflict between two writers' resulting ideas. Thus, once we determined that Nevins's later date of 1896 was the correct one, many consequences—Ford's greater skill in business than in invention, his fallible memory, and his desire for increasing his reputation beyond the facts—fall into place. Therefore, whenever you come across an idea conflict based on a fact conflict, you should try to resolve the fact conflict according to the criteria presented on pages 226–227.

Disputes over Selection of Facts   Because there are often more facts available than anyone can make full use of in any single book or article, each writer must choose what he or she considers the most important or relevant facts; thus the different choice of facts may lead to different conclusions. Each writer may have access to different facts or may be more or less careful about paying attention to all the available facts. At times, deeper differences between the thinking of different writers may predispose them to pay more attention to one fact rather than to another. The writer's selection of specific facts—from all those available—affects the ideas the writer eventually develops from the facts.

A typical conflict of ideas arising from a different selection of facts occurs between Sward and Nevins over the consequences of the Ford wage policy for the workers. Sward focuses attention on the number of workers who did not complete the six-month probationary period to become eligible for the five-dollar-a-day minimum. Sward cites many statistics concerning the rapid turnover of new employees and concludes that the Ford policy was not as generous as it first appeared and that Ford kept labor costs down by a deliberate policy of rapid turnover, enabling the company to pay the lower probationary wage to a large part of the work force. Nevins, on the other hand, focuses attention on the 70 to 80 percent of workers who did complete the probationary period and profited from the higher wage. Citing many instances of how workers' lives improved, Nevins concludes that the program was generous and beneficial to the workers. Sward concludes that, as far as the workers were concerned, the program was a fraud.

Which Set of Facts?   In this case, none of the facts are in dispute; neither writer presents any statistics or claims any facts that contradict those cited by the other writer. The differences only are in the facts they choose to attend to: the facts about the probationary employees versus the facts about the long-term employees. How can you evaluate the merit of conclusions made on such different bases of fact? The answer lies in evaluating how appropriate the initial choice of facts is in each case.

First, you should consider which of the authors gives a more complete picture by basing conclusions on a wider cross section of the available facts. An author who limits himself to a narrow range of facts, ignoring many other obvious aspects of the situation, is likely to come to a partial and distorted conclusion. In this respect, both Sward and Nevins share some degree of irresponsibility; each ignores half the picture. Sward, by focusing on the workers who did not meet company standards for permanent employment, entirely ignores the benefits to the workers who did make the grade. For him, the permanent workers become only the exploited tools of manipulative company policy. Nevins, on the other hand, is concerned only with the benefits to the permanent workers, who included many handicapped workers. In determining that the company demands were not excessive, Nevins dismisses those who could not meet the company standards of discipline: they simply did not deserve the job. It appears that neither author looked carefully at both sides of the picture. Later we will explore some deeper reasons why this might have happened.

The Complete Picture   Sometimes one author is able to present a fuller picture because he or she has fuller access to facts. Perhaps one author was able to interview a key figure in the story—a figure whom no other author was able to interview. Perhaps a later author has access to documents that were only recently discovered. Perhaps one author is a more careful scholar than another, searching harder for, and paying closer attention to, the facts available. If you find any of these situations, obviously you should give more credence to the author with fuller access to the facts.

Even if both authors paint equally complete pictures, you can ask which author tends to use the more representative and typical facts and which relies on more obscure, unusual facts. This distinction can actually cut both ways. At times the obscure facts may be the most important. A writer who wishes to expose hidden corruption will call into question all the more obvious and public acts of a famous politician by uncovering damaging data. At other times the obscure facts may simply be unrepresentative and distorting. A lengthy exploration of the childhood friendship between Abraham Lincoln and another boy who grew up to be a shady character would not paint a fair portrait of Lincoln's development. In determining whether the more obvious or the more obscure facts are most relevant, your own background knowledge of the subject enters the picture. The more you know about the subject, the better you can judge whether a particular writer's selection of facts is fair and representative.

Toward a Synthesis In comparing ideas based on different facts, you may decide that neither writer's set of facts adequately presents the true picture and that fair conclusions should be based on both sets of facts. You would then reject the extreme conclusions of each author and would develop your own *synthesis*—or your conclusion based on a combination of facts. In the conflict over whether or not workers benefited from the Ford wage policy, you might develop the following synthesis: "Although Ford's strict, perhaps meddlesome, regulations hurt some workers who could not or would not fit the company mold, the substantial number of workers who did comply with company regulations benefited by both a higher salary and an improved quality of life."

Different Reasoning In other cases, both writers agree on the facts and make roughly the same selection of facts, but they still disagree on the conclusions to be drawn from the facts. Here, as your criterion for evaluation, you should observe what the writers do with the facts. Both Sward and Nevins, for example, agree on the facts of the riot after the announcement of the wage policy: within a day of the announcement, ten to fifteen thousand unemployed workers gathered outside the factory gates looking for work. After a few days, the crowd turned violent; the rioting ended only after the police turned fire hoses on the men standing outside in the frigid weather. Although both writers agree on these facts, Sward takes the incident as another example that Ford could not have had the workers in mind when he formulated the policy, whereas Nevins simply blames the company's lack of awareness of the large numbers of unemployed people within a short distance of Detroit.

By examining the reasoning process that leads from facts to conclusions, you can determine which writer presents the more careful and logical argument. Sward's argument, in simplest form, is that workers were hurt; therefore, Ford could not have been concerned with the welfare of workers. Such an argument assumes that what a person intends is the same thing that ultimately happens and that events always turn out according to plan. But we all know that things do not always turn out as we intend, that plans go awry.

Even though intentions may be good, the results may be bad. Sward, in order to make his case about Ford's lack of concern, would have to show that Ford was aware ahead of time of the strong possibility that large crowds of unemployed would gather and riot. If Sward could present evidence to this effect and show that Ford still went ahead with his plans, disregarding the potential harm to workers, then his argument would be more convincing. Sward, however, presents no such evidence. Nevins relies on the more reasonable assumption that people do not always have complete control over the consequences of their acts and that sometimes events do not turn out quite as planned. The events were simply the result of a good idea that temporarily grew out of control.

In examining the reasoning behind conclusions, you may in some cases be able to apply the rules of formal syllogistic logic. In other cases you may have to rely on more common sense guidelines, such as the appropriateness of different assumptions to the circumstances. The varieties of logic available to writers and appropriate to different situations will be discussed in greater detail in Chapter 16.

Different Viewpoints   At times you will sense that differences of opinion come from deeper sources than just finite differences of fact or logic. Differences of opinion can arise from basic differences in the way people look at issues. You must already have sensed, for instance, that the disagreement between Sward and Nevins is part of some larger pattern than the detailed differences so far discussed. These deeper, more basic patterns are the subject of the next section. Even where such deeper, more systematic differences exist, you should—insofar as you can—evaluate and resolve specific conflicts of fact or logic. The more specific and precise you can make your evaluation of two conflicting opinions, the more persuasive your analysis and your conclusions will be.

Do Writers Differ in Perceptions?

The disagreement between two writers may be more than a matter of isolated facts and ideas. The disagreement may appear in consistent patterns that you can identify throughout both pieces of writing. Two writers may have such consistently different views that you may wonder whether they are actually discussing the same subject.

Keith Sward's book, *The Legend of Henry Ford,* consistently makes Ford out to be a villain, whereas Allan Nevins's *Ford: The Times, The Man, The Company* presents a complex man of talent and, at times, compassion. How can both books be talking about the same man?

If you examine these large differences, however, you can find a pattern to them. You will learn how different writers come to view the same subject differently, and you should be able to determine which viewpoint is the more accurate—or at least more compatible with your own perspective. The following pages present four types of deep-seated differences. You may discover others when you come to analyze conflicting sources in the course of your own research.

Same Evidence, Different Conclusions

First, after researching a subject and thinking about their research, all writers come to general conclusions about their subjects. These conclusions help them shape the argument of their entire writing on the subject. As you know from your own writing—and as we will explore in the next chapter—your thoughts on a subject help you select and interpret the evidence you find. The entire process of research and writing is in fact an interaction between the thoughts you are developing and the evidence you are amassing.

Once a writer starts to understand a subject in a particular way, the writer wants to share this perception and make as clear and convincing a case for it as possible—without distorting the material. A writer who has studied Ford's life and has come to see Ford as a social innovator who never lost touch with his grassroots origins may pay special attention to Ford's effect on American society and to his down-home opinions. Another writer, of equal integrity and intelligence, may come to understand Ford's distinctive qualities only as business shrewdness blessed with luck. This writer will be especially sensitive to Ford's corporate manipulations and good fortune in being in the right place at the right time.

The best way to evaluate this type of basic difference is to determine which writer has made the better case. A point-by-point comparison of the books will help you judge whose evidence seems convincing, who gives a more complete and balanced view of the facts, and who comes to the more reasonable conclusions from the evidence. When you sum up this point-by-point comparison, you may find that one author has indeed found the better pattern or interpretation. Or you may find that one book seems more accurate and perceptive on some points, whereas the other book makes more sense on other points. Using the evidence and ideas from both books, you may come to a synthesis, such as the following: Ford's shrewdness lay in adopting the innovations of others; although his grassroots attitudes sometimes worked against his business sense, they more frequently led him to make the right business decisions.

The more you know about a subject, the better you will be able to judge whose evidence and conclusions are better. For this reason, if you find basic differences of interpretation between two sources, you should look at additional sources if possible. These third and fourth sources may not provide easy answers, but they will give you a wider background of knowledge on which to base your own judgments.

The Viewpoint of Special Interests

The writing of authors who have a special interest in promoting a predetermined view often betrays a systematic pattern of bias. *Advocacy writing*—that is, writing to support one view and to attack its opposite, rather than to determine the truth of the matter— occurs frequently during political campaigns and in social-conflict situations when two groups clash over rights or power. The commitment to promote the cause at issue may outweigh the commitment to truth. Campaign biographies of candidates for the presidency are notorious for their flattering portrayal of the writer's chosen candidate and their systematic destruction of the opponent. In fact, in 1922 and 1923, when Ford was considering running for the presidency, a number of flattering biographies of him appeared, including *The Truth About Henry Ford* by Sarah T. Bushnell (Reilly and Lee, 1922), *The Amazing Story of Henry Ford* by James M. Miller (M. A. Donahue, 1922), and *Henry Ford: The Man and His Motives* by William R. Stidger (Doran, 1923). At the same time a highly critical pamphlet, *The Real Henry Ford* by E. G. Pipp (Detroit: Pipp's Weekly, 1923), tore into the candidate. Curiously enough, when Ford was no longer running for office and Pipp no longer perceived him as a political threat, Pipp wrote another, more balanced pamphlet, *Henry Ford: Both Sides of Him* (Detroit: Pipp's Weekly, 1926). Political and social issues do much to obscure objectivity.

Once you discover a pattern of advocacy in a piece of writing, you have found the explanation for many differences of fact and opinion compared to other sources, which either advocate a different side of the issue or do not advocate anything. Once you understand the advocacy purpose, you should be extremely cautious about accepting statements of fact and idea at face value from an advocacy source at face value. The arguments made and the facts cited in advocacy literature often do not evolve from deep research and careful thought.

The differences between two opposing pieces of advocacy writing may not provide the basis for an intelligent and careful judgment of the facts and issues but may, rather, present a battle in full swing. Advocacy literature often relies on unsupported assertions and unsubstantiated claims of evidence. Evidence may be distorted or falsified, and the reasoning may be slippery—designed to be immediately appealing and superficially sensible rather than logical and tightly argued. In comparing two conflicting pieces of advocacy writing, you may find large patterns of difference but little substantive material on which to base any evaluation at all.

Nonetheless, some advocacy literature does attempt to present accurate facts and careful reasoning. The writers of such pieces believe, to their credit, that the best way to gain support is by convincing readers of the truth. As a reader, you may gain important information from such sources, but you must be very cautious in weighing what is said against the contentions of other, less interested sources.

Although advocacy sources may not present much objective truth, they are the living documents of actual political and social struggles. By reading the 1984 campaign biographies of Ronald Reagan and Walter Mondale, you may not learn who was truly the better candidate, but you will learn how the candidates wanted themselves presented, what issues they stressed in the campaign, and to what voters they aimed their appeal.

Writers with Different Purposes

Different purposes will lead writers to focus on different facts and to develop different kinds of ideas, as discussed and illustrated in Chapter 6. Different purposes raise different questions for the writer to explore. Although advocacy is the most obvious and transparent kind of purpose, writers have many other purposes that involve fewer temptations to distort facts and warp logic. The differences between writers may simply be the result of the pursuit of different issues. For example, a writer who wants to study some general principle of business management will want to find out how Ford succeeded in business. A writer who wants to study American social history will want to analyze Ford's almost legendary public image during the Model T years. Each writer will come up with very different data and ideas. For the most part, the statements of these two authors will neither agree nor disagree; they will simply draw different lessons from different material. In passing, they may touch on a few shared issues—but only in passing. An analysis of social history will not tell you much about the development of the corporate structure within the Ford Motor Company, but it may give you some clues to why the Model T was such a success at first and why it eventually lost popularity.

Different Views of Life

Finally, writers may differ in fundamental ways of looking at and interpreting life. At times, basic differences in intellectual commitment, religious belief, philosophic outlook, cultural background, and even personality type can lead to different judgments about which data and ideas are most significant, how life is organized, and how human beings act.

A writer who believes in a particular school of psychological analysis may insist that the only way to understand the decisions made by an adult is to examine the basic structure of personality formed in childhood. This writer will pay close attention to any material that deals with the subject's childhood. Such is the case in Anne Jardim's *The First Henry Ford: A Study in Personality and Business Leadership* (Cambridge, Mass.: MIT Press, 1970). On the other hand, an author like Keith Sward, who believes that we can understand an individual's decisions only as part of large economic trends in the entire society, will pay close attention to material on financial interests and business cycles. Each writer will use different facts, ask different questions, interpret by different methods, and reach different conclusions. Jardim offers a psychological interpretation; Sward offers an economic interpretation.

In comparing the writings of two authors who have such basically different outlooks, you may be able to make some judgments about whose evidence is more accurate and complete and whose conclusions are more reasonable. But often the opposing lines of evidence do not intersect at enough specific points to allow such judgments. Examining the economic and psychological theories behind each writer's thinking will probably take more time and knowledge than you have. Of course, as you become more involved in a specific discipline that interests you, you will grow more familiar with the more important theories and approaches that are relevant to it. You may then come to some informed judgments about them. Bear in mind that some theories remain unresolved questions—even among the most knowledgeable. In the end, you may simply have to acknowledge the large differences of interpretation among writers.

Basic Patterns of Thought

By recognizing basic patterns of thought, you may not always discover which is right, but you can usually recognize which assumptions and approaches are close to the ones you can accept. Even more important, you may be able to understand how writers with beliefs that radically differ from yours perceive issues quite differently. Such recognition of basic differences may help you understand ideas you might otherwise reject as useless or absurd. With a broadened perspective, you can view conflicts impartially. Such an impartial overview is needed to understand the dispute that arose from Ford's famous statement that "history is more or less the bunk." Ford saw himself as a pragmatic man, interested in making life better for the average person now. Despite his success, he still counted himself among the common people. He had a rural distrust of journalists, fancy learning, "big shots," and international politics—all of which only made trouble for the ordinary person. When he rejected textbook history, he felt it described only the wars created by kings and queens and forgot the common people who actually fought the wars. Ford believed "official" history did not reflect real day-to-day life; consequently, he never paid much attention to the facts of history.

When Ford made his famous comments on history, the newspapers treated him as a country dolt. The educated people of the time were struggling to create in America an intellectual life to compete with Europe's. They were quick to disown what they considered Ford's ignorant, know-nothing attitudes.

When we consider the dispute impartially, we can see that Ford was far from ignorant about those things he considered important, such as manufacturing automobiles. Given the level of success he had reached, and given the great changes in society that he felt were the result of practical inventions, his practical, anti-intellectual attitude is understandable. At the same time, the journalists and other writers who were concerned about the development of an American intellectual life, felt they were not out to hoodwink the common people with fancy words. Each side advocated different ways to improve American life and perceived the other way as misleading and dangerous. Ford saw the issue as a practical concern for ordinary life versus the empty rhetoric of intellectuals; the journalists saw it as ignorance versus education. Both sides were unable to see the entire picture. With historical perspective, we are able to rise above this dispute to understand the attitudes and perceptions motivating each side.

The remainder of this chapter is devoted to writing assignments that will require you to resolve differences between authors. The first—an analytical comparison between two passages on the same topic—requires you to map out the difficulties of a small but confusing bit of terrain. Whenever you are engaged in any serious problem and find important disagreements between sources, you will need to do this kind of detailed comparative work. Business executives must field conflicting reports and proposals, police officers and social workers receive conflicting accounts of events, and academics encounter conflicting opinions about the truth. All must weigh the alternatives.

The second assignment—a synthesis of what several writers have to say on a subject—gives you the larger challenge of piecing together the best possible account of a complex event. All careers that use any kind of data or knowledge constantly require synthesis; that is, putting the information from a number of sources into a usable, coherent form, whether to give a picture of a company's financial stability or to write a newspaper story.

Writing an Essay of Analytical Comparison

In examining two sources that cover the same subject, you need to do two separate tasks: first, identify the specific agreements and disagreements between the two sources; second, analyze the patterns of agreement and disagreement. The first will let you know how much difference exists between them, and the second will help you resolve these differences. In preparing an *essay of analytical comparison,* the first step has to be completed before the second step is begun, because you must know the differences precisely and explicitly before you can analyze them. In your final version of the paper, the results of the two tasks may be intermixed as part of an overall evaluation of the two sources.

Selecting Two Passages

Unless two matched passages are handed to you by your teacher, you must first select the two pieces of writing that you will compare and analyze. This is no easy task. The passages should be short enough to allow detailed discussion. Often well-matched passages of only a few paragraphs provide enough material for a five- to ten-page discussion. In order to provide sharp comparisons, the passages should have more than a vague similarity; they should cover exactly the same issues within exactly the same limits. (One example would be the development of assembly-line techniques at the Ford company from the time of the introduction of the Model T until 1914.) Moreover, both passages should make directly comparable statements; for example, both should discuss Henry Ford's role in the introduction of assembly-line techniques.

Sometimes you can find short, self-contained selections in two separate versions of a news story published in various newspapers or contemporary affairs magazines. Or you might excerpt matched selections from longer works, such as biographies of Ford or sociological analyses of the role of the car in American life. When you are working with excerpts, your decisions on where to begin and end the selection are crucial. Try to match the subjects, the limits, and the claims of the two passages.

Occasionally, if you find some deeper comparison you wish to make—such as between basic ways of thinking—you may pick two selections that do not appear to resemble each other very much on the surface but do raise a basic issue sharply. For example, if you want to see just how much an economic interpretation of the decline of the Model T differs from a sociological one, you might compare two rather different passages from two rather different books. Such a comparison, however, is difficult, requiring much knowledge of the subject and clarity in defining the issues.

Whether you choose passages that offer many surface comparisons or that join issues on a deeper level, the best passages to select are those you come across in researching a paper for one of your courses.

Rear end of assembly line, Ford Motor Company Highland Park Plant, 1914. (Henry Ford Museum, The Edison Institute)

Then the conflict will be real to you—one whose resolution will clarify some issues of interest and use.

Making Apt Comparisons

Having chosen the two selections, you should try to understand each as fully as possible in its own terms. To do this, you may use any or all of the techniques presented earlier—reading journal, paraphrase, and so on. If you are working with selections from longer works, it usually helps to become familiar with the surrounding contexts as well.

Then identify the specific areas of correspondence between the two passages. For each claim or statement made in the first selection, take note of any corresponding claims in the second. You may keep track of these correspondences by numbering comparable claims of both writers with the same number or by annotating ("see line 24 of other"). Or you may want to compile a comparative chart of correspondences.

As you collect these correspondences, you will already be noticing patterns of agreement and disagreement. Once you have all of them collected, you can organize the various agreements and disagreements according to the categories presented earlier in this chapter. The following chart may be useful to you:

I. Facts
    A. Agreements
        1.
        2.
        3.
    B. Disagreements
        1.
        2.
        3.

II. Ideas
    A. Agreements
        1.
        2.
        3.
    B. Disagreements
        1.
        2.
        3.

III. Basic viewpoints and patterns of thought
    A. Agreements
        1.
        2.
        3.
    B. Disagreements
        1.
        2.
        3.

IV. Conclusions

As you sort out the matching items, you may see patterns start to emerge. For example, the two authors agree that specific events took place but disagree on the dates and order of the events. Or you may find absolute agreement on facts and total disagreement on conclusions. Or you may notice crucial issues on which the two writers turn to entirely different types of evidence. As patterns emerge, you will also gain more insight into the major differences between the writers regarding their purposes and their conclusions. The patterns you discover—of similarities and differences between the sources—will becomes the bases for your essay.

If the pattern is one of basic similarity, you might consider whether shared assumptions, common sources of information, or common purposes lie behind the similarity. If there is a mixed pattern of agreement and disagreement, you might try to determine whether the similarities or dissimilarities dominate—or whether the dissimilarities seem random and minor.

If many major disagreements leave you confused about where the truth lies, you should try to determine which writer presents the more credible or persuasive case. In each instance, you will have to decide what the appropriate criteria are for judging the kind of dispute before you; these criteria were discussed earlier in the chapter.

In the special case of two writers consciously arguing with each other (that is, each knows and discusses the other's views), you may also consider how effectively they argue against each other. Does each one answer the other's objections adequately? Does each successfully confront the other's main points? Or do they talk past each other, avoiding direct confrontations or missing the other's main objections?

You should explore these issues in journal entries, notes, outlines, or other informal ways until you come to some firm conclusions. At that point you are ready to begin writing the rough draft of the final paper.

The Final Essay

The final paper should begin by clearly identifying title, author, and publication information for the two passages being compared. If you are using excerpts of longer pieces, identify precisely where your excerpts begin and end. If the readers of your paper are not likely to be familiar with the material you are discussing, you would do well to include copies of both selections in their entirety as an appendix to the essay.

The introduction to the paper should present, in general terms, the overall pattern that will emerge in your comparison and possibly what you intend to prove about the relative value of the two selections. In other words, you should indicate to the reader where the comparison leads and what kind of analysis you will pursue.

The Body   The body of the paper should present the substance of the agreements and disagreements. You should expose the patterns and analyze the examples you have found. You need not discuss all the details from both selections, but you must use enough specific examples to support your general characterizations. You may refer to details in the two originals by quotation, paraphrase, summary, or line number if you have included copies of the originals. Whatever method you use, accuracy and fairness in representing the originals are particularly important because you will be setting details from two separate sources against each other. If too much gets changed between the originals and the discussion, you may wind up comparing products of your own imagination rather than the actual sources. Notice that, in the sample essay that follows, the information from the sources is integrated into the comparative discussion. Chapter 17 contains a complete discussion of appropriate and accurate reference.

Organization   The development and organization of the paper will, of course, vary with what you have to say. You may want to present the whole pattern of agreement and disagreement first, halting only to fill in representative details, and to follow later with a detailed analysis of underlying causes for the pattern. Or you may want to analyze and evaluate each disagreement as you come to it, and bring together the whole pattern at the end. If the sources describe a series of events, you may want to discuss the points of your comparison chronologically. Or you may find that you can produce a clearer comparison by separating differences of factual evidence from differences of interpretation. For example, you may want to compare the two authors' factual representations of Ford's campaign for president before comparing their interpretations of Ford's motives. Because there is no one best way to organize such a comparison, you should derive your organization from the patterns you have come to identify in the particular material before you.

Comparative Focus   You must take care, however, to keep your focus on *the comparison between the two sources.* Don't fall into the error of simply summarizing the two separate pieces—one after the other—or of just recounting facts about the subject covered in the two sources. Remember that your main subject is the relationship between two pieces of writing. Two techniques of sentence style should help you keep this task in mind. First, whenever you refer to details from one source, repeat the author or the title of the source—and do not continue the example for more than a few lines. For example, by repeating Henry Ford's name as author, you are constantly emphasizing that this is only *his* way of presenting the subject—only *his* claims about the events.

The second technique is to include many sentences that compare two ideas within the same sentence, as in this example: "Although Sward's view that assembly-line techniques developed gradually does not permit him to set a specific date for the 'invention' of the assembly line, Nevins's emphasis on the continuous movement of the main product along the line allows him to point to the installation of a conveyer system in 1913 as the key date." This placing of statements side by side within the same sentence will help you maintain the comparison throughout the essay.

The conclusion of the essay should develop from the issues you have raised in the body of the paper and should sum up the results of your analysis. If it seems appropriate, you might then sum up all the points of comparison to make an overall evaluation of the relative trustworthiness of the two sources. Alternatively, you might observe how two writers, approaching the subject from such different standpoints, come to the same conclusions.

Sample Essay

In the following sample essay, the student Carol Myer starts by indicating a large topic for comparison, but she soon focuses on a more specific aspect of the topic, limiting the actual comparison to only a few pages from each book. Thus she allows her argument to become more detailed and precise. After examining and evaluating specific differences between the two passages, she relates her findings to the general perspectives of the two books. Thus, she ends by analyzing the differences on many levels, while still noting specific, concrete comparisons.

Whose Assembly Line?

The innovative use of the assembly line is one of Henry Ford's main claims to fame, and most of his biographies describe the development of the assembly line in his factory in some detail. In <u>The Legend of Henry Ford</u>, Keith Sward devotes most of a chapter—about twelve pages (32–43)—to the topic. And in <u>Ford: The Times, The Man, The Company</u>, Allan Nevins devotes about sixteen pages to it across two chapters (369–372 and 464–476). Both see the emergence of the assembly line as a gradual process, involving borrowings from other industries and the contributions of many Ford employees. However, Nevins presents Ford as playing a significant role in the development of the idea and the management of a rapidly growing corporation, whereas Sward paints Ford as making no significant contribution, merely taking advantage of the work of others.

The typical differences between the two presentations of the development of the assembly line are revealed in the treatment of one of Ford's employees, Walter E. Flanders, who introduced some innovations into the manufacturing process. The two books disagree over some of the facts of Flanders's employment. They also disagree in their selection of what information to report and in their interpretation of Flanders's role within the Ford management team. The result is that in Nevins's book Flanders appears as a talented part of a talented Ford management, all of whom were involved with improving efficiency in many ways, while in Sward's version Flanders is presented as the main architect of the assembly-line concept.

Sward makes his primary presentation of Flanders's Ford career right at the beginning of the chapter on the assembly line, saying that he was hired in 1908 specifi-

cally to introduce manufacturing techniques for the popular Model T. At that time, Flanders was, according to
Sward, "then recognized as a foremost factory expert"
(32). He was "given a free hand," "turned the Ford factory inside out," and provided "the essentials of scientific mass production" (33). After Flanders left the
company, Ford opened a new plant using Flanders's ideas.

Nevins, on the other hand, has Flanders being hired in
1906 to work on the production of the earlier Model N.
Flanders is mentioned a number of times throughout the
book in various managerial roles (the index has eighteen
separate listings under his name), but his "program of
large-scale planned production" is presented on pages
334–336. Nevins lists several specific improvements
Flanders made, such as in machine alignment and in ordering and keeping track of stock, but he does not treat
these improvements as major turning points in the introduction of the assembly line.

Nevins seems to have the better evidence on both the
actual date of Flanders's hiring and Flanders's actual
contributions. The only source Sward cites is a 1921 magazine article by a Ford engineer, Clarence Avery, on "How
Mass Production Came into Being." Avery, himself involved with the design of certain aspects of the conveyer
belt system (according to Nevins), may have had some personal interest in how he portrayed the story of the innovations. Nevins, on the other hand, had access to all the
company records, which would include employment records,
and he cites in particular letters among Ford, Flanders,
and another executive. Moreover, his account is far more
detailed, recounting specific actions taken by Flanders
rather than settling for generalizations.

These differences of fact relate in two ways to the
interpretation of Flanders's role. First, if he was
hired in 1906 to work on the Model N and thus worked at

Ford for four years before leaving, he appears much more a regular Ford employee, concerned with ongoing managerial problems, than if he were hired in 1908, which makes him appear a short-term consultant brought in specifically to design Model T production. Second, Nevins's specific listing of Flanders's improvements tends to deflate the grandiosity of Sward's generalizations—while still giving Flanders significant credit. Moreover, Flanders's improvements can then be seen in the context of the many managerial and production improvements catalogued throughout Nevins's book.

Nevins also tells an anecdote that increases Ford's personal role in the realization of Flanders's plans, while Sward leaves the episode out, representing Ford as more passively receiving "the best technical advice money could buy" (33). The anecdote concerns a battle between Flanders and another executive, who claimed that the company could not afford to implement Flanders's plans. Ford had to struggle to make a decision over whose advice to follow and then had to go deeply in debt to carry out Flanders's plans. Thus the Ford of Nevins's book is given a major role as a decision maker, whereas the Ford of Sward's book is presented only as an opportunistic capitalist.

These differences seem consistent with the larger patterns in these books concerning both the issue of assembly-line mass production and Ford's general character. Sward constantly wishes to present Ford as a man of little talent who took advantage of the talent of others, whereas Nevins tries to present Ford as a significant decision maker in a complex world to which many people contribute. Not only does Nevins seem to have consistently better evidence, but his vision of the world seems more realistic, neither being unthinkingly anticapitalist nor making a simplistic capitalist hero out of the man.

Sources

Nevins, Allan. <u>Ford: The Times, The Man, The Company</u>. New
     York: Charles Scribner's Sons, 1954.

Sward, Keith. <u>The Legend of Henry Ford</u>. New York: Rine-
     hart & Co., 1948.

Writing Assignments

1. Drawing on a research project you are currently working on for this or another course, select two passages from different sources covering the same topic. Write an analytical comparison of about 500 words—or as long as necessary to cover all the pertinent issues. Your audience is other students doing research in the same area, who will be concerned with the extent of agreement and disagreement between the sources.
2. Excerpt two short passages for analytical comparison from the following three discussions, which all deal with Henry Ford's attempt to intervene in international politics just before the United States entered World War I. Write an analytical comparison of over 500 words. Your audience is your classmates, who by now know something about Henry Ford and something about an analytical comparison of sources.

Henry Ford and Grass Roots America

The role of Henry Ford in American politics in 1916 cannot be evaluated without reference to the "Peace Ship" episode. Although the basic facts in this venture are well known, the significance of these events needs further interpretation.

Henry Ford had grown up in a family that hated violence and war, and it was not surprising that he joined the American Peace Society in the fall of 1915. There he met Rosika Schwimmer, the Hungarian pacifist, in November of that year. Madam Schwimmer believed that any war which ended in a complete military victory for one side would eventually lead to further conflict. Therefore she wanted to stop the European war before the militarists were ready to quit fighting. She urged the establishment of an organization which would provide a forum for continuous mediation of international disputes. Neutral countries could provide this service by calling a conference. When Woodrow Wilson refused to call such a meeting, Madam Schwimmer and other pacifists toured the United States soliciting support for the idea. It was on one of these tours that Madam Schwimmer met Henry Ford, who was eager to help implement some program of direct action. Later in a meeting in New York, the Peace Ship venture was born. A group of delegates would go to Europe as negotiators to offer mediation to the warring parties.

Since the expedition needed passengers, telegrams were addressed to prominent people such as Thomas Edison, William Howard Taft, Luther Burbank, William Jennings Bryan, David Starr Jordan, and Ben Lindsey. Many refused the invitation, but the *Oscar II* pushed away from a Hoboken dock on December 5, 1915, with 83 delegates, 54 reporters, 50 technical advisers, 18 college students, and three photographers—an array which Charles E. Sorensen called the "strangest assortment of living creatures since the voyage of Noah's Ark."

Losing sight of the pilgrims' real mission, journalists stressed the bizarre, such as the prankster who sent two caged squirrels to Ford; the newsmen who organized themselves into the Friendly Sons of St. Vitus, and the cable to Rome to get the blessing of Pope Pius VII, who happened to have died in 983 A.D. Editors tossed off such phrases as "Ford's Folly," the "jitney-peace excursion," and "more innocents abroad." The Boston *Traveler* commented: "It is not Mr. Ford's purpose to make peace. He will assemble it."

During the fourteen-day voyage, morale plummeted. There was a divided reaction to President Wilson's message to Congress on December 7 which called for military preparedness; Henry Ford, the stabilizing influence among the leaders, came down with a cold and spent much of the time in his cabin; and Madam Schwimmer proved rather dictatorial and domineering. When the *Oscar II* reached Oslo, after surviving submarine-infested waters, Ford left the party on December 23 and returned to the United States on the *Bergensfjord.* This gave the impression that *he* was trying to get out of Europe by Christmas. The peace delegation visited Sweden and Denmark, however, and then received permission to cross Germany by train to Holland. A committee for continuous mediation scheduled other meetings in Stockholm and at the Hague. But by January 15 the peace party disbanded, with students and delegates returning to New York.

Obviously the Peace Ship adventure suffered from hasty planning, questionable actions, and a bad press on both sides of the Atlantic. The London *Times* referred to the members of the Ford Mission as faddists, propagandists-socialists, suffragists, and social reformers who tried to turn disgust into approbation. One news item merely announced that the Ford Peace Party arrived in the Hague to hold its meetings in the Zoological Gardens.

Although this mission was vilified in many quarters, the venture is now beginning to be seen in better perspective. The endeavor contained genuine idealism, with a desire to save humanity from war and death. One of the college students who made the trip, Christian A. Sorenson, of Grand Island College in Nebraska, spoke for youth when he gave a speech aboard the *Oscar II*. He warned against making America an armed camp, he opposed military conscription, he decried the wasted bodies on battlefields. Speaking metaphorically, he suggested gathering all the skulls of Europe's dead and building a pyramid a mile square and reaching to the clouds. With a giant pen dipped in the blood of Verdun he would write militarism as a monument to greed and war. He pleaded:

> Let us hear from the wives who will be widows and the young maidens who die of broken hearts. Let us hear from young men in shops and farms who will fall in trenches, there to die like cattle and be burned like piles of rubbish. The English verse puts it aptly; "Damn the army; damn the war. Oh what bloody fools we are."

More recently, Walter Millis saw the ridicule of the Ford Peace Ship as the "undying shame of American journalism." The idea of continuous mediation relied on the concept that the building of a new world depended on how the war ended. If one could read history backward and envision a negotiated peace in 1916 with neither Allies or Central Powers defeated, perhaps the postwar collapse of Europe might have been avoided. Had this occurred, governments might have been spared the forces of Communism, Fascism, and Nazism. Today the concept of continuous mediation lives in the charter of the United Nations. In this sense, Ford and his associates were ahead of the times. Perhaps Ford's expenditure of nearly half a million dollars in behalf of his principles did not represent failure. He could take consolation in the words of Rabbi Joseph Krauskopf of Philadelphia who attacked the critics of Ford in 1915, saying, he would "rather a thousand times be branded a fool in the service of humanity than be hailed a hero for having shed rivers of blood."

—Reynold M. Wik

Henry Ford

From the outbreak, in Europe, of the First World War, Ford had grown increasingly pacifist. His particular kind of success had depended on a free economy impossible in wartime. The interest in the country's development that Model T's exploits had aroused in him was sincere; it was unbearable to him that this progress should be interrupted. He had the aloof contempt that most citizens of what was then an isolationist stronghold felt for European politics. Finally, he had a very genuine hatred of killing in any form and, not having the equipment for the historical analysis of international behavior, the normal performance of an army was, to him, just plain murder.

His opinions were known to several prominent pacifists of the time. David Starr Jordan and Louis Lochner were anxious for the United States to carry on "continuous mediation" in Europe and, when President Wilson was cool to this proposal, they looked for a millionaire to finance a publicity campaign for the project. The Hungarian pacifist Rosika Schwimmer had already gained Ford's ear on the subject and when—after several luncheon meetings, in which Lochner and Mme Schwimmer were joined by Jane Addams, Oswald Garrison Villard, and a number of educators, editors, and clergymen— it was suggested that American delegates to a neutral commission in Europe proceed by special ship, Ford announced that he would finance the expedition.

> If I can be of any service whatever [he said] in helping end this war and keeping America out of it, I shall do it if it costs me every dollar and every friend I have.

He tried, personally, to persuade the President to give the pilgrimage official sanction and, upon Wilson's natural refusal, he released the full story to the press, with appalling results. Whether or not Ford himself made the promise to "get the boys out of the trenches by Christmas," the slogan was roundly ridiculed by the newspapers of the country—especially as November was then already well advanced.

The *Oscar II,* chartered by Ford, was scheduled to sail on December 4. In the weeks before the sailing a corps of stenographers in the Biltmore Hotel in New York who had sent out invitations to the voyage were busy opening declinations. Persons Ford and Mme Schwimmer had counted on sent late regrets: Bryan, Edison, John Burroughs, Ida Tarbell, and others. But the Biltmore suite was besieged, as Mark Sullivan tells, by "star-eyed enthusiasts as well as cranks, fanatics, butters-in and joy-riders of all sorts." And the reporters, the newspaper wags, the cartoonists were everywhere. "It was the answer," Walter Millis writes, "to an editor's prayer," and he adds:

> The famous "Peace Ship" had been launched, to the undying shame of American journalism, upon one vast wave of ridicule.

Other writers have since thought the laughter of the press shameful. Yet at the time, with the widespread pro-Allies feeling following upon the sinking of the *Lusitania* in May, and as some of the incidents of the preparation were unmistakably absurd, the often cruel laughter could hardly have been avoided. The American press is rarely gentle with such naïve idealism.

The *Oscar II* left on the fourth in a chaos that has repeatedly been described as "indescribable," with every sort of comedian on the dock and Henry Ford standing at the rail waving quite seriously and throwing American Beauty roses to the crowd. The whole affair was undoubtedly insulting to our future allies, thousands of whose young men were dying daily in the worst possible conditions of filth and horror. Its planlessness, its hurried, haphazard organization, its execrable publicity have since been thought by many earnest and intelligent pacifists to have put a stop to any possible peace movements later in the war. Yet, in retrospect, there is something deeply moving about the impulses behind it. Twenty-five years later, as William Simonds tells in his biography of Ford, the *Detroit Free Press,* on the December anniversary, said editorially:

> But we do not laugh any more, nor joke, when that unique argosy is mentioned. We mourn rather the disappearance of times when men could still believe in progress in human enlightenment, and thought that even those in the throes of blood lust might be led to reason. . . .
> No peace ship has sailed since the Second World War began. It could find no port either geographically or in the hearts of men.

In the Ford party was one who was strongly opposed to the whole affair. This was a prominent and intelligent clergyman, Dean Marquis, of Detroit's Episcopal cathedral. Marquis, a friend of the Ford family and Mrs. Ford's spiritual adviser, had left the church in order to accept employment in the company. At the request of Mrs. Ford and several of the company's executives he had pleaded with Ford not to go on the Peace Ship. It had been useless, so Marquis went along, hoping to persuade him to leave the pilgrimage and come back as soon as possible. His opportunity came when Ford, drenched by a wave on deck, got a severe cold and was confined to his stateroom. Marquis invaded it and again brought his persuasion to bear.

Until the party landed in Norway, however, Ford was adamant. In Christiania he added to his cold by insisting on walking to the hotel through a snowstorm. Finally, weak and tired, he gave in and admitted to Louis Lochner: "I guess I had better go home to mother. You've got this thing started now and can go along without me."

They went—to Stockholm, Copenhagen, and The Hague—and elected a permanent delegation, which Ford continued to finance until the break with Germany in 1917.

Ford returned to Detroit, where at the moment his company was producing two thousand Model T's a day. Late in the year the millionth Ford car had come off the line. Nothing quite like this production had ever been seen in the industrial history of the world.

—Roger Burlingame

The Legend of Henry Ford

In his first effort as knight errant, Ford ran up the standard of a militant pacifist. His debut in world politics began in the summer of 1915 when the European war was entering its second year. His first skirmishes over the new terrain were purely verbal. They took the form of statements to the press that were studded with passionate denunciations of war. Most of these bristling manifestos were, in reality, the work of Theodore Delavigne, a Detroit newspaper reporter, whom Ford engaged as his pamphleteer and "peace secretary." Issued in the name of his distinguished patron, Delavigne's broadsides were all the more noteworthy in that Ford was swimming upstream. Wall Street had already forged an alliance with France and Britain. Pro-British sentiment was deep-seated in America. The advocates of military preparedness were in the saddle. Against such a combination of social forces, Ford flung himself headlong.

His interviews and statements of 1915 read like socialist handbills. Hot with fervor, they branded Europe's war a capitalists' war. The instigators of the conflict, Ford said, were the money-lenders, the absentee owners and the parasites of Wall Street. At one press conference he exclaimed, "New York wants war, but not the United States." In another broadside he characterized the professional soldier as either "lazy or crazy." On the day that Couzens tendered his resignation at Highland Park, after having broken with Ford over this same issue, Ford released a statement on the causes of war that was the most trenchant thing he had yet uttered on the subject. This time he named names. With consummate scorn he denounced the Morgan firm for sponsoring a half-billion dollar war loan to the Allies. The Anglo-French bankers who were then negotiating with the Morgan syndicate, he said, "ought to be tin-canned out of the country."

Ford proposed a course of action. First, he castigated the war profiteers of America by saying what he would do in the event the conflict abroad were to spread to the United States. Under such conditions, he prophesied, before accepting a single order for cars that might be used for military purposes—even though he were offered three times the normal price—he would burn his factory to the ground. Next he issued a call to "the people" to stop the war by taking things into their own hands. He offered in August 1915 to pledge his entire "life and fortune" to the cause of peace.

Before long Ford's peace plans took more specific form, thanks to the persistence and colorful personality of Rosika Schwimmer, an American feminist of Hungarian origin. Brilliant, handsome and persuasive, Mme. Schwimmer was courting support for a movement to end the European war by mediation. It was her belief, shared by a number of notable colleagues, that the conflict in Europe could be halted through the intervention of a congress of peace delegates drawn from the neutral countries. The mediators whom she hoped to enlist were to convene continuously in some neutral capital until peace terms could be drawn up that would prove acceptable to the belligerents. Before they could hope to win recognition or any official standing, the proponents of the "Schwimmer" plan were well aware of the fact that they would first have to rally popular support in each of the participating neutral nations.

As the ablest and most energetic advocate of this proposal, Mme. Schwimmer went to Detroit in the hopes of enlisting Ford's aid. Her plan and the declarations of her prospective patron had much in common. Both were predicated on direct action and the will of the people. Both hoped to cut through the red tape of diplomacy and to do what no neutral nation either dared or cared to initiate officially. Nothing seemed more fitting to Mme. Schwimmer than an attempt on her part to solicit the support of America's most celebrated and most highly regarded millionaire. In November 1915, therefore, she proceeded to Detroit, determined to see Henry Ford in person.

On the alert, none of Ford's intimates, particularly the secretary Ernest Liebold, would permit any such interview. These social censors could readily identify Mme. Schwimmer as one of the "inadmissibles." The feminist was just about to give up in disgust when Liebold left the city on a business trip. Then she slipped through what remained of the protective cordon, with the aid of a newspaperman. Once admitted to Ford's office, Mme. Schwimmer made the most of her opportunity. She put her case so convincingly that Ford invited her to have lunch at his home the following day. This second engagement fell on November 17, 1915.

At the Dearborn luncheon, not all the guests gave a friendly ear to Mme. Schwimmer's eloquent pleading. Her sketch of the projected Conference of Neutrals struck a responsive chord in her host and in the mind of Louis Lochner, then a Chicago pacifist who had been included in the party, but it did not impress Ford's wife and two other important guests. The principal listeners whom Mme. Schwimmer was unable to sway were two intimates of the Ford family, William Livingstone, a local banker, and the Very Rev. Samuel S. Marquis, then Dean of the Episcopal Cathedral of the city of Detroit. Pulled this way and that in the table conversation, Ford was none too comfortable, Lochner reported later. He was ill at ease and seemed afraid to express any opinions of his own. When he spoke at all he took aim at "a certain banker" who he felt was responsible for the war. To Mme. Schwimmer, herself a Jewess, Ford offered the opinion that "the Jews" were the promulgators of the war. As he dropped this hint, he airily tapped one of his pockets and said he "had the papers" to prove it.

But despite the charged atmosphere of the reception at Dearborn, and despite the vagaries of her host, Mme. Schwimmer carried the day. Her triumph was complete and instantaneous. Ford was so impressed that he rushed pellmell to carry her scheme into execution. At her suggestion he leaped at the idea of financing a "Peace Ship" for the purpose of transporting a delegation of American pacifists to a projected Conference of Neutrals. At the same time he resolved to go direct to the President to solicit for the expedition either official sanction or at least the blessings of the United States Government. Moving with vigor and confidence, Ford left for New York several days later in order to prepare for the coming pilgrimage. Quartered at the Belmont in what a certain New York newspaper soon caricatured as "the nut suite," he chartered a private steamer, the *Oscar II*. Lochner, Mme. Schwimmer and their colleagues, meanwhile, were busy trying to give the *Oscar II* an impressive passenger list.

The quixotic voyage of the *Oscar II* could not have hoped for a favorable press, on any terms. The American economy was already deeply committed to the cause of the Allies. After having floated a $500,000,000 Franco-British loan in the United States, the Morgan firm was acting as purchasing agent for the beneficiaries of this credit. American corporations were about to reap a harvest of war orders. Adroit British publicists were winning American sympathies. Against so powerful a coalition of forces, Ford was now flaunting his wealth as well as his heresy. None of his current utterances was calculated to soften the blows that were about to rain down upon him. Shortly before putting out to sea, he suggested that the soldiers in the trenches should call a general strike. No conscientious objector could have excoriated the cause of war in more vitriolic terms. In a previous statement to the Detroit *News,* Ford had exclaimed, "Do you want to know the cause of war? It is capitalism, greed, the dirty hunger for dollars. Take away the capitalist," he said, "and you will sweep war from the earth."

Taking its bearings from such a compass, the Peace Ship was doomed before it lifted anchor. It set sail, moreover, in the face of an organized campaign of derision for which Ford himself unwittingly supplied the themes. His every gesture served to provoke a press that was only waiting for the kill. To Oswald Garrison Villard, then editor of the New York *Evening Post,* Ford averred, "All you need is a slogan." Villard said, "Yes, Mr. Ford, what kind of a slogan?" "Oh, something like—'We'll get the boys in the trenches home by Christmas.' What do you think of that?" Villard was one of the few editors in New York who was not scoffing at the expedition. He pointed out to Ford that the *Oscar II* was one of the slowest steamers on the Atlantic, and that if the war ended the moment this vessel docked in Europe, the feat of moving 10,000,000 soldiers back to their homes by Christmas would have to be over and done with within a period of nine days. Grateful for Villard's correction, Ford said, "Oh, I hadn't thought of that. Well, we'll make it, we'll get the boys out of the trenches by Christmas."

Sheathed in innocence and self-assurance, Ford blithely set out for Washington to see the President. With Lochner, he arrived in the capital hoping to get an endorsement from the White House. The audience with Wilson was described some years later in *America's Don Quixote,* Lochner's memoirs of the Ford expedition. The President carefully refrained from making any commitments. He was polite but evasive. When his guests were finally dismissed, they left empty-handed. Most of the time, said Lochner, Ford had sat in Wilson's presence, swinging his leg back and forth over the side of an armchair.

Irritated because of the President's noncommittal attitude, he had held his tongue until Lochner and he were alone outside on the steps of the White House. Then in a rage, Ford told his companion what he thought of Wilson. He snapped, "He's a small man."

Graciously rebuffed by the chief executive of the nation, the two men repaired to a theater in Washington for the purpose of addressing a women's peace rally. Here Ford made his second appearance as a public speaker. He managed to get out a single sentence. He said, "I simply want to ask you to remember the slogan, 'Out of the trenches before Christmas, and never go back,' and I thank you for your attention." Flustered by the applause, the manufacturer reddened and retreated to the rear of the stage.

Such artless behavior on Ford's part was rich material for a metropolitan press that was both cynical and pro-British. It was fodder for a merciless effort to make the peace mission sound like comic opera. For purposes of caricaturing the "rich fool" or the "rustic innocent," nothing was handier than Ford's own homely, unaffected speech. It was in the mouth of a rural oaf that hostile reporters at the Belmont put Ford's prophecy that when the war was over, Europe would "grow up as quick as an onion" or his ingenuous remark, "The Lord is with us . . . and we are going to follow the sunbeam right to the end."

Into the hodgepodge of reporting and editorial writing at Ford's expense went every bizarre incident that occurred at the Belmont. This patchwork-quilt of hostility included the reported visit of a woman who offered to contribute what purported to be a patent medicine guaranteed to heal wounded soldiers. Another reporter told of an odd character who wandered into the Belmont headquarters, flippantly greeting its principal occupant as "the champion bug hunter." No journalistic art was required to burlesque what happened when some practical joker forged an invitation from Ford and sent it to Dr. Charles G. Pease, then a notorious anti-nicotine crusader with a penchant for haunting public places and snatching cigars out of people's mouths. Pease never joined the Ford party, but he accepted the fabricated invitation and his acknowledgment was duly reported by the press.

Men of substance added their voices to the chorus of ridicule. Col. Theodore Roosevelt lambasted the peace ship as the "most discreditable" exploit in history. On the floor of the upper house, Senator Thomas of Colorado characterized Ford's delegation as "an aggregation of neurotics." Arthur Vandenberg, then a newspaper editor in Michigan, referred to the *Oscar II* as a "loon ship."

Mocked and pilloried on every side, Ford of necessity lost much of the support which might have graced his expedition with prestige and dignity. Most of the substantial liberals and intellectuals on whom Mme. Schwimmer had been counting, discreetly snubbed an invitation to book passage on the *Oscar II* at Ford's expense. Many distinguished Americans wired their regrets: Jane Addams, Julius Rosenwald, Zona Gale, Charles P. Steinmetz, William Dean Howells, Ida Tarbell, Thomas Mott Osborne, David Starr Jordan, Cardinal Gibbons, Morris Hillquit and Margaret Wilson, the President's daughter. From the roster of outstanding public figures, even Ford's closest friends refused to enlist as co-mediators of peace. John Burroughs, John Wanamaker, Luther Burbank and Thomas Edison respectfully declined Ford's invitation. Not a single college president would come forward, though nearly every one of consequence was invited. Of the forty-eight governors who were sought as guests, only Gov. Hanna of North Dakota saw fit to accept the offer.

On the final passenger list there were, consequently, few names of note. The guests included eighty-three peace delegates drawn somewhat at random from the tiers of the less renowned in public life. Outside of a determined minority, the passengers were by no means even agreed on the object of their undertaking as it had been projected by Mme. Schwimmer. The bulk of the delegates the New York *Times* characterized as "rainbow chasers," "crack-brained dreamers" and "tourists." For full measure, and all at Ford's expense, the formal delegation was accompanied by a body of fellow-travelers: eighteen college students, fifty clerks and technical attachés, and fifty-seven members of the press.

As the *Oscar II* prepared to sail on December 4, 1915, comedy continued to plague her. At the dock someone handed Ford a cage that enclosed within its wrapper two squirrels. Caviling newspaper reporters promptly christened the little animals "Henry F. Acorn" and "William H. Chestnut." When William Jennings Bryan came to see the boat off, he was kissed by an elderly woman who wore white streamers reading "Peace At Any Price." Edison's brief reception was every bit as droll. When the inventor put in an appearance, Lloyd Bingham, an actor and one of the passengers, installed himself on the deck, megaphone in hand, acting as unofficial master of ceremonies. At Bingham's command, the crowd of 10,000 on the pier first honored Ford with a "hip-hip, hooray" salute. The same tribute was repeated for Edison as the cheerleader called out, "Here's the fellow who makes the light for you to see by. Three cheers for Edison." A "hobo" poet and magazine writer who was an accredited member of the press corps boarded ship with his bride-to-be. They were wedded at once in the ship's salon, with the captain of the *Oscar II* officiating at the ceremony. Ford and Bryan signed the certificate of marriage. These solemn rites had to be repeated in mid-ocean because the first ceremony was illegal. The couple's marriage license had been issued by the State of New York and the first union, to which Bryan and Ford attested, had been consummated while the *Oscar II* was still moored at the port of Hoboken, New Jersey.

Still other grotesque events marred the sailing of Ford's vessel. A band concert alternated with hymn singing on shore. As Ford stood quietly acknowledging the cheers of the crowd, a dozen women gathered around him singing "America." When the steamer was a few hundred feet from the pier, Urban J. Ledoux, who chose to call himself "Mr. Zero," dived in after it. When the crew of a river tug fished him out of the Hudson, Ledoux explained that he had only wanted to swim after the *Oscar II* "to ward off torpedoes."

Up to the final moment of embarkation, Ford's wife and advisers tried every expedient at their command to keep the peace ship from sailing under Ford's auspices. Most of the night before he sailed, Ford spent in the company of his friends Livingstone, the banker, and Marquis, the Episcopal dean, both of whom had opposed Mme. Schwimmer's proposals from the start. Imploring their wealthy friend to desert at the last moment, neither of these family intimates had the least success. Unmoved by their appeals, Ford the following morning assigned his power-of-attorney to his son, Edsel, to provide for any emergency that might arise while he himself was at sea. Blocked on land, Mrs. Ford and several frantic Ford executives carried the fight to the Atlantic. They delegated to Marquis the task of weaning Ford from his fellow-travelers while the *Oscar II* was in passage. This practical-minded minister was promptly quartered in the King and Queen's suite of the *Oscar II*. He was to share this space with Ford and with Ford's bodyguard, Ray Dahlinger.

—Keith Sward

Writing a Synthesis
of Sources

The purpose of the *essay of synthesis* is to combine what a number of sources have to say into a coherent overview of the subject. In preparing the synthesis, you have to compare and analyze a number of sources in order to choose between conflicting statements, but the paper presents your final understanding of the subject—not your gropings. If, for example, you wanted to synthesize all that was known about the astronomy of the Aztecs of ancient Mexico, you would have to draw on facts, ideas, and interpretations from a number of different sources about the Aztecs, premodern astronomy, architecture of sun temples, and mythology. Your main focus, however, would be what you discovered about Aztec astronomy—and not the differences among your sources.

In the past, writing the essay of synthesis might have struck you as an easy task, much like the library report you may have done in junior high school. But by now you are much more aware of the problems of fitting multiple sources together in a coherent, consistent way. Not only do sources conflict but also they often omit just the information you are seeking. *You* become very significant at this point. Only you can make the connections between the information provided in different sources. Only you can search out additional sources to fill in the gaps. Only you can assemble the pieces into an intelligent whole. The sources remain quite separate until you bring them together.

In particular, the essay of synthesis will present you with five separate tasks: (1) framing a subject, (2) gathering material from varied sources, (3) fitting the parts together, (4) achieving a synthesis, and (5) unifying the style of presentation.

Framing a Subject

To frame a subject on which there is enough—but not too much—source material, you must find a question, issue, or subject on which a number of people have written, presenting facts and interpretations. But the number of sources should not be so great as to create a confusion of material. In other words, you have to find a limited topic that forms the center for a cluster of writing.

One place to look for such topics is within the structure of different academic disciplines. Each academic discipline is defined by a series of research questions that focus the attention of researchers in that field. For example, in anthropology much investigation centers on determining social roles within different societies. By selecting one type of society and one social role—such as the role of the shaman in American Indian tribes—you can define a cluster of research materials with which to work.

Sometimes a dispute over a controversial theory may excite much interest and lead to a flurry of new publications in support of one theory or the other. For example, much geological writing in the late 1960s argued for or against the controversial idea of continental drift. At other times a discovery or an invention may affect the work of many scholars and scientists, so that much new writing centers on the meaning of the discovery or the consequences of the invention. A major new discovery may have widespread consequences for an entire discipline. Such, for example, was the enormous effect of the discovery of the structure of DNA on all biological studies. Thus, within academic subjects, you can look for clusters of sources around topics defined by the structure of the field, around controversial theories, or around new discoveries and inventions.

In more popular writing, such as newspapers, general circulation magazines, and general nonfiction books, you can often find clusters of interest around social problems (juvenile delinquency in the 1950s or inflation in the 1970s), major historical figures and events (Abraham Lincoln or Pearl Harbor), social institutions (changes in the nuclear family), trends and fads (toga parties), or matters of political and public debate (the merits of national health insurance). In such areas of public interest and excitement, the different pieces of writing may not fit together in such clear-cut ways as they do in more organized academic disciplines. By sorting out the ways in which these different sources do relate to one another, you will find out much about the different attitudes behind the public interest.

Gathering Material from Varied Sources

Since you are trying to gather a composite view of the subject, you need to go beyond the most obvious sources for your topic and draw on the information and insights of a number of different viewpoints. If, for example, you are interested in what TV programming was like in the mid-1960s, you will get only a very limited view if you rely totally on the program descriptions in *TV Guide*. However, in an article in one of the old issues you may find mention of some criticism of TV quality. If you then follow up by finding out who these critics were and what their complaints were, you might discover the large public debate set off by Newton Minnow's remark that TV programming was a "vast wasteland." And you might also be led to find out about the movement that resulted in the Public Broadcast System. *One source will lead you to another* until you get many different ways of looking at the topic.

Fitting the Parts Together

If you find conflicting statements among sources, you need to judge which is the most reliable, according to the methods and criteria presented earlier in this chapter. A more frequent problem results when sources do not have any easily compared points—either of agreement or of disagreement. So it will be up to you to discover these correspondences. You may have to point out the relationship between the broad theoretical statement of one writer and the details of a case study by another. Or you may have to make explicit an indirect connection between two separate sources. Or you may have to identify a pattern that shows the similarity between the viewpoints of two articles.

The connection between facts and interpretations has been discussed throughout this chapter. In the final writing of your synthesis, you must explain these connections to your readers. To make the connection clear to someone who may have not recognized it before, transitions between sections are extremely useful. A transitional phrase or sentence, describing the connection between one idea and the next, can tie together seemingly diverse material, fill in gaps, and put the facts and ideas in sensible relationship. A careful writer will help the reader follow all the steps of his or her presentation.

Achieving a Synthesis

At this stage, you must add up all the information to discover significant patterns and to come to conclusions. These patterns and conclusions will be the shaping forces behind your organization of the final synthesis. You cannot simply rely on the patterns and the conclusions of your sources, for the limitations of purpose of each source determine the organization and ideas of that piece of writing. You are combining material from several sources—and you may well be broadening the scope of the subject—so your own conclusions and organization will necessarily take on a new shape.

Informal and formal outlines are, as always, useful as attempts to make coherent sense of all your journal notes and annotations. By trying different outlines, you can see in which way the information fits together best. As you approach a satisfactory outline integrating the ideas and information from the sources, you will be able to formulate an overview of the subject. A direct statement describing this overview—tying together the various parts of your synthesis— can serve as a thesis statement for your paper.

Unifying the Style

Unifying the writing style while remaining true to the sources will be your final task. Because the sources you use have their own separate purposes, the material in each may be presented in very different ways—from numerical statistics to anecdotes to highly detailed analyses. When you bring together such varying material, you must present all materials in a way that is consistent with the overall design of your paper, the *synthesis*. For example, if you are collecting information on the effects of the Supreme Court's Bakke decision, you may be drawing on a wide variety of materials: statistical charts of college enrollments by ethnic background, direct comments on the decision by college admissions officers, general policy statements by college boards of trustees, straight news reports, and analyses by journalists. You must bring together all these different kinds of writing into a single readable whole. Instead of copying an entire statistical table—with much unnecessary material— you must pull out the most relevant statistics and explain their bearing on your topic. You cannot simply string together the statements of college officials; you must rather bring out the official positions and hidden attitudes behind them. In other words, you must translate the separate kinds of language used in the various sources into a uniform style appropriate to your synthesis.

Even though you will often need to rephrase and rearrange the material from the original sources, you must be careful not to distort the original meanings. When you pull out only selected statistics and explain their meaning, you must be careful not to leave out other important statistics that might give rise to conflicting interpretations. In summarizing the argument of a newspaper column, you should not leave out so much of the context that the article appears to say something it could not possibly have meant. Chapter 17 gives more specific advice on how to present the ideas of other writers as part of your own coherent argument—without distorting the original meanings. Chapter 17 also covers the various methods for documenting the sources of your information. In a synthesis you must document your sources fully and carefully so that the reader can judge the credibility of your material.

An Example: A Violent Week

Each time you have to synthesize material from a number of sources— whether as a separate *essay of synthesis* or as part of some larger project—the tasks just described will appear in varying guises. Each time you will have to find different ways to handle them, so the advice we have given should serve as only the most general guidelines. The following sample paper, entitled "Protest and Violence," shows the way one student solved these problems in one particular case.

The assignment was to characterize any single social trend that took place in 1968 during a period of about a week. To do this, the student was to synthesize magazine and newspaper articles written during the specific week that she had selected. Because everyone in the class was doing the same task for a different week within that year, the papers combined to form a social history of the period, which all the students then read as background for their future research.

Dianne Pari found the focus for her paper in the violence that erupted out of the social protest movements of late March and early April 1968. Once she had found her theme, she was able to select a few relevant sources out of the immense number of newspaper and magazine articles on that subject. She interpreted the different instances of violent activities as examples of different responses by protestors and government officials to the same event. She was thus able to show a connection between many different incidents and the contrasting attitudes reflected in them. She was even able to fit in a campaign article by a political candidate, which on the surface seems quite dissimilar to the reports of incidents that provided the bulk of her sources. In the introduction to each section, she was careful to link one part with the next and to reassert the main focus of the paper.

All the varied material adds up to support her main synthesis: during the ten-day period, expression of dissent "led to increasing confrontation and violence." Although she uses several different kinds of sources, she maintains a consistent expository style to present her overall vision of the pattern of events. The reader never doubts that she is in control of her sources.

The documentation follows the Modern Language Association recommendations for endnote style.

Sample Essay

Protest and Violence

The decade of the 1960s was a period when the young people of this nation expressed their political and so—

cial ideas through public protest. They made their voices heard demanding an end to racial segregation, an end to the war in Vietnam, and a new concern for the environment. Desiring rapid change, they stated their demands in radical ways. The controversies caused by these radical demands led to increasing confrontation and violence. The ten days from March 28, 1968, to April 6, 1968, were a time when the violence was reaching its peak.

The period began with peaceful intentions of protest as Martin Luther King prepared a march in Memphis, Tennessee. The demonstration on March 28 was to protest a garbage strike that affected the black population of the city—but not the white. The Reverend Martin Luther King believed in nonviolence and intended to lead his 4500 followers in a peaceful march; however, a band of radical young blacks, calling themselves the Invaders, infiltrated the parade and began throwing stones and glass. The police reacted, made mass arrests, and shot a sixteen-year-old boy to death. Rioting followed, and the Memphis National Guard had to be called in to enforce a curfew.[1]

This escalation of peaceful protest into violent confrontation distressed the entire nation. President Lyndon B. Johnson's reaction was typical of the despairing hopes of most people: "The tragic events in Memphis yesterday remind us of the grave peril rioting poses. This nation must seek change within the rule of law in an environment of social order. Rioting, violence, and repression can only divide our people."[2]

The sad cycle of demonstration, violence, repression, and division recurred in a smaller incident involving a white radical group called the Yippies. Three thousand Yippies were on their way to a celebration of spring in New York City's Central Park when a few became violent as they passed through Grand Central Station. Arrests followed and the demonstration was broken up. Because the Yippies were already planning a similar gathering to be held in Chicago at the time of the Democratic National Convention in August, this incident increased police fears that the Chicago gathering would turn into an ugly confrontation.[3]

In an atmosphere of confrontation and violence, unexplained incidents appear frightening. On March 29, four large fires were set at Chicago department stores, Carson Pirie and Scott, Montgomery Ward, Wieboldt's, and Goldblatt's.[4] The next day suspicious fires or unexploded fire bombs were discovered in four major New York department stores (Bloomingdale's, Klein's, Macy's, and Gimbels'). At the same time, two other store fires were reported in Chicago. Although all these fires were suspicious, no direct evidence of conspiracy appeared, and no radical group was implicated.[5]

Violence seemed uncontainable. President Johnson decided that the only way he could bring peace to a divided country was to end the war in Vietnam. On the evening of March 31, he announced in a TV speech that he was halting all bombing raids on North Vietnam and calling for negotiations to end the war. In order to keep the peace negotiations out of politics, he announced that he would not run for re-election.[6]

National unity was not that easy to regain. On April 4, Martin Luther King was murdered in Memphis.[7] In reaction, a wave of violent rioting swept the cities of this country. Looting, arson, and general civil disorder tore apart Memphis, Chicago, Detroit, Boston, and Washington. The week ended with the National Guard patrolling American cities.[8]

Even out of such destruction and disorder, some good came about. Within a week, the Civil Rights Act of 1968,

ending racial discrimination in housing, was passed by
Congress and signed by the president.[9] A small bit of
justice was born out of great injustice. In addition some
members of the establishment were making themselves
available to the radicals and were trying to encourage
young people to involve themselves in organized politics. Senator Eugene McCarthy, running for the Democratic nomination for the presidency, wrote that he
placed great faith in the youth of this country. He
called them a "concerned generation" that, despite their
"exotic hairdos and occasionally eccentric behavior,"
demonstrated a deep moral concern.[10] He believed that
their rebellion came from "their sense of social commitment and their urge for involvement."[11]

During those few days of March and April 1968, this
"urge for involvement" led to violent conflicts that
seemed to be moving beyond control. It was a time when
young people were expressing their ideas actively—no
matter what the consequences.

Notes

[1]"Memphis Blues," <u>Time</u> 5 April 1968: 25.

[2]Max Frankel, "President Offers U.S. Aid on Riots,"
<u>New York Times</u> 30 March 1968: 30.

[3]"The Politics of Yip," <u>Time</u> 5 April 1968: 61.

[4]"Chicagoans Flee 4 Fires in Loop," <u>New York Times</u> 30
March 1968: 1.

[5]Murray Schumach, "Fires Set in Bloomingdale's and
Klein's," <u>New York Times</u> 31 March 1968: 1.

[6]Tom Wicker, "Johnson Says He Won't Run; Halts North
Vietnam Raids; Bids Hanoi Join Peace Moves," <u>New York
Times</u> 1 April 1968: 1.

[7] Earl Caldwell, "Martin Luther Is Slain in Memphis," New York Times 5 April 1968: 1.

[8] Ben A. Franklin, "Army Troops in Capital As Negroes Riot; Guard Sent to Chicago, Detroit, Boston," New York Times 6 April 1968: 1.

[9] "Opening the Doors," Time 19 April 1968: 20.

[10] Eugene McCarthy, "Opinion: On the Concerned Generation," Mademoiselle April 1968: 98.

[11] McCarthy, 98.

Writing Assignments

1. Write an *essay of synthesis* of about 800 words characterizing the social trends mentioned in print during one week out of the last fifty years. Use material from newspapers, news magazines, and at least one other kind of periodical. All members of the class should choose weeks within the same year, so that they will be informed readers of one another's papers.

2. Choose a minor historical event or a short period in the life of a famous person. Find what four reputable sources say on the subject and write a narrative combining the information. Imagine your reader to be a high school student with a strong interest in history.

3. Choose a news story that is currently breaking. Taking your information from several newspapers and magazines, write a narrative of the events as they might appear in a year-end summary of major news events. Direct your paper to a college-educated audience.

10 Writing the
Research Paper

The research paper is an original essay presenting your ideas in response to information found in library sources. As you gather research material, your ever-increasing knowledge of a topic will allow you to make informed judgments and original interpretations. At each stage of research, you will have a more complete idea of what you have already found and what you are still looking for. Midway through the process, the writing tasks of creating a review of the literature and a proposal will help you focus the direction of your research. This chapter addresses both the technical skills of finding and recording information and the intellectual skills of understanding the material, developing original ideas, and making informed judgments.

Your Ideas and the
Library's Information

Writing a research paper is a process of interaction between the materials you find in printed sources and the ideas you develop in yourself. Your ideas lead you to search out additional materials, and these new-found materials lead you to new ideas. Throughout this process, it is you who decides what materials you need, discovers the connections between different pieces of information, evaluates the information, frames the questions you will answer, and comes to original conclusions. Before you begin, you cannot know what you will find or what your conclusions will be; but as you proceed, your emerging sense of direction will give shape to the entire project.

In order to gain information and to discover other writers' thoughts on your subject, you will have to become acquainted with how material is arranged in libraries. Library classification systems, card catalogs, periodical indexes and abstracts, computer data banks, and similar information retrieval systems will tell you whether information is located on library shelves or on microfilm reels. But only your own growing knowledge of the subject can tell you what information is useful and how that information relates to questions you are raising. The secret to library research is to remember that the organization of material in books, journals, and reference documents differs from the new organization of facts and ideas that you will eventually achieve by your own thinking on the subject.

Writing an essay based on library sources takes time. You will spend time finding sources; you will spend additional time reading these sources and taking notes. Even more time will be required for your thinking to go through many stages: you will need to identify subjects, raise questions, develop a focus, formulate and reformulate ideas on the basis of new information, come to understand the subject, and reach conclusions. The vision of what your paper should cover will only gradually emerge in your mind. You will find your subject not in any book or card catalog but only in your own thoughts—and only after you have begun to investigate what the library books have to offer.

This chapter will present the typical stages you will pass through in preparing an original library research essay—that is, an essay in which you develop your own thoughts based on library research materials. The purpose of these stages is to isolate some of the complex tasks that go into the assignment and to allow you to focus on each skill one at a time. In reality, these stages are not so clearly separable. Everyone has an individual way of working, and the development of each essay follows a different course. To give an idea of the way the various stages interact in the development of one particular paper, I will describe how one student developed the ideas for a rescarch essay assigned in a writing course.

First Step: Finding
a Direction

Before you can do any research, you must set yourself a direction—a general area to investigate. That direction can, and probably will, change with time and knowledge—at the least it will become more specific and focused. But with the first step, as the cliché goes, begins the journey.

How can you set that first direction?

Interest Your Reader

The immediate context in which you are writing the paper provides one set of clues. If you are writing the research paper as part of an academic course, the issues raised in class and the particulars of the assignment given by the teacher establish the direction. If the teacher gives a detailed sheet of instructions defining the major research assignment, these instructions will suggest specific kinds of topics.

In addition to the appropriate topic and the stated expectations of the teacher, you should also consider the intended audience as part of the context. In some courses the teacher is the only reader; that teacher, already well informed about the topic you choose, may read your paper to judge how well you have grasped what you have learned and how well you express your understanding of the material. In this case, you would be wise to choose a topic in which you can demonstrate just such mastery. At other times the teacher, still the only audience, may request papers on topics with which he or she has only limited familiarity. In another class, the teacher may ask you to imagine yourself a practicing scholar writing for a well-informed professional community; your classmates may in fact be your primary audience—the community to which you report back your findings. Careful consideration of which topics might interest each of these audiences may help you choose an initial direction.

Interest Yourself

You should also look into yourself and into the materials to help you choose a general area of research. If you choose an area in which you already have some background knowledge, you will have some insight into the meaning and importance of the new materials you find. Some acquaintance with a subject will also give you a headstart in identifying useful sources. Even more important, if you already have an interest in the subject, you will have more motivation to learn and understand the subject in depth. If your interest in the subject makes you feel your questions are worth answering, that conviction will carry across to your eventual readers. On the other hand, if you pick a subject that is tedious to you from the start, not only will you probably drag your heels in doing the research, but also you will have a hard time convincing your readers that reading your paper is worth their time.

As you search for topics that will interest your audience and yourself, you must check to see whether enough of the right kinds of materials are available to make the topic possible. If there is too little information—if you have to use every scrap available—you will have no flexibility or selectivity in the development of your essay. You need a larger stock of information than you will finally use, so that you can select, focus, interpret, and consolidate the material in a new way. On the other hand, if material appears plentiful, the task of wading through all the relevant documents will require careful planning and strategy so that you can identify the most useful sources and use your time efficiently. You should also be careful about choosing topics that have already been treated from every conceivable angle. Unless you are remarkably ingenious, you may wind up only parroting the extensive work already done.

Two Quick Checks

Two types of preliminary checks will help you get a sense of how large your topic is. First, you should find an *overview of the subject* to read. A short, clearly written book, an article synthesizing current knowledge in a nontechnical journal, or an article in a specialized encyclopedia can give you—without too much investment of time— a sense of the range and possibilities of the subject. You will also start to see the difficult areas you may run into as your research develops.

Second, you should make a *preliminary search of your library.* By looking under the most obvious subject headings in the card catalog, in any specialized bibliographies, in periodical indexes, and in the indexes of microform materials, you can rapidly survey how much material is available on the subject. From the titles listed, you may also get some idea of the approaches taken in the various sources. These bibliographic library tools are discussed in detail on pages 277–282.

One Student's Progress

As an example of how one student developed the ideas and information for a research paper, we will follow the progress of Mark Green, a freshman interested in both politics and technology, through each stage of his work. The teacher stipulated only that the topic of the research paper had to grow out of some issue or event of 1957, a year chosen by the class after some preliminary investigation. The audience for the paper was to be the other members of the class, all of whom were simultaneously becoming expert in other topics relevant to 1957. The assigned length of the paper was ten typed, double-spaced pages, or approximately 2,500 words. The teacher assigned the paper two months before it was due, so students could pursue the research gradually while they did their other work for the semester. Smaller interim assignments based on the same research materials would also help the students develop their information and ideas for the large project.

From the class's preliminary research into the year 1957, Green knew that the Soviet Union launched the first artificial satellite then. Since he already knew from history class that this event had both political and technological significance, he decided to look further into the topic of space exploration. When the teacher assigned a smaller paper synthesizing a week's events (see Chapter 9, pages 266–270), he chose the week of the launching of the Russian satellite called *Sputnik.* From reading the week's newspapers and magazines, he noticed that the launching seemed to take the Americans by surprise. The big question on everyone's mind was "How did the Russians do it before we did?" Of course, no one had a definitive answer during that first week; there were only confusion and accusations from the Americans and propaganda claims from the Russians. Green thought he would try to answer that question from today's perspective.

He looked in the card catalog in the college library under *astronautics* and *artificial satellites.* He found, to his dismay, many books describing and analyzing both the American and the Soviet space programs. The books were written from all perspectives—from the official Soviet and NASA (the United States space agency) accounts of their programs' successes to critiques of the programs, pointing out the weaknesses, failings, and fraud on either side. The books, moreover, were written throughout the last twenty-five years, from 1957 up to the present. A quick scan of a few books convinced him that the question was still not resolved: people were still arguing all sides of the issue of who had achieved the most in space and why. Not only did he feel that he could add little to the already substantial debate, but he also suspected that crucial information was locked away in the files of both governments. Nonetheless, because these books contained much information about the background and development of the early space probes, he made a record of the books he looked at and took some of them home to make notes on.

Dejected at the loss of his first research question, Green was still sure the general topic of Sputnik would have something to offer. The technical problems of launching an earth satellite interested him, but on this issue most of the books agreed and presented pretty much the same material. Again Green judged that he could add little to the published discussion. Then he remembered all those articles he read for the week's synthesis. Clearly the launching of Sputnik had political and propaganda importance; newspapers devoted much space to the international reaction to the launching. This reaction surely would provide much original source material to discuss. After checking out the *New York Times Index* and *The Readers' Guide to Periodical Literature* for 1957 and 1958 under the subject headings *astronautics* and *artificial satellites,* respectively, he was doubly sure. Mixed in with the many, many articles on the technical aspects of the satellites, he found a substantial, but manageable, number dealing with the political reaction.

Finding the Needed
Information

Because even the smaller libraries have more material than users can locate by memory, librarians have devised various techniques for filing documents and for helping you find the information you need. A description of the more common information storage and retrieval devices follows, but don't forget that each library has its own selection of techniques.

Whenever you begin work in an unfamiliar library, take a few minutes to read any orientation pamphlets or signs prepared by the local librarian. Furthermore, do not hesitate to bring specific research problems to the reference librarian, who will know the special resources of the particular library as well as more general information-finding techniques. The more specifically you can define your research problem to the librarian, the more exact and creative solutions he or she can suggest. Although you will be working in your college library most frequently, you should also acquaint yourself with other libraries in your region, particularly those that have specialized collections in areas that interest you.

Locating the Sources You Want

The problem of finding materials in the library falls into two parts: you must discover what materials you want to examine, and you must find where in the library these materials are stored. The second task is easier, so we will discuss it first.

If you already know either the author or the title of a particular work—whether book, article, government publication, or other document—the various catalogs in the library will let you know whether the library has it and, if so, where and how it is stored. The main card catalog lists all books alphabetically in several places: under author, under title, and under one or more subject areas. Each entry card contains extensive bibliographic and descriptive information, as in the sample that follows. The most important piece of information is the *shelf* or *call number,* which is usually listed in the upper left corner of the card. This number tells you where you can find the item on the library's shelves.

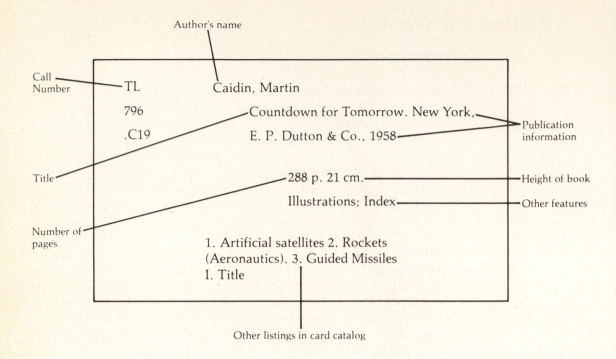

Author's name

Call Number

TL
796
.C19

Caidin, Martin

Countdown for Tomorrow. New York,

E. P. Dutton & Co., 1958

Publication information

Title

288 p. 21 cm.

Height of book

Illustrations; Index

Other features

Number of pages

1. Artificial satellites 2. Rockets (Aeronautics). 3. Guided Missiles I. Title

Other listings in card catalog

Library of Congress System   The call number on the sample card—TL796.C19—is from the Library of Congress Classification System, now used in most larger libraries in this country. In this system the first letter indicates the main category, and the second letter a major subdivision. The additional numbers and letters indicate further subdivisions. The main categories of the Library of Congress System are as follows:

A   General Works (such as general encyclopedias, almanacs)
B   Philosophy; Psychology; Religion
C   Auxiliary sciences of history (such as archeology, heraldry)
D   History: General and Old World
E   History: America (general)
F   History: America (local, Canada, Mexico, South America)
G   Geography; Anthropology; Recreation.
H   Social Sciences
J   Political Science

K Law

L Education

M Music

N Fine Arts

P Language and Literature

Q Science

R Medicine

S Agriculture

T Technology

U Military Science

V Naval Science

Z Bibliography and Library Science

Dewey Decimal System Smaller libraries tend to use the Dewey Decimal Classification System, based on a simpler and less differentiated all-numerical classification. The major categories are as follows:

000 General works

100 Philosoply and related disciplines

200 Religion

300 Social sciences

400 Language

500 Pure sciences

600 Technology

700 The arts

800 Literature

900 Geography and history

Some old and large libraries, such as the New York Public Library Research Collection, have their own numerical systems, which do not indicate any systematic subject classification but rather reflect the order in which the documents were received.

Serials File Some libraries list entries for newspapers, magazines, and other periodicals in a separate *serials file*. This file will list which issues of the periodical are available and whether the issues are loose, bound, or microform. The serials file entry will also give reference letters or call numbers, where appropriate. Because the serials listings offer only the titles and issues of the periodicals—and not the authors and titles of specific articles—you will usually have to consult the appropriate *periodical index* to find out exactly where and when any particular article appeared. You will usually also need to consult a specialized index to locate a government publication or any microform material. Each library offers a different selection of the many available indexes; some of the more common are in the following list.

Indexes to General Circulation Periodicals
Readers' Guide to Periodical Literature
Public Affairs Information Service
Humanities Index
Social Sciences Index
General Science Index

Indexes to Newspapers
New York Times Index
The Times Index (London)
Wall Street Journal Index
Washington Post Index

Indexes to Government Publications
Monthly Catalog of U.S. Government Publications
American Statistics Index

Indexes to Specialized Journals
Humanities

Art Index
Index to Art Periodicals
Film Literature Index
International Guide to Classical Studies
International Bibliography of Historical Sciences
Analecta Linguistica
MLA International Bibliography
Index to Little Magazines

Music Article Index
Popular Music Periodical Index
Index to Religious Periodical Literature
Philosopher's Index
Humanities Citation Index

Social Sciences

Anthropological Index
Accountants' Index
Business Periodicals Index
Criminology Index
Population Index
International Bibliography of Economics
Education Index
British Education Index
Current Index to Journals in Education
Resources in Education
International Bibliography of Political Science
Environment Index
Psychological Abstracts
Sociological Abstracts
International Bibliography of Sociology
Index to Current Urban Documents
Women Studies Abstracts
Social Sciences Citation Index

Sciences

Biological and Agricultural Index
Biological Abstracts
BioResearch Index
Chemical Abstracts
Computer and Control Abstracts
Bibliography and Index of Geology
Hospital Literature Index

Hospital Abstracts
Index Medicus
Physics Abstracts
Science Citation Index

Once you have the journal and the issue containing the article you want, you must return to the serials file to get the shelf number. Then you can locate the issue, microfilm, or bound volume on the library shelf. In some larger libraries you may not be allowed to fetch the materials directly from the shelves; instead you must file a request slip and an attendant will get the material for you. This closed stack system, though it makes it harder for you to browse, does allow librarians to maintain order in complex collections.

Pursuing Leads

The more difficult problem is to know what material you want in the first place. More ingenuity, imagination, and dogged persistence are involved than the simple following of procedures. The procedures suggested below can only serve as starting points that may lead you in many false directions before they lead you to a few good ones. You will probably have to look through much material before you find the few items that are directly relevant to your search.

Subject Headings   The first place to look is under the subject headings in the catalogs, indexes, and bibliographies we have described. Almost all are either arranged or cross-indexed according to subject. The trick is to find the right subject heading, because each topic can be described in many ways—and the catalogs and bibliographies have only a limited number of subject headings.

If you have trouble locating an appropriate subject heading, you may find the publication *Subject Headings Used in the Dictionary Catalogs of the Library of Congress* useful. Most libraries follow its system of headings. Sometimes you may have to try several different terms to describe your subject before you hit on the one used in the card catalog or in a periodical index. Sometimes merely rearranging the terms of a long subject heading may be enough to help you find the listings. For example, the subject of social aspects of American science would be phrased in a card catalog as "Science—Social aspects—United States."

Computer Search Increasingly, research libraries have access to computerized data bases that allow a researcher to search rapidly extensive bibliographies in most fields, including the natural and social sciences, humanities, law, medicine, business, engineering, and public affairs. Among data bases now available are *Biological Abstracts, Chemical Abstracts, Index Medicus, Magazine Index, Management Contents, National Newspaper Index, Physics Abstracts, Psychological Abstracts, Public Affairs Information Service, Resources in Education, Science Citation Index,* and *Social Science Citation Index.* Each record (or reference) provides complete bibliographical information (author, title, and publication information) plus, in most cases, an abstract and a list of descriptors—similar to subject headings (see the illustration on page 284). Computerized data bases have been compiled only in recent years, so you should be aware that you will usually not be able to retrieve bibliographical information much earlier than 1970. A few data bases begin in the 1960s.

The descriptors identify the main subjects covered in the article and are generally used to retrieve the reference from the data base. Because research in many fields changes rapidly, new descriptive terms are constantly needed. The currently used descriptors for each data base are usually listed in a special thesaurus for each data base. For example, the ERIC—the Educational Resources Information Center—system provides a frequently revised list of subject headings in *The Thesaurus of ERIC Descriptors.*

The secret to success in computer searches is to find the right descriptors and to combine them in an appropriate search strategy. First you must identify those descriptors that are likely to appear in articles you are interested in. Sometimes these will match the obvious subjects of your research, but sometimes the thesaurus will refer you to a synonym or other related word.

Once you have identified likely terms, you ask the computer to find out how many listings it has under one of them. You may find only a few listings or far too many. At this point the search strategy becomes important. You need to find the right combination of descriptors that will pull out all the articles you want without pulling out many you do not want. If a descriptor identifies too few listings, you might try to use additional terms, adding the files together. If a descriptor provides too many listings, you might instruct the computer to pull only those files that contain particular combinations of descriptors. For example, a search of the *National Newspaper Index* revealed 453 articles concerned with the space shuttle and 7,344 concerned with budget, but only 3 articles covered both of those concerns.

```
select space(w)shuttle and budget
             701  SPACE(W)SHUTTLE
            8584  BUDGET
      10      3  SPACE(W)SHUTTLE AND BUDGET
? t10/5/1-3
10/5/1
598938   DATABASE: NNI File 111
  Snags in shuttle schedule blamed on tight budget.
  Harsch, Jonathan
  Christian Science Monitor   v75  p22  March 30  1983
  CODEN: CSMOBF
  col 1   025 col in.
  illustration; photograph
  EDITION: Wed
  DESCRIPTORS:    aeronautics   and   state-economic  aspects;   space
shuttles-finance;   United   States.   National   Aeronautics   and   Space
Administration-finance; Challenger (space shuttle)-costs


10/5/2
598142   DATABASE: NNI File 111
  Tracing cracks in Challenger's engines to cuts in NASA's budget.
  Harsch, Jonathan
  Christian Science Monitor   v75  p3  March 7  1983
  CODEN: CSMOBF
  col 1   015 col in.
  EDITION: Mon
  DESCRIPTORS:    United    States.    National    Aeronautics   and   Space
Administration-appropriations   and   expenditures;   Challenger   (space
shuttle)-accidents, etc.; space shuttles-economic aspects


10/5/3
0176161   DATABASE: NNI File 111
  Carter budget refuels space shuttle effort; energy,  defense also winners
as support for 'R&D' resurges.
  Yemma, John
  Christian Science Monitor   v72  p1  Jan 30  1980
  CODEN: CSMOBF
  col 3   021 col in.
  EDITION: Wed
  GEOGRAPHIC LOCATION: Washington
  SIC CODE: 9311
  DESCRIPTORS:  budget-United States;  government spending policy-economic
aspects; research-United States; fiscal policy-United States; expenditures,
public-forecasts

? logoff
          7Jun84 14:11:23 User1927
    $9.91  0.118 Hrs File111 9 Descriptors
    $0.71  Uninet
    $1.20  12 Types
   $11.82  Estimated Total Cost



LOGOFF 14:11:25


*u012 000 disconnected at request of host
```

As you develop your strategy, you should test it out before asking the computer to provide the complete file or list. By looking at the first five items on the list, you can see if you are getting the kind of material you want. If not, you can adjust your strategy accordingly. If, for example, you find that about half the titles are useful, but the rest fall into one or two easily identified categories, such as articles in Russian or articles written before the events you are interested in, you can ask the machine to leave out articles in Russian or those published before a specific date. If you have difficulty finding the right descriptors or combination of them, you can call for the record of an author or specific article you know that handles the subject; then you can use the descriptors listed in that file.

In developing your search strategy, remember that the computer search can be a tremendous tool, turning up many useful references very rapidly. But without a correct strategy, your computer search will simply be a very expensive waste of time.

Newspaper Search   Because only a few of the major newspapers are fully indexed, you may need to begin your subject search with a newspaper that is, such as the *New York Times* or the *Washington Post*. Once you have identified the days when news stories appeared in the indexed papers, you can check those dates—and a few days forward and backward—in unindexed newspapers.

One Book Leads to Another

These first subject searches will give you an entry into the topic, but they will probably not provide all the material you will eventually need. Much of what you find will not be directly relevant to your interests, and you'll return these volumes to the shelves after a few moments of skimming. The material that you do find relevant probably won't tell the full story and may only serve to lead you to further material.

At this point, you need real ingenuity—to let the material you have already found lead you to more material.

First, one book or article can lead you to another through the references cited by the author. In footnotes, bibliographies, and passing mentions, authors indicate the work of other authors on which their own work is based. If you find a particular book or article important for your topic, probably the earlier sources it refers to will also be of some importance. Just because footnotes and bibliographies are sometimes in small print and tucked away in the back, don't ignore them. Sometimes the most fruitful thing a book yields is the title of another book that turns out to give you just the information you were looking for.

In your search, you should also develop the skill of selective browsing. If you find a few books on your subject clustered around a particular shelf number, browsing through nearby shelves—both before and after the shelf number—may help you turn up some related items. Similarly, if you find a particular journal that has published several articles over a short period of time dealing with your topic, skimming the tables of contents of earlier and later years may turn up a choice find.

After reading a few sources, you may discover that one or two scholars have written the major studies on which most other researchers have based their work. If this is the case, you may be able to locate other sources by finding out which other researchers have referred to these seminal writers. The *Science Citation Index, Social Science Citation Index,* and *Humanities Citation Index* will direct you to articles in professional journals that cite any particular earlier book or article by seminal writers. (The listings are arranged according to the work cited.)

Because each source teaches you more and more about your subject, you will be able to judge with ever-increasing precision the usefulness and value of any prospective source. In other words, the more you know about the subject, the more precisely you can identify what you must still find out. You will also become better aware of what other secondary subjects you need to investigate as background. As you move into your research, you will know more specific topics, key terms, and major figures. You can then return to the subject headings of the indexes, catalogs, and bibliographies for another round of more precise searching for sources. At some point, of course, you will have to stop looking and decide that you have enough information. But that decision is a story for later in this chapter.

Record Keeping

Throughout the long process of gathering raw material, you will need to keep track of specific sources, much varied information, and your developing reactions and ideas. While working on shorter papers based on just a few sources, you may be able to keep all the materials on the desk in front of you and store all your thoughts in your mind. But as research projects grow bigger and more complex, haphazard methods of record keeping lead to loss of materials, to loss of valuable ideas, and to general confusion.

Listing Sources   First, you need to keep careful account of the sources you use, not only because you will have to document them in the final paper but also because you may want to refer to one or another—for a piece of information you later realize is valuable. Depending on the size of the project and your own habits, you may record the sources on a continuous list or on separate index cards. The separate cards have these advantages: they allow you to sort out sources according to topic and to alphabetize the list for the bibliography; they also allow you to pull out individual titles to take with you to the library.

Whatever form the list takes, it should include (1) all the information you need to write the documentation for the paper, (2) all the information you need to locate the item in the library, and (3) enough of a description so that you will be able to remember what kind of work each source is. Book documentation requires

author(s)—full name
book title
publication information—city (state), publisher, year

Periodical documentation requires

author(s)—full name
article title
title of periodical
specific issue by date (or volume number)
inclusive pages

Other materials may require slightly different information. For detailed instructions, see pages 490–504.

To be able to relocate the information, you should record the library—or other place you found the material—and the shelf number. To help you remember the kind of information in the book, you should add a few descriptive and evaluative phrases.

On another list or another set of cards, you can keep track of sources you have not yet examined—promising leads from footnotes and bibliographies. Be sure to record any data that may help you locate a potential source. In addition to specific titles, you can record your future plans: types of information you still need and possible sources you might look into. For example, as Mark Green started to probe the reaction to Sputnik, he became aware of the significance of Russian propaganda attempts to influence international events. He then made a note to "check out Khrushchev's speeches and interviews to see how he uses Sputnik and missiles."

Maintaining a list of potential leads and sources gives you a sense of the direction in which your research is going, and you can organize the work ahead of you.

Note Taking   You must, of course, keep track of the relevant information you find in the sources by taking some kind of notes. The most precise form of note is an exact quotation. Whenever you suspect that you may later wish to quote the writer's exact words, make sure you copy the quotation correctly. And whenever you decide to copy exact words down in your notes—even if only a passing phrase—make sure you enclose them in *quotation marks*. In this way you can avoid inadvertent plagiarism when you are working from your notes.

Paraphrase, summary, and outline offer more selective forms of note taking than straight quotation. You can record only the most relevant information, and you can focus on giving your reader the essential ideas from the source rather than the author's complete argument. In each case, make sure your notes accurately reflect the meaning of the original, even though you are using your own words. In taking notes from any one source, you may use each of these forms of note taking—depending on how directly the passage bears on your subject. Again, if you borrow a phrase or even a key word from the original, identify it as original wording by quotation marks.

Early Notes   In the early stages of your research, before you have a specific idea of your final topic, you should record a wide range of information—even though you will not use all of it. In this way, you should not have to return to the source to pick up some useful data or detail that you ignored the first time around. As your topic gains focus, you may become more selective. In the last stages of research, you may simply be interested in a single fact to fill a gap in your argument.

Whatever form your notes take, be sure to keep an accurate record of where each piece of information comes from. Since you should be keeping a separate complete list of sources, you need

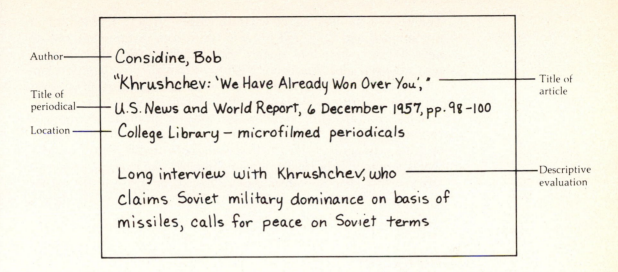

Author —————— Considine, Bob

"Khrushchev: 'We Have Already Won Over You'," ————— Title of article

Title of periodical —— U.S. News and World Report, 6 December 1957, pp. 98-100

Location ——————— College Library – microfilmed periodicals

Long interview with Khrushchev, who ————— Descriptive evaluation
claims Soviet military dominance on basis of
missiles, calls for peace on Soviet terms

only identify the source in your notes by a key word from the title followed by a specific page reference.

An easy—but potentially dangerous—way to retain information from sources is to keep the sources on hand, either by borrowing books from the library or by making photocopies. The danger in keeping the original or photocopy is that, once you have the information at home, you may never look at it until you begin writing the paper. In order for the information to be incorporated into your thinking on the subject, it has to be in your mind—not just on your desk.

The process of understanding the relationships among the many ideas that you read requires that you make sense of each bit of information as you discover it. If you own a particularly useful book or have made a photocopy of pertinent pages, you should read and annotate the material at the time you find it. By staying on top of the reading, you will think about the material at the proper time, and you will have complete, well-organized notes when you are ready to gather together all your information for the paper.

Notes on Your Own Reactions   Finally, you need to keep track of your own developing thoughts on the subject. Your thoughts will range from specific evaluations of particular sources, to redefinitions of your topic, to emerging conclusions that may become the thesis of your final paper. Hold on to these thoughts, however tentative.

They cover the essence of what you have already learned about the subject, and they will provide the direction for what you do next. What at first may seem a minor curious idea may develop into a central idea. Recording your own thoughts as they develop, you will discover the seeds of the internal organization of your material, and this new organization will make your paper original.

While you are still searching for sources, periodic attempts to restate your subject, to develop an outline, and even to write tentative opening paragraphs—long before you are actually ready to write the paper—will help you focus your thinking. The *proposal,* discussed later in this chapter, offers a more formal opportunity to gather your thoughts and to focus your direction.

Closing in
on the Subject

After reading on a subject for a time, you become familiar with both the subject itself and the writing on the subject. Both types of knowledge should help you define your specific approach to further research. Knowledge of the subject itself lets you know what issues exist and which issues are important. While becoming increasingly familiar with your subject, you gain substantive material on which to base your thinking. Simultaneously, your knowledge of the prior writing, or the *literature* on the subject, lets you know which issues have been fully discussed and which have not. In addition to helping you evaluate the early information you have come across, a study of the literature helps you sort out what kinds of data are available, what biases exist in the writing, what purposes other writers have had, and what areas of agreement exist between sources.

After several days or weeks of research, you may find that the questions that interest you have already been fully discussed in the literature. Or you may find—quite to the contrary—that no previous writer has had exactly your interest in the subject. You will also learn whether the available literature can provide you with enough information to pursue the questions that interest you. By seeing what approaches other writers have taken, you may discover a new approach to the subject that will lead to original questions. A study of the literature also may give rise to questions about why other writers have treated the subject in the way they have.

After this overview of both the literature and the subject, you are ready to choose a more specific direction for your research. The questions that you want to work on and that have promising sources will become more evident. Your research questions will help you decide what new information you need to locate and what kinds of sources you still need to seek out.

Finding Patterns and Making Sense

Mark Green's progress on his research into the political reaction to the launching of Sputnik illustrates how increasing knowledge of a subject helps you continually narrow your research direction because the material suggests certain interpretations and raises specific issues. As Green started looking carefully at the government response, he discovered that, although Congress seemed upset, President Eisenhower at first seemed to consider the launching of a space satellite a minor issue, of propaganda value only. After an initial comment, Eisenhower and his administration remained silent until he made two speeches a month later, admitting that U.S. space research needed more attention. Then it took another two months for him to present a concrete program.

It seemed strange that it took so long for the president to take the issue seriously. One source suggested that the time delay was just part of a large organizational problem in the Eisenhower administration. Green considered exploring the command structure and internal organization of Eisenhower's government, but he realized this would get him too far from his subject.

However, he did notice that, at about the time Eisenhower announced his new science policy, a number of other positive events occurred, including finally a successful U.S. launch of a satellite. Morale, as expressed in newspaper and magazine commentary, also started to look up. Within a few months, Congress passed education and research legislation that set the stage for the great American scientific advances of the next two decades. Green sensed that Americans felt they were bouncing back after that initial shock of Soviet success.

Another Side of the Story

He went back to see how bad a shock the launching of Sputnik was, looking this time at how Russia was taking advantage of the achievement. What he found was a well-planned propaganda cam-

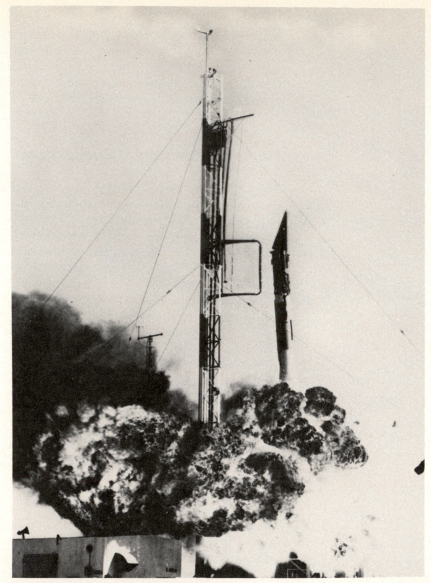

U.S. Navy Vanguard Launch Vehicle exploding on pad during unsuccessful launch attempt, December 6, 1957.

paign directed at undermining world support for the United States and forcing the United States into unfavorable negotiations. At this point all the events started making sense. By embarrassing the United States, the Soviet Union forced the United States to enter into a space race. It took a while for the United States to turn from confusion and embarrassment to more positive action, but when it did, it established the basis for a long-lived and successful program.

As Green started to understand the pattern of reaction, several other thoughts occurred to him. In an indirect way it seemed as though he had achieved an answer to his initial question of why the United States was beaten: the United States did not see space research as a clear commitment until this terrible embarrassment. Then he began to recognize certain parallels to today's situation, where scientific research, including space research, no longer seems a major government commitment and where some people are afraid that Japan might overtake us in several areas, especially computer research and development. He knew that the comparison with today could not be one of his major topics (that would require a whole new set of research and might double the length of the paper). Nonetheless, he found the parallels interesting to think about, and he thought he might be able to work them into the introduction and/or the conclusion.

Formalizing the Topic

Somewhere in the middle of your research—once you have a solid feel for what information is available—your attention should shift from what has already been said about the subject to the questions you set for yourself. Are any answers in sight? Your mind will be turning from other writers' statements to your own gradually forming ideas.

At this point you are ready to formalize the final topic of the project through a review of the literature and a proposal. The *review of the literature* sketches in the sources and background of your project; the *proposal* specifies the nature of your anticipated contribution to the subject. These two short pieces of writing help clarify the direction and the purpose of the research in your own mind, and they will reveal your research plans to others who might be able to give you useful advice—classmates, teachers, thesis supervisors, or research committees. These people may provide titles of valuable sources that you may not have come across. Or they may suggest ways to focus your thinking and research even more.

The Review of the Literature

The *review of the literature* surveys the available writing on a subject, indicating the patterns of current thought that the researcher has discovered. The review of a particular topic usually includes short summaries of the major pieces of literature and even shorter characterizations of less important material. The review also covers the connection or lack of connection among the various works in the literature.

In writing a review of the literature, cluster the discussion of similar books and articles. Explain as explicitly as possible the similarities within each cluster and the differences between clusters. Note such patterns as historical changes in thinking or conflicts between opposing groups of scientists. All the major opinions you have come across should be represented in the review. In this manner you will both organize the literature for your own purposes and demonstrate to the readers of the review that you are familiar with most of the material on your subject.

In some academic disciplines, the review of the literature may stand as an independent piece of writing, both at undergraduate and more advanced levels. In these disciplines, the literature may be so technical and may require so much detailed study that simply gaining a grasp of it is enough of a task for any student at any one time. Thus teachers in the sciences and the social sciences may assign reviews of literature on specific topics to familiarize their students with the most recent professional findings. Active scholars may write reviews of the literature for professional journals to keep their colleagues informed on proliferating research. When the review stands as a separate piece of writing, it may be quite extensive—upwards of twenty pages—and deal with the major sources in some detail.

Even the separate review of literature, in the long run, is in the service of new, original research. In the case of the undergraduate in a technical discipline, such original research may be postponed until the student gains a wider range of skills and concepts necessary to make a contribution at current levels of work. The review of the literature is a way of making the student aware of that level. In the case of practicing researchers, the professional review of the literature provides the starting point for future work by themselves or their colleagues.

When written as the introduction to a proposal for original research, the review of the literature can be concise, stressing the broad outlines of information available rather than revealing all the important details. The review serves as a background and a justification for the proposal.

Sometimes a review of the literature is needed as part of the final research paper or report on an experiment. In this case, the writer should be highly selective, raising only those issues and presenting only those findings that readers will need in order to understand the new work that follows.

The Proposal

The *proposal* states how you intend to build on, fill in, answer, or extend the literature you have just reviewed. In other words, the proposal should define a task that will result in something different from what has already been written. The proposal should also indicate how you intend to accomplish the task and your best estimate of the kinds of results you expect.

Identifying an Original Task   The setting of an original task for yourself in the proposal will lead to a final essay that goes beyond what others have written. Sometimes you may apply new information to an old question. Applying modern psychological theories to existing biographical facts may lead to an entirely new view of some notable person's work—for example, a re-evaluation of Emily Dickinson or Woodrow Wilson. Or newly reported data about crime in urban areas may be helpful in re-evaluating long-standing theories about the relationship between crime and unemployment.

You may take a new approach to a long-standing controversy. You may realize, for example, that one new approach to the question of whether TV has hurt children's reading skills is to compare the best-selling children's books before and after the advent of TV. None of the information or the basic question is new, but your new slant will lead to fresh answers.

You may also find an entirely new question to ask. This alternative is particularly attractive when you are at some distance in time from the other writers on the issue. The distance often results in seeing the subject from a different perspective—and that different perspective leads to new issues. For example, during the early sixties, most discussions on armaments in this country focused on immediate questions of practical defense, such as whether we were ahead of the Russians in the arms race or whether we had an adequate deterrent. Looking back on that period now, you will no longer be so caught up in the practical issues. You might ask whether the level of international fear during that period led to a special relationship between the U.S. government and the defense industry. By asking entirely new questions, you can examine the earlier source material and develop whole new lines of investigation.

In your preliminary research, you may also have discovered important areas of your subject that have been neglected or only half-explored. This is how Mark Green zeroed in on the final topic for his paper. Removed by twenty-five years from the panic over Sputnik that dominated most of his primary sources, he was able to discern a political pattern that he did not find discussed in any depth elsewhere. All the earlier writers were too caught up in the ongoing events to gain the kind of historical perspective that Green's research enabled him to adopt.

Practical Considerations   However you develop an original task for your paper, you need to keep in mind the limits of the resources available to you—in terms of both source materials and your own level of skills. From your review of the literature, you should be able to recognize the topics that would be extremely difficult to handle because of lack of substantive information. For example, any discussion about the Viking contact with native Americans would probably be very speculative and very short, for the simple reason that so little conclusive evidence remains. Similarly, if you are a student taking an introductory survey of psychology, you would be wise not to propose an entirely new theory of schizophrenia. A more limited task—the application of one existing theory to several published case histories—would allow you range for original thought but not overburden you with a task beyond your present skills.

Implementing Your Task   Having set yourself an appropriate original task, you need to explain in your proposal how you are going to accomplish it. This means indicating the sources you know you will use and the additional information you still need to seek out. If the additional information is to come from library sources, you should indicate what sources seem promising. If you need to conduct a survey, an interview, or an experiment—provided, of course, that it is appropriate to the course and possible within the assigned time—you should describe the precise purpose and the methods. You should also indicate the kinds of analyses you will apply to the findings you generate. At some point, you should indicate the general organization of your final argument. Thus the proposal will reveal all the issues you will deal with and all the means you will employ to accomplish your task.

Even though you have not yet completed your research, you should by now have some idea of the kinds of answers you are likely to find. These emerging answers will serve as tentative hypotheses, which you can evaluate as you gather and organize your evidence. These emerging answers will focus your thinking and lead you to consider the final shape of the paper.

Finally, you should discuss your interest in, or the importance of, the subject as defined in your proposal—to convince the reader (and possibly yourself) that the subject is indeed worthwhile. The more clearly you understand the value of your work, the more focused and motivated your work will be.

Sample Review of Literature

Review of the Literature on the American
Reaction to the Sputnik Launching

The Russian launching of Sputnik I on October 4, 1957, began the space race, but although the United States almost immediately felt the defeat, some months passed before it started to meet the challenge. The literature relevant to the U.S. reaction to Sputnik includes (1) some general background books placing Sputnik I within the larger history of rocketry, the space race, and the cold war; (2) the news reports of several launchings and attempted launchings and the immediate responses of public figures and various governments; (3) the more developed and changing political responses to be found in interviews and speeches; and (4) the contemporary analysis from political magazines and editorials.

The histories of the space programs are told from a number of perspectives that affect the account. Some, such as Project Satellite and From Vinland to Mars, treat the exploration of space as a great adventure of discovery. Thus they dwell on the accomplishments of all nations equally and tend to focus on the technical accomplishments and the substantial discoveries. In such books Sputnik is treated simply as part of the advance of

human knowledge. Other books present the accomplishments
of one nation in a partisan fashion. Some are official
government accounts such as NASA's <u>Chariots for Apollo</u>
or the official Soviet account, <u>Russians in Space</u>. Some,
though unofficial, take the same perspective, including
<u>The Future of the U.S. Space Program</u> and <u>Space Frontier</u>
from the American perspective and <u>Red Star in Orbit</u> and
<u>Soviets in Space</u> from the Soviet. These versions treat
only half the story and often dwell on the development of
agencies as well as scientific accomplishments. Sputnik
is treated very fully in the Soviet accounts, but not in
the American. On the other hand, the American versions present the development of the American Vanguard and Explorer programs as well as the early history of American
rocketry. Finally there are the histories written from a
kind of critical perspective, either as a critique of
America's failure to keep up, such as <u>Countdown for To-
morrow</u>, or as an investigation of Soviet policy and intentions, such as <u>The Rise and Fall of the Space Age</u> and
<u>The Soviet Space Bluff</u>. All these histories except the
critical ones are of only limited use to my topic, providing more institutional and technical background than
discussion of politics and political reactions.

Two books I have found place the space race and Sputnik
within the political context of the cold war. <u>A New History of the Cold War</u> tells the story from a Marxist perspective, blaming the United States for aggressive intentions. <u>Brainpower for the Cold War</u> is more pro-
American, concerning America's defensive attempts to
protect herself from an aggressive Soviet Union. In the
first, the United States is held weak by its failure to
be the first into space, whereas the latter focuses on
how the United States overcame the humiliation. Both
contain much important information about the political
struggle and political reactions to the space research.

The actual events of the Russian and American launchings are covered in much greater detail in the news reports in the New York Times and the news magazines Newsweek, Time, and U.S. News and World Report. There is much
duplication among their various accounts. The daily reports in the New York Times for several days following
each launch are most complete, both in technical information and in reactions from individuals and government
officials. The Times also reports reactions from the
press of other nations.

In interviews, news conferences, and speeches reported in newspapers and news magazines, President Eisenhower and First Secretary Khrushchev gave more complete reactions with obvious political intentions of
demonstrating strength and gaining political advantage.
Such items are useful to analyze as political moves. They
include interviews with Khrushchev in the New York Times
on October 8 and in Newsweek in the December 6 issue and
Eisenhower's speeches of November 6 and 13, his press
conference of October 9, and his State of the Union message the following January.

Finally there are the commentary, editorials, and
criticism of the American press, which I have sampled by
looking at the liberal magazines The Nation and the New
Republic and the conservative magazine the National Review. All three, curiously, were critical of Eisenhower's failure of leadership throughout most of this
period.

Sources

Brooks, Courtney G., James M. Grimwood, and Lloyd S.
    Swenson. Chariots for Apollo. Washington, D.C.: Na-
    tional Aeronautics and Space Administration, 1979.

Caidan, Martin. <u>Countdown for Tomorrow</u>. New York: E. P. Dutton, 1958.

Clowse, Barbara. <u>Brainpower for the Cold War</u>. Farmingdale, N.Y.: Greenwood Press, 1981.

Diamond, Edwin. <u>The Rise and Fall of the Space Age</u>. Garden City, N.Y.: Doubleday and Co., 1964.

Gatland, Kenneth W., ed. <u>Project Satellite</u>. New York: British Book Centre, 1958.

Gibney, Frank, and George J. Feldman. <u>The Reluctant Space-Farers</u>. New York: New American Library, 1965.

Lewis, Richard S. <u>From Vinland to Mars</u>. New York: Quadrangle, 1976.

Levine, Arthur L. <u>The Future of the U.S. Space Program</u>. New York: Praeger, 1975.

Lukacs, John. <u>A New History of the Cold War</u>. New York: Anchor Books, 1966.

<u>Nation</u>

<u>National Review</u>

<u>New Republic</u>

<u>New York Times</u>

<u>Newsweek</u>

Oberg, James E. <u>Red Star in Orbit</u>. New York: Random House, 1981.

Riabchikov, Evgeny. <u>Russians in Space</u>. Garden City, N.Y.: Doubleday and Co., 1971.

Smolders, Peter. <u>Soviets in Space</u>. New York: Taplinger Publishing Co., 1974.

<u>Time Magazine</u>

<u>U.S. News and World Report</u>

Vladimirov, Leonid. <u>The Soviet Space Bluff</u>. New York: Dial Press, 1973.

von Braun, Wernher. <u>Space Frontier</u>, new edition. New York: Holt, Rinehart and Winston, 1971.

Sample Proposal

Proposal

The early achievements and failures of the Soviet Union and the United States in orbiting artificial satellites have been well documented, as has the development of rocketry and space science. The space race has also been subjected to political interpretations as part of the larger cold war between the two superpowers. Even the early embarrassment of the United States by the Soviet launching of Sputnik I has been frequently told. However, I have not found the politics of those early moments of the space race discussed in detail, when the United States was facing its embarrassment. I propose to examine the mood and actions of the United States from the time of the launching of Sputnik I until the U.S. space program gained some momentum and had some success.

My research shows that, although the United States did have a satellite program, it was not well organized or a high government priority. It took the shock of embarrassment by the Soviet Union to get the Eisenhower administration and the country seriously committed to creating a strong space program. Even then the government seemed slow to act, as though it took a while for the impact of our defeat to sink in, particularly as Russia kept gaining more and more propaganda advantage through her successes.

Although I will be presenting this political process against the framework of the events of space launchings, the larger part of my paper will focus on political actions and reactions. I hope to show how Americans, particularly the Eisenhower administration, moved from confusion to a strong commitment to space research. One source relevant to this discussion that I still need to

look into is Eisenhower's memoirs, to see whether he reveals anything about his thinking during this period.

In addition, for my introduction and conclusion I may
want to draw some comparisons to today. Currently the Reagan administration seems to be weakening the government's commitment to space and other scientific research, even though other countries, especially Japan,
seem to be challenging our leadership in some branches of
science and technology. In order to get some facts to
back up these parallels, I will have to find some recent
news reports on the subject, probably through the New
York Times Index.

Such parallels point out the importance of my research
topic, for it tells more than the story of one key moment
in the recent history of our country and its technology.
It shows how our country reacts or does not react to scientific challenges and how, sometimes, even our military
defense depends on a broader approach to scientific
research.

Completing the Research

The proposal limits the research tasks remaining. The specific issues
outlined in it define the amount and type of information you still
need to find. In the course of completing the research, you may
find a few new leads, but you need to pursue them only if the new
information seems essential to an intelligent response to the issues.
One of the skills of doing research is knowing when you have
enough information. In considering too many side issues or too
many perspectives, you may lose the main thread of your subject.
A well-conceived proposal will, in most cases, mark the boundaries
of your task.

As the last few pieces of information fill in the picture, it is time to test specific ways of piecing the information together. The final shape of the paper may come to you in different ways, depending on your temperament, your habits, and the subject. This is the time for heavy use of scrap paper for jotting down your ideas, associations, trial sentences, and outlines. Some specific techniques that you may find useful follow:

- Write trial thesis sentences.
  What does all this information lead to?
  What are you trying to say in this paper?
- Write trial introductions.
  Where does the subject begin?
  How does it relate to other issues?
  What will interest your readers about this subject?
  How can you get the main argument of the paper moving?
- Make sketchy outlines.
  What are the main points?
  How do they fit together and in what order?
  How do they lead to your conclusion?
  How do the details of the research support your ideas?
- Phrase difficult ideas.
  How do you state your key points?
  Will certain ways of phrasing your ideas bring them more into focus?
- Let your thoughts flow freely in journal entries.
  What is your relationship to your readers?
  What will they want to know about the subject?
  What do you want them to find out?
  What will they find difficult or controversial?
- Make idealized outlines.
  Putting aside specific research material you have found, what are the main ideas you want to get across?
  What subordinate points do you need to make to support your main ideas?
  What would be the most effective organization of this idealized argument?
  How does your actual research material relate to this ideal paper?

Although you may not use any of these trial attempts directly in the final paper, each attempt will help you evolve the kinds of language, reasoning, and organization you will eventually use.

Outlining the

Argument

On shorter, less complex papers, a few organizational notes may be enough to fix the structure of the argument in your mind before you begin writing, but research papers are usually too long and too complex to organize by haphazard methods. An essay of anywhere from five to twenty or more pages, incorporating a range of ideas and information from many sources, requires conscious, careful planning. Preparing a full outline will let you think over your plans, consider them from several perspectives, and revise them accordingly.

The outline places in schematic form the main topic and issues you will discuss in the paper and arranges the subtopics and specifics underneath the major statements. It is the bare bones, the skeleton, of the paper you will write. As such, you should neither take it lightly nor arrange the material in a mechanical, automatic fashion. Rather you should consider what are the essentials of what you want to convey and what will be the most effective arrangement of the material.

The outline is your way of putting the subject together. Your major statements and the arrangement of them, although built out of your reading of sources, should *not* resemble the pattern of any source. If you borrow the skeleton of someone else's work, it will look like that earlier piece of work, no matter how you flesh it out. But because you have consulted many sources—and compared, evaluated, and synthesized them—your vision of the subject will not resemble anyone else's: your outline will be the result of a long line of original inquiry.

Actually, you may want to prepare an outline at any one of several stages of the research project. At each stage the outline serves a different function. Toward the end of the research period, as suggested earlier, you can make an *idealized outline* to help you determine whether your research material is adequate to the argument you have in mind. If not, you can either supplement your research or refocus your argument.

After you complete the research, but before you write a first draft, you should prepare a *working outline* to figure out the order and relationship of all the material. Then, as you actually write the paper, you can modify the working outline to solve problems, to take advantage of opportunities, or to develop ideas that you discover in the process of writing. If the organization of your paper changes significantly as you write the rough draft, you may wish to make a *draft outline* to make sure that the paper does hang together and makes the kind of argument you want it to make.

Finally, you can make a *formal outline* of the completed paper. Your teacher should let you know whether a formal outline must be submitted with the clean copy of your paper. The formal outline demonstrates to the teacher that your argument is well structured and can help guide the reader through your reasoning and evidence.

Usually you do not need to write all these levels of outlines for any one project. You can choose among them, depending on the nature of the project and your personal preferences. You should, however, outline at least once in the course of writing the paper to ensure a well-organized, coherent, purposeful argument.

You are probably familiar with the mechanics of the outline. At the top is a thesis statement, a statement that the entire paper argues for and supports. Listed underneath the thesis are the major statements that support or subdivide that thesis; these major statements are identified by Roman numerals. In turn, each major statement is supported or subdivided into secondary statements, which are listed beneath it and identified by upper-case letters. This subdivision continues as long as the material warrants, the smaller units being marked successively by arabic numerals, lower-case letters, numerals in parentheses, and letters in parentheses. Successive indentations visually separate the main points from the minor ones. Schematically, this is the framework of your outline:

Thesis statement
 I. First major statement
    A. Secondary statement
       1. Supporting claim
          a. Specific evidence
          b. Specific evidence
          c. Specific evidence
       2. Supporting claim
          a. Specific evidence
          b. Specific evidence
             (1) Example
             (2) Example
       3. Supporting claim
       4. Supporting claim
    B. Secondary statement . . .
 II. Second major statement
    A. . . .

Usually the major divisions will present ideas or generalized material. The smaller divisions will cover details, evidence, or references to supporting source material.

As a convenience in preparation for the final writing stage, you may want to cross-reference your notes to the numbers on the outline. In preparing the outline, you will also discover whether you need to seek out a few additional pieces of information to complete your argument.

The importance of the outline is that it forces you to arrange your thoughts in some order and then to think that arrangement over. As you outline and revise the outline, you should keep the following points in mind:

- *Support your thesis.*
  Does every part of the outline relate directly to the thesis by presenting your case, explaining an idea, or filling in *necessary* background?
  Do all the entries add up to a convincing argument for the claim you make in your thesis?
  Is the thesis broad enough to encompass all the important issues in your topic?
- *Clarify the order and relationship of the major points.*
  Are the statements in the most logical or effective order?
  Does one statement lead to the next?
  Does the argument maintain a consistent direction—or does it backtrack or even contradict itself?
- *Establish the relationship of major and minor statements.*
  Does each group of subheadings adequately develop the major heading?
  Does each piece of specific evidence have a clear relationship to some larger claim you are making?
- *Establish your task in the introduction.*
  Does the introduction show your awareness of the prior writing on the subject?
  Is a review of the literature necessary—to fill in the reader on background?
  Does the introduction raise the major issue you will discuss in the paper?
  Does it reveal how you will pursue that issue?
  Does the introduction indicate the importance and interest of your topic?
- *Frame an effective conclusion.*

Does the conclusion grow out of the major ideas you have discussed in the paper?

Does the conclusion reinforce your main thoughts?

Do you indicate how your findings relate to the findings of previous writers?

Do you suggest possible ways of pursuing the issue in future writing?

Does the conclusion show awareness that your own writing is part of a continuing conversation on the subject?

● *Check for coherence.*

Does the outline reveal a paper that holds together?

Will the final paper make the impact you desire?

Creating the Full Statement: Drafting, Revision, and Final Form

Writing a research paper demands all the skills discussed in this book, for the research paper is the synthesis of everything you can find from your reading and all the ideas you develop based on that reading. During the period of library research and the preliminary tasks of the proposal and outline, you will come to tentative conclusions. Reaching these early conclusions does not mean that you can put your concentrated thinking to rest and lapse into the mechanical task of filling in words to fit the outline. Quite to the contrary, all your powers of thought must remain alive until you have created the exact and final words of your message. That struggle to find the right words will lead you to new thoughts about the subject and cause you to reconsider—and perhaps sharpen—many of your earlier conclusions. You never know fully what you will write until you write it. The outline can serve only as a partial guide—a stage in your thinking. Even having a complete first draft does not complete the active consideration of your subject, because the refinement of language through revision will lead you to new meanings.

The last two chapters of this book, Chapters 16 and 17, are devoted to the thought processes and mechanical skills that come into play during the actual writing and revision of any essay. They apply in the fullest to the research paper. The next few paragraphs introduce the last chapters by presenting a few of the topics—logic, transitions, and word choice—that apply in particular to the research paper.

First, because the research paper rests on such a variety of source material and requires such an extended development, the step-by-step organization of your thoughts as they appear in the final paper is exceedingly important. You do not want your reader to get lost in the mass of information or the range of ideas you present. Beyond preventing confusion, you also need the reader to see the issues and subject from the perspective that you have finally reached. The pattern of your organization should reflect some real pattern you have discovered in the material. The orderly arrangement of ideas in a way appropriate to the material is the essence of the broader meaning of *logic,* as will be discussed on pages 441–447.

Once you have come to an organizational logic for your paper, you need to make that logic explicit for the readers, so that they know what you are trying to do. The longer and more complex the paper is, the more you need *transitions*—bridging phrases and sentences—to show the connection between one idea and the next. The importance of transitional phrases has already been discussed in other chapters that emphasize structure and connections (see pages 166–168).

The reader does not know your earlier thought processes, so your final choice of words fixes the meaning that will be conveyed to the reader. Because the statements of the research paper are the result of long work and long thinking, they should be among your most informed and thoughtful statements; naturally you want them to be understood precisely. Because the medium of presentation is words, the clarity of your ideas, the precision of your argument, and the seriousness of your intentions can be transmitted only through your choice of words. The discussion of revision in the next chapter includes more detailed comments on style.

Because the research paper is a structure of your own thought built upon the written statements of others, you need to be aware of the most effective method of presenting the material from each source and the proper ways of giving credit to the sources you use. These skills of referring to sources and documentation are the subject of Chapter 17. The techniques of referring to original sources discussed there will help you use the material to best advantage, while allowing you to develop your own thoughts. The research paper must, of course, be completely documented, as described on pages 486–504.

The last stage of preparing your paper for public presentation is the creation of a handsome final manuscript—neatly typed with generous margins. *Absolutely essential is a careful proofreading of the final manuscript.* These elements of formality and care are in themselves signs that you are making a well-considered public statement on a subject you have long wrestled with in private. Your thoughts deserve the best possible presentation.

Sample Research Paper

Mark Green
Writing II
Section JK4
May 3, 1984

The Beginning of the Space Race: The United States
and the Challenge of Sputnik

Outline

Thesis: Russia's early technological successes and propagandistic excesses forced America to enter the space
race energetically, but only after a period of embarrassment and confusion.

   I. Introduction—Commitment to space now and then

       A. Current lack of commitment

          1. Recent NASA funding cutbacks

          2. Space shuttle self-supporting

       B. 1957 U.S. embarrassment over Sputnik

       C. Thesis statement

  II. Sputnik I launching

       A. Technical details

       B. Announced Soviet lead in science and technology

          1. Dominated International Geophysical Year

          2. Satellite heavier and higher than U.S.
plans

          3. Military importance

 III. Immediate panic reaction in United States

       A. Press reaction of admiration and fear

       B. Loss of international prestige

       C. Jokes reflected fear

       D. Shook previous U.S. confidence

          1. Robert Goddard's pioneering rocketry

       2. Von Braun and other German rocket scientists in the United States

       3. Post–World War II missile and programs

    E. United States had ignored earlier warnings of Soviet plans

IV. American government confused

    A. Congress blaming the president and military rivalries

    B. Security questioned

    C. Military attempt to minimize Sputnik

    D. Journalistic criticisms

V. Eisenhower's attempts at reassurance fail to provide leadership

    A. October 9 press conference

    B. October 10 National Security Council meeting

    C. Eisenhower's later change in view

    D. Speeches on November 7 and 13

       1. Press criticisms

       2. Followed by stroke

VI. Khrushchev propaganda campaign

    A. Openness about data

    B. Need for positive image after 1956 events

    C. Russian claims of scientific leadership

       1. Pioneer Tsiolkovsky

       2. Sputnik II plans

    D. Offer of agreement on missile controls

       1. Seen as purely strategic

       2. No on–the–spot inspection

VII. Further events humiliate United States

    A. Sputnik II launched on November 3

       1. Technical details

       2. Again U.S. reaction of confusion and blame-finding

    B. U.S. Vanguard explodes on launch pad on December 6

    C. Vanguard II also fails on February 5

VIII. More positive response starts at end of the year
    A. Strong predictions for the next year
    B. Articles supporting U.S. accomplishments
    C. U.S. leaders calling for struggle
    D. State of the Union message outlines program
        1. Science education
        2. Control over military rivalries
        3. Intensified research and new space agency
 IX. United States finally enters space race
    A. Explorer I successfully launched, discovers Van Allen Belt
    B. Other launchings follow
    C. Soviet program slows down
  X. Conclusion——Current need for commitment
    A. Challenge from Japan
    B. Calls for scientific research and education

Introductory paragraph sets the subject within the context of significant events (the space race) and a similar current problem (funding for space research).

Passing references to recent news articles help establish the contemporary problem.

Transitional sentences pull the essay backward into the historical subject and introduce the main theme and meaning of the events to be discussed. The words back then *set the time frame for the paragraph.*

The space race, with us for twenty-five years, has gained new life through the recent successes of the space shuttle program. Yet Congress and the president do not seem committed to a continuing all-out space program. Funding for NASA (the National Aeronautics and Space Administration) has been severely cut in recent years ("White House"). Indeed the space shuttle program is intended to be a commercial venture, ultimately paying its own way by carrying payloads for industry, various governments, and other cash-paying customers (Reinhold). Not since the beginning of the space program has the U.S. government seemed less interested in space. The kind of international embarrassment caused by our lack of a space program then might hold lessons for the present.

Back then, in 1957, we were caught by surprise when in the fall the Soviet Union launched the first earth satellite. The United States was embarrassed to discover that our minimal program was far behind the Russians'. Our government was unable to respond intelligently, and a national panic grew. Russia took full propaganda advantage of her lead and our confusion. Only after the U.S. government gathered its wits and committed itself to a massive program of research and space flight did we embark on a path that led to U.S. dominance of space in the following years. Ultimately, Russia's early success and propagandistic excesses forced America's triumph, but only after that first international embarrassment.

On Saturday, October 5, 1957, Americans awoke to find that they were living in a new world dominated by Soviet technology and military prowess. On the preceding day, Russia had launched a 184-pound earth satellite called Sputnik. It was circling the earth every 95 minutes at a height of 560 miles and a speed of 18,000 miles per hour (Jorden, "Earth Satellite").

The Russian announcement coincided with an international conference of the International Geophysical Year, as through timed to upstage the rest of the I.G.Y. program and to announce to the world the Soviet Union had achieved world scientific dominance. Certainly the launching was the most dramatic event of the I.G.Y. Further, according to Dr. J. Kaplan, chairman of the United States I.G.Y. committee ("Device"), it not only beat a planned U.S. satellite, but it was eight times as heavy and had an orbit two hundred miles higher than U.S. plans called for.

The launch was a sign of military as well as scientific power, for the same rockets that launched the satellites could be used as missiles to carry nuclear warheads. In addition, satellites raised the possibility of aerial surveillance of the planet through so-called spy satellites--a possibility that soon became a reality.

With America clearly behind Russia in technology and rocket power, a panic swept America. Newspapers and mag-

This sentence provides transition from the technological events to the reaction to those events.

Different sources are synthesized to show the range of the reaction.

The joke is quoted in its original form for the most effective delivery. Because the source listed under "works cited" is longer than one page, a specific page reference for the quotation is needed here.

A transitional sentence moves the discussion to the deep background, summarized and synthesized from a variety of sources. This background is presented only because it relates to the theme of American complacency and surprise. It interrupts the chronological narrative of the paper, but belongs here thematically. If it were placed at the beginning, the reader would not understand the point of including the material.

The short form of the title of the anonymous source uses the opening words of the full title, so that the article can be found easily in the alphabetical listing of works cited.

azines were filled with mixed admiration for the Soviet achievement and fear (Shapely). People throughout the world were asking how Russia could do what America couldn't. The press in London, Paris, Italy, Spain, China, and Egypt commented on the U.S. loss of the lead in space science ("World Newspapers"). Overall it was seen as a "devastating blow to the United States scientific, industrial and technological prestige in the world" ("Blow to U.S. Seen").

On the lighter side, but still reflecting the U.S. fear, jokes swept the country, such as one describing a new mixed drink, "the Sputnik cocktail: one part vodka, three parts sour grapes" (Hazard 379).

There seemed to have been little reason for the United States to have been beaten so badly. The first pioneer in rocket research was an American. Dr. Robert Goddard in 1914, after seven years' work, patented the first liquid fuel and oxidizer rocket. He worked an additional nineteen years to perfect it ("History"). After World War II we also got the best of the German rocket scientists, including Wernher von Braun. His rocket launchings in Berlin in 1932 were the start of the German rocket program, which provided devastating weapons, including the notorious V-2 rocket, during World War II ("Spoils"). At the end of the war, bolstered by the surrendering German scientists, America clearly had the strongest programs, and the Soviet Union mounted a spy program to steal some of our secrets ("Missile Plans"). As soon as he was elected president in 1952, Eisenhower greatly expanded rocketry programs. Several rockets, including the Redstone, Viking, Vanguard, Jupiter, and Thor, were successfully tested (Gatland 59-92). In 1955, moreover, President Eisenhower announced that the United States would launch an earth satellite during the International Geophysical Year (Smolders 74).

The subject of ignored warnings reemphasizes the main theme of complacency and surprise. Parenthetical references to ideas and facts from books here require specifying pages.

With such a history of confident advance and success, it is no wonder that Americans had ignored warnings of Russia's upcoming achievement. On several occasions, starting in 1953, Soviet officials had announced their intention and ability to place a satellite in orbit. And in the months just preceding the launch, the Soviet Union was known to have been giving instructions to radio amateurs on how to receive signals from the planned satellite (Smolders 74–75).

The next level of response is presented through a mixture of summary and quotation from a wide range of sources to show the extent of unease and dissent.

America's eyes turned toward her government for direction and leadership. Instead they found confusion and blame. Congress was blaming the satellite lag on the withholding of funds by the administration ("Senators"), and members of the Senate Armed Services Committee were calling for "an inquiry into charges that interservice rivalries had harmed the [missile and satellite] programs" (Lawrence, "Senate"). Even American government

The paper returns to the main chronological line.

security was questioned, as an article in US News and World Report blamed the Soviet success on spies convicted six years before, Julius and Ethel Rosenberg (Greenburg). Some of the military attempted to minimize the Russian accomplishment. Rear Admiral Rawson Bennet,

Some sources are referred to not for the facts that they present but to show that such articles were appearing. The articles themselves are treated as events; their appearance is placed within a political context.

chief of naval operations, for example, said, "The Soviet earth satellite was a hunk of iron almost anybody could launch" ("Satellite Belittled"). But few Americans could feel so confident. The press of both the left, such as the New Republic ("Sputniks and Budgets"), and the right, the National Review ("The Moon"), as well as the

These periodicals are briefly analyzed in terms of political viewpoint.

middle, the New York Times ("Politics"), echoed the complaints of administration bungling.

The focus shifts to the president's reaction. As head of the government, he is a key actor in terms of political pressures and response.

President Eisenhower, again trying to instill confidence in America's strength, responded to the events and accusations at a press conference on October 9. He denied that there were interservice rivalries and viewed the Russian achievement as only a political one, not a seri-

The content of the press conference is summarized from a newspaper report.

The details of the National Security Council meeting were not reported in the press, so a later historical book is used as a source.

Eisenhower's later shift in opinion, taken from his memoirs, emphasizes his misjudgments at the time. Quotations are used to indicate his thinking precisely. Because the source is identified in the text, only page references are needed in parentheses.

This discussion of Eisenhower and the following one of Khrushchev interpret actions and statements as well as present them.

Eisenhower's actions are set against his later excuse of preserving government secrecy.

Criticism is quoted to show the barbed language firsthand.

ous military threat (Lawrence, "President"). But these denials did not quell the criticism, particularly of his defense policies and the organization of his government.

The next day, October 10, at a meeting of the National Security Council, Eisenhower again saw no cause for alarm in the events and declared satisfaction with current American programs and schedules (Clowse 10). Most members of the council, however, contended that Sputnik was making significant inroads on world opinion. The council recommended that the White House alter some priorities to meet the challenge or at least stop disparaging the Soviet accomplishment. Eisenhower, however, continued to belittle the Russian accomplishment, saying a few days later that our satellite would provide "more useful information" (Clowse 10). Years later, in his memoirs of the period, Eisenhower did give more credit to Sputnik, saying the "scientific achievement was impressive" (205). Moreover, he admitted in retrospect that Sputnik had created two problems: the "near-hysteria" of the American people and the need "to accelerate missile and satellite perspectives" (211).

Despite Eisenhower's hindsight, in the month after Sputnik he seemed to assume little positive leadership in either reassuring the American people or establishing new programs. In the memoirs, he claims to have been kept silent because of the secrecy of government secrets (225). On the evenings of November 7 and 13, he did make speeches outlining U.S. technological and military achievements and indicating that he would also be accelerating our missile programs (Richardson 130). But the *New Republic* accused him of sounding like "a man who realizes that his back is to the wall, even if he wants the country to think it isn't" ("Lecture One") and accused his leadership of being "indecisive" ("Lecture Two"). Then he suffered a stroke at the end of November; for three weeks he recuperated, unable to provide active leadership. Our government, lacking active and forceful response, seemed to be floundering. During three months of almost total American silence, the Soviet Union won propaganda victory after victory.

This sentence shifts our attention to the Soviet Union.

The head of the Russian government, First Secretary of the Communist party Nikita Khrushchev, made sure his country appeared open and friendly from the start. Orbital data and tracking information were made available almost immediately (Jorden, "Time Table"). Russia simply gave the appearance of the strong partner cooperating in the most important of the I.G.Y. ventures. This friendly, confident, and strong face was just what Khrushchev needed to reverse recent news of division and hostility in the Communist world. During the previous year, Russia had faced a Hungarian civil war, a Polish rebellion, and a hostile Chinese government accusing Russia of being run by "bourgeois chauvinism" (Lukacs 310). Thanks to Sputnik, for the first time in a while, the Soviet Union could project an international image of being united and strong.

Khrushchev's purposeful, active political role stands in sharp contrast to Eisenhower's apparent inaction.

Because many articles by Jorden are cited, short title is needed to identify the source.

The chronology backtracks slightly to present Russian actions in full. The analysis goes even further back to show the context in which Khrushchev was acting.

The Russians took full advantage of their triumph, declaring themselves world leaders in science and military rocket power ("Soviet Claiming"). They claimed to have invented space technology and dedicated Sputnik I to their pioneer, Konstantin E. Tsiolkovsky, who died in 1935 (Shabad). A week after Sputnik I was launched, Russia announced that a second satellite, two or three times the weight of the first, would be launched within a month or two (James).

The Soviet propaganda campaign is summarized from a number of news articles.

Khrushchev, feeling he occupied a position of strength, within three days of the first launch was asking for a general agreement on the international control of missiles (Reston). Again he was cultivating the image of the friendly strong man with only world peace in mind.

Interviews, presenting Khrushchev's political positions and also serving as his public platform to the United States, are summarized and quoted. These interviews were important events in themselves.

In an interview published in *Newsweek* on December 6, Khrushchev talked not only of banning the use of force for political gain, but of equipping the Russian military with nuclear weapons and of Russia's ability to strike against anybody. All he claimed to want was "a renunciation of war, with the necessary controls to follow" (Considine 99–100).

U.S. response is summarized to support the author's interpretations of the propagandistic nature of the Russian proposals and to highlight the cold war competition that surrounded these events.

But Khrushchev's bold offers were perceived here as only propaganda and traps. His offer to allow international control of missiles was interpreted by the American government as an attempt to keep U.S. missiles out of Europe and to create negotiations that the Soviet Union could stall endlessly (Schmidt). Further, his proposals did not include on-the-spot inspection, and some military analysts speculated that many of the missiles photographed from the air were dummies. No one could really be sure how strong the Soviet Union really was or how much of both the strength and the apparent peaceful intentions were just a propaganda display.

Sputnik II information and response are summarized rapidly because they follow the pattern already established by the discussion of Sputnik I. The story is capped by the Russian attempts to exploit their success.

Sputnik II, launched on November 3, 1957, strengthened the impression of Soviet dominance. The satellite weighed an astounding 1,120 pounds and, even more remarkably, contained a living dog (Jorden, "New Satellite"). Again the newspapers were filled with stories of congressional inquiries ("Demands") and impaired confidence in the United States. John Rinehart, assistant director of Smithsonian satellite tracking, dejectedly predicted, "No matter what we do now, the Russians will beat us to the moon" (Kenworthy). Then on November 7, Khrushchev predicted the Soviet Union would also outstrip the United States in the production of heavy machinery and consumer goods and again called for an end to the cold war (Jorden, "Khrushchev").

Giving the source of the quotation effectively shows the U.S. despair at this point.

The final humiliation came on December 6, when the first U.S. attempt to launch a satellite with a Vanguard

The third story of American humiliation is even more rapidly summarized. The headline encapsulates the mood.

rocket exploded on the launch pad after rising only two feet in the air (Bracker, "Rocket Burns"). The *San Francisco News* reported this event with the despairing headline "Cold War Pearl Harbor" (Diamond 14). Again the *New York Times* was filled with stories of adverse reaction from here and abroad, but this time the president was dismayed as well (Mooney). A second attempt to launch the Vanguard on the following February 5 ended when the rocket exploded four miles in the air (Bracker, "Crash").

The last humiliation is set against the first positive signs. The word but *sets up the contrast and marks the turning point in the story. Several positive statements are summarized and paraphrased from a variety of sources. The positive tone of the statements, rather than their content, is the subject of this paragraph.*

But by the end of the year, the United States finally seemed to be developing a response. Reports from Cape Canaveral predicted that the first U.S. launch of a twenty-pound satellite would take place in the spring of 1958, with heavier ones to follow in the fall and a promise of a thousand-pound satellite in 1959 ("Preview"). Other articles began appearing, supporting America's future space program and discounting the Russian one. Wernher von Braun stated that the United States had already sent man to where there was no atmosphere ("Interview"). At Cape Canaveral, on one day alone, five rockets were launched, including Vanguard's first stage and the Jupiter C ("Science").

Again, the fighting tone of these statements is the reason they are presented.

American leaders also began to gain strength and direction, calling for economic sacrifices to keep the United States strong and warning the public that the cold war could last indefinitely, clearly gearing up for a long struggle of which the space race was only part ("Nixon's Latest Word" and "Beware").

Eisenhower's political program is paraphrased from his memoirs. It is presented as important in setting a new government direction and in marking a turn-around from his former inaction.

Eisenhower's State of the Union message on January 9, 1958, was a major turning point. Recognizing the need to build the nation's scientific and military strength, he proposed a three-point program: strengthening American education; reducing interservice rivalries and increasing presidential control over military planning; inten-

The legislative actions emphasize the importance and success of Eisenhower's initiatives.

sifying research and establishing a space agency. These became the basis for a number of laws passed by Congress that year. The National Defense Education Act became law on September 2; on August 6 the defense reorganization law was signed; and on July 29, NASA was officially established. Thus the United States united all its space and missile programs under a single administration and set the stage for major growth in American science and technology (Eisenhower 239–53).

The actual accomplishments in space are presented after the political story to drive home the new American position. Note that, since the turning point several paragraphs back, the material has been organized in order of increasing significance: positive news stories, increasing morale and leadership from government officials, presidential leadership and political success, and at last the technological triumph of a satellite launching.

On January 31, the army finally launched Explorer I, a thirty-pound satellite, using the Jupiter C rocket (Belair). And the scientific instruments on board provided the first clues of the most important discovery of the International Geophysical Year––the Van Allen Belt, a zone of high-energy radiation beyond the earth's atmosphere. The belt was named after the scientist James Van Allen, who designed the experimental package on the satellite (Lewis 135–36). The United States was officially in the space race, even though it was a late start and even though von Braun later admitted that the Jupiter C was an undeveloped, last-minute collection of rockets clustered together to meet the need for greater launch power ("Spoils" 32).

This paragraph points to the continuation of American space achievement in the period following the events of this paper. The firm establishment of this new policy caps the main theme of realization and action only after embarrassment.

The year 1958 would see other American successes, along with some failures. On the third attempt, Vanguard finally put a satellite in orbit on March 17, and Explorers III and IV achieved successful orbits on March 26 and July 26. But Russia launched only one more satellite that year. Her great show of a space program, although it certainly had immediate propaganda value, in the long run only served to launch a more effective, far-reaching American space program that was to put men on the moon and create the space shuttle.

The last paragraph returns to the moral of the story

Once we decided to pursue the space program energetically, we proved that our science and technology could do *for contemporary problems, referring to well-known current news stories that need no citation.*

anything we wanted them to. But today we are again beginning to doubt our scientific strength. Today's lack of commitment is part of a larger problem that seems to be overtaking the United States. Japan, in particular, seems to be taking the lead away from us, especially in computers. Again we hear calls for more research and better scientific education. But will it take another major embarrassment and near panic to get our government to take serious action once more?

Works cited

Belair, Felix. "Army Launches U.S. Satellite into Or-
    bit." <u>New York Times</u> 1 February 1958: 1.

"Beware Russia's Soft Talk--Creed of Force Still Rules."
    <u>U.S. News and World Report</u> 14 February 1958: 104-
    05.

"Blow to U.S. Seen." <u>New York Times</u> 6 October 1957: 43.

Bracker, Milton. "Vanguard Rocket Burns on Beach; Fail-
    ure to Launch Test Satellite Assailed as Blow to
    U.S. Prestige." <u>New York Times</u> 7 December 1957: 1.

------. "Vanguard Crash Caused by Flaws in Engine Sys-
    tem." <u>New York Times</u> 6 February 1958: 1.

Clowse, Barbara. <u>Brainpower for the Cold War</u>. Farming-
    dale, N.Y.: Greenwood Press, 1981.

Considine, Bob. "Khrushchev: 'We Have Already Won Over
    You.' " <u>U.S. News and World Report</u> 6 December 1957:
    98-100.

"Demands Increase for a Congressional Missile Inquiry."
    <u>New York Times</u> 4 November 1957: 1.

"Device Is 8 Times Heavier Than One Planned by U.S." <u>New
    York Times</u> 5 October 1957: 1.

Diamond, Edwin. <u>The Rise and Fall of the Space Age</u>. Gar-
    den City, N.Y.: Doubleday and Co., 1964.

Eisenhower, Dwight D. <u>Waging Peace: 1956-1961</u>. Garden
    City, N.Y.: Doubleday and Co., 1965.

Gatland, Kenneth W. <u>Project Satellite</u>. New York: British
    Book Centre, 1958.

Greenburg, David. "Did Russia Steal Satellite Secret
    from U.S.?" <u>U.S. News and World Report</u> 18 October
    1957: 44-46.

Hazard, Patrick D. "Fast Buck on Sputnik." <u>Nation</u> 185:17
    (23 November 1957): 379-81.

"History--Coming of Rocket." <u>Newsweek</u> 4 June 1945: 90.

"Interview with Dr. von Braun." <u>U.S. News and World Report</u> 18 October 1957: 36.

James, Michael. "Second Soviet Sphere to Be Ready Soon." <u>New York Times</u> 11 October 1957: 3.

Jorden, William. "Khrushchev Asks East-West Talks to End 'Cold War.' " <u>New York Times</u> 7 November 1957: 1.

------ . "Soviet Fires Earth Satellite into Space." <u>New York Times</u> 6 October 1957: 1.

------ . "Soviet Fires New Satellite, Carrying Dog." <u>New York Times</u> 3 November 1957: 1.

------ . "Soviet Gives Satellite Time Table." <u>New York Times</u> 6 October 1957: 1.

Kenworthy, E. W. "Confidence in U.S. Is Held Impaired." <u>New York Times</u> 4 November 1957: 1.

Lawrence, W. H. "President Voices Concern on U.S. Missile Program, But Not on Satellite." <u>New York Times</u> 10 October 1957: 1.

------ . "Senate Inquiry into Interservice Rivalries." <u>New York Times</u> 9 October 1957: 1.

"Lecture One." <u>New Republic</u> 137:22 (18 November 1957): 34.

"Lecture Two." <u>New Republic</u> 137:23 (25 November 1957): 33.

Lukacs, John. <u>A New History of the Cold War</u>. New York: Anchor Books, 1966.

"Missile Plans Stolen." <u>Newsweek</u> 27 August 1945: 25.

Mooney, Richard. "Rocket Disappoints President." <u>New York Times</u> 7 December 1957: 1.

"Nixon's Latest Word on Foreign Policy." <u>U.S. News and World Report</u> 6 December 1957: 110-11.

"Politics of the Sputnik." <u>New York Times</u> 10 October 1957: 32.

"Preview 1958." <u>Newsweek</u> 6 January 1958: 21.

Reinhold, Robert. "With Technical Problems Solved, Shuttle Faces Fiscal and Political Hurdles." <u>New York Times</u> 5 July 1982: 8.

Reston, James. "Khrushchev Asks World Rule of the Satellite and Missiles." <u>New York Times</u> 8 October 1957: 1.

Richardson, Elmo. <u>The Presidency of Dwight D. Eisenhower</u>. Lawrence: Regents Press of Kansas, 1979.

"Satellite Belittled." <u>New York Times</u> 5 October 1957: 2.

Schmidt, Dana. "U.S. Skeptical on Missile Pact." <u>New York Times</u> 8 October 1957: 1.

"Science." <u>Newsweek</u> 4 November 1957: 66.

"Senators Attack Missile Fund Cut." <u>New York Times</u> 6 October 1957: 1.

Shabad, Theodore. "Launching Timed as If for Tribute." <u>New York Times</u> 5 October 1957: 3.

Shapely, Harlow. "Satellite Hysteria." <u>Nation</u> 185:13 (26 October 1957): 276–78.

Smolders, Peter. <u>Soviets in Space</u>. New York: Taplinger Publishing Co., 1974.

"Soviet Claiming Lead in Science." <u>New York Times</u> 5 October 1957: 2.

"Spoils of War: The Men Who Turned the Trick." <u>Newsweek</u> 10 February 1958: 32–33.

"Sputniks and Budgets." <u>New Republic</u> 137:17 (14 October 1957): 19.

"The Moon Is Up." <u>National Review</u> 4:15 (19 October 1957): 339–41.

"White House to Seek Budget Cuts of $40 Billion in 1982 Fiscal Year." <u>New York Times</u> 6 February 1981: 1.

"World Newspapers See Soviet Taking Lead from United States in Space Science." <u>New York Times</u> 7 October 1957: 17.

Writing Assignment

Write a research paper of 2,500 to 3,000 words (approximately ten typed pages, double-spaced); include notes and bibliography. The audience for the paper will be the other students in your class, who will be researching related topics. The teacher may present you with a list of specific topics or may ask you to develop an original paper from one of the following:

1. The class will be asked to investigate a specific year. Members of the class will first gather background material, perhaps by each student writing a synthesis of events for a week of the year selected (see pages 266–270). Each student will then pick an event, person, or issue in that year to investigate further. The scope of the final paper need not be limited to the original year but may trace the topic back or forward in time—as appropriate.

2. Each student will choose a local public or private agency, corporation, or other institution to explore, such as a local plastics company or day-care center. After gaining some background about similar institutions (for example, the development of the plastics industry or recent legislation affecting day-care programs), you should gather specific information about your chosen institution and then contact the institution directly to see whether you can obtain an interview or any additional information. For the final paper, you may focus on any issue, process, or problem that you discover in the institution.

3. Interview a person who has spent time in another region or country. Find out whether he or she has observed customs, attitudes, or ways of life significantly different from those where you live. Choose one of these differences to explore in your research.

4. Investigate an ecological problem in your region—perhaps a source of pollution or an animal species threatened with extinction. In your attempt to understand the problem, do not only investigate the local conditions and attempts to remedy the problem, but also look into background information that might shed additional light, such as the nature and ecological requirements of the threatened species or the operations and current technology of the industry that the polluting company represents.

5. For a novel or play that you have studied in a literature class, find out how the work was originally received when it first appeared. What was the author's reputation at the time, and

what did contemporaries think of this particular work? As you delve into original reviews and discussions of the author, compare them to your personal reaction to the work and the class response when you all studied the work. You may find your topic in the pattern of reception, in the comparison of original reaction with modern opinion, or in how the work's reception affected the author's life. Depending on how you focus the project, the follow-up research will vary.

Near the beginning of your research, you should submit to the teacher a short statement (one or two sentences) defining your intended research area. Midway through your research, after your topic has become focused, submit a formal review of the literature (of 300 to 500 words) and a formal proposal (of at least 200 words). Before you begin writing the rough draft, the teacher may also wish to see your research notes and outline.

3 Writing in Disciplines

11 Creating Knowledge

Statements of public knowledge differ from statements of private conviction. To produce claims that are likely to convince informed critical readers, you must go beyond the discoveries of personal experience to gather and analyze data according to currently accepted methods and standards. That data will help you develop your ideas and will become part of the evidence you present in your writing. A description of the methods you use may in fact be a necessary part of your final statement. The methods of gathering data and the formats for arguing for statements of knowledge vary through time, from discipline to discipline, and even within disciplines. Although much of this variation comes from differences in the objects studied and from the historical development of techniques, the most fundamental differences arise from the different kinds of questions asked by groups of researchers. These differences of fundamental questions lead to differences of concepts, procedures, and even ways of thinking.

Private Knowledge
and Public Knowledge

The first two parts of this book have treated you as consumers of knowledge—active, thoughtful, evaluative, selective consumers, but consumers nonetheless. You have learned to take knowledge in, understand it, and respond to it. You have learned how to discover the personal meaning and importance of texts. You have learned to evaluate and think about texts. And you have learned to make original statements using your reading.

Insofar as you have produced new knowledge, however, it has been private, personal knowledge. The reactions of Chapters 2 and 5 are reflections of your own mind and experience—important to you, interesting and possibly exciting to others, but still in the realm of personal opinion. The kind of introspective observation discussed in Chapter 8 helps expand your vision of the world, but it remains a personal vision. As personally satisfying and convincing as introspective discovery is, it alone cannot serve to convince other people because other people cannot live your experience. Even when others accept your word that your experience has led you to see things a certain way—for example, that your tiredness and sleep patterns fit Hartmann's model—they may not perceive their own experience the same way. You must provide them with a less subjective way of showing that the idea corresponds to the way the world actually is. That is, you must go beyond your feelings or internal conviction to develop the kind of argument and evidence others will accept. Charles Darwin and his followers, for example, had to engage in public debate (both spoken and on paper) for many years before his ideas gained general acceptance.

To gather data to test Hartmann's ideas, you might ask many people to observe their experiences of tiredness, or you might observe many people over time, or you might even create an experiment in which you tire your subjects in various ways under controlled conditions. Hartmann himself used a combination of these methods, including introspection, in developing his own ideas, as he states in the original text. But until other researchers find similar conclusions based on their own observations, Hartmann's conclusion will remain only suggestive—that is, his own idiosyncratic idea and not generally accepted theory.

Of all the assignments in this book to this point, the research paper has come closest to a statement that offers real, new, publicly acceptable knowledge. Using the best evidence you could find in already published sources, you have made a new argument, developed a new interpretation, or come to new conclusions on the basis of new synthesis and analysis. Your essay makes a statement about your subject that no previous piece of writing has made. Insofar as your evidence supports your ideas and is not significantly contradicted by equally good evidence in other sources, your argument may well convince a knowledgeable, thoughtful reader. In this case, however, the new knowledge you have produced is secondary, dependent on the evidence already available to everyone else. Sometimes major new statements arise solely from the reinterpretation of existing evidence (see Chapter 15 on theoretical disciplines). But more often new statements come from a fresh confrontation with the world and depend on new data to convince serious, critical readers.

Data both lie behind and stand right in the front of most new knowledge claims. Much of the data gathered in the research process are directly presented as evidence in the argument of the final statement. Without sufficient data, one would not have the evidence to present one's case. Even if a particular piece of information examined by the writer is not directly represented or mentioned in the final piece of writing, it has helped shape the more general knowledge claims. As we shall see throughout this part of the book, ideas and general statements arise out of contact with information about the world, and information about the world constrains what any writer can legitimately say. A writer seriously interested in developing knowledge takes the constraints of data as a way of finding which plausible statements do not fit the world. Further, a writer's work would have little chance of being generally accepted as knowledge if it consciously violates available evidence.

Methodology as Disciplined Data Gathering

Gathering convincing data is not easy. Almost every way of gathering information about reality presents problems. Consider interviews: does twenty people saying the same thing make it any truer than one person saying it? Or are the twenty people even saying the same thing? If each uses a slightly different set of words, do they all mean the same thing? Or if they are using the same words, are they really describing slightly different experiences? And have the questions you asked influenced the kind of answers you get? On the other hand, if you only observe individuals, you do not know how they are feeling inside. Nor do you know what happened earlier that might affect or explain the observed events. Moreover, in both interviews and observations, the variables may be so complex, with so many things happening at once, that you really cannot legitimately come to any clear-cut answers. If you try to design experiments, you get into whole new sets of problems.

Since academic disciplines set themselves the task of developing knowledge, that is, formulating and arguing for statements that reasoning people will accept as descriptions of reality, the disciplines have developed standards and procedures for identifying and reporting acceptable evidence as well as arguing for new ideas. The methodology—that is, standards and procedures for gathering and presenting information about the world—helps ensure that the evidence gathered and the conclusions drawn by one researcher will seem valid to another researcher. Moreover, use of accepted methods in most cases allows researchers to verify one another's results independently. They can examine the same documents, gather similar data, or run the identical experiment to see whether the new results coincide with the old. Thus a number of researchers may come to agree on whether the conclusions are supported by consistent evidence. The creation of knowledge is a group venture, requiring the work of many people. Mutual criticism helps develop reliable knowledge.

Method thus is part of the process that produces the final piece of writing. The quality, character, content, and function of the final statement of knowledge depend on the method that produces the evidence and ideas that appear in the paper. Different methods will produce different evidence, ideas, and arguments. Divergent methods among authors may produce disagreement. Unacceptable methods may produce unacceptable knowledge claims. Innovative methods may open up new areas of investigation and whole new kinds of statements to be made. Method is so central to the understanding and evaluation of the final written product that in many disciplines a writer is obliged to describe as part of the statement the method used to produce and analyze the data. In this way, many articles contain stories of how they were made.

Methods Vary

As important as method is, no single, fixed method serves for all kinds of statements. As the following pages indicate, methods vary through time, from discipline to discipline, and even within disciplines. As you take courses in different subject areas or even courses in two branches of the same area, you may in fact become rather confused about the many different ways people go about gathering and presenting knowledge. The differences among the branches of knowledge seem so great that at times you may wonder how people with different approaches to knowledge talk to each other. And even if they could talk to each other, you wonder what they might have to say that would be useful or acceptable to each other.

One strategy for dealing with this confusion of methods and knowledge is to commit oneself to one method, declaring all the others illegitimate. This strategy has been adopted with some success by many people. Adherents of a single method may call it "the scientific method" or "the humanistic method" or "the method of faith." Such a strategy, however, leads one to overlook the many significant contributions of the other methods; moreover, one overlooks the similarities and interplay among these methods. One may even overlook the fact that great variety exists even within a given method. Philosophers of science have had great difficulty coming up with a single definition of scientific method that consistently holds even for a single science such as physics, let alone all the natural sciences. Once the social sciences are brought into the picture, the concept of a single scientific method becomes even more troublesome.

A more fruitful strategy is to look at the methods used in each circumstance, try to understand why they are used, and then evaluate how appropriate they seem to the situation. That is the strategy pursued in this book. Not only will this strategy allow you to appreciate a greater variety of statements gathered by a variety of methods, but it will also give you the intellectual flexibility to consider many options in how best to develop statements about those questions you wish to pursue. At the very least you will understand why you are doing what you are doing, and thus you will do it better.

Methods Change with Time

As a field grows and changes, new methodological possibilities appear and ideas change. The invention of the telescope at the beginning of the seventeenth century made possible a new way of gathering information about the heavens, as did the invention of the radio telescope in this century. Each of these inventions opened up new kinds of data about the planets and the stars, but each also required the development of new standards and procedures to guarantee that the results would meet the approval of other practitioners in the field. One cannot simply look through a telescope and claim to see something. Rather, one can, but then one's word is not likely to be taken seriously. To be taken seriously, one must use a certain quality instrument in an atmosphere sufficiently clear of interfering contamination. Then one must record one's findings in such a way that other researchers can interpret them precisely and agree with the conclusions. Thus, members of the field must negotiate the appropriate methodology and the appropriate form of presentation.

Even without the invention of new means of observation or the refinement of old ones, methodological ideas may change just because the interests of a field change. For example, in the last twenty years, many historians have shifted their interests from the large public events—the histories of queens, kings, and wars—to the lives of ordinary people—the histories of families, sexuality, childhood, even eating. This has led to many methodological changes. Not only have certain kinds of documents become more valuable to scrutinize— such as the records of farm production or the birth and death registers of small villages—but statistical methods have been introduced to deal with trends involving many common people. The introduction of statistical material has also changed the form of the traditional historical narrative, so that now historians are arguing over how statistics should be presented, what kind of meaning they should be given, and how they should be discussed within a historical argument.

Changes in basic thinking in a field can even change whether a particular method is thought to give valuable or reliable results. As some clinical psychologists have come to believe that psychological behavior is influenced by the individual's social situation, they have come to distrust evidence from experiments that strip away realistic social situations. They prefer methods that preserve naturalistic settings in order to view the individual in the actual situation of his or her own life. Other experimental psychologists, however, still believe that such naturalistic methods contain so many variables that it is impossible to know what is really going on. Thus professionals may disagree not only on the ideas and the facts but on the very ways in which one can determine facts and present them to support ideas.

As disciplines evolve, modes of argument change in corresponding ways. The invention of the scientific journal in the seventeenth century, for example, necessitated the invention of the scientific article. The form of scientific articles evolved over the years, so that an experimental report published in 1665 bears little resemblance to one published today. In the deepest sense, the way anyone chooses to argue about knowledge reveals that person's fundamental concept of what knowledge is and how people can know it. If one believes that people's behavior follows regular patterns and that we can observe these patterns through statistical regularities in some quantifiable aspects of behavior, one will argue by presenting general patterns supported by statistical tables. If one believes that people's behavior results from complex individual choices taking into account many levels of human experience, one is likely not to argue for general patterns, but rather to lay out an individual's situation, options, and choices in one particular case.

Methods Vary with Disciplines

Some of the largest fundamental differences in what counts as facts and how one should obtain them stem from the differences among disciplines, or different branches of organized knowledge. Experimental psychologists go about producing knowledge in ways different from literary critics, historians, economists, or experimental physicists. To some degree the differences of the disciplines arise simply because disciplines look at different areas of reality. Biologists look at living organisms, physicists look at the behavior of physical matter, sociologists look at group behavior, and art historians look at objects of art and the artists that produced them.

Because paintings are different from electrons, they must be described in different ways, and evidence about them must be gathered and organized in different ways. Because electrons are small and move fast, one needs special detectors to find them and measure their energy. Paintings are large enough to be seen and usually stay still; they can frequently be found easily enough in museums. Electrons are all pretty much like one another, differing only in their energies and relations to other particles, so one looks for the patterns of their behavior. Paintings are different from one another, so one frequently looks for what makes a particular artist's work special. Electrons seem to operate on the basis of laws of nature, so one relates their behavior to general equations. Paintings seem to arise from the skill and imagination of an individual and they appeal to human observers, so one tries to analyze the skill and imagination of the painter and the appeal of the artwork. Electrons in Japan and America and on the moon all seem to be the same, but art varies from year to year and from culture to culture. Through such comparisons, one may be able to explain a number of differences in the procedures and knowledge of disciplines. The objects of investigation are different, requiring different kinds of data, different modes of description, and different methods of gathering data. Different special problems as well must be overcome.

Even more fundamental than the differences in objects of investigation, however, are the different kinds of questions the different disciplines are trying to answer. Chemists ask how elements combine to make more complex substances. Sociologists ask how social institutions and other groupings are developed and maintained, how they function and affect the lives of their members. Psychologists try to find out why people behave or think the way they do; clinical psychologists more narrowly wonder how people may feel better mentally and lead more successful lives. Literary critics want to explain what happens in a literary work; historical literary scholars want to know what the correct text is and how the text relates to events and other texts at the time of its creation.

These differences in underlying interests lead the different disciplines to approach the objects they investigate in different ways, even when they are looking at the same object. Many disciplines have, for example, looked at the phenomenon of the brutal murderer, but in rather different ways. The biochemist wants to find out whether such behavior can be linked to a chemical structure, perhaps within the genetic material. Legal scholars want to know how the crime should be defined and what constitutes adequate proof for conviction or acquittal. Psychologists are interested in finding out what thinking, feelings, or early events lead to the antisocial behavior. Sociologists want to know if certain classes of society or certain social situations produce more such criminals. Literary critics are interested in seeing how the criminal character acts within a literary work and perhaps serves some larger literary meaning. Last, but certainly not least, the criminologists want to know how to catch these evildoers, and penologists want to know how to deal with them once they are in prison.

The last example of criminologists and penologists reveal strikingly that the problems and questions a discipline addresses frequently derive from the social and political institutions they serve. Without legal and police systems as well as a criminal system, criminologists would not have a subject. Without prisons, penology would make no sense. This relationship to institutions of power appears not just in applied fields. Socialist economics differs from capitalist economics. Health and economic interests drive molecular biology to focus on some problems at the expense of others. Even such aesthetic, nonworldly subjects as art criticism often can be seen as the product of larger social issues; different countries and different ages, after all, produce different art.

In order to solve the kinds of problems they are interested in, disciplines develop different ways of thinking and different concepts. In order to predict how elements combine and the properties of combined elements, chemists try to understand and measure the binding forces in atoms and molecules. They try to determine models of how molecules fit together, and thus you may see them actually playing with oversize models that look like Tinkertoys, figuring out just how a particular molecule might fit together. Psychologists, treating the human mind and behavior as complex phenomena molded by learning, try to understand the different parts of individual perception and behavior and how they change through learning. Literary critics, concerned with how a literary text fits together, will consider how the separate parts of a story, such as character, setting, plot, imagery, and style, fit together into a consistent design. People in more applied fields, such as social work, criminology, or even medicine, will borrow ways of thinking and results from other fields, but only in relation to solving the practical problems that motivate their fields, such as making people healthy. Modern medicine, for example, borrows techniques and theory from engineering, physics, chemistry, biology, psychology, and even sociology, but only in the context of the practical task at hand.

These different ways of thinking, in turn, lead investigators in different fields to look at different aspects of phenomena and to gather different sorts of data. The medical doctor looking at a gunshot wound will measure the extent of blood loss and physical damage and the patient's pulse and blood pressure in order to determine how to treat the patient. The criminologist will look at the angle of entry, powder burns, caliber of the bullet, and even the extracted slug, in order to recreate the crime and identify the culprit. The sociologist will find out about the victim's class, income, and family structure, and perhaps inquire into how the victim was treated by the police and the hospital in order to see how these institutions relate to the condition of being a victim. The clinical psychologist will inquire into the victim's feelings and perceptions of the event, to help the victim cope with the trauma.

Methods Vary Within Disciplines

The same kind of variety that exists in the methods of different disciplines often exists within a single discipline, often for similar reasons. Different research groups may have different underlying assumptions about their subject, may be interested in different problems and questions, and may look at different aspects of the same general subject that defines the discipline.

In political science or government departments at your college, you may, for example, find many different approaches to the subject of government. Political philosophers, interested in such problems as the nature of political institutions, how political institutions affect human life, and what the best or most justifiable forms of government might be, approach their subject in a general philosophic way. They often begin with such questions as "what is the nature of human existence?" and "why do people form governments?" They may refer to historical examples, but they proceed largely through reasoning about a sequence of ideas (see Chapter 15).

Historical scholars in political science are interested in how particular political decisions were made in history and how political institutions developed through a historical process. Their studies, based on detailed examination of evidence from the past (see Chapter 12), reveal the actual historical institutions and decisions that developed through the complex forces in history rather than the general principles sought by the political philosophers. Sometimes, in a subfield like the study of the development of constitutional governments, the philosophic and historical issues come together, for that subfield tries to understand the development of different governments as a combination of philosophic and historical goals of people who shape constitutions and of the intellectual and political forces that surround them.

Some scholars now see the political process as not just a matter of institutions and obvious political decision makers (such as heads of state or members of legislative bodies) but of public attitudes and indirect public action. Some of these scholars study literary texts as a reflection of political attitudes, as a demonstration of how politics affect the whole of life as represented in literature, and as historical facts of political action and public opinion making. Much contemporary writing in Eastern Europe, for example, reveals both the political tensions and the difficulties of life within the Soviet satellites; the authors of this literature can as well be seen as a crucial part of the political opposition. These political scientists employ a kind of literary interpretation (see pages 377–384).

Other branches of political science, such as comparative international government, are more descriptive; they assume that we must understand how governments work before we can deal with them.

Today the most common branch of political science in the United States attempts to copy what it considers the scientific method and limits itself to issues that can be studied in mathematical or statistical ways. Data often come from survey research, and findings are usually reported in standard research-report format (see Chapter 13). Although the subject does not easily lend itself to experimental work, sometimes experiments are used to help elucidate political behavior (see Chapter 14). In this approach, researchers, who consider themselves behavioral scientists, typically ask questions about the relationship between voting patterns and economic, social, geographic, or other defining characteristics of voters. Similarly they study the way elected officials represent the interests of their constituencies and the means by which the constituents express their interests. These political scientists treat governments (or at least the governments of modern democracies, particularly the United States) as mass phenomena. Such studies do seem to fit in well with the realities of contemporary American politics and are of much practical use to political figures trying to gain and maintain the support of large numbers of voters.

We can see then, even within one field, that the same object of study can be approached from many angles with different assumptions and motivating questions. Sometimes communication may break down among these various approaches within a single discipline, for adherents of one approach may see adherents of another as totally misguided. But with proper appreciation for the assumptions, problems, and methods of different research groups, the chances for fruitful interchange increase.

Learning the Methods of Your Discipline

All these differences at all levels present a daunting array of methods and forms of presentations to become acquainted with. In order to test, support, and argue for statements in a particular field, you must use the kind of data or evidence currently accepted in that field, gathered and presented in the currently accepted ways. Fortunately, as you start to identify the disciplines you wish to work with and the kinds of underlying questions that interest you, the methodological range will narrow and you will begin to be trained in the methods and formats currently considered appropriate. Part of your methodological training in your chosen field will come indirectly through examples and through the standards you have to meet for your assignments, but part will be presented directly in laboratory and methodology classes.

In this unit we will look at some of the different methods of data gathering and data presentation used in some fields. This introduction to data gathering and presentation, however, barely suggests the range of methods available to different fields; moreover, it cannot live up to the true standards of any field in either rigor or comprehensiveness. You do not need to master all the possibilities of method, however, but rather at this point you need only be aware that many variations exist and each has its reasons, assumptions, and consequences. The discussion, examples, and exercises that follow will offer you a broad sense of how the statements you and others make may be grounded in forms of disciplinary methods and argument, so that as you enter into your chosen field of study and encounter readings from other fields, you will have a better understanding of what you and others are doing. By seeing how ideas are developed, tested, and presented in a variety of fields, you may gain a better sense of the meaning of what you read and write in the contexts of disciplines. You will see that the writing of knowledge is a dynamic process filled with choices.

Basically, most disciplines work with only three kinds of data: (1) accounts, artifacts, and remains of things that have already happened; (2) observations about current situations and events as they happen; and (3) observations of new, specialized situations created through experiments. The special problems, interests, and points of view of different disciplines lead them to collect and handle these kinds of data differently, but the basic categories are shared. This threefold division of the kinds of data organizes the next three chapters. A final chapter in this unit considers theoretical forms of inquiry, which attempt to address issues in the most general form, abstracted from any concrete data.

12 Writing About Past Events: The Humanities and Historical Sciences

Both reconstructive and interpretive disciplines use evidence from the past to come to new statements of knowledge. Reconstructive discipline—such as history, geology, and archeology—attempt to determine what happened in the past. Interpretive disciplines—such as literary criticism—attempt to understand creations made in the past by other humans. Guidelines for developing and organizing essays about the past and interpretive essays will help you understand and prepare your written work for courses in both kinds of historical disciplines. Sample essays are from journalistic history and interpretive comparison of drama and film.

Traces of the Past

In order to answer the questions they find interesting, fields as diverse as literary criticism, archeology, geology, history, evolutionary biology, and investigative criminology rely on the remaining traces of past events. Sometimes solid remnants like fossils or pieces of rock reveal the past; sometimes more fragile traces like fingerprints provide the only clues to what happened; and sometimes we must look at events through someone else's account, as in historical documents or paintings. Indeed, in some fields such as literary criticism the interpretation of the historical document (a poem, story, novel, or play) forms the very subject of inquiry.

Reconstructive disciplines, particularly history but also the historical aspect of any discipline, attempt to reconstruct what happened or what people did during past events. They necessarily rely on previous accounts of the same events or of reports of related information. *Accounts of people who witnessed the original events* (e.g., private journals as well as newspaper reports), *documents* instrumental to the unfolding of events (e.g., correspondence between two leaders negotiating a pact), or other *written records* (e.g., old bills found in a desk or the registration of a business contract) may be supplemented by *nonwritten objects* (e.g., archeological remains of a battlefield), but historians inevitably depend on the written record prepared by others. In using such written records, historians must constantly consider issues of meaning, interpretation, reliability, purpose, and bias of the primary documents and the secondary literature. *Primary documents* are those that come directly from the time of events under discussion, and *secondary documents* are those that follow afterward to discuss the earlier events. Thus the historian's basic problem of how to use the evidence of the written record resembles that of any person attempting library research; such problems are discussed throughout this book, but particularly in Chapters 6, 9, and 10. The guidelines below for writing an essay about the past and the example that follows on pages 347–353 show how one can harness the historical record to test statements from a wide range of disciplines.

Disciplines like archeology, paleontology, and historical geology, on the other hand, must *reconstruct past events and patterns of change and development* through physical objects that remain behind. Since these objects—a broken clay pot, a few bones, or an unusual rock formation—are rare and do not speak, the researcher may not know at first what to make of them. So these disciplines have developed many techniques for finding, identifying, and dating these objects.

Even more important, these disciplines have found ways of relating the individual object to others that are found at the same place or are in some other way similar. Thus an archeological dig starts to provide significant meaning only if all the objects and physical traces fit together to create a total picture, both of what was happening at a single time period and what happened before and after as revealed by traces found at other layers of the dig. Moreover, the dig is compared to other digs from the same region or similar cultures. Careful classification systems allow rigorous comparisons, so that, for example, paleontologists can decide whether a fossilized tooth found at one site is from the same species of animal as the jawbone found at another site.

Interpretive fields attempt to understand the creations left by other human beings, such as literature, music, art, or even ideas. Discussion in these fields always refers back to the *evidence of the poem, artwork, piece of music, or philosophic text* that is the subject of discussion. Although we can never be sure what the creator was thinking or feeling, or what the creator intended to accomplish by the work, we can know what has been passed down to us in the created object. So whenever we want to check the truth of anything we read about a human creation, we need to look at the creation itself. We need to consider how well the details of the created object fit the generalized interpretation. Consequently, to verify any interpretation, you must refer back constantly to the object you are analyzing through quotation, paraphrase, summary, and description of relevant examples. Doubtless you have had experience in English classes of writing analytical interpretations of literary works and evaluating the interpretations of others. In this book, the analysis of purpose and technique in Chapter 6 requires you to use the evidence of the analyzed text in just this way. Further advice on interpretive analysis follows in the latter part of this chapter.

The Essay About
the Past

In school you learn many things about what has happened and how events have led up to today's situation. You must judge much of this information simply on the basis of various accounts given in different books, for you may not have the opportunity to engage in a major archeological dig or read through the church records of a small French village. Other parts of this information, however, you can easily check out against your own judgment, and you too can make your own generalizations from the primary evidence. Just as the writer of the history book does, you can read through Abraham Lincoln's letters and other private papers to decide his exact motives for issuing the Emancipation Proclamation. All the relevant documents have been published and are probably available in your college library. By walking around your town, you can check out statements about its recent architectural history and come to your own conclusions. Television reruns of "I Love Lucy" and "Father Knows Best" provide easily available evidence for comments about cultural attitudes in the 1950s. Our world is filled with traces of the past for you to see. The following guidelines for developing an essay about the past show how you can reconstruct a general pattern from these separate traces.

1. *Know why you are interested in a particular topic.* Although the world is filled with things to look at, we usually look at only one or a few things at a time. We focus our attention because we are trying to solve a question or problem or because we believe a particular piece of information will help us understand a bigger issue. In the example below, the specifics of reporting on Jackie Robinson's first season shed light on the broader issues of bias in sports reporting and journalistic bias in general. (Because the essay on pages 347–353 will be used as an example throughout this section, you may wish to read the essay now.)

2. *Turn your general interest into specific questions.* Your underlying interest in the area will lead you to ask certain kinds of questions of the material you find. In the example below, Pat Washburn's interest in journalistic bias leads directly to the questions, "Where does bias enter into the newspaper accounts of Jackie Robinson's first year and where do the articles seem free of bias?" If the author were interested in a different kind of problem, such as the effects of social pressures on an athlete's performance, she would examine the newspaper accounts with different questions in mind, such as "At each point what pressures does Jackie Robinson feel and how does the baseball player's actual performance in the game as reported in the stories relate to the degree and kind of pressure?"

3. *Identify a statement or specific claim to be tested.* After examining the data, you should start to formulate an answer in a specific statement or claim. This statement might come directly from something you read; it might be a modification or expansion of something

you read; or it might be a totally new conclusion. The relationship of the statement to previous statements in the literature helps provide a continuity of thinking among people interested in the area and increase the likelihood that the different investigations will fit together in some larger structure, that they all will add up to something larger than a collection of totally separate pieces. Nonetheless, sometimes an examination of a specific case may lead your thoughts in very different directions than previous writing on related subjects. Strong new claims or ideas may persuade other writers to follow your lead, building a structure of knowledge on the basis of your work. That, however, does not happen as often as we would like to imagine.

The example presented below, in investigating racism in sports writing, tests only a narrow statement, based on the comment of the sports writer Roger Kahn. Kahn claimed that racist editing constrained his coverage of Jackie Robinson, the first black player in major league baseball. Pat Washburn wished to test an expansion of that statement—that coverage of Robinson's first year generally reflected such racial bias. The findings support Kahn's statement only in part and almost totally contradict the more extreme statement quoted in the concluding paragraph of the article.

4.   *Choose the kind of evidence.* Having decided on the statement to be tested, you must decide on the appropriate evidence. Will denials by sports writers and editors prove there was no bias? Or will those denials merely indicate they weren't aware of or won't admit to the bias? Pat Washburn thought the evidence of the actual sports stories would provide a more accurate measure, independent of people's self-perception or memories.

In considering appropriate evidence, you may find that certain statements are not really testable. Other statements may require evidence you cannot easily obtain. For example, the statement that "Jackie Robinson had greater personal courage than any other player in professional baseball's history" may possibly be true, but is absolutely untestable. No simple piece of evidence will tell you exactly how much courage any person has. For different people in different circumstances, courage may even be different things. No evidence can confirm or deny that statement, unless you reformulate it to depend on clear evidence—such as "No player in the history of baseball was subject to as many incidents of racial abuse as Jackie Robinson." Assuming you can clearly define "incidents of racial abuse," you may still not be able to test the statement because much of the evidence has been lost. As the *Journalism Quarterly* study suggests, many of the incidents involving Robinson went unrecorded; perhaps earlier in the history of baseball, other incidents, now lost to us, occurred involving other players. Certainly much of the history of the Negro leagues is lost.

5.   *Gather the evidence in an organized way.* You must gather the evidence methodically and carefully, organizing it in categories relevant to the issue you are testing and seeing what patterns they make. As Pat Washburn describes in the "Methodology" section of the paper below, a selection of newspapers covering the period in question were examined for specific indicators of racism, such as the number of pictures Robinson appeared in, and how often Robinson was identified as black and whether the identification was in the form of a noun or an adjective. These specific categories of information help indicate the presence and nature of racial bias, once all the information has been gathered and organized.

6.   *Analyze the data.* The analysis of the data involves seeing exactly what the data indicate about the statement you are testing. Pat Washburn finds that in some ways Robinson as an athlete received unbiased coverage, although he was excessively identified by race. However, the amount of racial harassment Robinson received appears to be substantially underreported, particularly after mid-May. The analysis reveals that editors kept the focus on narrow sports issues and buried the integration aspects of the Robinson story.

7.   *Organize the essay.* As in the following example from *Journalism Quarterly* the essay should identify the statement to be tested and its source near the beginning. Then the kind of evidence used and how it was gathered should be explained. The major findings should follow, either organized around major themes or around categories of evidence. Finally the meaning of the evidence and the conclusions to be drawn from it should be given. Dividing the essay into separate sections may help the reader understand the organization, although such formal divisions are not always necessary.

Throughout the essay, you should present and discuss your findings in as specific and concrete a way as possible, relying heavily on the evidence you have found. Remember that the main point of this essay is to see how specific evidence relates to or supports general claims. So keep returning to that evidence even as you interpret its meaning and pass judgments on the general statement being tested.

In historical essays, sometimes, a chronological narrative can present and argue for conclusions about events more effectively than an essay organized around general claims. By telling the story of how a series of events unfold you can frequently reveal what you consider the causes, meaning, and consequences of the events. In a chronological narrative, the events seem to speak for themselves, but you as a writer must work hard to present the story in the way you want the readers to see it. You should have a coherent vision of what happened and why; you should make that vision clear to the readers; and you should then show how all the factual details fit into that vision. Without such a controlling vision of the pattern and meaning of events, chronological narratives can deteriorate into pointless, rambling collections of disjointed facts. The three excerpts describing Henry Ford's Peace Ship episode (pages 251–255) illustrate the effective use of chronological narrative. Each controls the telling of the story to present its own coherent vision of the events.

An Example: Racial Bias in Sports Reporting

The following essay, published in *Journalism Quarterly,* is organized around a general claim. Pat Washburn used only evidence readily available to most students, whose college libraries usually contain files of several newspapers. Although the author has more background knowledge and methodological sophistication than you are likely to have in any particular area, the essay does not differ in kind from work you might do on a smaller scale in an undergraduate course.

Although the essay touches on a number of interesting topics— including baseball history, sports writing, racism, and integration— it focuses on its central issues of bias in sports reporting. The underlying issues that prompted the writer to investigate this material give coherence and meaning to the essay. As a result, this paper speaks to people interested in the operations and consequences of journalism—it rightly belongs in a publication like *Journalism Quarterly* and would be out of place in either a sports or a black history journal. The underlying interests and questions define a discipline and appropriate procedures, rather than simply the material examined.

New York Newspapers and Robinson's First Season

When Jackie Robinson was signed by the Brooklyn Dodgers in 1947, he became the first black in baseball's major leagues in modern times. He had impressive credentials. In 1946 with Brooklyn's Montreal farm team, he led the International League in batting at .349, was the league's best fielding second baseman and stole 40 bases.

However, most baseball owners still did not want him in the major leagues because of his race. That was no secret.[1] Some sportswriters felt the same way. But he silenced the critics by becoming a starter and batting .297 as the Dodgers won the National League pennant.

By the 1952–53 seasons, Robinson was an established star. Yet, Roger Kahn, while covering the Dodgers for the New York *Herald Tribune* in those two years, twice had problems with his "segregationist" editors when he wrote stories about racial incidents involving Robinson. On one occasion, they wired him: "Write baseball, not race relations."[2]

Kahn's recollections raise a question. If a major New York paper was prejudiced and/or biased (as Kahn suggests) in its coverage of Robinson after he was a star, was the coverage in his first major league season also prejudiced or biased?[3] Among the conflicting influences on sportswriters in 1947 were articles by their peers both for and against blacks playing in the major leagues, the fact that every writer covering professional baseball for the major New York papers was white[4] and the baseball owners' stated dislike of blacks.

[1]David Q. Voigt, *America Through Baseball* (Chicago: Nelson-Hall, 1976), pp. 116–117.

[2]Roger Kahn, *The Boys of Summer,* Signet (New York: New American Library, 1973), p. 135.

[3]There is disagreement on the function of a sportswriter. In the May/June 1976 issue of *Columbia Journalism Review*, Michael Novak chided sportswriters (pp. 37–38) for too much investigative reporting while not paying enough attention to what occurred at games. "The main business of a sportswriter is to describe what happened in athletic events. . . . Nothing should be hidden; everything should be reported. But not in the sports pages," he said. That brought a letter in the July/August issue of *Columbia Journalism Review* from one of the country's better-known sports editors, Sandy Padwe of *Newsday,* strongly disagreeing with Novak. "It is because sportswriters had little appetite for real reporting and little confidence in their reporting skills that sports pages have been so historically barren when it comes to good, solid work outside the realm of the game," he said (p. 54).

[4]According to Richard L. Tobin (former reporter and editor at the New York *Herald Tribune* from 1932 to 1956), private interview at Indiana University, Bloomington, Ind., November, 1979.

Methodology

The study examined the sports pages of the New York *Times,* New York *Herald Tribune* and New York *Daily News*[5] for 44 days in 1947. The days included the week before the baseball season began, the first and last weeks of the season and one day, immediately following a game, chosen randomly from each week between the season's first and last weeks.

The following items were tabulated for each story: number of times Robinson was identified as a black and whether the identifying word was a noun or an adjective; number of incidents reported that had racial connotations; and number of game stories in which Robinson's name did not appear (although he had played) and what his batting average was in those games. In addition, photographs were examined to see how many times Robinson appeared in pictures showing Brooklyn players.

These items were chosen as measurements of bias, based on racial prejudice, for specific reasons. Robinson complained after he was out of baseball about racial identifying terms being used as adjectives, and Roy E. Carter, in a 1957 segregation study, found that bias was shown by whether "Negro" was used as a noun or as an adjective.[6] The other items were measured because it was hypothesized that biased reporting would result in rarely mentioning incidents with racial connotations (so that readers wouldn't sympathize with Robinson) and non-use of Robinson's name in game stories and photographs, thus suggesting that he wasn't having an outstanding season.

Findings

Use of Robinson's Name in Game Coverage. In the 29 days' coverage of regular season games surveyed from April through September, the *Daily News* did not mention Robinson in only 21% of its stories. That was a lower percentage than in the other two papers. The *Times* did not refer to him in 24% of its stories, and the *Herald Tribune* did not mention him in 34% of its accounts. On all three papers, his batting average for the games in which he wasn't mentioned (most of which were in the last half of the season) was .057, which was far below his season average of .297.[7]

---

[5]These three New York papers were selected on the advice of Tobin because they represented three distinct types of sportswriting. The *Times* was the most conservative and least colorful; the *Herald Tribune* had a colorful, news-feature writing style; and the *Daily News* tended toward the sensational and had a reputation of being anti-black.

[6]Studying bias and/or prejudice by looking at whether race identifying terms are used as nouns or adjectives was suggested by Roy E. Carter Jr. in "Segregation and the News: A Regional Content Study," *Journalism Quarterly* 34:7-8 (Spring, 1957).

[7]The findings in this study are not statistically significant.

Jackie Robinson. (National Baseball Hall of Fame and Museum)

Identification of Robinson as a Black. In 144 stories surveyed on the three papers, there were 74 terms identifying Robinson as a black. Twenty-five of the terms appeared in 19 of the *Times'* 46 stories (41% of the paper's stories had at least one of the terms), 26 terms were used in 22 of the *Daily News's* 57 articles (39% of the stories) and 23 terms showed up in 15 of the *Herald Tribune's* 41 stories (37% of the articles).

The *Times* used 21 of the terms in 22 stories through May 10 and spread the final four terms over the other 24 stories. The same pattern existed in the *Herald Tribune*. Twenty-one terms appeared in 20 articles by May 10, and the other two terms were in the final 21 stories. The *Daily News* differed significantly, however, using 17 terms in 26 stories through May 10 and then putting nine more in 31 stories after that. This means that after May 10 the *Daily News* identified Robinson as a black 4½ times as often as the *Herald Tribune* and more than twice as much as the *Times*.

All three papers used race-identifying terms more often as an adjective, than as a noun. Thirteen of the 25 terms in the *Times* (52%) were adjectives, compared to 14 of the *Herald Tribune*'s 23 terms (61%) and 17 of the *Daily News*'s 26 terms (65%).

Incidents Reported with Racial Connotations. The three papers reported 46 incidents in 144 stories surveyed. The *Daily News* was the leader, using almost 2½ times more than the *Times* and about three times more than the *Herald Tribune*. The 26 incidents reported by the *Daily News* appeared in 18 of the paper's 57 stories (meaning that 32% of the stories cited an incident). In the *Times,* 11 incidents appeared in seven of the 46 stories (15% of the articles) while the *Herald Tribune*'s nine incidents showed up in six of the paper's 41 articles (also 15%).

As in the previous category, the majority of the incidents were reported by May 10. By that date, the *Herald Tribune* had used eight incidents (89%) in 20 stories while the final 21 stories contained only one incident. The *Times* noted eight incidents (73%) in the 22 stories through May 10, but only had three in the 24 articles surveyed after that. In the *Daily News,* 18 incidents (69%) appeared in 26 stories through May 10 and the other eight were in 31 stories after that.

Use of Robinson in Photographs Showing Brooklyn Players. In photographs of Dodger players, Robinson appeared in a higher percentage of the *Times*'s pictures than in the other two papers. He was in nine of the *Times*'s 25 pictures showing the players (36%). The *Daily News* had him in 39 of 135 pictures (29%) and the *Herald Tribune* showed him in nine of 36 pictures (25%).

In the *Times* and *Herald Tribune,* he appeared in pictures only in April and September. But in the *Daily News,* he appeared throughout the season.

Conclusions

The findings strongly suggest that the first part of May was a critical period in the coverage of Robinson by the three papers.

Until that time, all three papers avidly supported his entry into the major leagues.[8] There are a number of possible explanations for the undisguised enthusiasm. Over the past decade, talented blacks such as Jessie Owens, Joe Louis and Marian Anderson had been receiving more and more publicity; World War II had helped stress the inequities of asking blacks to die for America while not giving

---

[8]This is obvious from a quick reading of the sports pages in all three papers. For example, Jimmy Powers of the *Daily News* wrote (April 11, 1947, p. C17): "As we said before, and we repeat it here, everything El Cheapo (Branch) Rickey does is not wrong. He deserves a load of credit for his courage in bringing the first Negro into the big leagues. We wish Robinson the best of luck."

Jackie Robinson sliding into home plate. (National Baseball Hall of Fame and Museum/UPI)

them total rights at home; Robinson's pacifist personality caused him to avoid racist incidents on the field and kept him from being labeled "uppity"; and many sportswriters obviously placed athletic excellence above a player's color. As Red Smith of the *Herald Tribune* noted, "On most playing fields a man is gauged by what he can do and neither race nor creed nor color nor previous condition of servitude is a consideration."[9]

Against this backdrop, widespread conscious bias directed at Robinson would be surprising.

Not so conscious apparently was the casual manner in which each newspaper used race identification terms. The survey showed that none of the papers differentiated between using "Negro" as a noun or an adjective—but Robinson did, although he did not speak out until the mid-1960s.

Dodger writers gave generous space to my play, and were scrupulously fair. However, they fell into the habit of calling me "The Dodgers' Negro star" in their accounts of games. This was like

[9]Red Smith, "Views of Sports," New York *Herald Tribune,* May 10, 1947, p. 14.

calling Carl Furillo "Italian" or Gene Hermanski "Polish." Several years were to pass before copy editors blue-penciled Negro into limbo. Negro in newspaper stories should be used only as a means of identification, like "blue-eyed" or "red-haired."[10]

Another form of subconscious bias may be deliberately not printing all the facts. Reporters may omit certain facts from a story simply because of the sensitivity of the subject matter, thus distorting the truth.

Although Robinson's harassment by opposing players throughout the season is well documented,[11] the *Times* and *Herald Tribune* virtually ignored it. The 41 stories surveyed in the *Herald Tribune* never mentioned any harassment and the *Times* noted it only once in 46 stories. The *Daily News*'s record was only slightly better. In 57 stories, it mentioned harassment by opponents three times.

Not printing all the facts became more pronounced in the *Times* and *Herald Tribune* in the stories surveyed after May 10. On that date, the *Times,* in a separate story from its game coverage, revealed that Robinson recently had received a number of anonymous threatening letters which had been turned over to the police. The article also discussed a proposed player strike by the St. Louis Cardinals to protest Robinson's presence in the major leagues.[12] On the *Herald Tribune,* both columnists wrote lengthy pieces on the Cardinals and racism.[13]

These revelations apparently had a great effect on editors at both newspapers. Although no evidence has been found that there was a formal policy decision at either paper, coverage of Robinson changed after May 10—race identification terms and incidents with a racial connotation virtually disappeared. This suggests that the editors felt they were adding to racial problems, even though they were reporting only the facts, and therefore the responsible course was to delete anything that might inflame the situation further.

For whatever reason, their coverage shifted abruptly. Instead of covering Robinson extensively as a racial barrier breaker (as they did before May 10), they treated him as any other rookie, even leaving him out of game stories increasingly in the last half of the season when his performance wasn't notable. Subconsciously, this was biased reporting. Readers were given a rosy, sterile picture rather than the

---

[10]Jackie Robinson, *Baseball Has Done It* (New York: J.B. Lippincott Co., 1964), p. 53.

[11]One of the most thorough descriptions of the harassment is by Harold Parrot in *The Lords of Baseball* (New York: Praeger Publishers, 1976), p. 194.

[12]"Robinson Reveals Written Threats," New York *Times,* May 10, 1947, p. 16.

[13]Smith, *op. cit.,* p. 14. Stanley Woodward, "Views of Baseball," New York *Herald Tribune,* May 10, 1947, p. 15.

complete facts. While it may have helped cool racial tensions, this was a step backward in objective reporting, but it is not surprising in the 1940s considering the status of blacks at that time.

On May 10, the *Daily News* also carried a story on the threatening letters, the proposed player strike and the "riding" Robinson received from the Phillies.[14] However, no evidence was found to suggest that the editors felt the paper's coverage might contribute to racial problems. Instead, the paper's reporting on Robinson changed gradually until he was covered no differently than a white rookie by the end of the season.

There is ample evidence supporting this conclusion:

1. After May 10, the *Daily News* identified Robinson as black 4½ times as often as the *Herald Tribune* and more than twice as often as the *Times*. However, the paper's use of the terms declined significantly, from 17 terms in 26 stories through May 10 to nine in 31 stories after that date.

2. The *Daily News* not only reported far more events with racial connotations than the other two newspapers (almost three times as many as the *Herald Tribune* and 2½ times more than the *Times*) but it spread them out more over the season. Only a tenth of the *Herald Tribune*'s incidents and a fourth of the *Times*' incidents appeared after May 10, compared to almost a third in the *Daily News*.

3. The only paper to use pictures of Robinson throughout the season was the *Daily News*. While the *Times* and *Herald Tribune* had pictures of him only in April and September, the *Daily News* showed him in seven photographs (18 percent of the pictures in which he appeared) in May through August.

"It has long been established that the baseball writers of the 30s and 40s wrote fantasies about the great American pastime (baseball) and were generally apathetic about baseball's color," William G. Kelley wrote in 1976.[15] His unsupported assertion is not documented by this survey of the three New York newspapers. Instead of large, deliberate distortions of fact, as Kelley suggests, the writers basically covered Robinson fairly and comprehensively although there were numerous instances of subtle bias on all three papers.

—Pat Washburn, *Journalism Quarterly*
58 (1981): 640–644

---

[14]Hy Turkin, "Police Investigate Poison Pen Threats to Jackie Robinson," New York *Daily News*, May 10, 1947, p. 25.

[15]William G. Kelley, "Jackie Robinson and the Press," *Journalism Quarterly*, 53:138 (Spring, 1976).

The Essay of Interpretation and Analysis

The humanities and fine arts, unlike the sciences, have long memories. The creative works of the past continue to be of current interest, even though we may no longer produce works like them or agree with ideas presented in them. Students of architecture try to understand buildings of the past; students of art study art works; students of literature study literary texts; students of music study musical compositions and performances; even students of philosophy study the great philosophic texts of the past although some of these texts may no longer be considered to be correct or true. Interpretation helps us appreciate what others have accomplished; it also helps us create new works by seeing how older works convey their meaning. Both art historians and working artists gain by understanding the work of the great masters.

Whenever you study a human creation, an artifact left behind by another human being, you must interpret that creation—that is, you must find out exactly what the creation is and does. As part of that understanding you need to look beneath the surface meaning or surface effect of the work to see how that meaning or effect was evoked. In walking into the Lincoln Memorial in Washington, you may be struck by the somber mood and monumental scale of the sculpture. You may also feel close contact with Lincoln the man. Such sensations begin an appreciation of the monument. But until you can analyze how the controlled space creates a sense of largeness and intimacy at the same time, until you see how the central statue draws your attention through its placement and contrasting stone texture, until you notice the many other details that create the experience, you will not really understand the monument.

A monument creates meaning and effect differently from a piece of music or a work of philosophy. Some critics even suggest that a modern poem creates meaning in significantly different ways from an eighteenth-century poem. In studying particular kinds of creations, you will learn the different ways they work and the different levels on which they may be interpreted and analyzed. The critical tools of your specialty will give you the means to understand works on deeper and deeper levels.

Yet, however subtle and technical your understanding of particular modes of creative expression may become, you should never forget that first aesthetic experience of the creative work. That immediate experience begins all interpretation. An interpretation that ignores, say, the overwhelming fear you felt as you first watched a play does not help anyone understand the play you experienced.

The following guidelines suggest generally how to turn your immediate experience into critical interpretation. With the critical tools of your specialty, you can develop more specific procedures for writing interpretive essays. For example, combining standard types of literary analysis—analysis of character, conflict, and figurative language—can lead to an analysis of how a character's outward traits metaphorically reveal that character's internal conflict. Literature often works through complex and original interplay of its various elements. The experienced interpreter of literature discovers ways to reveal that complex originality.

The example of an interpretive essay that follows examines questions about how time is controlled in a theatrical and a cinematic version of the same story. The essay considers details of dramatic structure and film-making technique in order to explain how the dominant effect of the movie differs from that of the play. Those dominant effects come from the actual experience of watching productions in theaters.

1. *Choose a work or part of a work to interpret.* You should choose material that had a powerful effect on you, either positively or negatively, for then you will have something to understand. Obviously, you must experience the work before you commit yourself to studying it in detail. If a novel leaves you cold, then in a sense the novel has not worked for you, and you have no dominant effect or meaning to examine. In order to have something to say in your paper, you may be tempted to make up a meaning or effect that the work did not in truth have for you. If, however, you strongly sense that you missed some important element of the work, close interpretive attention may open up the meaning of a work that first eluded you.

2. *Make sure you understand the surface features, meaning, or events of the creation.* This step necessarily precedes any deeper look into a work. In a novel, make sure you know who the characters are and what happens to them. In a philosophic text, make sure you understand the words and can follow the ideas. For a piece of architecture, make sure you understand what kind of structure it is, what all the parts of it are, and how it is constructed.

3.   *Experience the work again to identify the dominant effect or meaning that you will be exploring in greater depth.* Successful works of art and thought often achieve many effects and meanings at many levels. In such cases, no interpretive essay can hope to encompass the entire work. Rather, you should focus your attention on that aspect that is in the forefront of your mind and experience. The example below—comparing the use of time in *Macbeth* and *Throne of Blood*—does not begin to tap all the richness of either work. Rather, it focuses directly on one aspect that came across strongly in this observer's experience of the two works. In seeing the movie for the first time after having seen a number of productions of the play, I was impressed by how rhythmic and filled with time urgency the film was compared to the play. In pursuing that sensation, I came to conclusions about the structure of the entire movie and even about the general differences between film and plays. Following a single issue to its end will usually lead you further than trying to cover all issues at once.

4.   *Identify the particular interpretive problem and the appropriate mode of analysis.* The effect or meaning you wish to explore will point you to particular technical issues to investigate. Depending on the interpretive issue and the particulars of the work, you will need to choose a level of analysis or interpretation. Some stories or poems raise issues of character more sharply, others of setting, still others the interaction of several elements. Unless your teacher assigns you a particular mode of analysis, you need to choose the mode that reveals the most crucial issues in the piece of literature.

For the particular interpretive issue that you wish to address, you may have to develop a less standard or combined mode of analysis. The peacefulness of a particular painting may suggest that you look at how colors and shapes are harmonized. Or, given the details of the painting, you may wish to consider the relaxed body postures of the figures portrayed. Or you may wish to examine all these and more, but only in relation to the issue of how the details of the painting reduce visual tension. The essay that follows, in trying to understand the rhythmic experience of *Throne of Blood*, considers a variety of technical issues, but they all directly relate to the control of time and its consequences.

5.   *Examine the work again to isolate details important for your chosen interpretive problem.* If you have decided to look at body postures in a particular painting, you need to go back to the painting to note all the details of body posture. In preparing the following

essay, I had to reread the Shakespearean play and watch the movie, taking careful notes about any detail that related to the control of time. In this reexamination, I discovered important aspects of the works that I had missed in previous, less focused experiences. For example, although I had been aware from the first viewing that the film had less talk than the play, I was not consciously aware, until I carefully compared the pacing of the scenes, that Macbeth's introspective soliloquies in the plays were eliminated in the movie and their function was taken over by dancelike movements.

6. *Consider all your evidence to find new levels to the meaning or effect of the work.* After finding all relevant details, look for the pattern that emerges from the evidence. The pattern may suggest a reconsideration of the text as a whole. In putting together the evidence about time in the movie, I realized the carefully paced time resulted in the externalization of emotion, conflict, and character in a kind of choreographed dance, I went back to the movie and my notes to see the effects of the externalization. Then I went back to the text of the play. The whole moral world of the movie, I then saw, had become simplified through this externalization. This sense of a simpler moral world formed part of my original experience of the movie, but until I had found the means to understand it through the interpretive process, I did not have the idea clearly focused enough to discuss it.

7. *Organize and write the essay.* The interpretive essay can be more flexible and open-ended in form than other types of disciplinary writing, in part because an interpretation may move through a number of levels and involve a number of side issues, as in the following example. Moreover, the meaning or projected effect of the work examined often deepens and becomes transformed as the interpretive essay proceeds. Again, the example below on the basis of an examination of technical matters of the use of time moves to a deepening view of character and an interpretation of the moral universe of the movie. In most cases, one cannot properly reduce the meaning of the interpretive essay to a single statement to be then expanded and supported in an obvious fashion. Nonetheless, you must present your interpretation in as clear, orderly, and coherent manner as possible.

In the opening paragraph, you need to identify the work to be discussed and raise the general interpretive problem. Depending on the complexity of the problem, you might explain the nature of the problem further or you might illustrate the importance of the interpretive issue for the work through a well-chosen example from the work.

The next paragraphs of the essay should present the details of the analysis, giving supporting evidence to show how the general ideas are realized in a concrete way. You want the reader to get a substantial feel for the work and your way of viewing it. The paragraphs may each look at different types of details, present a series of different levels of analysis, or follow through a series of related ideas, or they may take on some other organizational principle. As long as you can develop a clear and justified rationale for the progress of your argument and present the structure of your argument clearly enough for the reader to follow it, you may develop any organization for the paper that seems appropriate.

As your interpretation develops, however, you should be giving the reader a deepened sense of the work. Toward the end of the paper you should be able to make certain observations about the work that you could not earlier. The detailed work of the earlier part of the paper frequently prepares new levels of analysis that come later. The more powerful thoughts thus tend to come toward the end, once the reader has seen enough to understand the full importance of your statements. Certainly, by the conclusion of the essay you should give some sense of the importance of your interpretation for the meaning or significance of the work.

An Example: A Comparison of Artistic Forms

The following example looks at time and how an audience perceives time. Because the essay is an interpretation of artistic creations, however, the general topic of time is transformed into the questions of how the creators of different art forms can control the sensation of time and what the consequences of the differences in the control of time are for the nature and meaning of the artworks. Time is of interest because an artist can use it to create meaning and effect. As the essay progresses, the technical questions of the use of time merge into the questions of total meaning. The fundamental question of the essay remains *the* interpretive question: what are these works of art all about?

In order to compare how time can be controlled to create meaning in two different media, live theater and film, the essay compares two versions of the same basic story. *Macbeth,* as you know, is a tragedy written by William Shakespeare almost four hundred years

Book illustration from Act 1, scene 3 of Shakespeare's *Macbeth*. (The Bettmann Archive)

ago in England. The play presents the story of the rise of a Scottish noble to king. Egged on by his ambitious wife, Macbeth deceives, betrays, and murders in order to gain power. His conscience, however, troubles him deeply, destroying his desire to live even as supporters of the murdered previous king threaten Macbeth's ill-gotten throne and tormented life. Macbeth's destruction, both moral and physical, is agonizingly painful.

Throne of Blood is a film made about thirty years ago in Japan by the director Akira Kurosawa. Kurosawa takes the outlines of the *Macbeth* story and sets it in feudal Japan. Macbeth becomes the samurai warrior Washizu, and Lady Macbeth becomes Asaji. Asaji goads Washizu's ambition, but even as he rises to warlord he is thrown into psychological turmoil. He, like Macbeth, winds up physically destroyed by the friends of those he has murdered and morally destroyed by his misdeeds.

Scene from Akira Kurosawa's *Throne of Blood.* (Museum of Modern Art/Film Stills Archive)

In comparing the effect of time in these two works, the essay finds fundamental differences in the moral worlds, the senses of agony, and the aesthetic experiences. Even if you have not experienced these two particular works, the analysis will help you think about the role of time in other plays and films you may have seen. When we walk into live theaters and into film theaters, we walk into different kinds of worlds.

Time in Play and Film: *Macbeth* and *Throne of Blood*

The text of Shakespeare's *Macbeth*[1] as it has come down to us is approximately 2100 lines, five acts, long. When played on stage, *Macbeth* can take from one and a half to three hours to perform, depending on cuts, spectacle, mute action, scene changes and pace of delivery. *Throne of Blood*,[2] Akira Kurosawa's film adaptation of the same play, is one hour and forty-five minutes long. Barring commercial breaks on TV and movie buffs who steal film clips, performance of *Throne of Blood* will always take one hour and forty-five minutes: moreover, minute ninety-four will always show the exact same scene and speak the exact same words. The moviemaker has control of time that surpasses that of any other artist except the musician who has production control over his recordings. The moviemaker establishes the film's time relationships on the set and in the cutting room; these time relationships will stay the same for each performance and each viewer. The technical resources of film that allow precise control of time, furthermore, ultimately influence the basic nature of the drama presented. The possibilities of capturing performances, the controlled duration of shots, the creation of a rhythmic succession of images, and the setting of pace through cutting are so attractive and powerful as to encourage the filmmaker to choose one line of development of his story at the expense of another.

Certainly the playwright has some control over time. He knows whether he has written a short play or a long one; *Macbeth* is short by Shakespearean standards. So too he controls pace. The succession of long and short scenes sets up a rhythm, as the battle scenes of many Shakespearean plays, including *Macbeth,* illustrate. Pace can also be controlled by length of lines; for example, the nervous agitation of Macbeth and Lady Macbeth immediately after the murder of Duncan is reflected in a staccato interchange (II, ii). The nature of the action can also determine pace; compare, for example, the retarded pace of the scene when Malcolm and Macduff wait in England (IV, iii) and the swift pace of the scenes when they pointedly direct the battle (V, ii and iv). Repetition of word, situation or scene can tie together diverse moments and establish underlying rhythms of plot or emotion; the repeated prophecies of the witches, for example, keep the puzzle of Macbeth's fate constantly before the audience.

However strong these playwrights' controls over time may be, they are only approximate, filtered through the interpretation of individual directors and actors. Even if a playwright controls the production, he is limited by the vagaries of individual live performances, the lack of moment-by-moment control, and the technical restraints of what can appear onstage, how rapidly and with what precision.

In adapting *Macbeth* for the film, Kurosawa made full use of his freedom from these restraints. The precisely timed "permanent performance" of *Throne of Blood* creates a rhythmic interplay of events and images. The controlled motions, measured durations of shots, and the metrical pace of the succession of shots result in a movie almost dance-like in precision and most cinematic in form. As I will discuss later, visual choreography has consequences for the nature of the tragedy.

In comparing this cinematic adaptation to the Shakespearean script, however, we must recognize several important factors which stand in the way of a direct analysis of the changes wrought by film. First, *Macbeth* is a script, not a particular production; therefore, many of the new elements of Kurosawa's film may be discounted as the additions of spectacle and melody that any director of a stage or screen production must concern himself with. Further, script cuts and changes are common practice on both stage and screen, especially when the production is labelled an adaptation, so we cannot assume changes in plot, action or speech are the direct influence of film. Finally, with this particular Japanese adaptation we have additional changes wrought by translations of language, culture (particularly influential on this film is the *Noh* tradition), and historical setting (to fifteenth century civil war-torn Japan). The sorting out of these elements would be greatly aided if Kurosawa had, as Peter Brook had with *King Lear,* directed a stage production as well as a film version; unfortunately, the world does not always operate for the convenience of the critic.

Even as we recognize these complicating factors, we should not discount all but the most obvious and direct influences of film, for obvious influences may lead to less obvious ones. Consider, for example, the device of the series of messengers who follow on each other's heels with news of success or disaster. Shakespeare employs this device in many plays, but not in *Macbeth,* where the news of the hero's early heroism and of the opponent Malcolm's great power are brought by single messengers. In *Throne of Blood,* however, Kurosawa employs multiple messengers in both instances. Obviously this is the kind of script change available to any director, for stage as well as screen, but if we look more deeply into the matter, we can see how the resources of film encourage the addition. In *Throne of Blood* rapid cutting, precise timing, and the transitional "wipe"—where a new picture seems to wipe another off the screen—all emphasize the acceleration of events, heighten the effect of the device of repeated messengers and shorten the time necessary to complete the device. The messengers do not even have to enter and exit; they can be simply discovered in the center of the screen and wiped off by the image of the next messenger. The device of repeated messengers becomes more efficient, precise and effective on screen. The resources of film to control time enhance a stage technique relying on time control. In making the script changes Kurosawa was exploiting the potential of film to control time; as a result, the film makes the pace of events an important element in the experience of the scene. The measured duration of shots and cutting techniques have led to a script change which has led to a new affective element in the scene, a sense of urgency of time.

Kurosawa also exploits the film's potential for precise rhythmic control of motion and images in the scene where Washizu (the Macbeth character) sees the ghost of Miki (the Banquo character). As the banquet opens, a group of players is chanting a song and acting out the mime of a story that closely parallels Washizu's. Washizu listens with studied calm as he sips from a cup. He slowly lowers the cup to the saucer, then suddenly rises, stops the play and calls for light. The slow formal rhythm of the film, established by the mime and Washizu's deliberateness, is broken by the outburst. Washizu begins a dance of erratic motions; he notices Miki's ghost, charges around the banquet hall, calms into drunken passivity, sees the ghost again and tries to stab it with his sword. Rhythm and pattern emerge in the lack of symmetry of the sequence. The dance goes on. After his wife Asaji clears the hall, she mocks and berates her again passive husband. When the messenger arrives with Miki's head, however, Washizu again flares out in violence, for he finds that the son has escaped. There is no ease: Washizu kills the messenger. The precise sequence of motions, images and sounds become part of a cinematic choreography, a measured ordering of sense impressions through time.

Again the regicide sequence has the effect of a cinematic dance. Emotive rhythms are established by cutting, special shots, motions of characters with relation to the camera, and the intercutting of visual metaphors for the tense emotions. Silence punctuated by the sound of crows and spasmodic music accompanies as husband and wife alternate frantic action with almost catatonic stillness.

In both the haunted banquet and the regicide, Kurosawa externalizes emotional distress through movement, irregular rhythms and the sequence of images rather than through the verbal self-examination and self-doubts of Shakespeare's Macbeth. In fact, Washizu and Asaji have almost no soliloquies except for a terse version of the handwashing scene, which is more the portrayal of a deranged mind witnessed by others than a glimpse of internal conflicts by the audience. Whether to kill the Lord of Cobweb Castle takes the form of an argument between a simple, reticent Washizu and an ambitious, untrusting Asaji. Her transparent appeal is to Washizu's insecurity: rumor of the prophecy might get back to their lord, or the friend Miki may betray them. Mutely following his wife's goading, Washizu never verbally commits himself to the murderous course, unlike Macbeth, who expresses resolve and knowledge of his act.

The absence of psychological and moral self-examination in the film can with some justice be ascribed to a number of causes: the *Noh* tradition, the cultural transformation of the warrior hero into the plain *samurai,* the loss of Shakespeare's poetry in translation and Kurosawa's interpretation of character. But in light of the effectiveness of Kurosawa's use of cinematic technique to create the externalized characterizations of Washizu and Asaji, we must recognize some connection between cinematic form and the adaptation of Shakespeare's characterization. At the very least we must say that the film is admirably suited for Kurosawa's conception of the story and characters.

Moreover, Kurosawa is a filmmaker and as such chooses and transforms his subjects with at least some concern for cinematic potential. Having freed himself from the necessity of faithfulness to Shakespeare's text by labelling the film an adaptation, Kurosawa has freed himself to recast the story in such a way as to do what he feels cinema does best.

Closely related to the externalization of character and the attendant elimination of speeches of psychological and moral self-concern is the simplification of the moral framework of the film. Part of this simplification may be attributed to cultural translation, the replacement of the Western concern for the individual soul by the rigid social ethic of feudal Japan, which encouraged obedience within a well-defined framework of social and political obligations. Yet part must also be attributed to Kurosawa's choice of evocative external images of emotional distress rather than an examination of the psychological struggles within each of the characters. Without the intellectually powerful Macbeth to weigh the consequences of his actions to his soul, the play's moral tensions become reduced to a simple opposition between Asaji's goad to her husband—"No man without ambition is a man"—and the moral judgment expressed in the chorus that opens and closes the movie that the story is of a once "proud warrior murdered by ambition, his spirit still walking." The old hag sings a similar song, "Men are vain and death is long. Pride dies in the grave. Hair and nails grow when fame is gone." This content, and not the ambiguous other-world of the three sisters, provides the moral foundation of the film.

Among the many techniques Kurosawa uses to lend aesthetic and emotional depth to this simple moral theme are a number that rely heavily on cinematic control of time. We have already seen how these cinematic resources encourage evocative portrayals of emotions at the expense of exploration of thought, but precisely controlled time in film can serve the simple moral theme even more directly. The sequence where Washizu and Miki lose their way in forest and fog is a particularly clear example of how the manipulation of time-related elements can give affective weight to the metaphor of having lost one's way. By a few techniques of shooting and cutting Kurosawa achieves an absolute sense of disorientation to serve as an analogue for Washizu's moral confusion after having won the battle and being swelled with pride. It is in this state of moral confusion that he hears the hag's prophecy and is swayed by his own ambition and his wife's goading. Kurosawa creates this sense of confusion using simple riding shots, in which the riders keep disappearing and emerging from behind brambles and mists. Not only are rhythms of visibility established, but the sequence is broken up into many shorter shots (at least nine in the fog part of the sequence) so that the ride becomes disjointed. The path and duration of each riding shot vary with brilliant irregularity: hard rides to fixed spots end in baffled halts;

confused paths meander across the background, barely visible; one long tracking shot through the woods cuts to a close-up of the riders motionless. The shots are cut so that the riders seem to go off the screen at one point and in one direction and return from an entirely different one, often at an angle unusually oblique to the square of the screen. The rhythms within each shot, the contrasting pace of consecutive shots, the irregular duration of each shot, and the additive effect of the great number of varied shots all create a disturbed and disturbing visual rhythm of confusion. Thus the ability to control film time with duration and sequence of images makes the visual metaphor of disorientation evocative. When one loses one's way, time does not move forward in regular, predictable ways. Each new moment brings only greater disorientation.

All the cinematic techniques that control time, as we have observed in *Throne of Blood,* add up to a major difference in the overall sense of time between the play that Shakespeare wrote and the film that Kurosawa made. Between Macbeth's precipitous rise in the early scenes and equally precipitous fall in the closing scene, he ponders the ravages of illegitimate political power and pays the spiritual price of bloody ambition. In the long, tense middle of *Macbeth* we see a hero facing his acts and fate. In *Throne of Blood* the long middle is an extended evocation of fate overwhelming a hero too shallow to do anything but fear. The final movement of that cinematic chore-ography is Washizu trying to avoid the volleys of arrows while fran-tically attempting to rally the deserting troops. His long death agony is the last spasm of disorder, and calm returns with the regular rhythms of the final chorus.

Macbeth struggles as he tumbles into an abyss; his struggle provides the forward motion of the play. Washizu, however, loses his way and is called to task by a world of absolutes; he can only play out disordered rhythms against the solid regularity of *samurai* ideals. From *Macbeth* we tend to remember the great speeches, the moments of torment and self-revelation—the agonizing thoughts; from *Throne of Blood* we remember the sequences of shots, the eccentric rhythms, the haunting movements—the motions of agony. Because the film can so well control what we see from moment to moment, cinematic techniques of time control add new dimensions to adapted material, but these new dimensions may be at the expense of the old.

—*Charles Bazerman, Literature & Film*
Quarterly V (1977): 333–338

Notes

[1]All citations to *Macbeth* are from the Folger Library edition, 1959.
[2]Japan, 1957. My memory of the film was aided by the synopsis on pages 108–112 of Roger Manvell's *Shakespeare and the Film* (New

York, 1971). English subtitles quoted were translated by Donald Richie. I also wish to thank Audio Brandon Films of Mount Vernon, New York, for allowing me to see the film in private screening.

Writing Assignments

1. In the excerpt on pages 89–91, to show how conventions shape news reporting, Michael Schudson lists five conventions that he considers recent innovations. Using the historical files of one newspaper kept by your college library (probably on microfilm), test whether these conventions seem to have been followed at several points over the last century. Decide which kinds of stories at what intervals are likely to produce relevant evidence. Organize and categorize your data as you go along. Then report your findings in a short research report (300–500 words). Imagine you are writing the report for a journalism class.

2. Observe reruns of old television shows to test one of the following statements, and then report your results in a short paper (300–500 words), as though for a course on contemporary history. Be sure to define key concepts precisely.
   a. Television shows of the 1950s and 1960s had fewer incidents of violence than the shows of the 1970s.
   b. In the 1950s and 1960s, nonconforming or unusual characters on television shows were treated unfavorably as villains, comic fools, or otherwise unattractive persons more often than they were treated favorably as heroes and heroines or otherwise sympathetic human beings.
   c. Devise a statement of your own choosing.

3. Using a few selected issues of a magazine over the entire century, test one of the following statements about magazine advertising. Present your results in a short report (300–500 words), as though for a class in advertising.
   a. Over this century, magazine advertisements have increasingly used more art and fewer words.
   b. Over this century, the positive lure of becoming attractive, sexual, and successful has replaced the negative fear of being a social misfit as a major theme in magazine advertising.
   c. Devise a statement of your own choosing.

4. Discuss how a piece of music with which you are familiar (either classical or popular) uses time to create part of the effect of the music. You may consider such time-related aspects as rhythms,

tempi, pauses, and repetitions and variations of earlier sounds. As part of the analysis, you may compare how two musicians perform the same piece of music. Imagine you are writing this paper (300–500 words) for a music appreciation course.

5. Compare a novel or short story with its movie or television version in order to understand what changes occurred when the forms were changed. Consider what changes were simply an author's or film maker's decision and what were encouraged (or even necessitated) by the change in medium. Present your interpretive analysis in a paper (500 words) for a film studies course. Taking notes on a single viewing of the movie or television show may present difficulties. At least try to take some sketchy notes during the viewing to help your memory later. Then immediately after, supplement your notes from memory as much as possible. Sitting through a second showing of the movie or making a video recording of the television show certainly helps one make more detailed and accurate notes.

6. Analyze the presentation and use of time in Andrew Marvell's poem "To His Coy Mistress" or any other appropriate work of literature assigned by your teacher. The analysis (300–500 words) should help you interpret and experience the poem and should be written for a class in literary interpretation.

13 Writing About Current Events: Observation in Social and Natural Sciences

A researcher studying events happening right now faces what seems an infinity of potential data. The problem is to focus one's attention on only a limited kind and amount of data that will help answer the questions one is interested in and help reveal patterns in the complexities of the present. In order to make order of the potential chaos of observation, social and natural sciences have developed general procedures for focusing and presenting work, limiting the attention of both researcher and readers to narrow, testable issues. Within those general guidelines many variations exist. Both general guidelines and variations are presented and discussed to reveal their advantages and disadvantages. Examples from anthropology and sociology will introduce you to the range of the kinds of writing you will encounter and may be asked to produce in the observational sciences.

Collecting Data as
Events Unfold

Many disciplines investigate what is happening now in order to establish general processes and patterns of events as well as to record unique new events. The social and behavioral sciences consider how individuals behave as individuals (psychology), as a part of groups (sociology), as a part of cultures (anthropology), in relation to governments and other political institutions (political science), and with respect to material and financial goods (economics). These fields describe how people behave in various circumstances; what people actually do provides the ultimate test of the descriptions. Related disciplines such as management, counseling, and social work apply the general findings of the social and behavioral sciences to practical situations. Again, these applied disciplines test their prescriptions against actual behavior in specific situations.

Natural sciences, which study large uncontrollable physical phenomena such as astronomy, meteorology, and the geology of earthquakes and volcanoes, must collect data as the events unfold. One cannot stop an exploding volcano or a rapidly expanding distant supernova to run experiments on them. In some ways journalism and even contemporary history are like watching exploding volcanoes. The events can't be controlled or stopped; you just have to collect as much data of the right kind as things happen.

Advantages and Disadvantages of Unlimited Data

Obtaining evidence as events unfold presents special problems. You have the advantage of being able to gather as much data as you want and being able to choose what and how to record the data; you are not limited by the luck of what historical traces happen to be left behind. You can observe what happens; you can take measurements; you can even preserve aspects of the events through various recording devices. Moreover, if people participate in the events, you can ask the people questions. The amount of data seems potentially infinite.

So as not to be buried under masses of data, you must consider how to limit data to manageable proportions, how to select and record the data most appropriate to your purposes, and how to interpret and combine the many different kinds of data. If you collect too much data of too many different kinds, you won't be able to harness them to clear, significant generalizations. Events in the past have been simplified for us just because we have limited kinds of evidence about them, but events happening right now present themselves in all their complexity, so we must focus our attention to gain some clarity.

With newly emerging events, furthermore, you have the advantage and disadvantage of not knowing how things will turn out. With past events you know, in a sense, the meaning of the events, because you know the results: who won the war or which creatures survived the evolutionary struggle; thus you can try to figure out why one side prevailed or what anatomical features helped survival. You can put things together in a neat package, certain that events will turn out in the anticipated way.

But presently occurring events present uncertainties about where they come from and where they are going. Further events may prove anything you say wrong, foolish, or trivial. Historical material can easily mislead you to assume that what happened was the necessary and only possible consequence of prior events and that, moreover, it was all for the best; current material will keep you properly cautious. The uncertainty of the future, as well, allows you to test your ideas by seeing if your predictions come true. If what you learn about the present leads you to be able to tell what will happen in the future, you can have some confidence in your knowledge. But like meteorologists and economists, you must prepare yourself for the disappointment of many failed predictions.

Varying Methods, Standard Procedures

The methods currently used for finding out about ongoing events vary, of course, from discipline to discipline, depending on what information they find useful. They range from satellite probes measuring electromagnetic emissions of distant galaxies to interviews with gang members hanging out on a street corner. These methods can be very highly developed, requiring much training for their design and proper use—not only for technological hardware, but for such apparently simple things as questionnaires. Many advanced books discuss the problems and appropriate methods of survey research employing questionnaires. Moreover, the same basic method when applied to different disciplines or different problems may require quite different handling. Interviews of Nobel Prize–winning scientists to find out about their career paths require substantially different techniques than interviews with schoolchildren to discover the fears aroused by witnessing a violent event.

Although you will become familiar with the particular methodological concerns, problems, and techniques of your area of study, the following general guidelines for developing and presenting data should help you in a wide variety of situations.

1. *Know the underlying problem you are trying to solve.* The underlying problem is a basic issue or question you need to resolve in order to understand your subject. Anyone studying the sun, for example, needs to know if stars change through time and where in this cycle the sun is currently located. People interested in labor relations need to know why some industries are more highly unionized than others.

2. *Turn the general problem into more specific questions to be answered.* The underlying problem will frequently be too general to research directly. Narrowing the questions to more concrete issues makes meaningful answers more likely. The problem of why some industries unionize more than others, although important, suggests too many variable factors and too many possible solutions to handle in any single research project. However, narrowing the question to the influence of what are likely to be key factors in unionization can lead to a reasonable research project. Data and conclusions already in the literature may even be part of your answer. Typical specifying questions might be: "Do social and economic differences among workers in different industries make workers more or less likely to affiliate with a union?" or "Does the work environment, work task, or social relations among workers differ so as to influence union membership?" or "Do differences in management organization, planning, or policies affect union membership?"

3. *Choose a research site or source of data that will likely provide significant answers to your specifying questions.* Since the resources of any research project are limited, you must select only one or a few groups, incidents, or organizations to study. Insofar as you have control over the material you will study, you should try to choose a research site that highlights your particular questions. If, for example, you wanted to find out the effect of work environment on union membership, you should try to examine companies that

are similar in all ways except their work environment—perhaps in a partly modernized industry, all factors are similar except that some workers work in old and unpleasant facilities, whereas others work in modern, pleasant facilities.

4.   *Know exactly what claim you are testing.* Focus your attention on the particular data relevant to your interests. If you don't know exactly what you are trying to find out, you may wind up with a lot of data, but no clear knowledge about anything. Of all the things you could know, for example, about union members, their backgrounds, their companies, or their jobs, only a manageable few would be relevant to the specific claim that "the more power the worker has to schedule and organize his or her own work, the less likely he or she is to join a union." Specifically to test this claim you need gather data only about who makes scheduling and work decisions and correlate that to union membership.

5.   *Make the claim clear and simple enough to be tested.* Specific claims offer a manageable model of reality to work with. For the time being, they eliminate the overwhelming number of potential variables to allow a clear answer on one specific item rather than a fuzzy, indecisive conclusion about a more complex proposition. If a statement is too complex or offers no clear test, then you cannot gain a solid conclusion about its truth.

For example, the statement that "unhappy workers join unions" is both fuzzy and complex. First, what indicates happiness or unhappiness? Is it the percentage of time that workers frown? Is it the amount of complaining? Is it the number of nervous disorders they suffer? Is it simply whether they say they are happy? It could be all or none of these things. Workers of a particular social group may be more vocal in complaining; does this mean they are more unhappy than workers from a quietly suffering group? Even if all the fuzziness could be eliminated from the statement, happiness or unhappiness would be made up of many complex variables, such as sense of adequacy of pay, harmonious relations with fellow workers, perception of power or powerlessness with respect to many different aspects of the job and organization, and so on. In this case, you would not have reduced the number of relevant variables to manageable proportions.

In order to obtain manageably simple claims, researchers in many disciplines in the natural and social sciences work with self-consciously simplified models of the events they are studying. They know that the world is far more complex than their models and they are eliminating some potentially significant variables, but these simplifications do produce useful results. Indeed, the whole discipline of economics rests on the large simplification that all people always act in the economically most rational way to maximize gains and minimize losses. Economists do not consider what happens when you do business with your grandparents.

Although they appreciate the need for precision and clarity, however, some anthropologists, sociologists, and psychologists have resisted the simplifying assumptions of their disciplines. Particularly in recent years a number of researchers have been reminding us that culture, society, and the human mind are rich, complex phenomena and that simple descriptions seriously distort understanding. These writers have tried to present in their work a richer or thicker description of the events they analyze. They present multiple factors and multiple dimensions in their discussions, resulting in a more flexible, open sort of presentation, in some ways similar to the interpretive essay in literature or the other arts. The anthropological essay on pages 378–384 exemplifies this more humanistic approach to social science.

6. *Know the kind of data that will provide an adequate test.* Different kinds of statements require different kinds of data. Statements concerning worker feelings and perceptions about unions require evidence of what the workers themselves say, which could be provided by interviews or questionnaires. Statements concerning relationships between economic status and union membership require statistics concerning the economic status of members and nonmembers. Furthermore, different economic statistics present different interpretations of economic status. Earned income, total individual income, family income, family assets, home ownership, debt, and ownership of luxury items, such as a boat or videotape machine—each of these sets of statistics will give a different picture of economic condition. You have to decide exactly what you mean by economic status and decide which statistics will most accurately reflect your definition.

7. *Choose a method that will produce the kind of data you want. Know the biases, limitations, and character of the results of your method.* Many different techniques may be available to you, and each will produce different kinds of results. The social sciences raise this problem most critically in terms of how close you are intellectually and personally to the people you are studying. The price for getting inside the minds or experience of people often seems to be a loss

of objectivity; correspondingly, the price of objectivity often seems to be a limitation on the depth of the evidence. Here are some of the options with their advantages and disadvantages.

- *In-depth interviews* give the subject's conscious perception of events or a situation in great detail. You will learn the conscious thoughts, actions, and motivations of the subject. However, unless you compare the interview with other kinds of evidence, you may not be aware of the self-deceptions, unconscious thoughts, or limitations of the individual's perspective. One person's account, no matter how detailed and honest, is not necessarily a true and complete account of what happened. Further, the person being interviewed may not fully open up to the outside interviewer. And the interviewer, the kind of questions, and the manner of asking may influence the answers the subject gives.
- *Participant observation* tries to eliminate the "outsider" problem by having the researcher actually take part in events so that the other people being studied treat the observer as an insider and the observer also has his or her own experience to report. Although participant observation gets the researcher further into the actual experience of events, the researcher may lose objectivity of perspective and may not be able to see the events from the outside.
- *Case studies* view events from the outside by obtaining all possible information about a single event, but because the study focuses on a single complex event, general conclusions may not be warranted. The results from interviews and participant observation often suffer the same problem of lack of generalizability, because one obtains so much information particular to the situation being studied. That is, the individuality of the event appears more forcefully than its representativeness and typicality.
- *Questionnaire surveys,* by asking a large number of people exactly the same questions answered in a standard form, allow more generalized results, less influenced by the personal dynamics of the individual interview and the subjective impressions of the interviewer. However, such surveys tend to be rather removed from the events studied, so you have to rely on the word of the interviewee. Saying that you will vote for a particular candidate or that a particular issue is important to you is not the same thing as pulling a lever in a voting booth.
- *Behavioral observation,* that is, watching what people do and say, but not asking them questions and ideally not even letting them become aware they are being observed, also is an attempt to gain more objective data of the events, influenced neither by the per-

ceptions of the subjects nor by the presence and thinking of the researcher. However, what is gained in objectivity may be lost from the richness of the data.

- *Publicly available statistics,* such as census data or economic figures, are perhaps the least influenced by subjective considerations, the broadest in base, and most generalizable. But public statistics report only limited specific information, not necessarily directly relevant to your research questions. Also the figures usually refer only to external behavior and do not report feelings or perceptions.

8. *Carry out the method carefully so as to produce the best results possible.* Depending on your field of research and the methods you use, this may mean choosing an appropriate and adequately sized sample to work with, providing appropriate control groups, eliminating or taking into account various factors that might contaminate the results, and designing and tuning the instruments correctly. Proper instrument design and use refers not only to actual hardware such as Geiger counters, but also to intellectual instruments such as questionnaires. Extensive research has gone into how to design questionnaires and carry out surveys so as to get as honest, uninfluenced, and useful results as possible.

9. *Record and present your data in as objective a way as possible, free from your biases, personal viewpoint, feelings, or interpretations as possible.* Language is a powerful tool, allowing you to express moods, attitudes, feelings, judgments, concepts, interpretations, and conclusions at the same time as you describe an event. All these subtleties of expression, however, reflect your personal viewpoint. You need to record and present your evidence in such a way that everyone can agree on the data. The following sentence is loaded with personal judgments made by the observer: "The anxious man thought for a long time before making a defensive gesture." Do you *know* he was thinking just because he was silent? Is the movement of the hand necessarily a gesture with some implied meaning? How can you *know* that he was anxious and defensive, or even that anxiety and defensiveness are psychologically valid concepts to invoke? How long is a long time?

Social scientists and natural scientists, in order to avoid such problems, attempt to keep their language *value free and judgment free.* That is, they try to avoid words that imply any opinion, thought, or attitude about the factual material being reported. Frequently they attempt to find a *mathematical* or *statistical* way to represent their results, because numbers are free of connotations. Most dis-

ciplines, as well, have developed *specialized vocabularies* to express
information crucial to the field in terms that most members of the
field feel are objective and precise. In describing what they observe,
social scientists sometimes attempt to use what they call *behavioral
language*—that is, words that simply describe the external behavior
of the animals or people, carefully avoiding anything that implies
reasoning, thoughts, feelings, motivation, or intention. Thus they
might phrase the earlier example, "The man did not speak or move
his limbs for four seconds. His right arm then moved from hanging
straight down to a bent position, the upper arm horizontally straight
forward and the lower arm at ninety degrees, horizontally positioned
in front of the face, with the hand open and facing outwards."
Similarly, other scientists might use what they call *operational language*—that is, language that defines all concepts in terms of a
series of operations or actions so that any person will be able to
identify the same operations or actions and come up with the same
concept. Thus a cake would be defined by the recipe to make it.
If you follow the recipe precisely, what you will wind up with is
a cake.

In some kinds of studies and with some kinds of data, such as
when you are involved with participant observations that really
try to get at the inside of events, you will not be able entirely to
maintain value- and judgment-free language. As mentioned earlier,
a number of anthropologists, sociologists, and psychologists, seeing
the richness of human behavior, write their work in a more interpretive fashion, to get at the complex personal experience behind
the behavior. Some would even argue that the use of behavioral
and operational language implies a mechanistic view of humans as
both subjects and researchers and a more human-centered view
requires a different kind of language. In such situations, the language
is understandably somewhat less tightly objective.

Because objectivity of language is complex, difficult, and uncertain
does not mean you should give up the struggle. Objectivity can
remain an ideal goal, even when unreachable. You should always
attempt to eliminate the obvious biases of your language. Even
when presenting a highly personal perspective, you might begin
by stating what your perspective is so that readers will be able to
take that into account when they read your presentation of the
evidence.

10.   *Present and discuss your data so as to provide as specific an
answer as possible to the original question.* You must state the original
issue clearly and then specifically relate the data to the problem.

You must never let the data overwhelm the point you are trying to make. You must always keep your eye on the central issue and make sure the reader knows the connection between each piece of data and the overall point. In some fields, statistical techniques for combining and focusing the data facilitate clear-cut answers to the issue at hand. Yet no matter how technical the statistical methods you use, you should always return to a clear statement in words about the relationship between the statistics and the statement you are testing.

11. *Organize your presentation of the evidence according to the standard research report format unless you have strong reasons to organize differently.* Sometimes your ideas and evidence may suggest an unusual organization for the presentation of your results, but in general you should organize your paper in the following pattern, whether or not you formally divide your essay in separate sections with subheadings:

- Statement or thesis to be tested
- Source of the statement or review of the relevant literature
- Choice of evidence or data, including the specific situation or event being investigated (sometimes called the *research site*) and justification for the choice
- The method of data collection, including details of the interview technique, questionnaire, or observation method
- Presentation of the data, possibly including charts or other statistical displays, but always described or summarized in ordinary prose
- Discussion of the findings and conclusions

Even the more open organization of the essay that follows, "Ritually Changing the Seasons," observes this general pattern even while adding background discussions of the problem and the culture and life of the people described. The second example that follows, on sex roles and student assertiveness, follows the standard organization much more closely, even to the use of standard subheadings.

An Example: Culture Creates Time

The following paper presented at a professional conference looks at time from an anthropological perspective. That is, rather than treating time as a physical reality or an individually perceived passage, it raises the question of how cultures can create a sense of time, specifically here in terms of a sense of seasons. The culture of Ponape discussed here highlights the specific problem because the climate and agriculture of the tropical island do not define natural seasons strongly, so that whatever sense of seasonality that exists must be culturally created. The essay then explores how the seasons are created.

The paper begins with a general discussion of the problem as experienced in life and as developed in the anthropological literature. Then a focused discussion reveals how seasonality is created on Ponape. Although Glenn Petersen discusses the problem and describes the Ponapeans in as objective terms as possible, he finds it necessary to recreate in personal terms the sense of seasonality as experienced by all people and by the Ponapeans. Thus the essay begins with a literary quotation and includes discussions of how the Ponapeans experience and perceive themselves and their lives. Throughout Petersen makes evident his delight in the Ponapean's pleasant way of life. In considering the larger questions raised by his study, Petersen ends with philosophic thoughts about our experience of time.

Ritually Changing the Seasons

> He's not prepared for death. Even for our kitchens
> We kill the fowl of the season: shall we serve heaven
> With less respect than we do minister
> To our gross selves?
>
> *Measure for Measure*

The changings of the seasons—nature's self-imposed rhythms— seem to have deeply-rooted effects on humans' own culturally-organized rhythms. Our lives are orchestrated and compartmentalized, if not always by the climate, then by other forces symbolized in the metaphor of seasonality. This is particularly true for denizens of the temperate zones and those whose lives are subject to the rigors of desert, arctic, and mountain fastnesses. Even in the tropics, where the full complex of variations in temperature, precipitation, and day-length gives way to a much simpler alternation between wet and dry, this variation can be all-important in shaping subsistence cycles. Yet there are places in the tropics where even rainfall varies little. The people of Ponape, a Micronesian island where natural seasonal variation is minimal, reverse what we tend to think of as the natural order: they impose a cultural order on seasonal change. In doing so they not only change the seasons, they create them.

The Cultural Ecological Approach

Julian Steward (1938) and E. E. Evans-Pritchard (1940) developed an approach to the study of human societies, often called cultural ecology, that stresses the ways in which the basic problems entailed in making a living shape culture, including concepts of seasonality and time. Steward studied the Shoshone, a hunting and gathering people of Western North America, and Evans-Pritchard worked with the Nuer, East African cattle-herders. Both saw that under harsh environmental conditions, where seasons change radically and humans exploit natural resources directly, without the mediation of agriculture, rhythms of conceptualized time closely reflect the natural patterns. But Steward also argued that the anthropologist's task is an empirical one, meant "to ascertain whether the adjustments of human societies to their environments require particular modes of behavior or whether they permit latitude," and he suggested that agriculture to some extent frees humans from environmental exigencies (Steward 1972: 36–39).

Robert Murphy (1970: 155) points out that the process of work is of central importance in the shaping of culture because labor in its various forms represents the impinging of the social order on the environment and vice versa. Seasonality flows from this, we are told: "the concept of seasons is derived from social activities rather than from the climatic changes which determine them" (Evans-Pritchard 1940: 95). Since natural climatic changes significantly affect agriculture in most parts of the earth, it follows that labor and concomitant social organization are at least in part impinged upon by the natural order. If, however, we examine a situation where natural climatic change is almost nil, we might expect little culturally-conceptualized seasonality. Ponapeans do have marked notions of seasonality; since these are not truly determined by the natural order, we must confront the problem of locating some other source for these notions.

The Problem

More than fifty years ago, the Swede Martin Nilsson (1920) argued that in the tropics primitive time-reckoning was closely governed by wet and dry seasons rather than solstices and equinoxes. His study of the tropical Pacific tied conceptions of the seasons to an agricultural cycle that responds to the wet and the dry. He recognized that "the importance of agriculture is so great that the seasons in following it may sometimes depart from the changes of the climate" (1920: 56), but failed to see that agriculture is as much a culturally-determined activity as it is naturally conditioned. When seasons follow agriculture they are being shaped by culture rather than by nature. In parts of the humid tropics, where climatic variations are minimal or even negligible, seasonality becomes almost pure cultural artifice. The tropical Pacific offers just such circumstances. Working, respectively, in the Solomon Islands and the Bismarck Archipelago, Douglas Oliver (1955) and Hortense Powdermaker (1971) described systems where "there is no basis for the agricultural cycling which structures time for so many peoples" (Oliver 1955: 37).

Ponapean Agriculture

On Ponape, largest of the Eastern Caroline Islands, very similar conditions obtain. This high island, volcanic in origin, lies 6° north of the equator. Mean daily temperatures stay above 80°F and 81° throughout the year. Rainfall during each of the two months of what is optimistically called the "dry season" averages 11–12″, over two-thirds the monthly average for the rest of the year. There is, to be sure, climatic change on Ponape, but it is of almost negligible effect in determining subsistence necessities. And yet, Ponapean culture is marked by seasons, and by a host of first fruits rituals and rites of increase.

The Ponapean diet rests upon a foundation of breadfruit and fish. Pork, dog, and, now, tinned meats add to the animal protein. Bananas, yams, wet (*Cyrtosperma*) and dry (*Colocasia*) taros, and imported rice fill out the staple starches. Coconuts and a number of fruits complete the basic subsistence constellation. The heavy reliance on long-term tree crops means that farm land is in perpetual use.

The Ponapeans rely on breadfruit so thoroughly that the three periods during the year when breadfruit are in greatest supply are known as "times of plenty" (*rahk*), while the brief interstices between these are "hard times" (*isol* or *ansoun oapwahl*). However, in the course of a year and one-half's fieldwork on the island, I never saw a period when there was no breadfruit at all. By utilizing more than sixty-five named varieties of breadfruit, Ponapeans harvest year round. Bananas and taros are also harvested at any time during the year. Since pit or preserved breadfruit is easily made and stored, there really are no lean periods on Ponape. Indeed, several times Ponapeans told me that they prefer "hard times" to the "season of plenty" because then they are not so busy eating breadfruit and can enjoy a greater variety of other foods.

I repeat: there is seasonal change on Ponape, but its influence on subsistence activities is minimal. When breadfruit is ripe, which is most of the year, it is harvested. When it is not—or when there is a paucity—there are ample supplies of banana and taro to draw upon. Ponapeans are well-fed throughout the year and variations in most subsistence activities are matters of intensity rather than kind.

Nevertheless, certain Ponapean subsistence activities are markedly seasonal. In particular, the Ponapean calendar revolves around the yam season and complex host of activities which comprise it. Yams and yam cultivation are tremendously important to Ponapean culture. Along with kava (a mildly tranquilizing beverage) and pigs, yams play a central role in the competitive prestige politics of feasting that typifies Ponapean life and parallels the potlatching and big-man complexes of North America's Northwest Coast and Melanesia. Cultivation of yams is no less than an art. There are well over one hundred varieties and they are grown to sizes difficult to imagine without firsthand experience. Two-hundred-pound yams are common, I have seen four-hundred-pound yams, and I have reliable reports of yams that must have weighed over one-quarter of a ton. Much hard work and practical as well as esoteric knowledge is involved in raising such yams. They are a major topic of conversation and their cultivation is a key facet of the male Ponapean role pattern. But yams do not make a major contribution to the Ponapean diet.

Ponapeans say that yams are planted in order to provide food during the period when breadfruit is in shortest supply, November-February. But Ponapeans also maintain that an accomplished farmer has such great quantities of breadfruit and other foods that he does not need to rely upon yams during this period. Thus, great size indicates that a man has been able to leave his yams in the ground to grow, rather than digging them up for food.

Upon closer examination, one learns that the Ponapean yam season is largely a cultural artifice imposed upon the agricultural system. When one considers that Ponapeans can and do harvest yams as early as July and as late as April (and occasionally as late as May and June), it becomes clear that it is not nature that determines the Ponapean yearly cycle, but rather the Ponapeans themselves.

The period from November to March is known as "yam season" and is marked by an almost continuous series of feasts. Ponapeans say that there is "no rest during the yam season," referring to feasting activity rather than farming labor. Besides the various feasts made to honor chiefs and pay them tribute, a series of rites and minor feasts mark the many stages in the progressing yam season. Breadfruit, incidentally, is also subject to a whole series of rites of increase, not just a single first fruits ceremony. The Ponapean year is broken up by these events and considerable planning is involved in preparing for each season's events. We find, then, that in a case where natural seasons do not impose conditions significantly affecting labor processes, the people themselves do, and seasonality remains important to the orderly passing of life.

Time on Ponape

Steward's empirical method and a focus on the organization of labor provide us with an analysis of man-environment, or cultural, ecological relations in the Ponapean case, but the conditions are reversed from those more widely studied. Agriculture organizes labor as much as it harnesses nature. When humans are not forced by their environment to make seasonal responses, they simply overturn the relationship. Culture forces nature to respond.

Ponapeans ritually change their seasons, dividing up the year into breadfruit and yam intervals and embellishing these seasons with great ceremonial and political import. But why do they do this, when it seems not to be required by simple subsistence needs? To understand, we must turn from our images of the environment to our images of ourselves.

The conjunction of the Ponapean environment and agricultural system results in strikingly undemanding labor requirements. Ponapeans are not under pressure to complete specific tasks ahead of climatic or growth deadlines and the tempo of life there reflects this. Ponapeans work only a few hours a day at agricultural tasks, and spend much time doing very little. In particular, four- and five-hour kava sessions are daily occurrences. Being a good farmer, i.e., producing large yams and kava in quantity and raising pigs, is important for prestige—not subsistence—purposes, so agricultural work plays a major part in the Ponapean male identity. Work on Ponape is as much a way of passing time as it is a necessity; something to do as well as something to be done. In consequence, while Ponapeans speak of specific periods of time (e.g., mornings, days, and years), they must resort to the term *kulok*—"clock" (borrowed from English)— to deal with the daily passing of time. Feasts and other rituals, which serve to arbitrarily impose seasonality and a relatively pressing sense of time upon the otherwise timeless flow of Ponapean life, are significant precisely because of the structured contrast they create in opposition to most of Ponapean life.

Clifford Geertz (1966) has described the Balinese concept of time in much the same way. He speaks of "full" and "empty" days: days when important things, such as feasts, take place and days when nothing happens. Ponapeans live in similar empty and full times— periods when nothing happens and periods marked by feasts.

Edmund Leach (1961: 133–34) has argued that for "primitives" time is alternate, rather than flowing, and it is established through the "discontinuity of repeated contrasts." One function of regular festivals is the ordering of time, with the intervals between festivals providing named periods of time. Without such festivals these periods would not exist and all order would go out of life. While we speak of *measuring* time, as if it were something concrete, in fact, we *create* it by creating these intervals in social life.

My data from Ponape concur with such an approach, but only this far. For it has been generally argued that it is seasonal change which sets the pace for created time. Leach says that it is not astrological time which acts as man's chronometer, but "the year's round itself, the annual sequence of economic activities, which provide time" (ibid.). Van Gennep (1960: 179), who saw an "exact parallel" between seasonal rites of passage and rites of increase and propitiation, believed that the natural seasons were relevant to humans only through their "economic repercussions." And Evans-Pritchard wrote of Nuer time-reckoning that "it is a series of conceptualizations of natural changes, and that the selection of points of reference is determined by the significance which these natural changes have for human activities" (1940: 104). For these thinkers, time remains bound to natural seasonal change, even if it is not exactly the same as seasonal change.

As Geertz has remarked, "men are made aware, or rather make themselves aware of the passage of time" by marking many things, including not only the passing of seasons or the progress of plant life, but also by the measured cycling of rites, agricultural work, or household activities. The Balinese calendar largely ignores seasonal changes and turns rather on feasts and rites which mark out the full days from the empty (Geertz 1966: 42–52). Likewise, the Ponapean "calendar" turns free of any climatic demands from the natural seasons.

My point is that the social activities—the feasts and rituals— which man uses to "create" time, to "make himself aware of time," do not a priori follow from seasonal changes. Western—temperate— societies have assumed the priority of seasonal change in human awareness of time. And anthropological thought has accepted this. But it need not be the case. Seasonality can be ignored, as it is in Bali. Or it can be imposed where it is absent, as it is on Ponape. For Ponapeans, like all other people, must create time. And it is this, of course, which remains as the ultimate question. Why do we create time?

My research on Ponape leads me in retrospect to raise the question, but provides me with no answer. In closing, however, I would suggest that we might turn in the direction pointed to by some of the late eighteenth-century French *philosophes* (e.g., Rousseau, Diderot, Buffon), as summed up by Georges Poulet (1959: 24): "To exist, then, is to be one's present, and also one's past and one's recollections."

We do not possess infinite memories, and in order to hold onto the past that makes us what we are today, we divide it up into intervals that can be dealt with. It is thus that the Ponapeans make time by ritually changing and thereby creating the seasons.

Acknowledgments: The data on which this paper draws are based upon research done on Ponape, February 1974 to August 1975, supported by two grants from the National Institute for Mental Health. Further information on Ponapean economics and agriculture can be found in Bascom (1965) and Petersen (1976).

—Glenn Petersen

References Cited

Bascom, William
    1965   Ponape: A Pacific Island Economy in Transition. Berkeley: Univ. of California Press.

Evans-Pritchard, E. E.
    1940   The Nuer. Oxford: Clarendon Press.

Geertz, Clifford
    1966   Person, Time, and Conduct in Bali. New Haven: Yale
           Univ. Southest Asia Studies.

Leach, Edmund
    1961   Rethinking Anthropology. London: Athlone.

Murphy, Robert F.
    1970   "Basin Ethnography and Ecological Theory." In
           E. Swanson (ed.) Languages and Cultures of Western
           North America. Pocatello: Idaho State Univ. Press.

Nilsson, Martin P.
    1920   Primitive Time-Reckoning. Lund: Acta Societatis Hu-
           maniorum Litterarum Lundensis.

Oliver, Douglas L.
    1955   A Solomon Islands Society. Cambridge: Harvard Univ.
           Press.

Petersen, Glenn T.
    1976   Prestige Economy and Political Economics in the Eastern
           Caroline Islands. PhD dissertation, Columbia University.

Poulet, Georges
    1959 (1950)   Studies in Human Time. New York: Harper &
                  Bros.

Powdermaker, Hortense
    1971 (1933)   Life in Lesu. New York: W. W. Norton & Co.

Steward, Julian H.
    1938   Basin-Plateau Aboriginal Sociopolitical Groups. Wash-
           ington, D.C.: Government Printing Office
    1972 (1955)   Theory of Culture Change. Urbana: Univ. of
                  Illinois Press.

Van Gennep, Arnold
    1960 (1908)   The Rites of Passage. Chicago: Univ. of Chicago
                  Press.

An Example: Observing Student Assertiveness

The following example from the journal *Sex Roles* tests the idea that male and female college students behave with different levels of assertiveness and aggressiveness and that these levels vary depending on the sex of the professor. This statement itself greatly narrows the larger issues of sex roles raised in the article's introduction. Further, the attributes of assertiveness and aggressiveness are indicated, respectively, by the specific behaviors of speaking in class and interrupting others.

Such behavioral definitions—e.g., aggressiveness is interrupting someone else—allow the researcher, Virignia R. Brooks, to relate abstract personal qualities with measurable behaviors and to establish a series of procedures for observing and recording these behaviors. Quite simply, she has students record how many times and for how long students speak in class and who interrupts whom how frequently. She then sorts these data according to sex of the speakers and the teachers. She finds not only that there are differences between male and female students but that the differences depend on the sex of the teacher. When the teacher is female, the male students show more dominant behavior, but when the teacher is male, all the students act more or less the same. Her interesting findings may lead you to observe the behavior of yourself and your classmates a little more closely. You may even wish to collect similar data for your classes to see whether her findings hold true at your college.

After an opening summary, the untitled introduction presents an extensive review of the literature leading up to the specific statements to be tested and a description of the present study. The method, results, and discussion follow, each in a separate section labeled appropriately. Although the introduction presents abstract concepts and complicated discussion of the literature, the later sections describing the actual observations are rather straightforward, concise, and easy to follow.

Some readers may find the abstractions of the introduction phrased more difficultly than necessary, but such difficult passages frequently appear in theoretical discussions in the social sciences. Defenders of this style say it is necessary to keep the framework of ideas precisely defined. More familiar language, they contend, would encourage the imprecision of everyday thought and would lose the conceptual framework of the ideas. Whatever you think of the style, the concepts presented touch deeply on our social life, and the empirical work in the latter part of the article is presented simply and directly.

Sex Differences in Student Dominance Behavior in Female and Male Professors' Classrooms

Measures of verbal participation and interaction among graduate students provided a comparison of male and female dominance behavior in the classroom, and measures of the contextual effect of sex of professor provided further data on the interrelatedness of sex, status, and dominance behavior. Male students were found to exhibit significantly more aggressiveness (interruptive behavior) than female students in both male and female professors' classes, although significantly more male aggressiveness occurred in female professors' classes than in male professors' classes. Male students were significantly more assertive (frequency and duration of speech) in female professors' classes only. In student-to-student interaction, aggressiveness was predominantly exchanged between sexes rather than among same-sex members.

Negative effects of female sex-role socialization and stereotypes have been amply documented in recent years, particularly in areas of mental health (Bem, 1972; Cannon & Redick, 1973; Farberow & Schneidman, 1965; Gove, 1972; Gurin, Veroff, & Feld, 1960; Johnson & Terman, 1935; Knupfer, Clark, & Room, 1966; U.S. Department of Health, Education and Welfare, 1970) and achievement (Block, Von Der Lippe, & Block, 1973). One consequence of this reexamination of sex-role efficacy has been an increase in the scrutiny of verbal and kinesic behaviors that maintain and regulate the power differential of status quo sex-role ideology. Using the guiding principle that behavior is reciprocal, the microanalysis of sex-related behavior becomes an integral part of social change efforts.

Studies of sex differences in verbal assertiveness have shown that males consistently report themselves as more assertive than females (Hollandsworth & Wall, 1977). Greater assertiveness in males seems particularly evident in mixed group interaction in which the traditional pattern of male dominance and female deference has been found to prevail (Aries, 1974; Eisler, Hersen, & Blanchard, 1975; Hall, 1972; Richey, 1974; Skillings, Hersen, Bellack, & Becker, 1978). Results (Hall, 1972; Richey, 1974) indicating that women talk less both in frequency and duration, are more easily interrupted, and support and defend their own ideas less have import for academic performance for both female students and female professors.

This linkage between assertiveness, frequency of speech, and academic student participation in the classroom as measured by frequency of speaking was positively correlated with the College Self-Expression Scale, a self-report measure of assertiveness (Galassi, Delco, Galassi, & Bastien, 1974), course grade, and semester quality point index. Although this study (Kuhl, 1976) reported that participation did not appear to be related to sex of student, various contextual influences were not examined. Assertiveness is not a unitary dimension, but is functionally related to the social context of the interpersonal interaction (Eisler et al., 1975; Skillings et al., 1978).

The much-debated "fear-of-success" phenomenon initially investigated by Horner (1969) provided evidence that women expect social rejection as a consequence of academic success. The existence of this expectation continues to be explained as a consequence of ambivalence for women, created by their pull toward both achievement and affiliation with the other sex, and their "fear" that success in one rules out success in the other (Bardwick, 1971). Other evidence indicates that women have lower levels of academic self-confidence and are less competitive compared with men, although these characteristics seem not to appear until college (Maccoby & Jacklin, 1974). And women competing with men evidence performance decrements in some situations, but not in others (Medinick & Weissman, 1976).

What then, are some of the consequences of "success" for women who mount the obstacles of academic environs and achieve faculty status? Studies focusing on attitudes toward competent women spotlight the Catch 22 in vivo of women professors. Behavioral characteristics such as self-confidence, assertiveness, competitiveness, rationality, and ambition—which are intrinsic contemporary requirements of academic life are simultaneously defined socioculturally as male behavioral prerogatives. These behaviors in women have been found to elicit predominantly negative responses from men and, to a lesser extent, from other women (Hagen & Kahn, 1975; Shaffer & Wegley, 1974).

Although Spence and Helmreich (1972) found that the combination of competence and "masculine" interests in a woman received the highest appraisals from both men and women, subsequent research has found these appraisals to differ under different experimental conditions. Shaffer and Wegley (1974) found that although attractiveness to an employer was assessed by both sexes to be greater for a "competent-masculine" woman than a "competent-feminine" woman, the "competent-masculine" woman was also judged less socially attractive and less attractive as a work partner. Thus, Shaffer and Wegley (1974) concluded that an aspiring career woman might well adopt a "masculine" sex-role preference to impress her employer, but would do so at the risk of some social ostracism from peers of both sexes. Using more discriminant variables, Hagen and Kahn (1975) found that men only like a competent woman from a distance and not in competitive contexts. Employing Aronson's (1969) premise that expectancy disconfirmation affects one's self-esteem, Hagen and Kahn (1975) suggested that males who must interact with women of equal or higher achieved status would experience expectancy disconfirmation, the expectancy of ascribed secondary status not being met, and subsequently would experience reduced self-esteem. This threat to self-esteem may be countered by attempts to reassert dominance over the dissonance-creating woman.

The highly visible status characteristic of sex as a major variable in whether dominance behavior is elicited has been supported by investigations of both kinestic (e.g., Frieze & Ramsey, 1976) and verbal (e.g., Hall, 1972; Richey, 1974) behavior; and investigations of mixed-sex versus same-sex interactions have underscored the perceived status differential of men and women (Eisler et al., 1975; Skillings et al., 1978). The latter two studies indicate that both males and females comply with the wishes of males more frequently than those of females, and both males and females are more likely to ask a female to change her behavior than a male. One question that emerges from these findings is, at what point, if any, does female achieved status reverse or reduce male dominance behavior? Similarly, does female behavior toward other women of equal or higher status continue to demonstrate same-sex prejudice, as noted in earlier studies (Goldberg, 1968; Bernard, 1964)?

The present study combined aspects of the various lines of research discussed above—that is, women's "success" ambivalence and subsequent lesser assertiveness, negative perceptions of competent women, and the interrelatedness of status, sex, and dominance behavior. Specifically, it sought to ascertain whether dominance behavior in university classrooms would vary according to sex of student and/or sex of professor, and, if so, to identify which interactional effects would contribute most importantly to differences in dominance behavior. Dominance behavior refers to both assertiveness and aggressiveness, but assertiveness generally denotes behavior aimed at maintaining one's own prerogatives, while aggressiveness generally denotes behavior that attempts to usurp the prerogatives of others. For purposes of this study, frequency and duration of speech were viewed as indices of assertiveness, while interruptive behavior was viewed as an index of aggressiveness.

Method

The method employed assumed that quantification of spontaneous verbal behavior in a natural competitive setting would be a more accurate index of male and female dominance behavior and of interactional effects of sex and status than either self-report, role-playing, or videotape methods, which might allow misrepresentation of actual behavior.

Subjects were first-year graduate students in a social work master's degree program. Verbal behavior of students was recorded by tape and pencil-and-paper counts by two members of the first-year class in 16 separate class periods, each of three-hour duration. Thus, a total of 48 hours of classroom interaction was monitored, 24 hours each in male and female professors' classes. Three different female and three different male professors' classes were monitored to reduce the possible skewing of results by idiosyncratic influences. Professors included in the study were selected by the sole criterion of teaching courses in which the two students who collected data were enrolled. Subjects were not apprised of the recording function to avoid influencing spontaneous participation in class discussions. Overlap existed among students who were in monitored classes, so that although in all classes combined 72 males and 222 females were represented, the same individuals were often in more than one class being monitored.

Information recorded for each class period included (1) sex of professor, (2) number of male and female students present in class, (3) number of times a male or female student spoke, (5) number of times a male or female student interrupted a male or female student, and (6) number of times a male or female student interrupted a male or female professor.

Chi-square analyses based on grouped data from all the monitored classes were used to determine whether differences were statistically significant. Statistical computations allowed for the actual sex ratios in male professors' and female professors' classes (21% male, 79% female; 27% male, 73% female; respectively). Table 1 summarizes these data.

Results

In male professors' classes, no significant differences were found in number of times male and female students spoke or in duration of their speech relative to their proportion in the class. However, in female professors' classes, male students spoke significantly more

Table 1. *Summary of Data Comparing Male and Female Classroom Interaction*[a]

Verbal behavior	Male professors		Female professors	
	Male students	Female students	Male students	Female students
Number of times students speak	60 (26)	167 (74)	161 (51)	155 (49)
Length of time students speak[b]	14.24 (24)	44.39 (76)	49.34 (49)	51.02 (51)
Number of times female students interrupt other students	6 (86)	1 (14)	45 (83)	9 (17)
Number of times male students interrupt other students	0 (0)	7 (100)	6 (89)	47 (11)
Number of times students interrupt professors	8 (33)	16 (67)	23 (63)	13 (37)

[a]*Note.* The expected proportion of male to female students in male professors' classes was 21% to 79%; in female professors' classes, 28% to 76%. Numbers in parentheses indicate observed proportions.
[b]Total minutes and seconds in 48 hours.

often ($p < .001$) and significantly longer ($p < .001$) than female students.

Male students accounted for 33.3% of interruptions of male professors while representing 21% of the students, and accounted for 63.8% of interruptions of female professors while representing 27% of students. Thus, male students interrupted both male and female professors significantly more often than female students ($p < .01$ and $p < .001$, respectively), and interrupted female professors significantly more often than male professors ($p < .001$). From another perspective, 74.2% of all male student interruptions of professors were of female professors. By comparison, 55.2% of all female student interruptions of professors were of male professors, although female student interruptions of all professors were disproportionately less than male student interruptions.

Student interruptive behavior of other students was examined in relation to who interrupted whom and in what context. Of male student interruptions of other students, 90% were of female students. Interestingly, however, 83.6% of female student interruptions of other students were of male students.

For total student interruptive behavior of other students, male students again interrupted other students (male and female) significantly more often in both male professors' ($p < .001$) and female professors' ($p < .001$) classes. For interruptive behavior toward both other students and professors, 83.5% of male student interruptions and 74.4% of female student interruptions occurred in female professors' classes.

In sum, while male students comprised an average of about one-fourth (24.5%) of the student sample, they accounted for 40.7% of speech frequency, 39.8% of speech duration, and one-half (50.3%) of all interruptions. Finally, more than three-fourths (79%) of all interruptions occurred in female professors' classes.

Discussion

The results of this study emphasize the situation specificity of dominance behavior, as previously reported (Eisler et al., 1975; Skillings et al., 1978). They also support the consistent finding that males exhibit more dominance behavior than females in mixed-sex groups (Aries, 1974; Eisler et al., 1975; Hall, 1972; Richey, 1974; Shillings et al., 1978). The exception to this conclusion found in this study occurred in male professors' classes; in the presence of a higher status male, no differences were found in frequency and duration of speech between male and female students.

Male dominance behavior was significantly greater in female professors' classes than in male professors' classes in all areas, that is in frequency and duration of speech and in frequency of interruption. This result, coupled with the finding that although male students interrupted both male and female professors more often than did female students, they interrupted female professors significantly more often than male professors, suggests that the ascribed secondary status of women takes cognitive precedence among male students over their achieved status. This finding was further evidenced in the results showing that male dominance behavior was oriented predominantly toward females, including both professors and peers.

The fact that no significant differences in assertive behavior between male and female students were found in male professors' classes suggests that the attribution of higher status to male professors by male students tends to dampen these students' dominance behavior. Female students, although generally displaying less dominance behavior than their male peers, seemed not to differentiate between high status females and males, as no significant differences in levels of assertiveness were obtained between male and female professors' classes. However, female students were significantly more aggressive toward male students in female professors' classes. Two possible explanations are suggested. Male aggressiveness was also much higher in female professors' classes, and significantly higher than that of female peers. Thus, greater female aggressiveness may have been more reactive than proactive. Second, female students may have felt less constrained to react in the presence of a female authority figure than in the presence of a male authority figure. In either case, although speculative, these findings suggest that the women's movement has differentially impacted women's and men's behavior and attitudes toward sex equality. Its positive effects on women's self-concepts as well as their evaluations of other women may be reflected in females' greater competitiveness with males than females in the classroom, as indicated by the finding that most aggressiveness was exchanged between sexes rather than among same-sex members.

Another explanation for the sizable increase in male dominance behavior in female professors' classes involves the possibility of differential teaching styles of male and female professors. Some support for the speculation that male professors are more lecture oriented and female professors are more discussion oriented is found in the fact that student participation utilized nearly twice the amount of class time in female professors' classes compared to male professors' classes. This difference suggests that female professors may encourage and reinforce participation more than male professors; and as a product of differential sex-role socialization, male students as a group may take more initiative to respond than female students as a group. If this assumption of stylistic complementarity between female professors and male students were correct, however, the fact that no significant differences between male and female student assertiveness occurred in male professors' classes would remain unexplained. That is, the disproportionate dominance behavior of male students occurred only in female professors' classes. It also would not account for the greatly increased between-sex aggressiveness in female professors' classes. A more plausible explanation would concur with the Hagen and Kahn (1975) finding that men may like competent women at a distance, but not in competitive situations. Unfortunately for both women professors and students, the expectancy disconfirmation theory that males who must interact with women of equal or higher status experience a reduction in self-esteem, and react to this threat by attempting to reassert dominance over the same or higher status woman, appears to be supported by the present study's results.

—Virginia R. Brooks,
Sex Roles 19, no. 7 (1982): 683–690

References

Aries, E. Interaction patterns and themes of male, female, and mixed groups. *Proceedings of the 82nd Annual Convention of the American Psychological Association,* 1974.

Aronson, E. The theory of cognitive dissonance: A current perspective. In L. Berkowitz (Ed.), *Advances in experimental social psychology* (Vol. 4). New York: Academic Press, 1969.

Bardwick, J. *Psychology of women.* New York: Harper & Row, 1971.

Bem, S. *Psychology looks at sex-roles: Where have all the androgynous people gone?* Paper presented at the University of California–Los Angeles Symposium on Women, Los Angeles, May 1972.

Bernard, J. *Academic women.* University Park: Pennsylvania State University Press, 1964.

Block, J. H., Von Der Lippe, A., & Block, J. Sex-role and socialization patterns: Some personality concomitants and environmental antecedents. *Journal of Consulting and Clinical Psychology,* 1973, *41,* 321–341.

Cannon, M., & Redick, R. *Differential utilization of psychiatric facilities by men and women, United States.* National Institute of Mental Health, Statistical Note 81. Washington, D.C.: Survey and Reports Section, Biometry Branch, 1973.

Eisler, R. M., Hersen, M., & Blanchard, E. B. Situational determinants of assertive behaviors. *Journal of Consulting and Clinical Psychology,* 1975, *43,* 333–340.

Farberow, N., & Schneidman, E. Statistical comparisons between attempted and committed suicides. In N. Farberow, *The cry for help.* New York: McGraw-Hill, 1965.

Frieze, I. H., & Ramsey, S. J. Nonverbal maintenance of traditional sex roles. *Journal of Social Issues,* 1976, *32,* 133–141.

Galassi, J. P., Delo, J. S., Galassi, M. D., & Bastein, S. The College Sex-Expression Scales: A measure of assertiveness. *Behavior Therapy,* 1974, *5,* 165–171.

Goldberg, P. Are women prejudiced against women? *Transaction,* April 1968, pp. 28–33.

Gove, W. The relationship between sex-roles, marital status and mental illness. *Social Forces,* 1972, *51,* 33–44.

Gurin, G., Veroff, J., & Feld, S. *Americans view their mental health: A nationwide interview survey.* New York: Basic Books, 1960.

Hagen, R. L., & Kahn, A. Discrimination against competent women. *Journal of Applied Social Psychology,* 1975, *5,* 362–376.

Hall, K. *Sex differences in initiation and influence in decision making groups of prospective teachers.* Unpublished doctoral dissertation, Stanford University, 1972.

Hollandsworth, J. G., Jr., & Wall, K. E. Sex differences in assertive behavior: An empirical investigation. *Journal of Counseling Psychology,* 1977, *24,* 217–222.

Horner, M. Fail: Bright women. *Psychology Today,* 1969, *3,* 36–38.

Johnson, W. B., & Terman, L. M. Personality characteristics of happily married, unhappily married, and divorced persons. *Character and personality,* 1935, *2*(June), 305–315.

Knupfer, G., Clark, W., & Room, R. The mental health of the unmarried. *American Journal of Psychiatry,* 1966, *122,* 841–851.

Kuhl, E. C., Jr. Assertion training effects on oral classroom behavior of college students (Doctoral dissertation, University of Maryland, 1976). *Dissertation Abstracts International,* 1976, *37,* 810A–811A. (University Microfilms No. 76–18, 822).

Maccoby, E. E., & Jacklin, C. N. *The psychology of sex differences.* Stanford: Stanford University Press, 1974.

Mednick, M. T. S., & Weissman, H. J. The psychology of women—Selected topics. In S. Cox (Ed.), *Female psychology: The emerging self.* Palo Alto: Science Research Associates, 1976.

Richey, C. A. *Increased female assertiveness through self-reinforcement.* Unpublished doctoral dissertation, University of California, Berkeley, 1974.

Shaffer, D. R., & Wegley, C. Success orientation and sex-role congruence as determinants of the attractiveness of competent women. *Journal of Personality,* 1974, *42,* 586–600.

Skillings, R. E., Hersen, M., Bellack, A. S., & Becker, M. P. Relationship of specific and global measures of assertion in college females. *Journal of Clinical Psychology,* 1978, *34,* 346–353.

Spence, J. T., & Helmrich, R. Who likes competent women? Competence, sex-role congruence of interests, and subjects' attitudes toward women as determinants of interpersonal attraction. *Journal of Applied Social Psychology,* 1972, *2,* 197–213.

U.S. Department of Health, Education and Welfare. *Selected symptoms of psychological distress, United States.* Washington, D.C.: U.S. Public Health Service, Health Service and Mental Health Administration, August 1970.

Writing Assignments

1. Following the methods described in the article on dominance behavior in the classroom on pages 385–393, but using data from your own classes, repeat the kind of observations described to test the author's findings. Then write a short report (300–500 words) either confirming or disconfirming Virginia Brook's conclusions.

2. Design and carry out a series of observations to test the claims of sexism in children's learning about computers, as presented in the article "Second Class Citizens?" excerpted on pages 119–121. Report your results in a short article (300–500 words) for the same journal, *Psychology Today,* the original article appeared in.

3. In the excerpt on pages 83–85, Daniel Boorstin describes some basic characteristics of the pseudoevent, which he claims is being increasingly reported in the news. Using his defining characteristics of the pseudoevent, make observations to see whether pseudoevents are reported as frequently as he claims in newspapers and on television newscasts (both local and national). You may wish to count both the number of stories of pseudoevents and the time or space devoted to them. You might also consider these as percentages of total reported news. Report your findings in a short essay appropriate for a class in journalism.

4. Design and carry out a series of observations to test the following ideas from Erving Goffman's *Relations in Public.* Then write up your findings in a short report to your classmates.

Pedestrian Traffic

A few comments about pedestrian traffic seem possible. In American downtown streets, traffic tends to sort itself out into two opposite-going sides. The dividing line is somewhere near the middle of the sidewalk but is subject to momentary shifting (to accommodate sudden bunching of traffic in one direction) and to longer term displacement caused by the tendency for the journey to and from work to involve a large volume going in one direction in the morning and the reverse at night. As in road traffic, the side going in one's direction tends to be on the right of the dividing line. However, pedestrians on either side who desire to walk quickly sometimes move to the curb and there manage two-way flow. The innermost part of the street tends to be slowest, perhaps because of the obstruction produced by window shoppers and those entering and leaving buildings. Apart from these considerations, lane formation *within* the right- or left-hand side tends not to be marked, although when an individual momentarily shifts from a lane to facilitate traffic flow, he is apparently likely to shift back into it after the interference is past. It might also be added that at crosswalks the side-division tends to break down, and those going in one direction will take up both sides at the curb, thus facing across the street a broad front of others ready to come toward them. Contrariwise, there are steps and tunnels that physically mark and thereby consolidate two-lane flow.

When routing by divided two-way flow is not used to avoid collision during opposite-direction passing, pedestrians tend (in America) to use the road traffic device of veering to the right, although this practice is breached for many reasons, among which are the principled ones that males should take the road side when passing females and that pedestrians have the right to cut across the sidewalk at any point, there being no full equivalent of periodic road intersections.

The workability of lane and passing rules is based upon two processes important in the organization of public life: externalization and scanning.

By the term "externalization," or "body gloss," I refer to the process whereby an individual pointedly uses over-all body gesture to make otherwise unavailable facts about his situation gleanable. Thus, in driving and walking the individual conducts himself—or rather his vehicular shell—so that the direction, rate, and resoluteness of his proposed course will be readable. In ethological terms, he provides an "intention display." By providing this gestural prefigurement and committing himself to what it foretells, the individual makes himself into something that others can read and predict from; by employing this device at proper strategic junctures—ones where his indicated course will be perceived as a promise or warning or threat but not as a challenge—he becomes something to which they can adapt without loss of self-respect.

The term "scanning" does not have to be defined, but the way it is done in pedestrian traffic needs to be described. When a pedestrian in American society walks down the street, he seems to make an assumption that those to the front of a close circle around him are ones whose course he must check up on, and those who are a person or two away or moving behind his sight-line can be tuned out. In brief, the individual, as he moves along, tends to maintain a scanning or check-out area. (By angling his own head so as not to be directly obstructed visually by the head of the pedestrian ahead of him, he can ensure his maintenance of this view.) As oncomers enter the individual's scanning range—something like three or four sidewalk squares away—they are commonly glanced at briefly and thereafter disattended because their distance from him and their indicated rate and direction of movement imply that collision is not likely and that no perception by them of him is necessary for his easily avoiding collision. A simple "body check" is involved, albeit one performed more circumspectly (at present) by women than by men. This check tends to occur when the individual making it can introduce a large directional change through a small and therefore undemeaning angular correction. Once others have been checked out satisfactorily, they can be allowed to come close without this being cause for concern. Thus the individual can generally cease to concern himself with others as soon as they have come close enough abreast of him so that any interference from them would require a very abrupt turn. And further, since he apparently does not concern himself with oncomers who are separated from him by others, he can, in dense traffic, be unconcerned about persons who are actually very close to him. Therefore, the scanning area is not a circle but an elongated oval, narrow to either side of the individual and longest in front of him, constantly changing in area depending on traffic density around him. Note that even as the individual is checking out those who are just coming into range, so they will be checking him out, which means that oncomers will be eyeing each other at something of the same moment and that this moment will be similarly located in the course of both; yet this act is almost entirely out of awareness.

When an individual deems that a simple body-check is not sufficient, as when a collision course is apparent or there is no clear indication of the other's course, then additional assurances are likely to be sought. He can ostentatiously take or hold a course, waiting to do this until he can be sure that the other is checking him out. If he wants to be still more careful, he can engage in a "checked-body-check"; after he has given a course indication, he can make sure the signal has been picked up by the other, either by meeting the other's eyes (although not for engagement) or by noting the other's direction of vision, in either case establishing that his own course gesture has not likely been overlooked. In brief, he can check up on the other's eye check on him, the assumption here being that the other can be relied on to act safely providing only that he has perceived the situation. Finally, a brief face engagement may be initiated in which one party signals what he proposes they do and the other party signals agreement. (A strategic device here is to signal a collaborative routing in which the other has a slight advantage, this usually assuring agreement.) In all of this maneuvering, two special moments can be found. First, there is the "critical sign": the act on the part of the other that finally allows the individual to discover what it is the other proposes to do. Second, there is the "establishment point": the moment both parties can feel that critical signs have been exchanged regarding compatible directions and timing, and that both appreciate that they both appreciate that this has occurred. It is then that movements can be executed with full security and confidence; it is then that those involved can feel fully at ease and fully turn their attention elsewhere.

14 Writing About Designed Events: The Experimental Sciences

Experimental sciences attempt to simplify the problems of observation by creating new, narrowly focused, carefully controlled events to provide specific types of data. Not all questions can be studied by experimental techniques, but when applicable, experiments provide powerful tools for developing and confirming knowledge. Experimental methods and laboratory techniques vary, of course, from field to field and problem to problem. But all experiments share four features: minimizing personal factors, measuring precisely, controlling extraneous factors, and testing theory. Guidelines for the format of the experimental report should aid you in your work in experimental disciplines. Sample essays come from developmental linguistics and medically oriented psychology.

Controlling Events

The scientific experiment simplifies and focuses observations by simplifying and focusing the event itself. Because the experimenter designs the initial conditions (but not the results) of the event, he or she can control personal and other extraneous factors and can maximize precision of measurement. Moreover, the experiment can be designed to test a particular theory or hypothesis.

Not all events can be studied through experiment; for example, no one has yet been able to create an earthquake under laboratory conditions nor a political revolution. Moreover, laboratory conditions may so distort some events that the experimental results, stripped of natural complexity and context, may be misleading. Studies of writing done under laboratory conditions, for example, have been questioned because the artificial laboratory atmosphere both changes the behavior of the writers studied and divorces them from the reality of the writing task. Particularly in studying human behavior, experiments might not tell what you would want to know about behavior in naturally occurring situations. But for those situations where experimental techniques apply, the experiment can provide a definitive, focused test of a claim.

Experimental methods vary among disciplines and even among different approaches within the same discipline. Different research questions, different objects under study, different equipment, different procedures, and different modes of analysis lead to different criteria of precision and validity. What counts as an experimental fact in one discipline may be of little interest to another, understandably enough; somewhat more surprisingly, that same fact may not even be considered valid in another field—and not just because some disciplines may be more rigorous than others. A physicist may find it hard to accept certain results in experimental psychology because the results do not directly relate to a strong theoretical framework; at the same time, the experimental psychologist may find the physicist's results too dependent on a long chain of theoretical reasoning and not based on a large enough set of occurrences.

You will have to study long at the laboratory bench of an experimental discipline to be able to produce results that would be considered valid. Experiments and experimental reports do, nonetheless, share some common elements in all disciplines. The next few pages will discuss these common elements.

Experimental Methods

Minimizing Personal Factors

The best way to understand what scientific experiments try to achieve is to explore the limitations of ordinary observations. First, as pointed out earlier, an individual's observations are affected by that person's beliefs, prejudgments, and interests. To some extent, a person will see what she expects to see or thinks she should see. In an experiment, therefore, the experimenter tries to minimize personal factors by establishing objective measures that can be recorded without requiring interpretation by the observer. Statistical counts, machine readings, chemical tests, and descriptions using a specified technical vocabulary all reduce the interpretive role of the observer. The results produced by such techniques are less likely to be criticized as "just one person's way of looking at things." The results of the experiment have even better claims to objectivity if other experimenters in other laboratories produce the same results when they repeat the experiment.

Measuring Precisely

A second problem in ordinary observations is the lack of precision of human senses and of ordinary language. For example, assume you have two lumps of metal, each about the size of a baseball. You might hold the first lump of metal in your right hand and hold the second lump in your left; by feel, you might be able to sense that one lump was heavier than the other. You might even be able to say that the second was "very much heavier than the first," but that is as precise as you are likely to get unless you were to use some measuring device, perhaps a balance scale. You would then measure the difference in terms of grams or ounces, which have specific values, rather than the vague *heavier* or *very much heavier*. Scientific experiment replaces the imprecise sensations and terms of ordinary observations with more precise and universal measures.

Controlling Extraneous Factors

Decreasing personal interpretation and increasing precision of observation are only half of what experiments do, for a well-designed experiment puts in focus what is to be observed and attempts to eliminate other factors that would interfere with the results. In informal daily observation, many factors beyond what you are interested in knowing enter into what you see and feel. For example, the comparative weighing of the two metal lumps may have been affected by different strengths of your two arms or even by the fact that you just pitched a baseball game so that your pitching arm was more exhausted than the other one. If you wanted to compare the two different substances that made up the lumps, you would also have to worry about whether the two lumps were exactly the same size and even the same temperature, for metals expand when heated. You would also need to know whether there were air bubbles or other impurities in the metals. The altitude at which the measurements are taken is also a factor, because weight becomes less as the center of the object moves away from the center of the earth.

An experiment tries to make all these other factors equal so that the other factors will not influence the results. In the above example, you can eliminate other factors by measuring the purity of the samples (making sure that one is 99.99 percent pure iron and the other is 99.99 percent pure lead), by matching the volumes of the two lumps (perhaps by using a water displacement device), by keeping both samples at the same temperature, and by making all the measurements on the same scale placed at a constant altitude. Thus the variable factors are limited to only one, the density (mass per unit volume) of the two substances.

Testing Theory

Finally, these specific variables isolated by the experiment have been chosen specifically because they test a particular theory. In order to test his theory that all objects fall at the same speed, Galileo is said to have designed the experiment of dropping two unequal weights from the top of the Tower of Pisa. The observation that the objects released at the same time did, in fact, land at the same time confirmed Galileo's hypothesis and contradicted an alternative hypothesis that heavier objects fall faster.

To test the hypothesis that obedience to authority is such a strong motivating force in many human beings that they will even follow orders to hurt strangers, Stanley Milgram set up a laboratory situation where subjects were ordered to administer strong—even lethal—electrical shocks to punish other subjects. You may be happy to learn that the shocks were not real; on the other hand, you may be distressed to find out that most people obeyed orders even past the point where the victims would have been killed had the shocks been real.* These experiments set up situations that are not like everyday circumstances in order to highlight only those unknowns that will test a particular theory—whether of gravity or of obedience.

By these four methods—eliminating personal factors, increasing precision, controlling extraneous factors, and testing theory—experimenters drive reality to extremes not ordinarily experienced. Experiments are said to "twist the tail of nature" to make nature reveal its secrets. The conversion of matter into energy through atomic fusion, for example, although it is the source of the sun's energy, is observable on earth only under the most extraordinary circumstances that have to be set up intentionally by physicists.

Experimental Reports

Even though experimentation varies from field to field, a few general features of the writing of experimental results are common throughout most disciplines. Reports of experiments almost always include these steps: (1) a statement of the researcher's purpose and hypothesis, (2) a description of procedure, materials, and apparatus, (3) a report of results, (4) a discussion of the meaning of the results, and (5) a conclusion about the validity of the hypothesis and the implications for further study. Sometimes these parts are further broken down and expanded; sometimes they are presented in a continuous narrative. No matter what form they take, these parts are usually found in the experimental report.

The introduction presents the background of previous work—

*Stanley Milgram, *Obedience to Authority: An Experimental View* (New York: Harper & Row, 1974), p. 35.

both in theory and experiments—that led to the current hypothesis being tested. The hypothesis may be an original one or one taken from a previous writer in the field. In college laboratory courses, you will usually be given a hypothesis to test; as you advance to more independent work, you will most likely have to develop hypotheses of your own. The introduction, establishing the logic and purpose of the experiment in terms of prior work published in the field, helps the reader see exactly what you are trying to prove by the experiment.

The experimental design should be explained in the section on procedure, materials, and apparatus in order to indicate how the experiment isolates those factors to be measured and eliminates any possible interfering factors. The description of the experimental design should also indicate a method of observation and measurement that will achieve precision and decrease personal bias. Finally, the description should be clear and precise enough to allow another experimenter to recreate the experiment and confirm your results.

The report of results should, of course, be as accurate as the experiment allows: you should indicate the degree of accuracy of your claims, and you should never claim to have found more than you actually did find. In some cases a narrative of the actual progress of the experiment helps put the results in better perspective.

The results, however, are not sufficient in themselves; they must be discussed and interpreted. What kinds of patterns emerged? Were the results as anticipated? Were there any anomalies? How do these results compare with those of previous experiments? How strongly do the results support or contradict the original hypothesis? Do they suggest some other theoretical possibility? Would information from another kind of experiment or a repeat of this one be useful in verifying the hypothesis further? Answers to these and similar questions will draw out the full meaning of the experiment and contribute to advancing knowledge in the field.

Thus, although researchers may, to the uninitiated, seem to gain knowledge entirely on the basis of first-hand experience, the experiments only make sense in a framework of theory, verification, and criticism presented in the literature of the field. Study of published research helps the new researcher define problems that need investigation and provides the information necessary to carry on that investigation profitably. Afterward, the research report connects the results of the experiment with the rest of what is known in the field, making the work available for future researchers. In this way scientists build on one another's work—checking and developing the findings of all the separate researchers.

An Example: How Infants Understand Language

The following experimental report from *Science* magazine tells of an experiment to find out what an infant knows about language. The basic problem of developmental linguistics forms the background for this particular study: how do people learn to understand and use language? But the study of infants' understanding of language presents special difficulties. Simple observation will not reveal the infant's thoughts and understanding, nor can the baby answer questions. An infant's mind is a curious and seemingly inaccessible place.

To test whether infants perceive language bimodally—that is, through coordinating sounds with visual lip reading—the researchers here have devised a clever set of experiments. These experiments present the infants with carefully controlled sight and hearing stimulation to see whether the infants coordinate the information from the two modes of perception. Particularly, the infants are tested to see whether they prefer sound (auditory) and sight (visual) stimuli that are synchronized to those that do not fit together.

Although this report does not formally separate and title individual sections, it clearly follows the standard organization, with minor modifications to allow two experiments to be discussed together. After an introduction presenting the hypothesis of bimodality as found in the prior literature (paragraph 1), the report describes the first experiment and the specific apparatus and methods used (paragraphs 2–4). The results of the first experiment are reported in paragraph 5. Paragraph 6 describes the second experiment, and paragraph 7 the second set of results. The remainder of the article discusses the results and, in the final two paragraphs, presents the conclusions.

The Bimodal Perception of Speech in Infancy

Abstract. Infants 18 to 20 weeks old recognize the correspondence between auditorially and visually presented speech sounds, and the spectral information contained in the sounds is critical to the detection of these correspondences. Some infants imitated the sounds presented during the experiment. Both the ability to detect auditory-visual correspondences and the tendency to imitate may reflect the infant's knowledge of the relationship between audition and articulation.

In conversation, speech is often produced by talkers we can both see and hear. We see talkers' mouths move in synchrony with the sounds that emanate from their lips and recognize that the sequence of lip, tongue, and jaw movements correspond to the sounds we hear. Our recognition of these correspondences underlies our ability to lip-read. Recent experiments have demonstrated the impact of vision on speech perception and suggest that in adults speech is represented, at some level, bimodally (*1*).

The experiments reported here show that 18- to 20-week-old infants can detect the correspondence between auditorially and visually perceived speech; in other words, they too manifest some of the components related to lip-reading phenomena in adults. This demonstration of the bimodal perception of speech in infancy has important implications for social, cognitive, and linguistic development.

The infants were shown two side-by-side filmed images of a talker articulating, in synchrony, two different vowel sounds (Fig. 1A). The sound track corresponding to one of the two faces was presented through a loudspeaker directly behind the screen and midway between the visual images. The visual stimuli consisted of two 16-mm film loops, each containing a face repeating a sequence of ten /a/ vowels (as in *pop*) and ten /i/ vowels (as in *peep*). The articulations were produced once every 3 seconds by the same female talker (*2*). One film loop displayed the /a/ face on the left and the /i/ face on the right; the other loop displayed them in the reverse orientation. The faces were 21 cm long and 15 cm wide: their centers were separated by 38 cm. The auditory stimuli were 16-mm sound tracks containing sequences of /a/'s and /i/'s presented at an average intensity of 60-dB sound pressure level (range, 55 to 64 dB). Either sound track could be played with either film loop. Stimulus durations fell within a narrowly constrained range (*2*), assuring, together with the precise alignment of the sound and film tracks, that each sound track was temporally synchronized to both faces.

The experimental procedure was one of familiarization and testing (Fig. 1B). During familiarization, an infant was shown each face separately for 10 seconds without sound. Following this 20-second period, the faces were briefly covered until the infant's gaze returned to midline. Then the sound (either /a/'s or /i/'s) was turned on and both faces were presented for the 2-minute test phase. The sound presented to the infants, the left-right positioning of the two faces, the order of familiarization, and the sex of the infant were counterbalanced. The subjects were 32 normal infants ranging in age from 18 weeks and 0 days to 20 weeks and 1 day ($\overline{X} = 19.3$). The only source of visible light in the room was that provided by the films themselves. An infrared light was suspended above the test cubicle. An infrared camera and microphone provided audiovisual recordings of the infants. The infant's visual fixations were scored from videotape by an independent observer who could neither hear the sound nor see the faces presented to the infant (*3*).

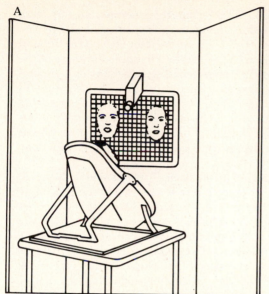

B	Familiarization			Test	
Visual stimuli	Face 1	Face 2	Midline gaze	Both faces	
Auditory stimuli	. . .	. . .		/a/.../a/.../a/.../a/	
Time	10 seconds	10 seconds		2 minutes	

Fig. 1. (A) Experimental arrangement of an infant placed in an infant seat within a three-sided cubicle, 46 cm from the two facial displays. (B) Experimental procedure.

We hypothesized that the auditorially presented vowel would systematically influence the infants' visual fixations. Specifically, we predicted that if infants detected the correspondence between the auditorially and visually perceived speech information, they would look significantly longer at the face that matched the sound. The results were in accord with this prediction. The percentage of total fixation time devoted to the matched versus mismatched face was calculated for each infant. The mean percentage devoted to the matching face was 73.6 percent, which is significantly different from the 50 percent chance level [t (31) = 4.67, $P < .001$]. Twenty-four infants looked longer at the face that matched the sound presented than at the mismatched face ($P < .01$, binomial test). There were no significant left-right preferences, face preferences, or familiarization order effects.

Experiment 1 demonstrated that 18- to 20-week-old infants detect a cross-modal relationship between the auditory and visual products of articulation. It did not isolate the auditory information necessary for the detection of these correspondences. Experiment 2 constituted an initial attempt to do so. The original auditory stimuli were altered to remove the spectral information necessary to identify the vowels (formant frequencies) while preserving their temporal characteristics (amplitude and duration). These computer-generated signals were pure-tone stimuli centered at the average frequency of the female talker's fundamental (200 Hz). Their onset-offset characteristics and their amplitude envelopes were synthesized to duplicate those of the original vowels: If infants in experiment 1 were relying on temporal information to link particular face-voice pairs, then they should still look longer at the "matched" face, even though it was represented only by its sine-wave analog (4). Alternatively, if the spectral information contained in the vowels was necessary for the detection of these auditory-visual correspondences, performance should now drop to chance.

Thirty-two infants ranging in age from 18 weeks and 1 day to 20 weeks and 0 days ($\overline{X}$ = 19.4) were tested using the same procedure as experiment 1 and the new stimuli. The mean percentage of fixations to the matched face dropped to chance (54.6 percent, $P > .40$); only 17 infants looked longer at it. Experiment 2 thus suggested that some aspect of the spectral information was necessary. It will now be important to determine if perception of the vowel's identity is required to produce the effect, or whether an auditory signal approximating the spectral pattern of the vowel without identifying it is sufficient.

An infant's ability to detect equivalences between auditorially and visually perceived speech has implications for theories of social, cognitive, and linguistic development. From a social perspective, the recognition that a given auditory signal emanates from a mouth moving in a particular way may help direct the infant's attention toward a specific speaker. This in turn may play a role in coordinating joint actions between infants and caretakers (5). These results are also relevant to an emerging view of infant cognitive development. In this view, young infants are predisposed to recognize intermodal equivalences in the information picked up by different perceptual modalities, and that this ability underlies their success on a variety of cross-modal tasks (6, 7).

The results are particularly relevant to theories of linguistic development. They suggest that infants relate specific articulatory postures to their concomitant speech sounds. These findings could reflect isolated auditory-visual associations that were learned by watching caretakers speak. Alternatively, they could reflect a more general knowledge, learned or inherent, of the relationship between audition and articulation. Such knowledge might be quite broad, encompassing information about the auditory, visual, and motor concomitants of speech. This latter alternative would imply that in addition to the auditory-visual equivalents demonstrated here, young infants may be cognizant of auditory-motor equivalents, exemplified by vocal imitation, and visual-motor equivalents exemplified by the imitation of visually presented articulatory movements (8). Such an intermodal representation of speech would be especially conducive to vocal learning (9).

During these experiments we made two observations concerning vocal imitation that support this broader interpretation. (i) Ten infants who heard the vowel stimuli (experiment 1) produced utterances typical of babbling (*10*), whereas only one infant who heard the pure-tone stimuli (experiment 2) did so. The speech stimuli thus seemed more effective in eliciting infant babbling than nonspeech stimuli. (ii) The infants in experiment 1 produced sounds that resembled the adult female's vowels. They seemed to be imitating the female talker, "taking turns" by alternating their vocalizations with hers.

Figure 2 displays a single infant's imitation of the prosodic features of the adult's vowels—their intonation contours and overall durations. The adult produced a "declarative" contour; that is, a rise in the fundamental frequency followed by a longer, more gradual fall in the fundamental frequency. The infant mimics this rise-fall contour producing a pitch pattern that resembles the adult's (although it is higher in frequency because the infant's vocal cords are shorter than the adult's). Rise-fall contours of this type are not common in the babbled utterances of infants at this age (*10*). The overall durations of the vowels, each about 1 second, are also similar. Sustained vowels of this duration, produced without consonant-like elements, are again infrequent in the babbled utterances of infants at this age (*10*). Such vocal productions suggest that infants are directing their articulators to achieve auditory targets that they hear another produce, in other words, that they are capable of vocal imitation (*11*).

We suggest that both the detection of auditory-visual correspondences and vocal imitation reflect a knowledge of the relationship between audition and articulation (*12*). Furthermore, we suggest that these abilities have a common origin—the infant's intermodal representation of speech. Future studies should test the extent to which auditory-visual and auditory-motor equivalence classes are related and the extent to which experience plays a role in their development.

Our findings go beyond these theoretical issues and extend to clinical concerns. On the basis of the data reported here and in other

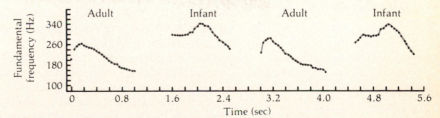

Fig. 2. The fundamental frequency (pitch) of the adult's and infant's vowels are shown as a function of time. Both the adult's and infant's contours are characterized by an initial rise and then a gradual fall in the fundamental frequency. Their durations are also similar. This display illustrates the infant's tendency to take turns. The infant's first vocalization was produced 1/2 second after the adult's, the second, 1/4 second after.

recent infant studies (6, 7), we suggest that the bimodal delivery of speech information may facilitate language learning because infants are predisposed to represent information in this way. In particular, infants born deaf might well be aided by the codelivery of visual and tactual information about speech. Such sensory substitution approaches have proven effective in improving speech reception in artificially "deafened" adults, who combine visual information provided by lip-reading with spectral information provided by a tactile aid (13).

Infant speech perception has traditionally been studied as an auditory phenomenon (14). Here we presented data and arguments showing that it may be profitable to investigate infant speech perception as an intermodal event. Studies of infants' intermodal organization of the auditory, visual, and motor concomitants of speech may bring us closer to understanding the development of the human capacity to speak and comprehend language.

—Patricia K. Kuhl
and Andrew N. Meltzoff,
Science 218 (10 December 1982):
1138–41

References and Notes

1. N. Erber, *J. Speech Hear. Discord.* **40**, 481 (1975); H. McGurk and J. MacDonald, *Nature (London)* **264**, 746 (1976); Q. Summerfield, *Phonetica* **36**, 314 (1979); R. Campbell and B. Dodd, *Q. J. Exp. Psychol.* **32**, 85 (1980).
2. The average durations of the vowels, measured acoustically, were 1120 msec for /i/ (range, 1050 to 1220) and 1150 msec for /a/ (range, 1060 to 1270). The average center frequencies of the first three formants for /i/ were 416, 2338, and 2718 Hz; comparable values for /a/ were 741, 1065, and 3060 Hz.
3. The observer recorded when the infant was looking at the left or right visual display. Both inter- and intraobserver reliability was assessed. The mean difference in the percent-fixation scores for the left (or right) face was 3.3 percent (interobserver) and 1.8 percent (intraobserver).
4. B. Dodd [*Cognit. Psychol.* **11**, 478 (1979)] provided data suggesting that infants detect gross temporal misalignment between mouth movements and sound. While we argued that our alignment procedure effectively ruled out temporal cues as a potential explanation for the effect obtained in experiment 1, experiment 2 addressed this temporal hypothesis directly.
5. J. Bruner, *Cognition* **3**, 255 (1975); D. Stern, J. Jaffe, B. Beebe, S. Bennett, *Ann. N.Y. Acad. Sci.* **263**, 89 (1975).
6. A. N. Meltzoff and K. Moore, *Science* **198**, 75 (1977).
7. T. Bower, *Human Development* (Freeman, San Francisco, 1979); A. N. Meltzoff and R. Borton, *Nature (London)* **282**, 403 (1979).

A. N. Meltzoff in *Infancy and Epistemology*, G. Butterworth, Ed. (Harvester, Brighton, England, 1981).

—— and K. Moore, in *Advances in Infant Research*, L. Lipsitt and C. Rovee-Collier, Eds. (Ablex, Norwood, N.J., 1982), vol. 2.

8. Meltzoff and Moore (6) demonstrated imitation of oral gestures in infants less than 1 month old. The gestures were silently produced by an adult model. Since their mouth-opening gesture is similar to the articulatory posture adopted for the production of an /a/ vowel, these data support the hypothesis that infants are capable of imitating some speechlike gestures produced in the absence of vocalization.

9. P. Marler, *J. Comp. Physiol. Psychol.* **71** (1970); F. Nottebohm, *Am. Nat.* **106,** 116 (1972).

10. D. Oller, in *Child Phonology*, Vol. 1. *Promotion*, G. Yeni-Komshian, J. Kavanagh, C. Ferguson, Eds. (Academic Press, New York, 1980), p. 93; R. Netsell, in *Language Behavior in Infancy and Early Childhood,* R. Stark, Ed. (Elsevier, New York, 1981).

11. These observations underscore the need for careful experimental studies on the development of vocal imitation. Previous reports of vocal imitation in young infants have not provided acoustic analyses of either the model's or the infant's vocalizations [J. Piaget, *Play, Dreams and Imitation in Childhood* (Norton, New York, 1962); I. Uzgiris and J. Hunt, *Assessment in Infancy* (Univ. of Illinois Press, Chicago, 1975); W. Kessen, J. Levine, K. Wendrich, *Infant Behav. Devel.* **2,** 93 (1979)].

12. The motor theory of speech perception also outlined an argument in which the auditory and articulatory levels of representation were closely linked [A. Liberman, F. Cooper, D. Shankweiler, M. Studdert-Kennedy, *Pscyhol. Rev.* **74,** 431 (1967)]. Specifically, the model addressed the issue of speech-sound categorization in adults and argued that it was based on motor mediation. The infant data presented here do not bear on this issue. We posit that at a functional level, 5-month-old infants are cognizant of auditory-articulatory equivalence classes, and we do not suggest that the metric linking the two is defined in motor terms.

13. D. Sparks, P. Kuhl, A. Edmonds, G. Gray, *J. Acoust. Soc. Am.* **63,** 246 (1978).

14. P. Kuhl, in *Handbook of Infant Perception,* P. Salapatek and L. Cohen, Eds. (Academic Press, New York, in press).

15. We thank A. Anderson, D. Grieser, R. Baarslag-Benson, K. Merrick, P. Cameron, and C. Harris for assistance in the experiment, and A. Ross, K. Lee, K. Mighell, and M. Sweeney for technical assistance. I. Hirsh, D. Klatt, J. D. Miller, K. Stevens, and Q. Summerfield provided helpful comments on an earlier version of this manuscript. Supported by NSF grant BNS 8103581 to P.K.K.; A.N.M. was supported by grants

from the Spencer Foundation and the National Institute of Child Health and Human Development (HD-13024).

An Example: Time, Psychology, and Health

The next example, from the *Journal of Abnormal Psychology,* applies a psychological approach to medical issues. People with certain types of behavior patterns (called type A) have been found to have higher risk of heart attack than people with different behavior patterns (called type B). The medical problem of improving health through better diagnosis of risk, treatment, and prevention through behavioral changes motivates the study. But the immediate research question fits within a standard problem in experimental psychology: the problem of human perception. In the experiments, standard perceptual measurements reveal that people with type A personality have a more rushed sense of time than those with the B personality.

The article follows the format recommended in the American Psychological Association *Publication Manual* for both article organization and references (see pages 503–504). In accordance with the manual's recommendations, the article is headed by an abstract of the whole article and then contains the standard parts of the research report, identified by subheadings (except for the untitled introduction and review of the literature). The report of methods and results, moreover, is split into separate sections for the two experiments, as also indicated by subheadings.

The report of the results contain not only statistics of the findings but statistics concerning the reliability of the findings. The chi-square analysis mentioned in the results tests how consistent the results are with predictions from the hypothesis. The *SD, F,* and *p* numbers measure how reliable or significant the calculated values are. Statistical methods are essential to many disciplines; if you pursue any subject that uses numbers (including business and economics as well as experimental disciplines), you will probably take at least one course in statistics. The proper use and honest presentation of statistics are an essential part of the subject as individual statistical techniques.

Time Urgency Among Coronary-Prone Individuals

Coronary-prone individuals (Type A) are characterized as relatively more hard-driving, competitive, hostile, and time urgent in comparison to non-coronary-prone individuals (Type B). This article addresses differences among Type A and B subjects in impatience. Two different tasks were employed that measure time urgency. In Experiment 1 subjects were required to signal the passage of 1 minute while engaged in a reading task. The results indicated that Type A subjects perceived time as passing significantly more quickly than Type B subjects. A second experiment assessed the relative work rates (completion of inventories) among Type A and B subjects. It was found that Type As worked significantly more quickly than Bs. Both experiments lend support to the hypothesis that Type A subjects are more impatient or time urgent than are Type Bs. Explanatory hypotheses and recommendations for future research are discussed.

Research on the coronary-prone personality (Type A) has proliferated over the past 10 years. One important dimension of the Type A behavior pattern is an exaggerated sense of time urgency in which the person attempts to accomplish more and more in less and less time (Friedman & Rosenman, 1974). Several indexes of time urgency have been investigated in relation to the coronary-prone and non-coronary-prone (Type B) designation.

Using a DRL schedule (differential reinforcement of low-rate responses), Glass, Snyder, and Hollis (1974) found that Type A subjects committed more errors than did Type Bs in that they tended to respond before the waiting period was over. Gastorf (1980) reported that As arrived earlier than Bs for a scheduled experiment. Assuming that the impatience of As will lead to an experience of time passing slowly, Burnam, Pennebaker, and Glass (1975) asked subjects to estimate the passage of 1 minute while engaging in a reading task. Type As signaled the passage of 1 minute sooner than did Bs. However, Burnam et al. did not record reading rate during the task. Because Frankenhaeuser (1959) found that increasing the number of stimuli or stimulus changes decreases perceived time duration, different reading rates between As and Bs instead of impatience can account for the differential time estimations.

Thus, Experiment 1 was designed to replicate the Burnam et al. (1975) time-estimation data while controlling for reading rate.

Experiment 1

Method

Twenty-two female introductory psychology students were run individually. After removing their watches subjects read aloud from a technical paper in social psychology and signaled when they believed 1 minute had elapsed. In the absence of a time piece, it was deemed unlikely that subjects would be able to mark time through other means (e.g., counting or finger tapping) during the reading task. The dependent variables consisted of time estimation, reading rate (words per second), age, and race (dummy coded). Subsequently, subjects completed the student version of the Jenkins Activity Survey (JAS; Glass, 1977). Subjects were thus seen without knowledge of their A/B designation.

Results

Subjects were assigned to Type A/B categories using a median split of the JAS scores (As $\geq$ 7, Bs < 7), yielding 11 As and 11 Bs.[1] Mean time estimation for As was 61.4 sec (SD = 17.24) and 77.2 sec (SD = 16.16) for Bs, $F(1, 20)$ = 5.10, p < .01 (one-tailed test). Analyses of variance performed on reading rate (for As, M = 2.06, SD = .44; for Bs, M = 2.29, SD = .52), age, and race failed to reach significance (all Fs < 1.6, ps < .50). These data strongly support the time urgency hypothesis noted here and in Burnam et al. (1975) because the findings cannot be attributed to perceptual and demographic artifacts.

An additional behavioral measure that converges on the construct of time urgency is the time taken to complete a task under unspecified time constraints. Experiment 2 was conducted to assess the relative work rates of Type A and B subjects.

Experiment 2

Method

One hundred and twelve introductory psychology students (80 males, 32 females) were run in groups of 10 to 30. Each subject completed a battery of four inventories (presented in counterbalanced order, one of which was the student version of the JAS). Immediately on completion subjects returned their packets to the experimenter, whereupon the packets were placed in sequential order, thus allowing for a rank ordering of completed time. For purposes of data analysis, each subject received two designations. Based on the total sample, subjects above or at the median (*mdn* = 8) were As, those below were Bs. Second, inventories obtained from subjects in each group were dichotomized as being in the fastest or slowest half of completion time relative to the other subjects in the room.

Results

The results showed that 66.7% (n = 36) of the subjects with the fastest completion times were Type As, whereas 65.5% (n = 38) of the subjects with the slowest completion times were Type Bs. A 2 × 2 chi-square analysis (Type A/B × Fastest/Slowest) on the total

---

[1]Normative data from our laboratory indicates population medians of 7 for 263 female undergraduates and 8 for 240 male undergraduates. These are consistent with the sample medians we employ in dichotomizing Type A/B groups: The median in Experiment 1 is 7 (100% female subjects) and 8 in Experiment 2 (71% male subjects). See also Glass (1977) for a discussion of the median-split method.

sample was highly significant, $\chi^2 (1) = 11.59$, $p < .0001$. Further, a 2×2 chi-square analysis (Male/Female $\times$ Fastest/Slowest) failed to reveal a sex effect, $\chi^2 (1) = .70$, *ns*. Moreover, the proportion of male As to male Bs was not significantly different from the proportion of female As to female Bs, $\chi^2 (1) = 2.8$, *ns*.

Discussion

The results of the present experiments lend increasing support for the contention that coronary-prone individuals are more impatient than their non-coronary-prone counterparts. Experiment 1 rules out the hypothesis that Burnam et al.'s (1975) time estimation differences between Type As and Bs was due to response rate. The data are more congruent with Fraisse's (1963) findings directly relating impatience with the perception of elapsed time.

Experiment 2, despite the use of a different method, revealed the same Type A/B differences in impatience and is consistent with Burnam et al.'s (1975) finding that Type A subjects fail to modulate productivity under shifting environmental demands. Whether Type A individuals perform quickly at the expense of errors is not known.

The present findings are consistent with the observation that Type A subjects strive to achieve as much as possible in the shortest period of time. An unequivocal explanation for this style of responding among Type As has yet to emerge. One hypothesis is that Type A subjects set higher performance standards irrespective of the task. The results of research by Grimm and Yarnold (Note 1) clearly show the tendency of Type As to establish higher goals for quality-based performance. The present findings and those of Burnam et al. (1975) and Snow (1978) are consistent with the hypothesis that Type As set higher standards for the production of quantity. The role of standard setting in the Type A's impatient mode of responding as well as Glass's (1977) mastery and control hypothesis is deserving of additional research. However, at this point there is no reason to place a valence on the Type A's impatience because this dimension of the coronary-prone behavior pattern has not been shown to be pathogenic nor have treatment studies indicated that modifying time urgency reduces the risk of cardiovascular disease.

—Paul R. Yarnold
and Laurence G. Grimm,
Journal of Abnormal Psychology 91,
no. 3 (1982): 175–177

Reference Note

1. Grimm, L., & Yarnold, P. *Performance standards and the Type A behavior pattern.* Manuscript submitted for publication, 1982.

References

Burnam, M. A., Pennebaker, J. W., & Glass, D. C. Time consciousness, achievement striving, and the Type A coronary-prone behavior pattern. *Journal of Abnormal Psychology,* 1975, *84,* 76–79.

Fraisse, P. *The psychology of time.* New York: Harper & Row, 1963.

Frankenhaeuser, M. *Estimation of time: An experimental study.* Stockholm, Sweden: Almqvist & Wiksell, 1959.

Friedman, M., & Rosenman, R. H. *Type A behavior and your heart.* New York: Knopf, 1974.

Gastorf, J. W. Time urgency of the Type A behavior pattern. *Journal of Consulting and Clinical Psychology,* 1980, *48,* 299.

Glass, D. C. *Behavior patterns, stress, and coronary disease.* Hillsdale, N.J.: Erlbaum, 1977.

Glass, D. C., Snyder, M. L., & Hollis, J. F. Time urgency and the Type A coronary-prone behavior pattern. *Journal of Applied Social Psychology,* 1974, *4,* 125–140.

Snow, B. Level of aspiration in coronary prone and noncoronary prone adults. *Personality and Social Psychology Bulletin,* 1978, *4,* 416–419.

Writing Assignments

1. If you are currently taking or have recently taken a laboratory course that used a laboratory manual with prepared forms on which to report the results of your experiments, rewrite the results of one experiment according to the experimental report form described in the preceding pages.

2. In order to test the claim by Edward Hall (*The Hidden Dimension*) that people will try to maintain a sense of personal space around them when they work, carry out the following experiment, which is modeled on one reported in N. Felipe and R. Sommer, "Invasions of Personal Space," *Social Problems* 14 (1966): 206–14.

   a. Go to a study area in your college. For thirty minutes, observe all people sitting alone, that is, with no one sitting within two seats in any direction. How long do they continue to sit there? Calculate the rate of leaving.

   b. In a second session, make the same observation, except that after a few minutes you or a friend should sit down in the chair next to each person studying. Calculate the rate of leaving now with a person sitting nearby. You may also notice any behaviors that might be considered defensive after someone has sat nearby, such as fidgeting, stacking books between the two people, or moving the chair slightly away.

Write up your results in a short report (300–500 words), as though for a psychology class.

3. Test the old saying, "first impressions may be lasting ones," by carrying out the following experiment modeled after one performed by S. E. Asch, and reported in "Forming Impressions of Personality," *Journal of Abnormal and Social Psychology* 41 (1946): 258–90.

a. Ask ten people to volunteer as subjects. Split the ten people into two groups of five each.

b. Distribute to the first group the following list, presented in the exact order as given. Tell them that these characteristics describe a particular person. Then ask each subject to write down a rating from 1 to 10 for the person so described, with 1 being very unfavorable and 10 being most favorable.

c. With the second group follow exactly the same procedure, except that the list should be presented in reverse order.

d. Compare the rankings of the two groups.

List of Characteristics for Personality to Be Rated

Intelligent
Industrious
Impulsive
Critical
Stubborn
Envious

Write up your results in a short research report (300–500 words), as though for a psychology class. You may also repeat this experiment, telling some subjects that the person so described is a man and others that it is a woman, again using both the forward and the reverse versions of the list. This latter version of the experiment will also tell you whether men's and women's personalities are judged differently.

15 Writing About Events in General: Theoretical Disciplines

Some disciplines and parts of disciplines attempt to formulate statements that are generally true across many different kinds of situations. Theoretical statements can be developed in a purely abstract way, independent of any observations of the world, or they can be developed as generalizations from many specific empirical findings. Theoretical disciplines vary in their connection to empirical evidence. Theoretical writing varies in form from situation to situation, often depending on the mode of analysis being used. In general, however, theoretical writing follows a sequence of ideas, with thought being the primary organizational device. Examples from philosophy and economic social theory give a sense of both the form and the importance of some typical theoretical arguments.

The Range of Theory

The last several chapters have offered ways of developing and presenting statements of knowledge using data gathered through various methods. But knowledge advances by general theoretical statements as well as by narrow claims closely related to specific evidence. Theoretical disciplines try to form statements that are generally true across many kinds of situations and are abstracted from the specifics of any particular case.

Some disciplines, such as pure mathematics and formal logic, develop pure theory. Writings in these fields argue through abstract rules, independent of particular observations of the world. A geometric proof, for example, proceeds by a series of generally true mathematical statements derived from other generally true mathematical statements, using acceptable procedures of mathematical manipulation. Formal logic never asks whether the premises or assumptions actually tally with conditions in the world; it only follows out the formal consequences of those assumptions.

Certain other theoretical disciplines, although they proceed primarily by general forms of argument, incorporate common sense experiences or other familiar observations about life. Much of philosophy operates by relating general ideas to ordinary experiences. In the Platonic dialogues, Socrates constantly asks people to consider everyday events, such as how a cook makes food taste good or how we tell a good thing from a bad one. This tradition continues today when linguistic philosophers ask us to consider how we use words in everyday contexts.

Other more empirical disciplines use theory to generalize from many specific findings. Disciplines like physics have in fact been able to establish general rules, often expressed in mathematical form, that seem to apply to all the observed examples and can predict future events. On the basis of laws of motion, we know when Halley's comet will next appear near the earth and when the next solar eclipse will occur. Physicists have even been able to predict that particles never before observed could be found under precisely defined circumstances. And in some cases the particles are right where they are supposed to be.

No matter how elegant the theory gets in empirical disciplines, however, it ultimately relies on the proof of empirical evidence. If the particle cannot be found, the theory falters. Although the theory article may never mention any experiment or data, somewhere down the line it must fit with observation and experiment. To be testable, theories must have specific real-world consequences to be compared with empirical results. Albert Einstein's general theory of relativity, first proposed in 1913, had as one of its consequences that gravity bends light. In 1919, during a solar eclipse, the astronomer Arthur Eddington took photographs confirming that light from stars was bent as it passed the sun's gravitational field. These confirming results persuaded many scientists of the theory's validity. If a theory does not offer such concrete consequences, it is untestable, unpersuasive, and of only limited value.

Because theoretical statements in the physical sciences offer such specificity of results and rest on strong confirming evidence, they can become treated as laws, statements that are always true. Complex deductions follow with great certainty and precision from these laws without the need of checking every step against empirical results. Of course, theories change and surprising (or anomalous) empirical results appear, but within normal practice these events are the exceptions.

Other empirical disciplines rely on a looser connection between theory and observations or experiments. Theory can serve to gather together and organize what people have found. Theory can even speculate about a discipline's fundamental questions for which currently no firm answers exist. But the theory's lack of precise, thorough, and unquestionable support in empirical evidence makes complex deduction and prediction on the basis of the theory more risky and less fruitful. Sociological theory can help illuminate many social events, can stimulate research, and can even suggest powerful answers to questions about how society is organized and people behave. But many competing sociological theories exist with none persuasive enough to convince most sociologists of a single point of view. A sociological argument based only on pure theory will find few adherents.

Most fields that do not have a more rigorous theory usually have one form or another of this kind of conjectural theory. Of course, conjectural theories are more tightly tied to empirical data in some disciplines than in others. Legal theory, although interpretive, is frequently well grounded in the actual legal systems in the world, whereas literary theory tends to be more speculative. Also, as some fields make certain discoveries and develop new methods of observation opening up new classes of data, speculative theories can be replaced by more firmly grounded ones. For example, the identification of DNA as genetic material and the advances in the techniques of analyzing DNA have turned the field of genetics from speculation toward an exact science.

Despite the lack of certainty of the conjectural theories, they have been used as the basis for practical action, particularly in the social sciences. Economic theories, although in conflict with one another and all to some degree unreliable as predictors, guide decision making in governments and businesses. In fact, two competing theories of economics (with the political, historical, social, and psychological consequences) guide the major political divisions of our world: capitalism and communism. On a less monumental scale, psychological and social theories guide many professionals in helping people improve their daily lives.

Theoretical Writing

Theoretical writing is built on methods of analysis specific to each discipline. Social-class analysis, behaviorism, and syntactic analysis are for their disciplines defined methods of arguing just as much as geometric proof, formal logic, and mathematical derivations are for theirs. Great innovators of theory provide not only theoretical systems or specific theoretical statements; they provide new methods of analysis: the calculus, quantum analysis, analysis of the subconscious, the analysis of language in use.

All theoretical writing, nonetheless, in its presentation follows a sequence of ideas, with thought being the primary organizational device. Since theory presents a general line of reasoning rather than a description of a specific event, the narrative and descriptive elements evident in more empirical work tend to vanish. Specific descriptive and narrative details, where they appear, clearly must be subordinated to the progress of the overall thought. The formal sequence of the thought will, however, vary with the mode of analysis appropriate to the problem and the discipline. Some of the more common patterns for organizing thought found in theoretical articles include the following:

- *Synthesis*—presenting a set of already accepted or plausible claims to see how they fit together or add up into a unified whole
- *Derivation*—transforming one statement or set of statements to another using a specific set of approved transformation techniques, often from mathematics or formal logic
- *Causation*—showing how one system or state of affairs transforms by a series of steps into another
- *Division*—breaking a problem, statement, or system down into its component parts

- *Speculation*—proposing a new idea or thought experiment and showing what the consequences of such an idea would be
- *System building*—proposing a speculative overall model for a subject and then showing how this model fits existing knowledge and what the further consequences of the system might be

Although formal patterns of the presentation of theoretical arguments can be identified and you must be careful to justify every significant step in the formally presented thought, the actual process by which you think through and develop a theory is not so easily specified.

Theories are often great achievements of the imagination, relying on many modes of thought—conscious, subconscious, unconscious, and just plain lucky. The only general advice that seems to hold in most cases is that you should be thoroughly immersed in the work of others and you should define the problem you are attempting to solve as carefully as possible. The definition of the problem will let you know the kind of answer you are looking for and the immersion in other work will let you know some of the pieces you have to work with. Then when a plausible answer comes along—whether when you are working at your desk or when you are dreaming or when you are reading the newspaper—you can recognize that this is what you are looking for.

An Example: Time in the Abstract

In the following excerpt, the philosopher R. G. Collingwood considers some misleading imprecisions in the way we ordinarily talk about time in order to clarify our understanding of what time is. The passage begins by defining what a theory of time would be: a discussion of the difficulties in thinking about time. Having defined his philosophic task, Collingwood accordingly presents his central difficulty. He finds that all the usual ways we talk about time contain obvious lies about the nature of time. To elaborate on his central difficulty, he analyzes four common misleading types of statement about time: (1) statements that imply that time moves, (2) statements that say that time can be measured, (3) statements that claim that time is continuous, and (4) statements that claim that time is infinite.

Collingwood's analysis leads to a general conclusion, that the untruths all come from a common mistake—conceiving of time as a line. This error of linear time he attributes to misunderstandings of the concepts of memory, the past, and the future, all of which refer to events that are not happening right now. Although the events of memory, past, and future appear real to the imagination, they cannot be said to exist or be real in the present moment. Collingwood, consequently, suggests that time consists only as an ever-changing present.

In trying to clear up our understanding of the term *time,* Collingwood refers only in a general way to our common use of the term and to our experience of time. He does not take a survey about what people think nor does he discuss how specific historical writers—literary or philosophic—have discussed time. He rather discusses categories of statements, which he assumes we all have heard. In analyzing the four common misleading statements about time, he draws out their logical entailments and assumptions and then shows how these are logically inconsistent with what we know of time. Then once he has located the central error of spatializing time, he follows out the logical consequences of that error and tries to derive a definition of time that eliminates the error.

Throughout this passage, one thought clearly leads to the next, and no thought is expressed until the groundwork has been established by previous analysis. Although Collingwood may have told us no specific "thing" about time, he has helped us think about the general concept. Although his conclusions may at first strike us as bizarre and unreal—the result of an artificial word game— as we ponder what he says we may start to see how our senses of memory, past, and future are only personal constructs residing in our minds. The only moment we have any hope of knowing concretely is the present, and that present moment changes even as we experience it. Previous moments experienced and future moments anticipated exist only in shady representations of the mind, perhaps spurred by tokens that manage to exist in the present moment. If we watch a home movie of ourselves as a child and start to remember what it felt like then when our parents were taking that movie, have we really made that child live again? Does that child still exist? Where is the child that existed back then? How real can we say that child now is? Perhaps by trying to imagine time as fixed and linear we are trying to give more certainty to the meaning of history and our lives than they perhaps warrant.

Whether or not you understand Collingwood's argument in all its details and whether or not you agree with all his points, his thoughts can make you wonder.

Some Perplexities About Time

I.

. . . . No doubt time, like knowledge and goodness and number, is *sui generis* [in a class by itself]; but it does not follow that there cannot be a "theory" of it, if that means a reasoned discussion of the difficulties which are encountered when we try to think about it. And that is the only sense in which I ask for a theory of time or of anything else.

II.

My central difficulty is this: — *All statements ordinarily made about time seem to imply that time is something which we know it is not, and make assumptions about it which we know to be untrue.*

a. Thus, we say that time flies. But what is the air in which, or the ground over which, it flies? Nothing, surely, but a system of reference, a temporal system of reference; in fact, time itself. The movement of time can only be a movement relative to something that is itself time—time regarded as stationary and existing *totum simul* [everywhere the same]. That, relatively to which time moves, cannot be space; for what moves relatively to space can only be a spatial object or body. We have, therefore, two times, a moving and a stationary; and since to be stationary implies permanence in time, we have a third time in which the stationary time remains stationary, and so *ad infinitum*. If I am told to accept this result in a spirit of natural piety, I reply that I cannot, because it had contradicted the thesis on which it depends: for it now appears that time as such does *not* fly, but that some times fly while others remain at rest. If I am told that my difficulty comes from taking a popular metaphor literally, I gratefully accept the confession that to speak of the flight, lapse, movement, &c., of time is a mere metaphor, and that in using it we are saying what we know to be untrue.

The difficulty is not removed if we say that events move "in" time. Here either (i) the time is regarded as moving with the events, in which case the difficulty recurs in the same form; or (ii) events are regarded as moving past a stationary frame of temporal references: in which case it recurs in a new form. For events must carry their own time-determinations with them—*e.g.*, an hour's journey, however far it recedes into the past, remains an hour long; and thus we have once more two times, one moving and one stationary, with results as before. It is not merely events but times that move in time; which is absurd. (The same difficulty arises in the conception of a body moving in space; the fact that it recurs there does not make it less serious here.)

b. Again, we say that time can be measured. But how can it be measured? We measure (not abstract space, but) bodies by laying measuring-rods against them: that is, by juxtaposing two bodies and thus measuring one by reference, through the other, to a third. This could not be done unless we could move a rod from one place to another; and the hypothesis of the Lorenz-Fitzgerald contraction brings home the fact that the constancy of the length of the rod is an assumption and no more. But in the sense, which is the natural sense of measuring, we cannot measure temporal events at all. We can observe a rough simultaneity between the beginnings and ends of two events (*e.g.,* the rotation of a minute-hand and a journey), but only if the two events are going on at the same time; or, I ought to add, appear to the measurer to be going on at the same time. But we cannot then move the rotation of the minute-hand to another part of time and thus compare the length of the journey with the length of a symphony. For that, we have to use a different rotation of the hand. It is as if we were unable to move our measuring-rods at all, but were compelled to use a fresh rod for every fresh measurement. Then how could the rods be standardized? Obviously, they could not. But our clocks *are* standardized. Does the difficulty, therefore, vanish? No; for we can only standardize two clocks by observing that *at a given time* their hands are travelling at the same pace, and this does not prove that they will travel at the same pace at any other time. And in the nature of the case there can be no possible means of showing either that they will or that they will not; in other words, there can be no possible method of measuring the time taken by one event relatively to the time taken by another event not simultaneous with it.

If I am told in reply that, after all, it is reasonable to assume that a clock, wound up and kept in order, continues to move uniformly, and that pragmatic results justify the assumption that one "hour"— meaning one rotation of the minute-hand—is the same length as the next, I agree; but a pragmatic assumption is not quite the same thing as a measurement, and once more it appears that we have said one thing while meaning another.

c. Suppose, again, we say that time is continuous. What, in saying this, are we denying? Presumably, that time is discrete. If it had been discrete, it would have had gaps in it. But what would the gaps have been made of? Nothing but time: any gap in a series of events must be a gap consisting of time, for if there is no time in the gap there is no gap. Clearly, then, time is continuous.—But this does not seem to follow. That which must be either discrete or continuous must be a quantity. But if time cannot be measured,[1] it is doubtful whether we ought to call it a quantity; it is, in any case, an un-

---

[1]There may, evidently, be quantities which *we* cannot measure. But the difficulty in measuring time is not of this kind.

measurable quantity, and in this phrase it is reasonable to suspect a *contradictio in adjecto* [contradiction in attribution]. We must inquire further.

When one event in time is said to be continuous with the next, the statement is either meaningless or false. Meaningless, if "the next" is simply "that with which it is continuous"; false, if it is assumed that events in time are really packed side by side with no intervals between them. In actual history, events overlap; you cannot, except by a confessed fiction, state the point at which the event called the Middle Ages ends and the event called the Modern Period begins. This is not because our notions of the distinction between the mediaeval and the modern worlds are vague and confused. There is no sequence of events, however clearly conceived, that does not show the same overlap; and it is only when our knowledge of events is superficial and our account of them arbitrary that we feel able to point out the exact junction between them, or rather, feel that there *is* an exact junction if only we knew it. In the actual history of events there is, as the theory of compact series insists, no nextness; not so much because there is always something between (though in a sense the facts may be put that way—you may distinguish an intermediate period between the Middle Ages and the Modern Period, and so *ad infinitum*) as because there is no clear beginning or ending.

But if it is said that, whatever is true of concrete historical events, the parts of *abstract* time are continuous, a new difficulty arises. To know that two bodies are continuous, we must know that their separate lengths are together equal to their length overall. This we can only know by measuring and adding the measurements; and this, as we have seen, cannot be done in the case of time. To put this objection differently: the continuity of any two things presupposes a system of reference other than themselves, by appeal to which we can assure ourselves of the absence of a gap. In the case of spatial bodies, this system consists of the marks on a measuring-rod. In the case of temporal events, it consists of continuous time with its clock-marked divisions. But in the case of time itself, there can be no system of reference except another time, concurrent with but distinct from the first. This second time, assumed to be continuous, can guarantee the continuity of the first by a one-one correspondence of its parts. But how do we know that *it* is continuous? There is no way of *even assuming* that it is, unless we suppose the existence of yet another time, and so *ad infinitum*. Hence, far less prove, we cannot even assume the continuity of time without surreptitiously assuming another time as a background to it, and assuming the continuity of this other.

d. A difficulty of the same kind attaches to the statement that time is infinite. This presumably means that time is temporally infinite, *i.e.*, everlasting. But to say that something is everlasting means that it lasts all the time; it implies two terms—that which endures, and the time in which it endures. Hence to say that time is everlasting is to say that, in addition to the time which goes on, there is another time during which it goes on; and to say that it goes on always means that it goes on as long as this other time goes on. Once more, we are involved in the fallacy of a reduplicated time-series.

This cannot be avoided by pleading that when time is called infinite we only mean that after any given part of time another always follows. For to say this is already to say that one part of time follows after another, and this implies a system of reference by appeal to which we can say that a change or lapse has taken place. We are, in fact, back in the perplexities that arose out of the notion of time as flying or moving.

If, instead of saying that abstract time is infinite, we say that temporal events are infinite, it must again be asked whether we mean infinite in number as succeeding each other in a series of mutually external terms. If so, it must be pointed out that events are not related to one another in this way, as has already been shown; and the infinity of time seems from this point of view to be only a metaphorical phrase to describe the infinite complexity of that one event which is the history of the world.

III.

It is hardly necessary to pursue further the quest for a statement about time that shall be anything but a conscious and more or less deliberate falsehood; we should be better employed asking what it is in all these statements that makes them false. Perhaps part of the answer lies in the habit denounced by Bergson (and others before him) as the "spatializing" of time. We imagine time as a straight line along which something travels. Without inquiring too closely what it is that does the travelling, we may ask whether time is at all like a line; and, obviously, it is not. "Thought of as a line, it would only possess one *real* point—namely, the present. From it would issue two endless but imaginary arms, Past and Future" (Lotze, *Metaphysic,* Section 138). It is difficult to uproot from one's mind the illusion that somehow the past and the future exist, or that the past somehow exists, even if the future does not. Have we not, in memory and in historical inference, *knowledge* of the past? Have we not, in scientific prediction, knowledge of the future? And is it not self-evident that what we know must be real? This seems to be the argument on which we rely when we try to bolster up our belief in the reality of past and future against the attacks of the obvious common-sense reflection that what has been, and what is to be, do not in any sense exist at all. No doubt, the present would not be what it is if the past had not been and if the future were not to be; but it is a childish confusion of thought to argue that therefore the past and the future are now real. On the contrary, they are just therefore *not* real. It is just because I have left Euston and hope to get to Carlisle that I am at Crewe and not now in any sense whatever either at Euston or at Carlisle. Euston and Carlisle still exist, but they are not past or future events; the past event of my leaving the one and the future event of arrival at the other are not happening, and an event when it is not happening is just nothing. It is true that the whole of which they are parts is happening, and that the parts, as we said, overlap one another in the structure of the whole; but this does not mean that the past *as past* continues to exist. What does continue to exist is the contribution it has made to the present.

The point may be illustrated by the way in which many theories of memory have broken down through confusing my present memory of a past event with the present effect of that past event on my bodily or psychic organism. To go about short of a leg is not the same thing as remembering the loss of it, and to suffer a neurotic disability as the result of fear is not the same thing as remembering the fear. Memory is a kind of knowledge, if it is knowledge, having this peculiarity, if it is a peculiarity, that its objects have no existence of any kind whatever, and that they are known to have no existence. This may seem strange to people who believe that all thought is of a real object existing independently of the thought of it; but the alternative, to take literally the fairy-tale of the place where all the old moons are kept, is surely a good deal stranger.

To spatialize time is to fall into the illusion of thinking that past and future exist but are not "present to us" at the moment. And this fallacy seems to underlie all the ordinary statements about time— that it has one dimension, that it lapses uniformly, that it is continuous and divisible and measurable and infinite and so on—all of which rest on the assumption that a great deal of time, if not the whole of it, exists at any given moment and that we can somehow "go over" it in the same kind of way in which we go over a spatial object with a foot-rule: which we obviously could not do were it not present to us, as a whole, *now*. If this were not so, time could not be a quantity, for a quantity must exist somewhere, somehow, at some time; and when we say that from 1800 to 1900 is a hundred years, we are assuming (what we know to be untrue) that these dates exist now and that we can measure the interval between them. Nor is it better to say "from 1800 to 1900 *was* a hundred years." Was *when*? Obviously, at no identifiable time: in fact, never.

The first condition of clearing up our conception of time, then, is to stop thinking of it as a special kind of one-dimensional space and to think it as what it is—a perpetually changing present, having somehow bound up with it a future which does not exist and past which does not exist. Poetic imagination may think of the future as lying unrevealed in the womb of time and of the past as hidden behind some screen of oblivion; but these are metaphors, and the plain fact, obvious to anyone who will open his eyes and look at it, is that both future and past, consisting as they do of events that are not happening, are wholly unreal.

—R.G. Collingwood, from
*Proceedings of the Aristotelian
Society,* 1926

An Example: An Economic Theory of History and Society

In the opening of *The Communist Manifesto,* Karl Marx and Friedrich Engels formulate their theory of history as class struggles, the fight between those who hold power and those denied it. This theory, as presented over 135 years ago, has had powerful consequences for what many people believe about the world; many of the political and social conflicts of this century involve people acting on or acting against this vision of human organization. In a less dramatic way, this theory has had serious impact on the study of history, politics, economics, sociology, and even art and literature. Although modern communism has spawned repressive, ugly political systems, the thought and theories of Marx and Engels continue to excite intellectual controversy. The impact of these theories on the world demonstrates forcibly that theories are not just empty abstractions, with little relation to reality. Theories can come from a vision of the world and can in turn influence the shape of the world that follows.

The passage opens with a bold and simple statement about the meaning of all history. A series of elaborations fleetingly suggest how the general concept of class struggles apply to the many different periods and situations of history. Then Marx and Engels discuss in a bit more detail the class structure they saw in nineteenth-century Europe: the bourgeoisie (or capitalist class) dominating the working class. In sweeping historical generalizations, they present the rise of the bourgeoisie and then analyze several aspects of the political advance of the bourgeois class. The consequences of bourgeois dominance for the structure of society and economy are then revealed in equally sweeping, general terms. In a sense, Marx and Engels create a model of history, which they then use to analyze how we got to the current situation and to reveal its structure.

Karl Marx. (Brown Brothers)   Friedrich Engels. (Brown Brothers)

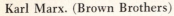

Although the model is drawn in the most sweeping terms, it is meant to apply to all the details of history, society, and economics. Many, many volumes have been filled by theoretical and empirical attempts to show exactly how this general theory explains all aspects of human life. And just as many volumes have been written attempting to show where the theory fails in both theoretical and empirical terms. Because, however, the theory makes claims about complex topics about which we have not been able to come to simple, definite conclusions, no straightforward way to resolve the issues raised by this theory exists. It remains something of a matter of belief. Certainly in communist countries, belief in Marxist thought takes on the character of a religious belief not to be questioned.

I. Bourgeoisie and Proletarians

The history of all hitherto existing society is the history of class struggles.

Freeman and slave, patrician and plebeian, lord and serf, guild-master and journeyman, in a word, oppressor and oppressed, stood in constant opposition to one another, carried on an uninterrupted, now hidden, now open fight, a fight that each time ended, either in a revolutionary reconstitution of society at large, or in the common ruin of the contending classes.

In the earlier epochs of history, we find almost everywhere a complicated arrangement of society into various orders, a manifold gradation of social rank. In ancient Rome we have patricians, knights, plebeians, slaves; in the Middle Ages, feudal lords, vassals, guild-masters, journeymen, apprentices, serfs; in almost all of these classes, again, subordinate gradations.

The modern bourgeois society that has sprouted from the ruins of feudal society has not done away with class antagonisms. It has but established new classes, new conditions of oppression, new forms of struggle in place of the old ones.

Our epoch, the epoch of the bourgeoisie, possesses, however, this distinctive feature: it has simplified the class antagonisms. Society as a whole is more and more splitting up into two great hostile camps, into two great classes directly facing each other; bourgeoisie and proletariat.

From the serfs of the Middle Ages sprang the chartered burghers of the earliest towns. From these burgesses the first elements of the bourgeoisie were developed.

The discovery of America, the rounding of the Cape, opened up fresh ground for the rising bourgeoisie. The East-Indian and Chinese markets, the colonization of America, trade with the colonies, the increase in the means of exchange and in commodities generally, gave to commerce, to navigation, to industry, an impulse never before known, and, thereby, a rapid development to the revolutionary element in the tottering feudal society.

The feudal system of industry, under which industrial production was monopolized by closed guilds, now no longer sufficed for the growing wants of the new markets. The manufacturing system took its place. The guild-masters were pushed to one side by the manufacturing middle class; division of labor between the different corporate guilds vanished in the face of division of labor in each single workshop.

Meantime the markets kept ever growing, the demand ever rising. Even manufacture no longer sufficed. Thereupon, steam and machinery revolutionized industrial production. The place of manufacture was taken by the giant, modern industry, the place of the industrial middle class, by industrial millionaires, the leaders of whole industrial armies, the modern bourgeois.

Modern industry has established the world market, for which the discovery of America paved the way. This market has given an immense development to commerce, to navigation, to communication by land.

This development has, in its turn, reacted on the extension of industry; and in proportion as industry, commerce, navigation, railways extended, in the same proportion the bourgeoisie developed, increased its capital, and pushed into the background every class handed down from the Middle Ages.

We see, therefore, how the modern bourgeoisie is itself the product of a long development, of a series of revolutions in the modes of production and exchange.

Each step in the development of the bourgeoisie was accompanied by a corresponding political advance of that class. An oppressed class under the sway of the feudal nobility, an armed and self-governing association in the medieval commune. At first, an independent urban republic (as in Italy and Germany) or a taxable "third estate" of the monarchy (as in France), afterwards, in the period of manufacture proper, serving either the semi-feudal or the absolute monarchy as a counterpoise against the nobility, and, in fact, cornerstone of the great monarchies in general, the bourgeoisie has at last, since the establishment of modern industry and of the world market, conquered for itself, in the modern representative State, exclusive political sway. The executive of the modern State is but a committee for managing the common affairs of the whole bourgeoisie.

The bourgeoisie, historically, has played a most revolutionary part.

The bourgeoisie, wherever it has got the upper hand, has put an end to all feudal, patriarchal, idyllic relations. It has pitilessly torn asunder the motley feudal ties that bound man to his "natural superiors," and has left remaining no other nexus between man and man than naked self-interest, than callous "cash payment." It has drowned the most heavenly ecstasies of religious fervor, of chivalrous enthusiasm, of philistine sentimentalism, in the icy water of egotistical calculation. It has resolved personal worth into exchange value, and in place of the numberless indefeasible chartered freedoms, has set up that single, unconscionable freedom—Free Trade. In a word, for exploitation, veiled by religious and political illusions; it has substituted naked, shameless, direct, brutal exploitation.

The bourgeoisie has stripped of its halo every occupation hitherto honored and looked up to with reverent awe. It has converted the physician, the lawyer, the priest, the poet, and the man of science into its paid wage-laborers.

The bourgeoisie has torn away from the family its sentimental veil and has reduced the family relation to a mere money relation.

The bourgeoisie has disclosed how it came to pass that the brutal display of vigor in the Middle Ages, which reactionaries so much admire, found its fitting complement in the most slothful indolence. It has been the first to show what man's activity can bring about. It has accomplished wonders far surpassing Egyptian pyramids, Roman aqueducts, and Gothic cathedrals. It has conducted expeditions that put in the shade all former Exoduses of nations and crusades.

The bourgeoisie cannot exist without constantly revolutionizing the instruments of production, and thereby the relations of production, and with them all social relations. Conservation of the old modes of production in unaltered form, was, on the contrary, the first condition of existence for all earlier industrial classes. Constant revolutionizing of production, uninterrupted disturbance of all social conditions, everlasting uncertainty and agitation distinguish the bourgeois epoch from all earlier ones. All fixed, fast-frozen relations, with their train of ancient and venerable prejudices and opinions are swept away, all newly formed ones become antiquated before they can ossify. All that is solid melts into air, all that is holy is profaned, and man is at last compelled to face with sober senses, his real conditions of life, and his relations with his kind.

The need of a constantly expanding market for its products chases the bourgeoisie over the whole face of the globe. It must nestle everywhere, settle everywhere, establish connections everywhere.

The bourgeoisie has through its exploitation of the world market given a cosmopolitan character to production and consumption in every country. To the great chagrin of reactionaries, it has drawn from under the feet of industry the national ground on which it stood. All old, established national industries have been destroyed or are daily being destroyed. They are dislodged by new industries, whose introduction becomes a life and death question for all civilized nations, industries that no longer work with indigenous raw material, but raw material drawn from the remotest regions, industries whose products are consumed, not only at home, but in every quarter of the globe. In place of the old wants, satisfied by the productions of the country, we find new wants, requiring for their satisfaction the products of distant lands and climes. In place of the old local and national seclusion and self-sufficiency, we have intercourse in every direction, a universal interdependence of nations. And as in material, so also in intellectual production. The intellectual creations of individual nations become common property. National one-sidedness and narrow-mindedness become more and more impossible, and from the numerous national and local literatures, there arises a world literature.

The bourgeoisie, by the rapid improvement of all instruments of production, by the immensely facilitated means of communication, draws all, even the most barbarian, nations into civilization. The cheap prices of its commodities are the heavy artillery with which it batters down all Chinese walls, with which it forces the barbarians' intensely obstinate hatred of foreigners to capitulate. It compels all nations, on pain of extinction, to adopt the bourgeois mode of production; it compels them to introduce what it calls civilization into their midst, *i.e.,* to become bourgeois themselves. In one word, it creates a world after its own image.

The bourgeoisie has subjected the country to the rule of the towns.

It has created enormous cities, greatly increased the urban population as compared with the rural, and thus rescued a considerable part of the population from the idiocy of rural life. Just as it has made the country dependent on the towns, so it has made barbarian and semi-barbarian countries dependent on the civilized ones, nations of peasants on nations of bourgeoisie, the East on the West. More and more the bourgeoisie continues to do away with the scattered state of population, means of production, and property. It has agglomerated population, centralized means of production, and concentrated property in a few hands. The necessary consequence of this was political centralization. Independent, or but loosely connected, provinces with separate interests, laws, governments and systems of taxation, became lumped together into one nation, with one government, one code of laws, one national class-interest, one frontier and one customs-tariff.

The bourgeoisie, during its rule of scarcely one hundred years, has created more massive and more colossal productive forces than have all preceding generations together. The subjection of nature's forces to man and machinery; the application of chemistry to industry and agriculture; [the development of] steam-navigation, railways and electric telegraphs; the clearing of whole continents for cultivation; the canalization of rivers and the conjuring of whole populations out of the ground—what earlier century had even a presentiment that such productive forces slumbered in the lap of social labor?

We see then: the means of production and exchange, on whose foundation the bourgeoisie built itself up, were generated in feudal society. At a certain stage in the development of these means of production and exchange, the conditions under which feudal society produced and exchanged, the feudal organization of agriculture and manufacturing industry, in one word, the feudal relations of property became no longer compatible with the already developed productive forces; they became so many fetters. They had to be burst asunder. They were burst asunder.

Into their place stepped free competition, accompanied by a social and political constitution adapted to it and by the economical and political sway of the bourgeois class.

—Karl Marx and Friedrich Engels,
from *The Communist Manifesto,* 1848

Writing Assignments

1. In an essay of 300 words for a philosophy class, clarify the meaning of one of the following commonly used abstract terms: *honesty, love, virtue, despair, sin* or *evil*. With your teacher's permission, you may substitute any similar word. In your discussion,

examine what you consider incorrect or inaccurate uses of the term, and present a better way of understanding the concept.

2. If you are taking a course in mathematics, logic, or one of the physical sciences, explain a proof or derivation from your textbook or class lectures. Explain the meaning of each step in the proof or derivation, how the author moves from one step to the next, and why that logical progression is justified. Your explanation can be in the form of a fuller rewriting of the original proof or derivation (at least twice the length to allow for explanatory additions) or in the form of annotations to a photocopy of the original. Consider the purpose of this explanation to be to demonstrate to the teacher of the subject your full understanding of the proof or derivation.

3. A friend, considering taking a course you are now taking, asks you to describe what that course is really all about, what the underlying ideas are. In an essay of 300 words, explain the basic theory of the subject as presented by the teacher, and relate that theory to the kinds of material that are taught.

4. Imagine you are taking an introductory course in the philosophy of knowledge and you have been assigned to read and discuss the four examples of writing about time presented in this unit: the essay on play time and movie time (pages 360–365), the anthropological essay on time in culture (pages 378–384), the psychological study of time perception (pages 410–414), and the philosophical discussion of the concept of time (pages 422–427). In an essay of about 500 words, compare the differences and similarities with which the four essays approach the subject of time. Relate the approach of each article to the basic ideas and purposes of the discipline it comes from.

5. For a discussion group on ethics and belief, prepare a 300-word statement of some general principle or idea that you consider important to your life. Explain what the principle or idea is, why it is a good principle or idea, and how it affects your thought and/or behavior.

6. Write a letter to me, the author of this book, presenting some of the concepts about writing that you got from using this book. Then explain whether you believe these concepts are valid or useful. Defend your position. I want very much to receive your comments, for I want to know what students are getting or not getting from the book. Mail the letter to: Charles Bazerman, c/o College Text Division, Houghton Mifflin Company, One Beacon Street, Boston, Massachusetts 02108.

4 The Craft
of
Writing

16 A Guide to the Writing Process

*W*riting is a process with many parts. Much of this book has been devoted to advice on the early stages, or prewriting, and to descriptions of the final essay, or product. This chapter, however, is concerned with the problem of putting words on the page and improving those words to make a more effective statement. Drafts and revisions help you concentrate on one level of language at a time: getting the ideas down, tightening the logic, refining your relationship to the audience, and sharpening the details of paragraphs, sentences, and words. In the latter stages of the writing process—the public presentation of the essay and the readers' responses—the writing moves from the privacy of the writer's workshop out into the social world.

Writing Takes Time

Few essays pop into a writer's head fully developed, word for word, as they appear in the final paper. Unlike speech, which often seems to flow spontaneously and where the first thought is rarely far from public utterance, writing needs time, thought, and many conscious choices to move from your first conception to a public document. Writing can be extremely frustrating as you try to turn vague ideas into a full statement that will mean what you want it to mean to the reader. Because you do not start out with anything that resembles a completed statement, you may doubt that you have anything to say, but you will find that you are frequently mistaken. If you gather the courage to put down your beginning thoughts and if you have the patience to work through the many stages of developing these thoughts, that vague beginning will lead to a precise and full final statement. You may also mistakenly assume that your first thoughts are adequate for the final statement that will communicate with and convince your reader. Good writing requires you to apply yourself on many levels.

Much of this book is devoted to explaining the process of pre-writing: all those things you need to do before you put a blank piece of paper in your typewriter. Chapters give advice on how to understand a writing task, how to gather ideas and information from books, how to evaluate that information on the basis of experience and evidence, and how to think about that material. The chapters also describe particular assignments. Advice about what you should accomplish in those assignments and what the finished product should look like provide goals for your work; furthermore, suggestions about the stages of preparing each assignment give you some guidance in the process.

No matter how much guidance you are given about any particular assignment, you must still face the universal problem of putting words on the page and then revising them. You still have to do the actual writing.

Fortunately, writing is something of a private act, even though its goal is public communication. You can think about your writing for a while, correct it, revise it, and put it through several stages. You may show early versions of your writing to friends and advisers for help, but in the end only the final version counts. Not only can you use the earlier versions of your writing to develop and clarify your meaning gradually, but also you can experiment in the early drafts, trying out ideas, organizations, and various ways of constructing sentences to find the most effective ones. If the experiment fails, you can always rework the passage before you create the final version.

In the process of writing, of working out how to put your ideas and information together in language, you can discover many new things. Ideas that hid in the back of your mind as you did your research or planned your essay suddenly may become clearer as you start putting words on the page. Seeing your thoughts in black and white gives them new impact. One thought may lead to the next, and you may find yourself making a new and more powerful argument than you had previously imagined. The problem of finding precise words to explain vague ideas may force you to sharpen your thoughts and come to new, more precise conclusions. Putting words on the page allows you to examine them and ask new questions. You can see how exactly ideas match evidence and whether you need to reformulate parts of your argument. You may find opportunities to analyze or explain your ideas in greater detail—and thus take those ideas further. Sometimes even a phrase you use in passing may open up new insights.

Thus writing is far more than a mechanical skill: it is an open-ended process of discovery. The more you have prepared yourself in the prewriting period—by analyzing the writing task, by gathering materials, by thinking and planning—the more exciting the writing becomes. All the parts of your preparation come together to make something new. The more pieces you have to work with, the more original you are likely to be. The better prepared your mind, the more readily it will recognize the importance and power of the new ideas you come up with.

Each writing task is an individual problem, and the final version is your solution to the problem. Unlike math problems, writing problems have many acceptable solutions. No one knows what your essay will be like until you create it. In the process of developing and revising your writing, you invent a new solution. Through tackling new writing problems resourcefully and developing new solutions to these new problems, your skill as a writer will grow.

Drafting

Drafting—writing an essay in several versions, each time limiting your attention to only a few factors—is necessary for good writing because writing is both a complex competence and a demanding art. You have by now acquired many skills that go into writing, from the mechanics of spelling and the formal rules of grammar to the strategic use of examples and the logical organization of the entire paper. Even if some of these skills are second nature to you, it is quite difficult to keep them all in mind simultaneously while you are trying to write. Even a professional juggler can keep only a limited number of objects in the air at one time. Even if you could pay full attention to all the skills at once, that effort would leave you very little mental room to devote to the actual subject of the writing—your individual ideas on a topic and the invention of new ways to develop your topic. The more you can devote your mind to each of these tasks, one at a time, the more likely you are to discover a good solution to each. Your writing will develop most efficiently if you limit yourself to one problem at each stage, starting with the basic issue of developing ideas and working through to the final task of neat typing according to conventional formats.

Many prewriting activities, such as gathering notes, developing ideas in journals, and organizing an outline, already begin to shape what you read, see, and think into written words, as described in previous chapters. Ideas, phrases, and even longer passages from these early materials may wind up in your final paper. However, as you enter into the actual period of writing, you focus directly on producing a coherent, unified text. These later stages of developing a full written statement consist of:

1. Fleshing out the thoughts in words
2. Tightening the relationships between statements
3. Defining the relationship to the audience
4. Sharpening the language
5. Satisfying the formalities of public presentation

One additional stage occurs after you are finished with the writing, but it is as much a part of the writing process as the earlier stages:

6. Dealing with response to your writing

The actual separation of these stages into drafts—and revisions of these drafts—varies, depending on the kind of writing you are doing, its difficulty, your own skills, and your preferences and habits. In actual practice the stages often overlap.

You may sometimes work on several levels simultaneously. At other times you may find yourself going back to an earlier stage as you recognize new problems to work on. Sometimes, for example, a phrasing problem may reveal an underlying problem with the logic of the argument. No matter how your own drafting methods vary from the idealized stages presented here, you should follow the general pattern of working on the deeper structural issues first—your ideas and their organization—and moving gradually toward the more surface issues, such as polishing the language.

The First Full Draft:
Fleshing Out Thoughts
in Words

No matter how complete and formal, an outline can provide only a loose scheme for your writing—an anticipated order of major and subordinate thoughts. Only when you turn the approximate plans of an outline into a continuous and complete first draft will you discover all that you want to say on the subject. Only then will you need to clarify the precise relationship of all the parts to the whole; only then can you judge the appropriateness of your specific examples for illustrating the points you wish to make.

In writing your first complete draft, the most important consideration is to create a continuous line of words—a thread of argument that covers all you feel must be said on the subject. This first full draft may be ungrammatical, inelegant, redundant, and even a bit obscure, because you should concentrate mainly on setting down on paper everything you have to say on the subject. This objective will be met if you follow these three guidelines:

- Be as complete as possible. Don't worry about being too long, overly explicit, or repetitious. Write something as many times and in as many ways as you need to until you feel you have stated it correctly. You can always choose the best of these options later and cut out the excess at that point. Right now, you just need to make sure you have a full set of words to work with later. If you try to be complete in the first draft, you won't have to worry later that you have left something important out.

- Try to support every generalization through detailed examples, and make sure that each specific detail is closely related to a general statement made in the paper. Specific examples tie down the meaning of your generalizations, helping both you and your reader see exactly what you have in mind. This procedure will not only help you bring out your ideas more sharply but also will force you to look more carefully at those ideas that you have only vaguely formulated. Conversely, by making sure every specific is related to a generalization, you will make certain that your paper never drifts away from its point. Details can sometimes be so all-consuming in themselves that they may cause you to forget the main direction of the paper. Generalizations give meaning to the specifics. Again, don't worry about too many examples or about too much explicit explanation making your paper repetitious. You can always eliminate the excess in later drafts.

- Pay attention to step-by-step continuity. Justify to yourself why one point should follow another. Decide how each individual piece fits in with the overall design. Then bring out the connections between points as explicitly as possible by using transitional words or phrases, by referring to other related points, or by repeating the main points of the argument. Don't worry if these connecting devices seem obvious, self-evident, or cumbersome. You can always either delete them or make them less obtrusive later.

Logic: Tightening the Relationships Between Statements

Your essay is not a kite's tail, where one scrap of cloth is tied to another unmatched scrap of cloth to form a long chain held together only by bulky knots. The statements of your essay should bear important structural relationships to one another—more like the parts of the well-defined body of a kite than the scraps of its haphazard, trailing tail. The study of the relationship of statements is *logic* in its broadest sense, and the logic of an essay is the way in which its parts fit together.

There are many different kinds of logic—many different rationales for drawing statements together in a coherent essay. Each of these logics is an entire study in itself, far beyond the scope of this book. One type, formal logic, you may have studied in school. Another type, associative logic, you may have seen incorporated into some of your reading. And you may have acquired a practical understanding of transactional logic from your daily interactions with other people. Obviously, the more you know about each type of logic, the more effectively you can use and control logical statements in your writing.

In revising your first draft, you must recognize what kind of logic is most applicable to the kind of writing you are doing, and then you must attempt to bring out that logic sharply and consistently throughout the piece of writing. That is, you must choose the most appropriate kind of logic, adhere to it throughout the piece (unless you have a strong rationale for shifting), and finally let the reader know exactly what connections are being made and why.

Formal Logic

Formal logic (or *deductive logic*) is governed by a set of rules that define what conclusions follow precisely from a given set of propositions. In their most familiar form, deductive arguments appear as *syllogisms,* which consist of a series of *premises* and a *conclusion* that follows from the premises. Consider this example:

No human being has feathers.
Johnson is a human being.
Therefore, Johnson does not have feathers.

Actually, there are four types of deductive arguments. The above example is called a *categorical argument* (where the conclusion is based on the general category to which the specific example belongs). The next example is a *hypothetical argument* (in which the conclusion depends on some hypothetical condition being true):

If gas supplies are short, gas prices will rise.
Gas supplies are short.
Therefore, gas prices will rise.

The third type is the *alternative argument* (which is based on the elimination of a limited number of possible alternatives):

Either Jones is evil or he is stupid.
Jones is not stupid.
Therefore, Jones is evil.

The final type of deductive argument is the *disjunctive argument* (where a situation is shown to be impossible):

A person cannot be in two places at one time.
Lucretia was in Washington last Saturday evening at 10 P.M.
She was not in Boston last Saturday evening at 10 P.M.

Such formal logic serves very well for determining all that can be inferred from a given set of *propositions,* or first statements. In abstract fields of study, such as mathematics and formal logic itself, chains of syllogistic logic can produce complex conclusions of great certainty. Deduction plays a role in most areas of study.

However, formal logic does not help you in judging the truth of first propositions or in making statements beyond those that are implicit in the first propositions. That is, formal logic will not help you prove whether, indeed, human beings do or do not have feathers or whether Johnson is the name someone has given to a pet parakeet. Moreover, such a set of propositions will not help you discover why human beings do not have feathers. Formal logic does not cover most arguments, questions, and statements that people are actually interested in. In practice, formal logic at most tells you what you cannot do—what is a breach of basic ground rules of rational argument—rather than what you should do.

Further, there are dangers in relying too heavily on deductive logic in any but the most abstract disciplines. Although some mathematical propositions—such as *parallel lines never meet*—are true by definition, most propositions about actual things in the world are only simplifications and approximations, such as *politicians must pay attention to the interests of their constituents if they hope to be re-elected.* The specifics of any situation referred to by this general statement are much more complex than the general words indicate; for example, the politician's constituency may include many conflicting interests. Even in such an abstract field as theoretical physics, the basic propositions of Newtonian mechanics were found to be only approximations that did not apply under extreme conditions, such as speeds approaching the speed of light. Even Einstein's revisions of the propositions of mechanics are held by many physicists to be only simplifications and approximations. If you take these approximate statements and combine them with other approximate statements and run them all through many deductive operations, the possible errors can compound dramatically. You may wind up with conclusions that are not at all reasonable. Thus you should not try to deduce too much from simplified statements about the world.

Inductive Logic

Inductive logic is reasoning from observed events rather than from abstract propositions. Consequently, it is the main logic of experimental science. The principle of induction is that if, every time you observe a particular thing, it behaves in a certain way, then after many such observations, you can assume that the next time it will behave the same as before. That is, if you have seen Johnson many times and never once was he growing feathers, you can assume that the next time you see him he still will not be growing feathers. In even more general terms, if Johnson is a human being and if you have never observed any human being growing feathers, you can assume—even before seeing this particular human called Johnson—that he is not growing feathers. Induction is not without limits. Here, for example, Johnson may be a freak of nature. But, given all the accumulated observations of science on this subject, such an aberration is extremely unlikely. Induction is very useful for developing generalized descriptions of repeating and patterned events. Induction keeps your attention on the actual shared characteristics of phenomena. If, however, you are describing random, unpatterned, or unique events, induction is useless if not misleading. Furthermore, induction by itself leaves you close to the surface of things as they appear and may not be appropriate for inquiry into deeper causes or meanings.

Analogical Reasoning

Analogical reasoning is the drawing of conclusions on the basis of the similarity between two things. It is a way of applying what you know about one thing to another. Thus, if you notice that a corporation is in some ways organized like a sports team, you may be able to understand some of the more confusing aspects of the company's organizational structure through the more clear-cut and familiar sports example. All analogies, however, are imperfect: a corporation is not a sports team, and the two differ in significant aspects. Thus you should say precisely what the similarities are, and you should limit the conclusions you can draw from the similarities. Analogies may be useful in an early stage to help you gain an understanding of an unfamiliar subject; you can find your bearings by making comparisons to things you already know. However, an argument based purely on analogy is weak, for it does not establish the distinctiveness of the new subject under investigation. Analogies are best used only to introduce your readers to a topic with which they are unfamiliar. Before incorporating one into your final paper, you will already know the subject quite well, so you will be able to judge just how far you can legitimately extend the analogy.

Ordinary Argumentation

Ordinary argumentation, according to philosopher Stephen Toulmin, follows none of the patterns we have already described but rather draws conclusions from given data by means of *warrants,* which act as bridges between data and conclusions. For example, starting with the information that Marianne Hodge has made *A*'s throughout the semester in her writing course, we draw the usual conclusion that she will receive an *A* as the course grade. The warrant that allows us to go from data to conclusion is that students who receive *A*'s all semester long receive a final grade of *A*. If we were pressed to give *backing* for this warrant, we might further say that the final grade in this particular course is based on a straight average of all grades for the semester, except for special circumstances that do not occur more than one time in a hundred. The last phrase "except for . . ." gives the necessary qualification to the conclusion. Schematically, the argument would appear as follows:

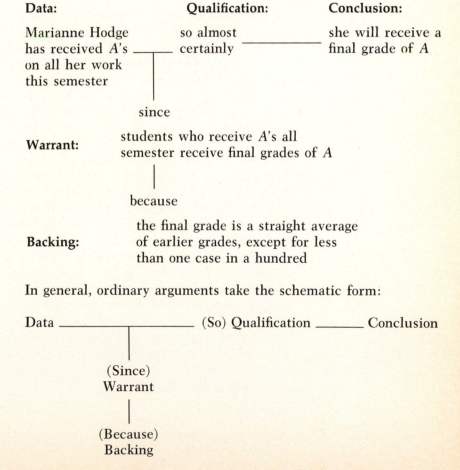

Data: **Qualification:**   **Conclusion:**

Marianne Hodge has received *A*'s on all her work this semester   so almost certainly   she will receive a final grade of *A*

since

Warrant: students who receive *A*'s all semester receive final grades of *A*

because

Backing: the final grade is a straight average of earlier grades, except for less than one case in a hundred

In general, ordinary arguments take the schematic form:

Data ——————— (So) Qualification ——— Conclusion

(Since)
Warrant

(Because)
Backing

In order to make a convincing argument, you must have warrant and backing for your argument that your particular audience finds acceptable. If, for example, a student believes that Professor Jones assigns final grades by randomly pulling letters from a fishbowl and not by taking an average of the grades, our warrant and the conclusion that follows will not be convincing to that student. In writing arguments for any of the academic disciplines, you must use warrants and backings that are accepted as valid and relevant by the appropriate discipline.

Persuasive Logic

At times your purpose may not be to convince your readers through reason. Instead you may want to persuade them through appeals to their emotions, beliefs, or interests. The *logic of persuasion* requires you to consider what moves the reader and then to build your argument around that. The order and relationship of the statements in such a persuasive essay will be based on getting the reader more and more involved with your side of the issue—rather than on laying out an impersonal argument. This kind of persuasion is useful when you want others to act with you or support your cause, provided it is not important that you achieve intellectual agreement. However, most academic writing presumably aims at intellectual agreement. You would be unwise to frame your next paper in economics as an appeal to your professor's emotions.

In one academic situation, it may make sense to pay some attention to the attitudes of your readers. If you foresee that your readers may be so set against your ideas that they will not even entertain your point or pay attention to your arguments, you might first try to establish some common ground of agreement with them. You should try to imagine how they will receive your ideas; put yourself in their position. Then state the ways in which you agree with them. In this way a sense of trust and communciation will be established before you try to convince them of more controversial matters. This attempt to remove threat and hostility from communication is the essence of *transactional logic,* as presented by the psychologist Carl Rogers.*

---

*Carl Rogers, "Communication: Its Blocking and Facilitation," in Richard Young, Alton Becker, and Kenneth Pike, *Rhetoric: Discovery and Change* (New York: Harcourt Brace Jovanovich, 1970), 284–89.

Other Logics

At other times, you may not be trying to convince your reader of anything. You may instead be presenting a set of feelings or a state of mind, perhaps yours or perhaps another individual's. You may, for example, be trying to recreate for a history paper how an eighteenth-century Englishman would have responded to news of the rebellious colonists in America. Here you would have to pay some attention to the *logic of emotions*.

In writing a narrative of the growth of the French-speaking separatist movement in Quebec, you would have to pay attention to the *logic of events,* the *logic of group dynamics,* and the *logic of nationalist sentiment.* Indeed, the connection and sequence of statements in your own paper may necessarily follow these logics rather than the more traditional logics discussed earlier. One may even speak of something as strange as *dream logic,* whereby events that seem disordered by waking standards may make sense in some deep symbolic way. If your psychology teacher or perhaps your creative writing teacher asks you to keep a record of your dreams, your writing will have to reflect dream logic.

If you are writing an informal essay speculating on connections among ideas, events, and feelings, the relationship of statements may follow an *associational logic*. For this type of essay, you will have to show only that there is some tangential connection between two statements—not necessarily an ironclad structural link. If you are interpreting a piece of writing, *interpretive logic* demands that you explain explicitly the structure and meaning of each part of the original.

Different kinds of essays call for different kinds of logic. In each case you must decide which is the appropriate form of logic to connect and integrate all your statements into a whole. When you revise for logic, you must then clarify and bring out the specific type so that your readers will know which of these many forms of logic governs your thinking. The most exquisite logic in the world will remain unconvincing if your readers cannot follow it.

Refining Your
Relationship to
the Audience

You must keep the audience—the ultimate readers of your writing—clearly in mind throughout the writing process, from the very first decision to write through the development of your ideas to the final drafting of sentences. Without an audience to communicate with, you would have little motivation even to begin to imagine writing. Moreover, your reasons for communicating with a particular audience should shape the piece of writing as it develops. In revision, however, you need consciously to define your relationship to the audience so that you can rework your paper to have a maximum effect on your readers. Not only for persuasive writing but for all writing, the more you know of your readers' attitudes, dispositions, and knowledge, the more effectively you will be able to communicate with them.

As discussed in Chapter 1, the basic definition of the writing problem you are addressing depends on your relationship with and intentions toward your readers. In fact, a constant theme of this book is how each piece of writing attempts some kind of social action within a particular social setting (see especially Chapter 6, "Analyzing the Author's Purpose and Technique," and Part 3 on the writing within different disciplines). In revision, however, you must reassess your relationship with the audience in order to judge how your words can have maximum effect on readers. The more you know of your readers' attitudes, predispositions, and knowledge, the more effectively you can communicate with them.

Your Responsibility

The first aspect of your relationship with your readers is your responsibility to them. And your first responsibility is not to write nonsense, lies, or unwarranted statements. For each statement you make in your paper, you should ask yourself whether it is a true statement and whether it makes sense. If the reader discovers you being less than truthful or sensible, you will lose that reader's trust and patience. You may have a hard time getting either back. Part of truthfulness is letting the reader know how certain or uncertain you are of any claim you make. Ask yourself how much you need to know, or what kind of proof you should have, to make any particular claim with absolute certainty. If you have that knowledge and proof, you should present them to the reader. If you don't have either, don't bluff. You can still make the statement, but let the reader know that you are not yet certain of it, that you are only mentioning the idea to raise questions, or that you are presenting a speculation open to further evaluation. The more honest you are about the strength of your proof, the more the reader will respect your conviction at those times when you write with absolute certainty.

Another part of your responsibility to the readers is to take into consideration their expectations. This does not mean you always have to give them what they want or expect; often you will want to—and should—tell them something quite different. But it does mean you should recognize and, if necessary, explain the way in which you are disregarding reader expectation and your reasons for so doing. You can see how reader expectation operates, for example, when you write an essay in answer to a test question. The grader, or reader, of the essay expects to find a direct and full answer to the stated question; any failure to meet that expectation will be reflected in your grade. If you believe that the question is improperly framed—and genuinely feel that you can get to the most important issues by answering a different question—you had better begin your answer with a very clear and convincing explanation of how and why you are changing the question. In almost all writing situations, you must pay attention to some reader expectation, whether it is your supervisor's desire for a clear-cut recommendation in a business report or the mystery reader's anticipation of being amused and baffled by your detective story.

Your final responsibility to your readers is to make good on all that you promised. The title and introduction of a piece of writing are usually filled with implicit promises. If you title a paper "A Comparison of Mass Transit in New York, San Francisco, and Dallas," you are promising to give a comprehensive overview of all forms of mass transit—bus, subway, and train—in the three cities, to make specific comparisons among the systems, and finally to draw conclusions about the advantages and disadvantages of each city's system. If you intend to do less—to tell only about the buses in each city—you need to choose a less ambitious title. Similarly, if in your introduction you write "the importance of speech act philosophy for understanding spoken agreements cannot be underestimated," you are obligated to explain what speech act philosophy is, what it has to do with spoken agreements, and why it is so important to the subject of spoken agreements. Promises can even be implicit in the tone of your language; for example, if you initially adopt a humorous tone, you had better live up to it by actually being funny. If you choose to write with unusual words and long, intricate sentences, you are implying that your subject is so difficult and complex that any less tortuous language could not convey your precise meaning. Your actual content had better live up to this elaborate technique—unless you want to be thought pompous and obfuscating.

Your Opportunities

In addition to your responsibilities, you have opportunities to enlighten and convince your reader. To enlighten the reader, you must carefully consider what the reader needs to know in order to understand everything you discuss in your writing. To increase the reader's understanding, you may have to provide more background or you may have to offer more specificity—persuasive examples or telling details. In order to judge how much background or specificity your audience can profitably use, you have to draw on your knowledge of the audience—what your readers already know, what they believe, and how they think. You can gain some sense of what a professional audience is likely to know from seeing what ideas and information are common in the professional literature of the discipline. For a more general audience, you can look to the cultural beliefs, educational level, and common experiences of your anticipated readers. If you are writing for an instructor, you probably have substantial personal knowledge to go on. What students call "psyching out" a teacher is worthwhile if it is done in the spirit of figuring out how best to communicate to a teacher whose views differ from your own.

Introductions and conclusions are particularly useful places for letting the reader know the significance of your subject. A well-written introduction can draw your readers into the subject and let them know how the subject relates to the surrounding issues and to their personal interests. With professional audiences, a review of the literature placed immediately after the introduction will help place your subject against the relevant background so that the reader can see what you are hoping to accomplish in the essay. The conclusion can drive home the major ideas of the paper and pinpoint their importance and essential implications. The conclusion can help readers see what meaning they should take away from the writing and what action, if any, they should consider.

Finally, you must ask yourself what will convince this particular audience of your ideas. What kind of evidence is most compelling with this audience—statistics, theoretical analyses, personal experience, introspection, or what? Do readers harbor ideas that conflict with yours so that you have to demolish these competing ideas before you can argue for yours? Are there certain objections readers are likely to raise, so that you can anticipate the objections? It is important to remember that just because readers understand your argument does not mean that they will be convinced by it. Also remember that just because certain evidence convinces you does not mean that it will convince all readers—whether they are reasonable or otherwise.

Exercises

1. For each of the following passages, analyze how one statement leads to the next. Can you categorize each connection according to one kind of logic or another? Discuss whether the logic in each case is appropriate to the situation.
   a. The opening of the Declaration of Independence on page 62
   b. The discussion by Medawar and Medawar on pages 55–56
   c. De Tocqueville's comments on pages 51, 55
   d. Mort Rosenblum's discussion on pages 77–78
   e. The sample essay of synthesis on pages 266–270
   f. One of your own essays
2. Write short statements (two or three sentences each) on the topic of either fear or joy, using each of the following logics:
   a. Formal (or deductive) logic
   b. Inductive logic
   c. Ordinary argumentation
   d. Analogy
   e. Associative logic
   f. Narrative logic
   g. Dream logic
3. Identify the ways in which the following paragraph violates reader expectations or otherwise acts irresponsibly toward the audience. Then rewrite the paragraph to correct these problems.

The four reasons for the popularity of television soap operas all derive from the lack of social experience people have today. First, because young people lack social experience, they are unsure about what they can expect from life as they take on adult roles. The soap operas provide a picture of the world, which the young people can imagine as their futures. Using the TV image as the model for the world, the viewers also learn about how they might behave in society. They aren't confident about their own behavior and about how to interpret other people's behavior. They let TV tell them what they should have learned on their own more realistically in actual life. But that's all a big joke, isn't it? I mean real people don't act like those cardboard idiots on the tube, always staring off in space wondering about what will happen to an illegitimate twelve-year-old sister now that she has run off with a disbarred lawyer who is accused of murdering his wife. I mean, is that any way to behave? What a joke. But back to my main point, I've heard people say they even look at soap operas to see how the people dress and how they furnish the houses. People, old and young, must have pretty empty lives to need that to fill up their imaginations. I guess soap operas give them make-believe communities to worry about, just like when they were kids and had make-believe friends to play with. It's all fantasy.

4. Identify the ways in which each of the following writers shows awareness of the audience.
   a. Dale Carnegie in an excerpt from *How to Win Friends and Influence People* on pages 117–118
   b. James Lewis, book review on pages 182–183
   c. Ludwig Wittgenstein, preface on pages 147–149

Fine-Grained Revision: Sharpening the Language

By this stage you should know what your paper will say and how you would like it to affect the reader. But until you have pored over each sentence, each phrase, and each word, your meanings may be much murkier to the reader than you imagine. Writing communicates only through language. *Only detailed attention to language makes your message precise and clear.* This painstaking and detailed revision of language may at first seem unrewarding, but in struggling with obstinate words and sentences, you may create a more sharply defined statement than you had thought possible. As with people you know well, the beauty, character, and interest of writing are expressed through details.

A skillful writer attends to the details of language on three levels: (1) the intelligent and logical progression of statements within the paragraph, (2) the clear, concise, and graceful phrasing of sentences, and (3) the choice of precise words. Although we will treat the three separately, in practice they are interrelated. By finding a single right word, you may eliminate a long awkward phrase. By showing the relationship of statements through well-controlled sentence structure, you may solve problems of paragraph organization and you may solve problems of clarity, precision, and gracefulness at any of the three levels.

Anatomy of a Paragraph

Each well-written paragraph contains a number of sentences brought together because they share a *common element.* The art of writing paragraphs is to make evident this common element by the arrangement and connection of the sentences. Then each statement will shed light on the previous one, and each will carry forward the meaning of the whole.

Sometimes the common element is obvious, particularly if the paragraph is built around a well-developed topic sentence placed in the most prominent position. The topic sentence may then be exemplified, proved, explained, or otherwise supported in the remainder of the paragraph. In earlier writing courses, you may have studied a series of paragraph types built around a topic sentence in lead position. Some common paragraph types are known as comparison and contrast, cause and effect, classification, statement supported by multiple arguments, and statement supported by extended example. You may also have studied easily recognizable patterns for organizing details within a paragraph: time order, space order, and order of importance. All these are good and useful tools for making order out of otherwise disorganized statements.

By now, your writing and thinking may have advanced to a stage where what you have to organize is more complex than these simple patterns allow. What brings your statements together may be more subtle than simple support of an explicit topic sentence: you may now wish to establish a cluster of different relationships within a single paragraph. To move beyond the basic patterns you have learned, you need to create new patterns to fit your new, more complex meanings. Paragraph structure does not have to be rigid or limiting; it just has to make sense.

The early chapters of this book contain examples and analyses of paragraph structures that appear in professional writing. These examples appear as part of the discussion of such tasks as paraphrase, summary, and analysis of writing technique. Understanding the organizational structure of other writers' work is part of intelligent reading. If you expect your readers to pay close attention to your most serious statements, you should work toward a control of paragraph structure that will reward close attention by revealing precision of meaning. You must write intelligently to deserve intelligent reading.

More advanced forms of paragraph structure are frequently hybrid combinations of simpler, more easily recognized patterns. As you become more adept at reading and writing, you can blend several kinds of organization together in a single paragraph and still maintain a common core of meaning. If you do create such hybrid structures, it is especially important to keep relationships clear; otherwise, the reader may not see any reason behind what appears to be a muddle of very different types of statements. In the following sample paragraph from Leon Edel's biography of the novelist Henry James, the writer maintains coherence, flow, and clarity as he introduces many kinds of background information about the relationship between Henry James and the writer Oscar Wilde.

> The bulky figure of Oscar Wilde had crossed Henry James's path at infrequent intervals during the previous decade. They had met long before—in 1882—in a drawing room in Washington, during Oscar's circus-like tour of America. James had confided to friends at the time that he thought Wilde "an unclean beast," and found him "repulsive and fatuous." Thereafter he referred to him usually in terms of the animal kingdom. There was however no ill will or animosity between them. Oscar simply irritated James; and the novelist regarded with curiosity and a certain amused condescension the public antics and public wit of the younger man. Wilde on his side spoke with respect but with understandable reservations concerning the fastidious American. His own relaxed amateurism, his emphasis on talk and performance rather than on creation, caused him to feel that James treated art as "a painful duty" rather than as one of the amusements of life. They had no common bonds of temperament; and they represented two diametrically opposed attitudes toward life and the imagination. If Wilde insisted on putting his talent into his art and his genius into his life (as he later told André Gide),

Henry James. (Brown Brothers)

Oscar Wilde. Photo by N. Sarony, 1882. (The Bettmann Archive)

Henry James did exactly the opposite. James's drawing-room wit was merely the surplus of his genius—and he lived for his art. He was eleven years older than Wilde; he worked hard and was highly productive. Wilde had a lazy facility that James found "cheap"—the cheapness of the actor who knows how to provoke applause: he had written very little and the American deplored the public display which had made the young Wilde the subject of Gilbert and Sullivan and of George du Maurier in *Punch.* There has been speculation that Gabriel Nash, the talkative aesthete in *The Tragic Muse,* incorporated some of Wilde's qualities: if this was so, James had drawn a singularly generous portrait. Nash's cultivated ineffectuality might be that of Wilde; his wit is that of Henry James, and so is his sentience. Whether James read *The Picture of Dorian Gray* when it came out in 1891 we do not know. What we do know is that Wilde turned to the theatre at the very time that James did; and from this moment on, they were—from James's point of view—rivals, or fellow-contenders in the same arena.

The paragraph begins with what can only be very loosely called a topic sentence; the first sentence is more like an introduction to a story of many parts. The second sentence seems to be leading into a retrospective narrative, but the next few sentences turn first to the effect of the first meeting and then to James's general opinions about Wilde. After presenting Wilde's opinions of James, Edel redirects the paragraph into a comparison of the two men. The comparison leads back to James's distaste for Wilde, which Edel links to a character analysis of a Wilde-like character in James's writing. The character analysis raises the historical question of how much James knew of Wilde's writing. The paragraph ends with the last moment of a chronological sequence, but the information conveyed is more like the logical conclusion of all that came before it. Although this last sentence is not the total topic of the paragraph, it does demonstrate the consequence of all that came before it—like the conclusion of a story.

Despite the complexity of the paragraph structure and its lack of an explicit topic sentence, the meaning, coherence, and progress of the paragraph are clear. We gain a many-sided picture of how things stood between Wilde and James up to the time they both began writing plays. The paragraph, in fact, serves as an introduction to a chapter discussing the period when they both were writing plays.

The Well-Arranged Sentence

Sentences bring words together. The art of writing sentences is in bringing out the connections among the words essential to the intended meaning—while at the same time keeping the sentence as simple and easy to understand as possible. Your control of sentence structure largely determines your control of meaning. Carelessly thought-out sentences may present irrelevant or even false ideas; tangled sentences may convey little of your meaning to the reader. On the other hand, a well-shaped sentence can clarify a previously murky concept or can make a vivid and memorable impression on the reader.

The main tools for your artful control of sentence structure are the rules of syntax, which define the well-established ways of putting words together. Syntactical rules are the means by which your readers recognize the relationships you are establishing in your sentences. Even if you occasionally break the rules for particular stylistic purposes, the shock effect works only against a background of conventional sentences—the shock of the unusual. In the next few paragraphs, we will present some of the uses and strengths of various syntactic forms.

The Key Spots   The subject and the verb are the most important parts of any sentence. Do not squander them on anything less than the most important words of your statement. Subject and verb can, by themselves, often carry a very complete message.

Ralph yawns.
Philosophy lives.
I came. I saw. I conquered.

Words other than the subject and verb typically modify or complete the primary statement of the subject and verb. Consider, for example, this sentence:

Net profits after taxes dropped slightly this year.

The central meaning is contained within the subject and verb: *profits dropped.* The other words only let us know what kinds of profits (*net, after taxes*), how much (*slightly*), and when (*this year*).

A poorly constructed sentence wastes the subject and verb on minor information and pushes the important words into spaces that should hold only minor modifiers. Many meaningless words creep in, and the reader has a hard time figuring out what the sentence is trying to say. See what happens when we take the previous example and push the main words to the far corners of the sentence.

Concerning the post-tax remainder of net profits during the current annual period, our ledger books reveal a change of small proportions downward.

The subject and verb tell us only that *books reveal.* What do they reveal? A change, but what kind of change? Of small proportions, but in which direction? Downward. We get the key information only at the end of a long string of modifying phrases.

If you search for the key words to convey your idea and then put these words in the most important positions in your sentences, your meanings will become clearer and your sentences simpler. Short, simple sentences—with strong subjects and verbs—can frequently convey your full meaning.

However, you will sometimes need to put two or more statements into a specific relationship with one another within the same sentence. In time, the complexity of your thoughts will inevitably require the use of more complex sentence structures. The first point to remember in combining two statements is that you must know the exact purpose of the combination. A loose continuity between two ideas ("and another point is . . .") is not enough to warrant combining them. *You must have a specific and substantial reason for combining sentences.*

Coordination   In *coordination,* two or more sentences are brought together to emphasize their equality:

Jack is taking notes on the statistics lecture, and *Carol is outlining the textbook.*

You can spend the money for repairs, or *you can learn to live without a car.*

I want very much to go to the concert, but *I have already promised to go to the play.*

As these examples illustrate, the two statements can be additive, alternative, or contrary.

Coordination through the use of a semicolon emphasizes the parallel nature of two statements:

Economics is now one of the more popular courses of study; fifteen years ago literature courses had the largest enrollments.

This parallelism of meaning can be further emphasized by parallelism of phrasing:

Premedical programs require a concentration in science; prelegal programs require a concentration in liberal arts.

With tightly parallel phrasing, you may even leave out some of the repeated words, marking the *ellipsis* (or words left out) by a comma:

Premedical programs require a concentration in science; prelegal, a concentration in liberal arts.

Using a semicolon for coordination, you can emphasize the relationship between two equal statements by coordinating adverbs and phrases, such as *however, moreover, on the other hand, for example,* and *nevertheless:*

The study of the French language has been decreasing; however, *the study of Chinese has been on the rise.*

Subordination   Combining sentences through *subordination* makes them unequal. One statement, the dependent clause, modifies the other statement, the independent clause. The main statement of the complex sentence is found in the independent clause; the dependent clause only modifies this main statement. In relative constructions, introduced by the relative pronouns *which, who, whom,* and *that,* the subordinate clause modifies a noun in the main clause, as in the following:

The criminal who brought about this misery *shall receive the punishment* that he deserves.

The two subordinate clauses in the sentence tell us a bit about the criminal (the subject of the main clause) and a bit about the punishment (the object of the main clause). The main statement remains, however, the simple statement *the criminal shall receive punishment.*
     Other subordinate clauses are introduced by subordinate conjunctions, such as *because, while, if,* and *before.* These clauses act as adverbs, modifying the action of the main clause, letting us know when, how, why, or under what conditions the action takes place:

If you dare to speak that way, *you will challenge the authority of the supervisor.*

After I resigned, *I celebrated.*

     In a third kind of subordinate construction, the entire subordinate clause acts as a noun within the main clause, as in this example:

I know what you are doing.

The subordinate clause *what you are doing* serves as an object of the main verb *know.* These noun clauses often begin with interrogative pronouns, such as *how, why, who, where,* or *what.* Noun clauses are particularly useful in relating complex series of events, causes, or thought processes, as in the following example:

How Moriarty escaped unseen *baffled Sherlock Holmes until the detective remembered* why he had been called in on the case in the first place. *The secret of* where Moriarty had hidden *would be found in the construction plans of the sewer system, the plans stolen by Moriarty himself.*

In this example, noun clauses serve as subject of the main clause (in the first sentence), as object of the verb *remembered,* and finally as object of the preposition *of.*

Shortened Forms   Frequently, you can eliminate many words of the subordinate clause, leaving only a short modifying phrase. Notice in the following examples how shortening the subordinate clause— by eliminating obvious or repetitive words—makes tighter sentences that still retain all the original meaning.

Because Fleur was excited by the chance to win the lottery, she forgot to pay for lunch.
Excited by the chance to win the lottery, *Fleur forgot to pay for lunch.*

Calvin analyzed the political situation as it continued sliding into chaos.
Calvin analyzed the political situation sliding into chaos.

After the Mets had settled in last place, they no longer had fans.
Having settled in last place, *the Mets no longer had fans.*

Karen, who was the outgoing president, tried to hide her feelings.
Karen, the outgoing president, *tried to hide her feelings.*

Doris Lessing, who is the author of many distinguished novels, was born and raised in Rhodesia.
Doris Lessing, the author of many distinguished novels, *was born and raised in Rhodesia.*

Technically, the first three shortened versions contain participial phrases of different kinds; the last two shortened examples contain appositives. A participial phrase is a modifying phrase built on either the present participle of a verb (the *-ing* form) or the past participle (the *-ed* form for regular verbs). An appositive is additional information placed directly after a noun. It is usually set off by commas. These constructions allow you to bring in modifying information while keeping a simple sentence structure.

Gerunds   The present participle of a verb (that is, the *-ing* form) can be used as a noun:

Running *tires a person.*

The technical name of this verb form used as a noun is *gerund.* Gerund phrases can include all the objects and modifiers the verb could have in an independent clause, so that gerund phrases can operate much like the shortened subordinate clauses discussed in the last paragraph. The following example from baseball shows how complex a situation you can describe by using a gerund phrase as subject:

Intentionally dropping a fly ball when there are two or more runners on base *was eliminated by the infield fly rule.*

The subject of the sentence is the gerund phrase *intentionally dropping a fly ball when there are two or more runners on base.* This subject includes the gerund *dropping,* the object of the gerund (*a fly ball*), and the adverb *intentionally;* moreover, the gerund is modified by an entire subordinate clause, *when there are two or more runners on base.* The entire complex gerund phrase serves as the subject of the main clause; this entire complex situation "was eliminated by the infield fly rule."

Colon   One often neglected—but powerful—tool of sentence combining is the colon. When used to connect two sentences, the colon indicates that the second sentence explains or sums up the first, as in the following examples:

Group membership imposes responsibilities: club members must pay dues, attend meetings, and owe obligations of loyalty and mutual help.

The four people living in the apartment share work, decisions, and concern for one another's welfare: they form a voluntary family.

The colon also serves to introduce quotations and lists or series. In all cases, the items after the colon should fill out the statement before the colon.

In the fully revised essay, each sentence should make a specific contribution to the overall argument. Each sentence's contribution should be expressed in as clear, direct, and readable a form as possible. Complex thoughts may require lengthy, complex sentences for their accurate presentation, but you have a repsonsibility to the reader to make the sentences no more difficult than they need be. And no matter how complex the sentences may be, they should never be confusing. If, after many attempts to tighten your sentences, they remain tortured and murky, the problem may be with the thought and not the phrasing. To help yourself, try to express the thought by using an entirely different kind of sentence; if you still are baffled, rethink the thought from the very beginning. If you cannot state your idea clearly, you may not know yet what it is you want to say.

The Right Word

Choosing the right words can be frustrating. Ernest Hemingway rewrote the ending of *A Farewell to Arms* thirty-nine times; the problem was, he explained, "getting the words right." Either you cannot pinpoint the words for the idea you want to express, or you think of too many alternatives and cannot choose which one. To make matters worse, there are no absolute guidelines to tell you what choice is right in all circumstances. What is the right choice in one sentence may be the wrong choice further down the page— and certainly wrong in another paper.

The three things that will most help you choose the best word for each circumstance are knowing your subject well, knowing what you want to write about it, and knowing what words other writers use to discuss the subject. In other words, you need to know the subject, your mind, and the relevant vocabulary. This is a tall order, and rarely does anyone live up to it completely. But, given what you do know at the time you are writing, you have to make the best choices you can. Consider the factors discussed below when choosing.

Dead Wood Your first consideration should be to evaluate how much each word adds to your overall statement. Words that take up space without contributing anything should be eliminated— except where they are necessary to avoid awkwardness or confusion. Two common groups of words that can usually be eliminated without loss are vague intensifiers (such as *really, very,* and *quite*) and weak subjects (such as *the fact that, there are,* and *one of the things that*). Repetitious words, covering material already covered elsewhere, also should be deleted. Words that provide information irrelevant to the point of your writing should also be eliminated. You may, for example, be proud of the thirty-eight miles per gallon obtained by your car, but mentioning the mileage would be out of place when describing how much your dog loves to ride.

Some phrases add only a little information at the expense of many words. By isolating the few bits of substance, you may be able to state the point more concisely. Consider, for example, this sentence:

Being of grouchy disposition, I lacked the patience to listen to the entire story to the end.

Only a few words—*grouchy, I, lacked, story*— convey all the substance. The sentence can be phrased more concisely:

My grouchiness kept me from hearing the full story.

Concrete or Abstract You also want to consider how concrete or abstract a word is. The more concrete a word is, the more it identifies an actual thing that exists in the world; the more abstract a word, the more it refers to an idea or quality rather than to an actual thing. The word *strawberry* is more concrete than the word *fruit;* the word *food* is even more abstract than *fruit.* The more concrete the words you use, the less likely they are to be misunderstood. For example, *strawberries* cannot be mistaken for *blueberries,* and neither can be confused with *apples.* But the abstract word *food* gives the reader only a vague picture of what you have in mind. In using abstract terms, you run the risk that your reader will not understand what you are referring to exactly. Unless well defined and used with the greatest care, the grand abstractions, such as *freedom, truth,* and *justice,* can result in gross misunderstandings and confusions.

Concrete words also leave readers with more vivid impressions than abstractions. A reader can easily imagine the taste, texture, sight, and smell of a strawberry, but what can the reader imagine from the unspecific word *food?* On the other hand, it is very difficult to discuss ideas without abstractions. Without the abstract term *food,* agricultural economists would have difficulty discussing how to provide something to eat for everyone in the world. Thus, in choosing between abstract and concrete words, you must decide whether an unmistakable, vivid impression of an actual object or the idea behind the object is more appropriate for your discussion.

Specificity and generality are closely related to concreteness and abstraction, but there is a difference. The more specific a word is, the more it pinpoints the items it refers to. The specific phrase *the strawberry I am holding in my hand* refers to one, and only one strawberry, but the concrete word *strawberry* by itself is general, for it can potentially refer to billions of strawberries—not just in this year's crop, but throughout the history of agriculture. Specific words tend to be more vivid and less mistakable than general words, but general words are useful for discussing repeating phenomena or categories of things.

Word Precision In most circumstances you will want to choose precise words—that is, words that offer clear limits to their meaning. As we have just seen, words that are concrete and specific tend, by their nature, to be precise. *Abraham Lincoln* is obviously more precise than *president* or *leader*. Problems of precision are more likely to occur with words that are abstract, general, or both. Make sure that you know exactly what you mean whenever you use a general or abstract word, and then let the reader know. Sometimes you can achieve this precision by being careful to use the troublesome word in exactly the same way each time you use it. At other times, giving more concrete or specific examples of your more abstract or general statements will help tie down the difficult words. If the problem is very sticky, you can give explicit definitions of all the important terms you will use in the paper; however, you must make sure that your usage throughout the essay is consistent with your definitions. Technical terms are especially useful for increasing precision, but only if you are writing for a professional audience familiar with the technical language; otherwise, the unknown terminology will serve as a barrier—rather than an aid—to communication.

Another aspect of precision is identifying with what certainty you are making the statement and how absolutely the statement holds for all cases. You need to take care in choosing words that accurately express your degree of certainty about the claims you are making. In the following example, whichever word in the parentheses you select implies a specific level of certainty—how complete you feel the evidence is.

This paper (suggests, identifies, describes, demonstrates) *factors influencing the onset of viral diabetes.*

Even the choice of *a, the,* or *one of the* indicates a level of definiteness. Such qualifying words as *tendency, partial, under some circumstances,* and *almost* help limit the extent to which a statement can be held true.

Hedging   As necessary as qualification is for precision, it can be improperly used to hedge statements that should be made with more certainty. Unless you can justify your every use of words like *perhaps, possible,* and *probable,* you are hiding behind these weak words. You should have, as the saying goes, the courage of your own foolishness.

Another kind of hedging is for the writer to use a more general word or phrase than is necessary. In particular, words like *relate, depend,* and *connect* can apply to a host of situations. Do not use the general word to avoid thinking out the specific word or to avoid committing yourself to a definite statement. Use the general term only when you mean precisely the entire large category of things encompassed by the general word. When used to avoid making a clear-cut statement, both overly general words and uncalled-for qualifiers go by the name of weasel words—and for good reason.

Imagine you have been investigating Adolf Hitler's motivation in the mass murder of millions of Jews. After studying what many psychologists and historians have written about Hitler's upbringing and personality and about the social and economic conditions prevailing in Europe when he came to power, you decide to write about the psychological factors in Hitler's actions. Consider these three ways of stating your conclusions:

1. *Hitler's persecution of Jews was related to his own deep-seated desire to purge himself of any traces of Jewish ancestry.*

2. *A deep-seated desire to purge himself of any traces of Jewish ancestry contributed to Hitler's persecution of Jews by adding personal passion to cultural prejudice and political manipulation.*

3. *A deep-seated desire to purge himself of any traces of Jewish ancestry caused Hitler to persecute Jews.*

The first alternative hedges and thereby loses specificity and impact. To say that one thing merely *is related to* another sidesteps the responsibility to explain the nature of the relationship. The third alternative is forceful—at the price of oversimplification. Not only does this sentence present a simplistic concept of psychological causation, the sentence does not allow for any contributing factors, such as a deliberate political plan to unite Germans by making Jews scapegoats for the Germans' economic suffering. The second alternative specifies the causal relationship while respecting other factors. It is the best choice of the three.

Don't assume, however, that the most forceful word choice is necessarily the wrong choice. If the facts back up the contention and you have defended it well, it is misleading and confusing to your readers to shrink from expressing your thought firmly and clearly. Courage!

Emotions and Judgments   Another scale against which to judge your choice of words is the continuum from highly emotional words to impersonal words. At times it is appropriate to report on your own emotions, as in autobiography and—less obtrusively—in reviews of art and literature. In some situations you may want to report on the feelings of others—in analyzing some of the personal motivations behind a historical event, for example. In other circumstances, such as in describing the behavior of subjects in a psychological experiment, comments reflecting your own or others' feelings are totally inappropriate.

The continuum of judgmental and nonjudgmental words overlaps somewhat with the emotional-impersonal continuum, for reports on your emotions often reflect your values. *Values* are those deeply held principles and beliefs on which you base your opinions of worth and quality. Judgments of value and morality are carried in such words as *good, bad, virtuous,* and *evil;* judgments are also carried in expressions of causes ("His negligence caused the accident"), nonobservable connections ("Where there is life, there is hope"), and imposed categories ("He is a painter of the decadent romantic school"). Much intellectual discourse would be impossible without these judgments; nonetheless, if you are writing within any of the scientific disciplines, you must eliminate such judgmental statements and rely as much as possible only on what can be observed or can be directly deduced from observations.

Denotation and Connotation   A final continuum against which to consider the impact of your words is the scale from purely denotative meaning to heavily connotative or associative meaning. Denotative meaning is the explicit, defined reference of a word; for example, *snake* denotes a scaly, legless reptile with a long, cylindrical body. Connotative meaning, on the other hand, refers to all those other associations we have about a word beyond its literal meaning; for example, *snake* connotes something untrustworthy, sneaky, poisonous, and generally evil. At times you will want to use words with strong connotations in order to evoke a mood or a reaction on the reader's part. At other times you may have to make sure that the connotations of a word do not conflict with the tone or attitude of the whole paper. Whether you call a particular ancient king an *absolute monarch,* a *dictator,* or a *tyrant* depends on how benevolent a picture you wish to draw. If you have previously described him as enlightened, well-intentioned, and successful, the word *tyrant* would evoke connotations that are not consistent with the image you are creating. In situations where you want to keep the meaning as explicit and denotative as possible—in certain kinds of philosophical and scientific argument—you will want to choose words that have very little connotation. Much of the unusual technical language of the social sciences is an attempt to describe the facts of everyday life in a way that will not evoke the everyday connotations. For example, clinical psychologists who must regularly describe the behavior of persons institutionalized with a psychiatric disorder often characterize problem behavior as *inappropriate,* rather than using such value-laden terms as *vicious, criminal, crazy,* or *disgusting.*

Consistency of Style

The three levels of attention to language that we have discussed in the past few pages—paragraph, sentence, and word—are the major elements of style. But style is not a fancy decoration pasted on during the final revision; style is the natural outgrowth of the process of addressing individual writing tasks. Apt metaphors, phrases of remarkable clarity, graceful turns of thought, surprising wording—all take on meaning only in the context of the total piece of writing. In fact the more clearly you know what you wish to accomplish, the more likely you are to come up with those passages of inspired style that grab the reader and do not let go.

A clear conception of the purposes of a piece of writing should lead you to a consistent style—a way of telling your story to your audience. After you have established the basic style of your paper through initial work on the details of paragraphs, sentences, and words, you need to make a further revision for *stylistic consistency.* In this revision, you look for and work on those spots that are not yet up to the high level you have achieved in the rest of the paper. Be particularly suspicious of those spots where you are proud of turning a phrase or making a clever joke. Those may be just the spots where you bring in considerations that are irrelevant to the main task of the paper—no matter how amusing or pleasing to your own mind. All the language of the paper must work together.

Public Presentation
of Your Paper

Throughout the process of forming your thoughts, organizing them, and putting them into words, your mind will be fully occupied. You probably will have little time for or interest in such matters as correct spelling, punctuation, grammar, and footnote form. By this point in your writing career, such mechanics should be largely automatic, but people do make mistakes, especially if they have heavier matters—like creating a statement—on their minds. I know that in my own rough drafts I become so involved in setting down my thoughts that I seem to forget the basic mechanics: I write *there* when I mean *their* or I drop a verb ending. Such errors don't matter much in the early drafts, for the drafts are only for my own use. But if such silly errors stayed in my final copy, I'd be more than embarrassed. I'd probably have to turn in my red pen, my badge as an English teacher. Nevertheless, I would not want to break the trend of my thought by checking every spelling I was unsure of or by proofreading every half-formed phrase in early drafts. I might not even use those words and phrases in the final paper.

The solution, of course, is doing a final revision with grammar in mind and dictionary in hand. With your full attention on the basic mechanical skills, the revision for correctness should clear up all remaining mistakes. During this final revision, you should also mark where footnotes are required and then write a draft of the notes in the appropriate format, as described in the next chapter.

After the final revision, everything going into the paper should be set, so that making a clean copy is only a matter of accurate typing. But however accurate your typing, you need to *proofread* the final copy to correct any errors that may have slipped in. If you must make minor corrections, write them in as neatly as possible. The clean copy is the public presentation of your work: it should present as few obstacles to the reader as possible. Generous and consistent margins and a generally neat appearance make the paper more inviting to the reader. However, excessive prettiness, such as unusual typefaces or colored paper, is as much of a barrier to objective reading as smudged and crumpled pages.

Dealing with
Response to
Your Writing

After you have placed the clean copy in your teacher's hands—or put the report on the boss's desk or slipped the manuscript into an envelope addressed to the publisher—you breathe the usual sigh of relief, let the subject slip to the back of your mind, and turn to new endeavors. You feel you have made your statement, and the cycle of writing is complete.

At a later time, the conversation is reopened: comments return to you. In school, papers return with a grade and comments evaluating where you went right and where you went wrong. Using marginal annotations, the teacher may begin a discussion about ideas that you raise. A friend who has read your paper may want to argue with you. Response can come to you in many ways.

Writers at all levels have two common reactions to the response of readers. The writer may either react too strongly to the reactions of others, despairing at criticism and rejoicing at praise. Or the writer may discount anything a reader may have to say—on the theory that the writer knows what he or she was trying to do and knows the best way to do it.

Much more is to be gained from a middle course, a serious but measured consideration of readers' responses. If someone makes a criticism or suggests a change, consider whether the criticism is justified. Ask yourself whether the reader understood what you were doing; ask yourself from what perspective the reader made the comment. You may conclude that the critical comment was right, in whole or in part. With this new perspective, you may begin to rethink the subject or just revise a few words. Even if you reject the criticism, you may learn much: if the reader misunderstood your meaning, you might ask whether the fault was in your writing.

It is part of the writing process to learn how your writing appears to different readers. Although gaining approval is always pleasant, you should be more concerned with whether you have communicated fully. Response from readers is a very special kind of information, for it alone can tell you what you have and have not achieved through your writing.

Exercises

1. Analyze the paragraph structure of each of the following:
   a. The excerpt by Bertrand Russell on pages 47–49
   b. The passage by Margaret Mead on pages 7–8
   c. The excerpt by James Madison on page 60
   d. Several paragraphs from one of your own essays
2. In the excerpts by Susan Wagner on page 159 and by Maurice Corina on page 161, underline the main subject and the main verb of each sentence. Then circle the words conveying the most important information in each sentence. Do the subject and verb coincide with the most important information? If not, try revising each sentence to make better use of the main positions.
3. Using any techniques that are grammatical and appropriate, combine the sentences in each group below. Also shorten the combined sentences if no important information will be lost.
   a. The network was faced with a dilemma.
   It could report on the secret negotiations.
   The government would accuse it of irresponsibility.
   It could bury the story.
   The public would accuse it of irresponsibility.
   b. It is difficult to shoot a science fiction movie.
   You must coordinate special effects and acting.
   Large budgets are expended on special effects.
   The actors must make totally imaginary scenes seem plausible.
   c. Sergei Eisenstein was a great Russian film maker.
   He coined the term *montage*.
   Montage is an important film technique.
   One shot follows another.
   The image on the screen changes abruptly.
   The viewer sees a connection between images.
   A new meaning develops from the combination of the shots.
   d. Old movies challenge new moviemakers.
   The new moviemakers try to outdo scenes in the old movies.
   Woody Allen saw an old slapstick joke in many old movies.
   An unsuspecting character slips on a banana peel.

Woody Allen made a movie called *Sleeper*.
Sleeper is set in the future.
The fruits and vegetables of the future are giant-sized.
Woody Allen slips on a fifteen-foot banana peel.

4. The following passage is based on an essay by Winston Churchill, the famous British political leader, discussing the movies of Charlie Chaplin. In the original passage Churchill compares British and American tramps, but here Churchill's complex, polished sentences have been broken into choppy little statements. You are to rewrite the passage, recombining the statements to recreate all the connections between the statements.

Charlie Chaplin portrays tramps. People go to the cinema. Every one of these people is familiar with these tramps. I wonder about something. How many of these people have reflected about an idea? These tramps are homeless wanderers. These tramps are characteristically American. The English tramps are dwindling in number. In their ranks one finds all sorts of people. One finds the varsity graduate. His career has ended in ruin and disgrace. One finds the illiterate. This illiterate is a half-imbecile. He has been unemployable since boyhood. But they have one thing in common. They belong to a great army. The army is defeated. They still pretend to look for work. They do not expect to find work. They are spiritless and hopeless.

The American hobo existed twenty-five years ago. He was of an entirely different type. Often he was not much of an outcast. He was not cast out from society. Rather he was a rebel against society. He could not settle down in a home. He could not settle down in a job. He hated routine. Regular employment was a routine. He loved the road. The road had changes and chances. He had an old adventurous urge. This urge was behind his wanderings. The same urge sent covered wagons. Covered wagons lumbered across the prairie. They went towards the sunset.

5. Revise the following sentences to make more appropriate word choices and to eliminate unnecessary words.
    a. It is a fact that in the experiment scientists observed an evil-looking, snarling rodent devour three heads of Boston lettuce, which comprised the entire harvest of the garden grown by the seven-year-old daughter of one of the scientists.
    b. This guy placed an order for some stuff, which the pharmacist refused to sell without a prescription, probably because he didn't want to do anything that was illegal or otherwise against the law.

c. Somebody wanted to learn charcoal sketching, water colors, oil painting, sculpting, design, space relations, color, scale, proportions, graphics, etching, wood blocks, and other things like that, but he had to support his parents, so he got a job listing numbers in columns in order to see how much the company took in and spent.

d. Carol thought Kevin's habitual slacking of the mandibular muscles to produce an invariable three-centimeter aperture between his upper and lower facial labial flesh was the most sensual thing she had ever seen.

6. Select an essay written by you earlier this semester that has been heavily marked and annotated by a teacher. For each comment or correction, either write an answer defending your original statement or revise the original to conform to the teacher's suggestions.

17 A Guide to Reference and Documentation

By making explicit the sources of your ideas and information, you let the reader know the full extent of the conversation in which you are taking part. You may use sources for many purposes, and the ways in which you refer to the source materials depend on those purposes. Whenever you cite another writer's work, whether by paraphrase, summary, or direct quote, you must document it. Proper documentation makes your use of source materials legitimate and allows the reader access to those sources. In this chapter, the documentation rules of both parenthetical reference systems and notes are presented according to MLA and APA formats.

Revealing Sources

The informed writer draws on knowledge gained from many sources. Writers use existing knowledge as a storehouse that provides examples, evidence, and quotations from respected authorities as support for their ideas. The writer also uses existing knowledge as a foundation upon which to construct an orderly base of facts and ideas that most educated people will accept as reasonable—so that the writer doesn't have to prove every point from the beginning. On this shared foundation the writer can build new and ambitious structures. If the writer ignores the solid foundation of existing knowledge and builds instead on the shifting sands of fad and whim, the structure is likely to collapse and few readers will put much faith in it.

The uses of knowledge go beyond metaphorical storehouses and foundations: the knowledge you discover in sources provides the context and much of the content for your informed writing. Other writers' ideas can inspire you to continue your research or rouse you to debate their points in your writing. As we have mentioned, you must decide whether your sources should be accepted, rejected, or compared to other sources. Several authors can provide multiple perspectives on your subject, or your research can put the writings of these authors into new perspective. Perhaps you have not considered that your writing may serve as your reader's entry into the ideas of previous writers. In short, informed writing takes place within a complex world of continuing reading and writing.

The people who read your writing may not be aware of all the facts and ideas you have discovered through your own reading. In fact, they may have come in contact with very different information through other books. For this reason you need to make explicit what source materials you are relying on. You must identify, through reference and documentation, those points of connection between your thoughts and the thoughts of other writers who came before you. *Reference* is the art of mentioning other writers' words, ideas, or information in the course of your own argument. *Documentation* is the technique of accurately identifying the precise source of these words, ideas, and information. Through skillful reference and correct documentation, you can demonstrate the relationship of your own comments to the ongoing written conversation, making it easier for you to say what you want to say and easier for your reader to understand your meaning. Your reader will come to see the full discussion instead of just eavesdropping on one disconnected fragment.

There are other narrower—but still important—reasons for proper reference and documentation. First, you will be more likely to convince your readers of the validity of your ideas if you can show that you are building on the solid foundation of respected earlier work and that you are taking into account what is already known about your subject. Second, you should repay a debt of gratitude to those earlier writers whose work you have used; they are the ones who stocked the storehouse for you. Finally, intellectual borrowing without giving credit is a form of theft called *plagiarism*. Plagiarism is passing off someone else's work—whether in the exact words or in paraphrase—as your own. There should, however, be no need to hide any of your sources if you are actively working with the material and are using the sources to develop your own thoughts. Indeed the more clearly you identify what others have said, the more sharply your own contribution will stand out.

The Uses of References

During the periods when you are selecting a subject, gathering information, and developing your thoughts, you will look at many sources with only a vague idea of the eventual use you will make of the material in your final paper. Many of those sources you may never use directly. As you give shape to your final statement, *you must decide not only what source material you will mention but also the purpose of each reference*. You must know how each bit of cited material advances the argument of your paper, for if you lack a clear idea of why you are mentioning someone else's work, your paper is in danger of losing direction. You do not want your paper to deteriorate into a pointless string of quotations that leaves your readers wondering what you are trying to say.

The purpose of any reference must fit in with the argument you are making and with the kind of paper you are writing. Otherwise the reference is an intrusion, distracting the reader from understanding and evaluating your main point. For example, in the middle of a technical paper reporting the chemical analysis of a new pesticide, it would not be appropriate to quote the political statements of the producer or of environmental groups. But you might want to mention—and even describe in detail—a new method of chemical analysis developed by another chemist, particularly if that new method allowed the user to obtain more precise and trustworthy results. The reference must be more than loosely connected to the subject: it must fit the exact logic of the argument you are making at the place where the reference is made.

In the past, you probably have used references most frequently to quote or paraphrase the words of some authority who agrees with a statement you have made. In political debates and other situations where you are trying to persuade the audience on less than totally rational grounds, the fact that a respected person has said something similar to what you have said—only perhaps more elegantly—may lend some acceptability or believability to your claims. In persuasive debate, citing authority remains an effective tool, particularly if you can embarrass the opposition by showing that one of its heroes really supports your side on this issue. Political journalists delight in such tactics. However, persuasion through passing mention of an authority will not lend strength to a scholarly analysis for a professional audience. For a scholarly paper your argument must stand up to scrutiny on its own merits without regard for the graceful words of poets or the reputation of the idea's supporters.

In more serious academic writing, you can use the authenticated findings of other researchers to support your own findings—but only in carefully limited ways. One way is to follow your general point by citing another researcher's specific data or a case study as evidence. Another way is to present all your own evidence and reasoning and then compare your conclusions to those of other researchers, showing how both studies—yours and theirs—are consistent and confirm each other. In both these situations you retain primary responsibility for your argument and use other studies only to show that your conclusions agree with what others have found.

As you look to other writers for support, you may turn on them— to attack what you consider wrong-headed nonsense. In persuasive debate situations, where destroying your opponent's arguments is almost as good as making your own case, quoting the opposition's ideas as the first step in tearing them apart is often a good tactic. While attacking, you may sometimes have the opportunity to bring in your own, more praiseworthy ideas. But in academic or professional writing, where your purpose is establishing the truth and not gaining votes, you should attack only in limited circumstances, such as when an error is so convincing and so firmly believed by most experts that it stands in the way of more accurate thought. Then you should show why the cited ideas are wrong, but you should not ridicule them as outrageous or foolish. Ridicule may be an effective political tool, but it undermines the cooperative community necessary for rational discourse. The insults traded by nineteenth-century German philosophers may be amusing to read in retrospect, but they only created deeper divisions among philosophers than were necessary. If, however, you do find a fair critique of another writer's argument a useful way to advance your own argument, you should refer as precisely as possible to the specific ideas you are criticizing—even to the extent of lengthy quotation. This detailed reference should then become the starting point for specific and carefully argued criticisms.

At times your essay may call for interpretation or analysis of primary source material. One example would be a paper in which you were trying to understand Thomas Jefferson's thinking through an examination of his letters. In this kind of textual analysis, as with critiques, you need to make specific reference to the exact ideas or passages being analyzed, by quotation, paraphrase, or summary, along with page and line reference. This reference identifies exactly what material you are working with and allows the reader to compare your interpretation and analysis to the original in order to judge whether your arguments are convincing. Similarly, if you are comparing the thoughts of two or more writers, you need to present enough indication of the originals so that the reader can understand and evaluate your comparison. Put yourself in your readers' position and analyze how much they need to know of the originals. Such specific comparisons of two arguments can serve as the basis for your own synthesis, resolving the conflicts between the two earlier writers. Extensive comparison, interpretation, and analysis of the thoughts of a number of writers may be necessary if you are tracing the evolution of ideas on a particular issue. In all the uses of reference mentioned in this paragraph, opinions expressed in the sources are what is being studied. That is, you are analyzing the opinions rather than just citing them in support of your idea. The sources are part of the subject you are discussing.

At other times, various writers' works may serve as a general background for your own ideas. You may be building upon someone else's theory; or your own findings may be understood fully only when they are set against other research findings; or you may borrow a method of analysis from another writer. In all such cases you may have to discuss the original sources at some length in order for your readers to understand the ideas, assumptions, information, and methods that lie behind your own approach. Even more specifically, your paper may present an experiment or argument testing someone else's theory; you must then certainly let the reader know the source of the theory in question.

In the course of your own reading and writing, you may discover many other uses for mentioning the work of others. You will also develop a sense of the most effective and important places to bring in references. In citing source material, you must always know why you are citing it and how it fits most effectively into your ongoing argument. You must never let your use of sources overwhelm the forward impetus of the main statements of your paper.

Two structural devices can help you maintain the forward motion of your writing while still discussing all the relevant references: a review-of-the-literature section and the content footnote. In many essays a *review of the literature,* limited to those items specifically relevant to the essay, can provide most of the necessary background (see pages 293–295). Such a review, usually presented early in the essay—perhaps directly after the introduction—frees the writer to follow his or her own line of thought, with fewer interruptions, later in the essay.

If some sources develop interesting sidelights to your main issue or if other sources make points you want to answer, discussing either might interrupt the flow of your main argument. In that case, you can place the secondary discussion in a *content footnote.* Such footnotes are also the place to discuss detailed problems with evidence, further complexities of background, and additional reviews of literature limited to a specific point made in passing.

Methods of Reference

Each time you refer to another writer's work, you need to decide in how much detail to report the content of that reference. You have a range of options, varying in explicitness from identification of a thought or concept by its name only (Freudian Oedipus complex) to lengthy quotation of the writer's original words. Each option has advantages and disadvantages that must be weighed in each separate reference situation. The decision of which option to use should be based on the nature of the material cited, the need to provide your reader with a precise understanding, and the role the reference takes within your larger argument. The following more specific considerations may help you choose among the alternatives.

Reference by Name Only

In each field the writings of certain key individuals are so well known that any person familiar with the field will recognize a concept—or even a whole series of findings—just from a short *tag name*. Sometimes the tag names include the name of the original author or researcher, as in *Bernoulli's effect* or the *Michelson-Morley experiment;* at other times the name is more generalized, as in *the second law of thermodynamics.* The three examples just cited all have complete and precise meanings to trained physicists. Similarly *Turner's thesis* has a definite meaning to any historian, and *Grimm's law* is recognized by any linguist. Such tag names allow you to bring in a concept quickly without any pause in the forward motion of your ideas.

However, you must consider not only whether all your readers will recognize the reference but also whether they will understand it exactly the way you do and grasp the way you are applying it to the subject under discussion. Philosophers will recognize Plato's *allegory of the cave,* but they will probably disagree on its meaning. Turner presented his thesis concerning the role of the frontier in American history in several different versions. The reader could easily mistake which aspect of Turner's thought you have in mind and therefore misinterpret how that thought fits in with the point you are making. If the references used are even more indefinite, the potential for confusion increases. Just think of the grab bag of different meanings different readers attach to the term *constitutional guarantees of freedom* or to a reference to *President Reagan's foreign policy.* In short, you should rely on tag names only when their application is so limited and self-evident in the context of your argument that the reader will not mistake your meaning. If any possibility for confusion exists, you should use a more explicit means of reference.

Summary

As described fully in Chapter 4, a summary allows you to explain in a short space those aspects of the source material that are relevant to your argument. You can focus on the most important points pertaining to your discussion, letting the reader know how you understand the ideas you are referring to. You can also adapt the summary to fit into the continuity of your prose and the organization of your essay. The summary is particularly useful for establishing background information, for reviewing an established theory, and for reporting supporting data from other studies. In these situations the reader frequently does not need all the details of the original and is not likely to question your interpretation of the original.

However, in those situations that require a detailed examination of the source material or where you are presenting a controversial interpretation or critique of the original, you may need to give a more complete paraphrase—or even a direct quotation. Particularly if you are using the summary to introduce a source you will then attack, you must not make your task too easy by exaggerating the weaker parts of the original and leaving out the stronger points, the qualifications, and the explanations necessary for an accurate assessment. Such "straw man" tactics keep you from confronting the more basic points of dispute and lead readers to suspect the integrity of your argument.

Paraphrase

Detailed restatement of a passage in the form of a paraphrase lets you keep control of the style and continuity of the writing (see Chapter 1). Paraphrase allows you to move smoothly from your own points to the source material, preventing the disconcerting shifts of tone of voice that often result from excessive quotation. You can also keep the focus on your main argument through emphasis in the paraphrase. Paraphrase is indispensable when the original source never makes an explicit and complete statement of the relevant ideas in one place; you must then reconstruct the important material in a single coherent paraphrase. Two other kinds of special material, transcripts of spoken conversation and the condensed prose of reference books, usually must be paraphrased in order to be easily readable. Because of the importance of sustaining the logical order of your argument and keeping your own statement sharply in focus, you should generally prefer paraphrase to exact quotation for reporting sources in detail.

Quotation

Direct quotation is the most obvious and most abused form of referring to another writer's thoughts. It should be strictly reserved for those times when you will later analyze the exact words of the original text or when the meaning is so open to interpretation that any change of words might lead to distortion. Occasionally you may want the direct testimony of other writers if their phrasing is so precise and stirring that the rhetorical effect strengthens your own argument or if you need to recreate the mood of some historic confrontation. In any case, it is not enough just to quote and move on: you must work the quotation into the line of your argument. You need to underscore the relevance of the quotation to the point you are making and to indicate what the reader should understand from the quotation. You must therefore select the quotation carefully to make the point you wish to make—and no more. Keep the quotations short and relevant; always explicitly indicate their relevance. Unless you can give good reasons for reading the quotation, the reader may skip over it. The greatest danger of using quotations is that they may remain foreign, undigested lumps interrupting your ongoing argument.

Depending on the needs of your paper, you may want to use several methods of reference within a short space. For example, you may use a summary to introduce the context of a reference, followed by a paraphrase of the key points and a quotation of an important phrase you will analyze later. Such a mixture of reference methods occurs in the sample passage from Freud's *On the Interpretation of Dreams* on pages 99–100.

Whatever methods you use to refer to source materials, you should give an accurate representation of the original. Moreover, you should use the material in ways that are consistent with the original form, intent, and context. The greater the detail in which you present the source material, the less chance there is that you may—unintentionally or intentionally—distort, twist, or unfairly deride the material. Even direct quotation can turn a meaning around by leaving out an important context or a few key words. Reasons of intellectual honesty should keep you on guard against the possible unfair use of sources. More practically, if the reader knows the original and catches you distorting it, the penalty is steep: loss of the reader's trust in your judgment and honesty. In matters of communication, losing the reader's trust is losing the whole game.

Punctuating
References

When you refer to sources by name, summary, or paraphrase, you are using words and sentences that are your own and are therefore punctuated in the same style as the rest of your writing—except for the documentation of bibliographic information, discussed later in this chapter. You need to be careful, however, to make clear through the phrasing of your sentences exactly where the borrowed material begins and ends. It is necessary to distinguish your own thoughts and ideas from those you obtained from other sources.

Direct quotation, because it promises accurate reproduction of the words of the original source, presents special problems of punctuation. First, the other writer's words need to be set off from your own. Whenever you use the exact words of your source, even for just a short phrase, you must set off the quoted words. For short quotations—that is, quotations of five or fewer typed lines—this may be done through quotation marks, as I am now doing in quoting the theoretical physicist John Ziman, "A scientific laboratory without a library is like a decorticated cat: the motor activities continue to function, but lack coordination of memory and purpose."

For quotations within short quotations, the interior quotation should be marked with *single* quotation marks, as in the following example: "Toulmin shares Kuhn's view that there are periods in science when knowledge does not cumulate. He calls them 'recurrent periods of self doubt,' during which scientists tend to question whether science can explain anything."

Longer quotations need to be set off from the main body of your writing by triple-spacing, indenting ten spaces, and double-spacing the entire quoted passage. Triple-space before returning to your own words. This form of quotation is called a *block quotation*. When you set off the quoted material in this way, do *not* use quotation marks to begin or end the quotation, for they would be redundant. As an example, I will quote what the sociologist Robert Merton has to say about the use of reading in his field.

> No great mystery shrouds the affinity of sociologists for the works of their predecessors. There is a degree of immediacy about much of the sociological theory generated by the more recent members of this distinguished lineage, and current theory has a degree of resonance to many of the still unsolved problems identified by the earlier forerunners.
>
> However, interest in classical writings of the past has also given rise to intellectually degenerative tendencies in the history of thought. The first is an uncritical reverence toward almost any statement made by illustrious ancestors. This has often been expressed in the dedicated but, for science, largely sterile exegesis of the commentator. It is to this practice that Whitehead refers in the epigraph to this chapter: "A science which hesitates to forget its founders is lost."

The second degenerative form is banalization. For one way a truth can become a worn and increasingly dubious commonplace is simply by being frequently expressed, preferably in unconscious caricature, by those who do not understand it. (An example is the frequent assertion that Durkheim assigned a great place to coercion in social life by developing his conception of "constraint" as one attribute of social facts.) Banalization is an excellent device for drying up a truth by sponging upon it.

In short, the study of classical writings can be either deplorably useless or wonderfully useful. It all depends on the form that study takes. For a vast difference separates the anemic practices of mere commentary or banalization from the active practice of following up and developing the theoretical leads of significant predecessors. It is this difference that underlies the scientists' ambivalence toward extensive reading in past writings.

Notice that the beginnings of paragraphs within the quotation are doubly indented and that the quotation from Whitehead within the block quotation is set off by double quotation marks. For quotations within a quotation typed in block form, use single or double quotations—as in the original.

Because you are claiming to present the exact words of the original, you must clearly mark any additions, deletions, or other changes. The only unmarked change you may properly make is converting the opening letter of the quotation to a capital or a lowercase letter in order to fit the grammatical context of your introductory sentence. If you delete some words from the quotation because they are not relevant to your argument, you must indicate the deletion by an *ellipsis,* which is three dots (. . .). If the ellipsis begins at the end of a complete sentence, you must use a fourth dot—where it normally belongs—to indicate the end of the complete sentence. The material deleted from the following quotation by the anthropologist Jack Goody requires the use of both three-dot and four-dot ellipses:

> There are two main functions of writing. One is the storage function that permits communication over time and space, and provides man with a marking, mnemonic and recording device. . . . The second function of writing . . . shifts language from the aural to the visual domain, and makes possible a different kind of inspection, the reordering and refining not only of sentences, but of individual words.

In the original text this quotation was preceded by the phrase "We have seen that . . ." but because the deletion did not come in the middle of the quotation, it did not require an ellipsis. Further, since the remaining part of the sentence could stand independently as a grammatical sentence, the *t* of the first word, *there,* was capitalized. You may also have noticed that there was no double indentation for the paragraph beginning; double indenting is needed at the beginning of a quoted paragraph only when the quotation extends to a second paragraph.

You should avoid adding anything to the exact quotation. Your comments on the quoted material should be placed either before or after the quotation. However, you may occasionally have to add a word or two of explanation to clarify the meaning of the quotation, either because the quotation uses material clarified earlier in the original text or because you need to summarize deleted material to bridge two parts of the quotation. All added material must be put in square brackets—[interpolation]. If your typewriter does not have brackets, add them by hand. Do not use parentheses, because they may be confused with parentheses used by the original writer. The historian Elizabeth Eisenstein, for example, in discussing the chilling effect of censorship on scholarship, notes that on "hearing of Galileo's fate in 1633, he [Descartes] stopped working on his grand cosmological treatise and perhaps clipped the wings of his own imagination by this negative act."

If the quotation contains an error of spelling, grammar, or fact, you should not correct the error. Rather place the italicized or underlined word *sic* in square brackets directly after the error. The Latin word *sic* means *thus* and indicates that the original was phrased exactly thus, including the error. As one third-grader remarked, "We must all sometimes eat our missteaks [*sic*]."

On rare occasions you may wish to emphasize a word or phrase in a quotation by underlining or italicizing it. If you do, you must indicate that you—and not the original author—are assigning the emphasis, as in the following quotation from the political scientist Paul Boller: "Quotemanship—the utilization of quotations to prove a particular point—has in recent years become a highly *skilled* art [emphasis added.]"

Making the Most
of References

Beyond you yourself knowing why and how you are using a reference, the reader must understand what you want to show by the reference and what conclusions you have drawn from it. A reader may find material drawn from sources puzzling—or even interesting for the wrong reasons. Therefore, you must give the reader specific guidance as to the relevance of the material to your argument and the full set of implications for your thought. You need to introduce the reference—that is, to show how the material fits into the continuity of your essay—and then you need to follow the reference with interpretation, analysis, or other discussion.

The introduction to the reference serves as a transition between the ideas you were developing at this point and the material you are bringing in from the outside. You need to connect the material with your previous statements and then to indicate where the material comes from. Even though the details of the source may be fully stated in a footnote, the reader usually needs to be given at least a general idea of the source in the text in order to evaluate the material. So that the reader may properly understand the reference, you may also have to include some background information in the introduction.

Transitions are, of course, necessary throughout your writing, but they are unusually important before references because you are bringing in material foreign to your own statement. That external material, particularly if it is quoted in its original form, may seem quite distant from what you are saying unless you show the reader the point of connection. In fact, unless you make the justification for the material obvious to the reader, the material may appear so digressive that the reader will skim over it to get back to what seems to be the main line of the argument. Further, the inserted material may have a number of possible interpretations for your statement so that you must indicate which interpretation you want the reader to attend to.

Depending on the material and the function of the reference, the introduction may be short and direct, such as: "These findings concerning growth rates are confirmed by a similar experiment conducted by Jones." Or the introduction can be quite complex, incorporating much background, interpretation, and directiveness:

> This long-standing ambivalence Smith felt towards authority figures can be seen even in his letters as a teen-ager. The following passage from a letter to his father, written when Smith was only fourteen, shows his desire to be respectfully at odds about his father's opinions. Notice particularly how the polite phrases at the beginning of sentences almost seem ironic by the end when he starts to assert his own contrary opinion.

Here the introduction was lengthened by the necessity of indicating the exact feeling "at odds" and the particular features of the quoted material that indicate the conflict.

Once you have presented the reference, you should not leave the reader in the dark about the specific conclusions or inferences you want to draw from it. You must draw out the conclusions and relate them to the larger points of your essay. If you include a quotation to be interpreted or analyzed, you must carry out those tasks in full detail—and not simply rely on a few brief general comments. Similarly, if you cite a set of detailed data, you must let the reader know exactly what you have found in the mass of specifics. You have gone to the trouble of presenting quotations or data, so you should go to just a bit more trouble to wring all the meaning out of them that you can. Often you will find that, in the process of making your analysis or conclusions explicit for your reader, you yourself will become more precise about the consequences of the cited material. Only rarely will the meaning of the reference be so clear-cut and self-evident that no discussion is needed. What you may at first consider tedious belaboring of the obvious may turn out to be the kind of attention to detail that leads to interesting new thoughts.

The introduction and discussion of sources are the main means you have of showing how other writers' thoughts and information can be assimilated into your own argument. No matter how much you have thought through your reading, your references will appear only pedantic quote-dropping to your reader unless you tie them directly into your argument. Only through thoughtful transitions and discussions of the material can you maintain the continuity of your thoughts and keep everything under the control of your main argument. No matter how many sources you use, yours must be the controlling intelligence of the paper.

Documentation:
What and How

You must give full documentation—that is, specifically identify the source you are using—each time you directly refer to the work of another writer. You must also do so each time you use material—facts, statistics, charts, ideas, interpretations, theories, or the like—from another writer, even though you do not directly mention the writer's name. In other words, whenever someone else's work appears within your writing—whether undisguised through direct reference and quotation or submerged through paraphrase and summary into your own argument—you must give credit to the specific source, either in the form of in-text documentation or in notes.

You can decide for yourself whether to document those sources that you have not explicitly used in the final version of your essay. If certain ideas or information from other sources lie behind your own original ideas, you may want to identify such sources in a bibliographical discussion within a footnote. In the bibliography, you may mention all the books you have consulted, or only those that you found useful, of all those that other readers may find useful, or only those that you have actually cited in your essay. Choosing which kind of bibliography is appropriate to each piece of writing will be discussed later.

There are only two exceptions to these general rules: common knowledge and deep sources of your thinking. *Common knowledge* is the information that most people familiar with your subject would already know and that few experts would dispute. (For example, most people know—and few would dispute—that separation of powers is one of the principles behind the United States Constitution.) If a number of your sources mention the same fact or idea with little discussion and with no disagreement among them, you can generally assume that this fact or idea is part of common knowledge and therefore does not need documentation.

What you should consider common knowledge does depend, to some extent, on the particular audience. In addition to the general shared knowledge of our culture, each subgroup has its own shared common knowledge, which may be unknown to other groups. To students of English literature, for example, it is common knowledge that T. S. Eliot was partly responsible for the revival of metaphysical poetry in this century. But readers without a specialized interest in English literature might not even know what metaphysical poetry is, let alone whether it was revived by T. S. Eliot, whoever he might be. If you were writing as one expert to another, you would not need to document your claim about Eliot. But if you were writing as a nonexpert to other nonexperts, you would need to document the claim and to indicate what expert you are relying on.

The *deep sources* of your thinking are those ideas and information that you came in contact with long before you began work on the essay in question. Even though you did not have your current project in mind when you read those materials—perhaps many years ago—they may have influenced how you approached the current problem and how you interpreted the material that you did search out particularly for this project. However, such influences may be so far in the back of your memory that there is no way to identify which writers helped shape your thinking with respect to your current project.

At some point in your intellectual growth, you may find it interesting and enlightening to try to reconstruct your intellectual autobiography and to trace how your thoughts and interests grew in relation to the books that you read at various points in your life. Such self-searching may lead you to reread and rethink the sources of your ideas. But for most of your writing, you need not go back to these earlier sources; such a deep search may, in fact, distract you from the immediate task at hand. So it remains a matter of judgment whether or not to include any deep sources, even in cases where you know them. Include them only if they will increase the strength and clarity of your argument. Generally your direct responsibility is only to document those sources that you sought out and used for the current project.

By In-Text Mention

Every time you mention or quote a source—or any idea, fact, or piece of information from that source—you must indicate at that point in the text the documentation of the reference. The documentation includes author, title, and publication information for general references to a work. If the reference is to a specific fact, idea, or piece of information, you must also include the exact page on which the original item appears.

If the bibliographic information is concise and can be incorporated smoothly into the text of your writing, you may do so and thereby avoid excessive notes. In the following example of in-text documentation, the information fits naturally into the flow of the discussion.

> The publication in 1962 of Thomas Kuhn's challenging study *The Structure of Scientific Revolutions* (Chicago: University of Chicago Press) caused historians and philosophers of science to re-evaluate their ideas about how scientific knowledge advances. From the very first page of the book, Kuhn takes issue with the traditional view of scientific growth, which he claims derives from "the unhistorical stereotype drawn from science texts."

Parenthetical Systems

Many academic disciplines now document through a short reference in parentheses in the text linked to fuller information in a list of works cited or references at the end of the paper or chapter. A number of similar systems of parenthetical references currently exist. The most common system, used throughout the social sciences, is the *author-date system* recommended by the American Psychological Association (APA). In this APA style, each piece of information or quotation requiring documentation is immediately followed by the author's last name, the date of the publication, and (if necessary) the specific page reference. If the author and/or the date is clearly mentioned nearby in the text, such information should not be repeated in the parentheses. The reader can then easily find more complete bibliographical information in the references list. The APA format for the reference list is described on page 504. The following sample illustrates the APA system.

> Some studies have indicated that perceptual distortion is multi-causal (Jones, 1958; Smith and Smith, 1965; Brown, 1972). Green contested this, claiming "only a single cause stands behind all the perceptual distortion observed in earlier studies" (1979, p. 158). In 1983, however, Green reversed his opposition when he found some errors in his own laboratory procedures.

Also used are the *author-title system* (Kinney, "New Evidence on Hinckley's Theory," p. 357) and the numerical system (35, 357). In the numerical system, each item in the list of references is given a reference number. In the parentheses this reference number is underlined or italicized to distinguish it from the page reference that follows.

Recently the Modern Language Association (MLA) has also recommended the use of a parenthetical system, suggesting that the parenthetical reference contain only the minimum amount of information necessary to identify the item on the list of works cited (which should be prepared according to MLA bibliographical form, as detailed on pages 499–504). In many cases the author's name will suffice as a parenthetical reference, but that may need to be supplemented by a short version of the book's or article's title if several different items by the same author are referred to. If the source is adequately identified in the text itself, no parenthetical information is needed. Page references, however, should be supplied if appropriate, as in the following illustration of the MLA system.

The question of influence has been approached historically (Jones), but the psychological approach has recently been argued (Smith, *A New Approach*). Green has even suggested that influence is "entirely a matter of psychological projection" (137). But Smith, in his case study of Coleridge's influence on his friends (*Romantic Forces*), finds a wider range of psychological issues. Even though this study has been called "nonsense" (Edwards, 236), Smith has continued the argument in his latest book, *Coleridge, Once Again*.

By Notes

Although it recommends a parenthetical system, the Modern Language Association still recognizes the note form of documentation as *endnotes* gathered together at the end of the paper or chapter. Because many publishers, scholars, and teachers still rely on the note system, we will now explain it in greater detail, following the style suggested by the MLA. Sample student papers in this book follow either the MLA note style or the MLA format for parenthetical examples. Other published examples follow the documentation style of their own disciplines. For example, the article on pages 410–414 follows the style of the American Psychological Association. Other commonly used style manuals are prepared by the American Chemical Society, the American Institute of Physics, the American Mathematical Association, and the Council of Biology Editors. Because so many styles of documentation are available, you should inquire which system your teacher or the journals in your discipline prefer. Often, on the page describing submission procedures, journals include a short statement on their documentation style. Whichever system you choose, you should be consistent and use it throughout the piece of writing.

Note Numbers   Notes should be numbered consecutively and should correspond to numbers in the main text of the paper or chapter. The numbers in the main text should be placed consecutively at the places requiring documentation, starting at the beginning of the article. There should be no repetition of numbers and no numbers out of sequence. Repeated use of a single source at several places in the text requires a new note number at each place. The reference number in the main text should be placed *after* the material to be documented, usually after a final period or the closing quotation mark, and typed slightly above the line.

Stephen Toulmin observes that the difference between thoughts and concepts is the difference between the personal and publicly shared.[7]

Stephen Toulmin discusses the distinction between thoughts and concepts: ''Each of us thinks his own thoughts; our concepts we share with our fellow-men. For what we believe we are answerable as individuals; but the language in which our beliefs are articulated is public property.''[8] We may consider such a distinction . . .

If several references occur within a single sentence, you may combine the citations into a single footnote and put the single reference number at the end of the sentence. If the combined footnote will lead to confusion about who should receive credit for which ideas, place the reference number at the end of an appropriate phrase— just after the mark of punctuation. The reference numbers in the next example separate source material from the new commentary added by the writer of the paper.

Toulmin's distinction between private thoughts and public concepts necessarily articulated in the common language[9] on the surface appears to be consistent with Popper's view that sciences strive toward ''objective knowledge,''[10] but public language does not guarantee objectivity.

Note Format   The documentation in notes should contain four kinds of information: author, title, publication information, and specific page reference, where applicable. For books, publication information consists of city of publication (and abbreviation of state if the city is not well known), publisher, and year of publication. For articles in periodicals, publication information includes the name of the periodical, its volume number, and the date of the periodical. This book follows the style prescribed by the Modern Language Association in the *MLA Handbook* for both notes and bibliography. In most other note styles, the order and content of the information in the note is similar; variations are primarily in preferred punctuation.

Basic Note Punctuation

For a Book

- First line indented
- Reference number elevated slightly
- Comma between author and title
- Publication information in parentheses
- Last number is page reference
- Period at end

   [1]Jane Author, <u>Any Old Title</u> (Metropolis: Metropolis Univ. Press, 1980) 17.

For an Article in an Anthology

- Article title in quotation marks
- Book title underlined
- Editor after book title (ed. abbreviated)

   [2]Jane Author, ''The Articulate Article.'' <u>The Scholarly Collection</u>, ed. Joseph Editor (Metropolis, Metropolis Univ. Press, 1980) 17.

For an Article in a Periodical

- Article title in quotation marks
- Periodical title underlined
- Volume number included
- Date of issue in parentheses
- Colon before pages

   [3]Jane Author, ''This Month's Title,'' <u>Metropolis Monthly</u> 35 (June 1980): 17.

Modifications of Basic Form

Depending on the bibliographic information of your sources, you may have to modify the basic models in the following ways:

Author

If no author is given, begin directly with title.

If two authors: *Jane Author and John Writer,*

If three authors: *Jane Author, Joan Scribbler, and John Writer,*

If four or more authors: *Jane Author et al.,*

Multivolume set

If part of a multivolume set, include the volume number after the book title. Also list the set title if different from the volume title.

Author, *My Childhood,* vol. I of *My Life* (publication information) 73.

Edition

If other than the first edition, list edition number or edition name after the title and set information.

Author, title, *2nd ed.* (publication information) 4.

Translator and/or editor

List after edition information.

Author, title, edition, *trans. Jane Jones, ed. John Jones* (publication information) 2–6.

Series

If book or set is part of a series, list series title, editor, and number of this volume in the series after all the above additions, but just before the publication information.

Author, title, edition, translator, editor, *American Biographical Classics* 37 (publication information), pages.

Date of Publication

This is the date of the first edition unless another edition is specified. Reprint date should be placed after the primary date.

Author, title (*1957;* City, state if city unfamiliar: Publisher, *1976*), pages.

Type of Periodical

For popular magazines and newspapers, delete the volume number and set off the date of issue in commas instead of parentheses. For scholarly journals with continuous pagination throughout the volume, delete the date and give only the year.

Author, "Title of Article," *Time 17 June 1968:* pages.
Author, "Title of Article," *Renaissance Quarterly* 33 (*1979*): pages.

Book Review

If an article is a book review, directly after the title place *rev. of* followed by title of book and author. If the article has no title, simply use *rev. of.*

Author, "Title of Article," *rev. of Disaster, by S. Smith,* periodical information: pages.

Specific samples of book and periodical notes appear at the end of this chapter.

Second and Later Mentions

You need to give the complete bibliographical information only the first time you cite a work. In later citations you need only indicate in short form which document you are citing and the specific page reference. Usually you can indicate the document by using only the last name of the author.

[6]Toulmin 39.

If you cite two authors with the same last name, you should distinguish them by first initial as well.

[7]R. Cole 456.
[8]S. Cole 123.

Similarly, if you cite more than one work by the same author, you should add a shortened form of the appropriate title in second and later references.

[9]Kuhn, <u>Structure</u> 24.
[10]Kuhn, <u>Tension</u> 143.

Generalized Documentation— Bibliographies

Bibliographies are lists of sources related to the subject of your writing. However, in a bibliography you do not indicate the specific information you have used or the location of that information in the sources. Thus a bibliography serves only as a general listing of the sources that you have used or that your readers may wish to use.

Because bibliographies can vary in completeness and selectivity, it is better to label the bibliography in your paper with one of the more specific names presented below than to use the loose overall term *bibliography*.

The two most common types of bibliographies indicate the sources you actually used in preparing your paper. A *Works Consulted* bibliography lists all the materials you looked at in the course of your research on the subject, although you usually omit the titles that turned out to be irrelevant to your subject. A *Works Cited* or *References* bibliography presents only those sources you actually refer to in the course of your paper. Both the *Works Consulted* and the *Works Cited* bibliographies demonstrate the quality of your research and the bases of your own work. They also allow readers to search out any of your references that seem of potential use for their purposes. These two kinds of bibliographies are those that are usually attached to formal essays.

Bibliography for the Reader

The other kinds of bibliographies are directed more toward reader use. In the *Complete Bibliography* you list all works on the subject— even if you did not consult them for the present project and even if you have never seen the publications. The preparation of such a complete listing requires such an exhaustive and extensive search for materials that it is frequently a project in itself. The primary purpose of compiling a *Complete Bibliography* is to help future scholars on the subject quickly discover the materials relevant to their new projects. Thus a *Complete Bibliography* must meet high standards for completeness and reliability.

The kind of bibliography usually titled *For Further Reading* is directed more toward the nonscholarly reader who would like to know more about the subject but who does not intend to go into the subject as deeply as the writer. This list of books is therefore usually short and selective, presenting those books that expand topics raised in the preceding work but that are not too technical for the general reader.

If you feel that a few comments on each source listed might make either the *Complete Bibliography* or the *For Further Reading* list more useful to the reader, you can turn either into an *Annotated Bibliography*. In your annotations you may comment on the content, quality, special features, viewpoints, or potential uses of each source. The annotations should come right after the formal bibliographic listing of each book, and your comments may range from a few fragmentary phrases to a full paragraph. The following examples of annotated entries are from the bibliography at the end of H. C. Baldry, *The Greek Tragic Theatre* (New York: Norton, 1971).

> R. C. Flickinger, *The Greek Theater and Its Drama* (Chicago University Press, 1918; 4th edition 1936, reprinted 1965). Greek Drama explained through its environment. Detailed discussion of technical problems.
>
> A. E. Haigh, *The Attic Theatre* (Oxford University Press, 1889; 3rd edition revised by A. W. Pickard-Cambridge, 1907; New York, Haskell House, 1968). Still useful in part, but out of date on many aspects.
>
> A. W. Pickard-Cambridge, *The Theatre of Dionysus in Athens* (London & New York, Oxford University Press, 1946). The standard work, fully documented and illustrated, on the history of this theatre down to the Roman Empire.

If you wish to discuss relationships between works or problems that arise in a number of sources, you may want to write a *Bibliographic Essay* instead of simply presenting a list. The bibliographic essay is closely related to the *review of the literature* discussed on pages 293–295, except that the bibliographic essay is done after the project is completed rather than in the early stages. As such, it should focus either on the usefulness of particular sources for your project or on the potential usefulness of the sources for future readers—either scholarly or nonprofessional.

Bibliography Format

Bibliographies are basically organized as alphabetized lists by the last name of the author (or the first word of the title for anonymous works). For the sake of clarity and usefulness, the bibliography sometimes can be broken up into several titled categories—with the items still alphabetized within each category. For example, the works by an author who is the main subject of the study may be separated from critical and biographical works about the author. Or extensive archival sources may be listed separately from more conventional print sources. The bibliographic essay is, of course, organized around the topics discussed and is the only exception to the general rule of alphabetical listing.

Each bibliographic entry contains three kinds of information: author, title, and publication information. Thus it contains the same information as the footnote or endnote, except that the bibliographic entry does not have the final item of specific page location. The main differences between bibliographic entries and footnotes are in the order of the author's name and the consequent changes in punctuation. Because bibliographies are alphabetized, the author's last name must be put first; a comma follows the last name to show that the order is reversed. Because the comma is required for that function, *periods* must be used between the major divisions of information.

Basic Bibliography Punctuation

For a Book

- First line flush with left margin; second and following lines indented
- Author's last name first, followed by comma and first name
- Book title underlined
- Periods between major parts and at end

```
Author, Jane. Any Old Title. Metropolis: Metropolis
        Univ. Press, 1980.
```

For an Article in an Anthology

- Article title in quotation marks; book title underlined
- Editor after book title, name in normal order
- Inclusive pagination of article at end

```
Author, Jane, ''The Articulate Article.'' The Scholarly
     Collection. Ed. Joseph Editor. Metropolis: Metrop-
     olis Univ. Press, 1980, 12-26.
```

For an Article in a Periodical

- Article title in quotation marks; periodical title underlined
- Date of issue in parentheses
- Inclusive pagination of article at end

```
Author, Jane. ''This Month's Title.'' Metropolis Monthly
     35 (June 1980): 12-26.
```

Modifications of Basic Form

Depending on the bibliographic information of your sources, you may have to modify the basic models in the following ways:

Author

If no author is given, begin directly with title.

If two authors: *Author, Jane, and John Writer.*

If three authors: *Author, Jane, Joan Scribbler, and John Writer.*

If four or more authors: *Author, Jane, et al.*

Multivolume set

If multivolume set, use title of entire set for main entry, followed by number of volumes; use inclusive dates for main publication date. List separate volume titles and dates at end of entry.

Author. *My Life. 3 vols.* City: Publisher, *1962–1968.*

If you are referring to only one volume of a multivolume set that uses a separate title for each volume, give the title of the single volume, followed by the volume number and title of the multivolume work. Give the publication date of the separate volume.

Author. *My Childhood.* Vol. 1 of *My Life.* 3 vols. City: Publisher, 1962.

Edition

If other than the first edition, list edition number or name after the main title.

Author. Title. *2nd ed.* Publication information.

Translator and/or editor

List after edition information.

Author. Title. Edition. *Trans. Jane Jones. Ed. John Jones.* Publication information.

Series

List series title, and number of this volume in this series just before the publication information.

Author. Title. Edition. Translator. Editor. *American Biographical Classics 37.* Publication information.

Date of Publication

This is the first edition date unless another edition is specified. Reprint date (such as for a paperback edition) should follow the primary date.

Author. Title. *1957.* City: Publisher, *1976.*

Samples of Modern
Language Association
Documentation

Book, Single Author

note   [1]Bruno Bettelheim, *The Uses of Enchantment* (New York: Knopf, 1976) 285.

bib.   Bettelheim, Bruno. *The Uses of Enchantment.* New York: Knopf, 1976.

Book, Two Authors, Translator, Part of Series

note   [2]Carl G. Jung and Carl Kerenyi, *Essays on a Science of Mythology,* trans. R. F. C. Hull, Bollingen Series 22 (Princeton: Princeton Univ. Press, 1963) 126.

bib.   Jung, Carl G., and Carl Kerenyi, *Essays on a Science of Mythology.* Trans. R. F. C. Hull. Bollingen Series No. 22. Princeton: Princeton Univ. Press, 1963.

Book, Group Authorship, Translator

note   [3]Zuni People, *The Zunis: Self-Portrayals,* trans. Alvina Quam (New York: New American Library, 1974) 83.

bib.   Zuni People. *The Zunis: Self-Portrayals.* Trans. Alvina Quam. New York: New American Library, 1974.

bib.   Kirkwood, G. M. *A Short Guide to Classical Mythology.* New York: Holt, Rinehart and Winston, 1959.

Article in an Anthology

note   [10]Stanley Edgar Hyman, "The Ritual View of Myth and the Mythic," *Myth: A Symposium,* ed. Thomas Sebeok (Bloomington: Indiana Univ. Press, 1955) 143.

bib.   Hyman, Stanley Edgar. "The Ritual View of Myth and the Mythic." *Myth: A Symposium.* Ed. Thomas Sebeok. Bloomington: Indiana Univ. Press, 1955. 136–153.

Article in an Encyclopedia

note   [11]Andrew Lang, "Mythology," *Encyclopaedia Britannica,* 1911 ed.

bib.   Lang, Andrew. "Mythology." *Encyclopaedia Britannica.* 1911 ed.

Article in a Scholarly Journal

note   [12]Dale F. Eickelman, "Form and Composition in Islamic Myths: Four Texts from Western Morocco," *Anthropos* 72 (1977): 452.

bib.   Eickelman, Dale F. "Form and Composition in Islamic Myths: Four Texts from Western Morocco." *Anthropos* 72 (1977): 447–464.

Article in Popular Magazine

note   [13]Daniel Goleman, "Greek Myths in Pop Fiction: Jason and Medea's Love Story," *Psychology Today* April 1976: 84.

bib.   Goleman, Daniel. "Greek Myths in Pop Fiction: Jason and Medea's Love Story." *Psychology Today* April 1976: 84–86.

Article in Newspaper (unsigned)

note   [14]"Origins of Walt Disney Cartoon Character Mickey Mouse in Mythology Noted," *New York Times* 3 December 1977: 23.

bib.   "Origins of Walt Disney Cartoon Character Mickey Mouse in Mythology Noted." *New York Times* 3 December 1977: 23.

Book, Anonymous Author, Joint Editors and Translators

note   [4]*The Mwindo Epic,* trans. and ed. Daniel Biebuyck and Kahombo C. Mateene (Berkeley: Univ. of California Press, 1969) 59.

bib.   *The Mwindo Epic.* Trans. and ed. Daniel Biebuyck and Kahombo C. Mateene. Berkeley: Univ. of California Press, 1969.

Multivolume Work (separate titles for each volume, partly revised)

note   [5]Joseph Campbell, *Primitive Mythology,* vol. I of *The Masks of God,* rev. ed. (New York: Penguin, 1969) 216.

bib.   Campbell, Joseph. *The Masks of God.* 4 vols. New York: Penguin, 1962–1969.

Multivolume Work (only one title)

note   [6]Theodore H. Gaster, *Myth, Legend, and Custom in the Old Testament* (New York: Harper & Row, 1969) II: 811.

bib.   Gaster, Theodore H. *Myth, Legend, and Custom in the Old Testament.* 2 vols. New York: Harper & Row, 1969.

The Bible and Other Sacred Scriptures

Cite chapter and verse instead of page location; indicate edition.

note   [7]Proverbs 3: 13–15 (King James Edition).
bib.   The Bible. King James Edition.

Unpublished Dissertation

note   [8]Herbert Paine Edmondsen, Jr., "Aspects of the Prometheus Myth in Ancient Greek Literature and Art," diss., University of Texas at Austin, 1977, 135.
bib.   Edmondsen, Herbert Paine, Jr. "Aspects of the Prometheus Myth in Ancient Greek Literature and Art," diss., University of Texas at Austin, 1977.

Pamphlet

note   [9]G. M. Kirkwood, *A Short Guide to Classicial Mythology* (New York: Holt, Rinehart and Winston, 1959) 27.

Review in Magazine (unsigned, untitled)

note   [15]Rev. of *Zalmaxis, The Living God* by Mircea Eliade, *Choice* 10 (June 1973): 604.
bib.   Rev. of *Zalmaxis, The Living God* by Mircea Eliade. *Choice* 10 (June 1973): 604.

Congressional Record

note   [16]*Cong. Rec.* 15 March 1980: 3751.
bib.   *Cong. Rec.* 15 March 1980: 3751.

Court Cases

note   [17]Clagett v. Daly, 87 S. Ct. 311 (U.S. Supreme Ct. 1966).
bib.   Clagett v. Daly. 87 S. Ct. 311. U.S. Supreme Ct. 1966. (87 *S. Ct. 311* refers to the volume, name, and page of the journal reporting the decision.)

Interview

note   [18]Romila Thapar, personal interview, 9 June 1977.
bib.   Thapar, Romila. Personal interview. 9 June 1977.

Film

note   [19]Henrik Galeen and Paul Wegener, dir., *The Golem,* Germany, 1920.

bib.   Galeen, Henrik, and Paul Wegener, dir. *The Golem*. Germany, 1920.

Radio or Television Program

note   [20]"On the Road in Oscaloosa," narr. Charles Kuralt, CBS Evening News, 28 January 1980.

bib.   "On the Road in Oscaloosa." Narr. Charles Kuralt. CBS Evening News. 28 January 1980.

Recording

note   [21]Alfonso Cruz Jimenez, *Folk Songs of Mexico,* Folkways Record FW 8727, 1959.

bib.   Jimenez, Alfonso Cruz. *Folk Songs of Mexico*. Folkways Record FW 8727, 1959.

American Psychological Association Bibliographic Form

As discussed on page 489, the American Psychological Association recommends linking in-text parenthetical documentation to a complete reference list at the end of the paper or chapter. Following are the basics of the recommended style for that reference list. For more complete details, see the *Publication Manual of the American Psychological Association,* third edition (Washington, D.C.: American Psychological Association, 1983).

For a Book

- First line flush with left margin; second and following lines indented
- Author's last name first, followed by a comma and initials (no full name)
- Date of publication in parentheses, following author's name

- Book title underlined, only the first word capitalized (except for proper nouns)
- Colon between place of publication and publisher
- Periods to separate major divisions and at end

```
Author, J. (1985). Any old title. Metropolis: Metropolis
     University Press.
```

For an Article in a Periodical

- Year in parentheses follows author's name.
- No quotation marks for article title, only first word capitalized.
- Journal title underlined, followed by volume number and inclusive pages separated by commas
- Volume number underlined

```
Author, J. (1985). This month's title. Metropolis
     monthly, 35, 12-26.
```

Sample Reference List

- References are alphabetized by first author's last name.

REFERENCES

```
Gerwin, D. (1974). Information processing, data infer-
     ences, and scientific generalization. Behavioral
     sciences, 19, 314-325.
Greeno, J. G. (1976). Indefinite goals in well-struc-
     tured problems. Psychological review, 83, 479-491.
Klahr, D. & Siegler, R. S. (1977). The representation of
     children's knowledge. In Reese, H. & Lipsitt, L. P.
     (Eds.), Advances in child development (Vol. 12).
     New York: Academic Press.
Newell A., & Simon, H. A. (1972). Human problem solving.
     Englewood Cliffs, N.J.: Prentice Hall.
Polanyi, Michael. (1967). The tacit dimension. Garden
     City, N.Y.: Anchor Books.
```

Exercises

1. For a research paper you have written or are currently working on, list the sources you refer to in the course of the paper. Explain (1) why you have included each reference, (2) what you hope to accomplish by the reference, (3) whether you have presented the reference through quotation, paraphrase, summary, or name only, and (4) why you have chosen each method listed in (3).

2. In the following excerpts from *A Study of Writing* by I. J. Gelb, identify where each reference is made to source material and the method used to present the reference. Then discuss the reason for each reference and the appropriateness of the reference method used.

   a. Simple ways of communicating feeling by the sense of touch are, for instance, the handclasp, the backslap, the lovestroke. A fully developed system of communication by handstroking is used among blind deaf-mutes, for which the best-known example is provided by the case of Helen Keller, the American writer and educator.

   b. Objects are used as memory aids for recording proverbs and songs among the Ewe Negroes in a form quite similar to that which they achieved by means of written symbols. Carl Meinhof relates that a missionary found in a native hut a cord on which were strung many objects, such as a feather, a stone, etc. In answer to his query as to the meaning of the string with the objects the missionary was told that each piece was supposed to stand for a certain proverb. Another custom is related by Mary H. Kingsley from West Africa about native singers who carry around in a net all kinds of objects, such as pipes, feathers, skins, birdheads, bones, etc., each of which serves the purpose of recalling a certain song. The songs are recited with pantomimes. Persons in the audience choose a certain object and before the recital they bargain about the price to be paid to the singer. In a way, the net of the singer can be considered the repertoire of his songs.

   c. A modern illustration of the use of objects for the purpose of communication is contained in the story from the Hungarian writer Jókai, according to which a man sent a package of coffee to another man to warn him about danger from police. The story can be understood on the basis of the phonetic principle by noting that the Hungarian word for coffee is *kávé* and that it resembles in sound the Latin word *cave*, "beware!"

   A most interesting usage from the comparative point of view

is reported from the same Yoruba country, where the cowrie mussels are used so frequently for communicating messages. During an attack of a king of Dahomey upon a city of the Yoruba one of the natives was taken captive and, anxious to inform his wife of his plight, sent her a stone, coal, pepper, corn, and a rag, conveying the following message: the stone indicated "health," meaning "as the stone is hard, so my body is hardy, strong"; the coal indicated "gloom," meaning "as the coal is black, so are my prospects dark and gloomy"; the pepper indicated "heat," meaning "as the pepper is hot, so is my mind heated, burning on account of the gloomy prospect"; the corn indicated "leanness," meaning "as the corn is dried up by parching, so my body is dried and become lean through the heat of my affliction and suffering"; and finally, the rag indicated "worn out," meaning "as the rag is, so is my cloth cover worn and torn to a rag." An exact parallel to this usage is reported in the fourth book, section 131 ff., of Herodotus, "The Scythian kings sent a herald bringing Darius the gift of a bird, a mouse, a frog, and five arrows. The Persians asked the bringer of these gifts what they might mean; but he said that no charge had been laid on him save to give the gifts and then depart with all speed; let the Persians (he said), if they were clever enough, discover the signification of the presents. The Persians hearing and taking counsel, Darius' judgment was that the Scythians were surrendering to him themselves and their earth and their water; for he reasoned that a mouse is a creature found in the earth and eating the same produce as men, and a frog is a creature of the water, and a bird most like to a horse; and the arrows (said he) signified that the Scythians surrendered their weapon of battle. This was the opinion declared by Darius; but the opinion of Gobryas, one of the seven who had slain the Magian, was contrary to it. He reasoned that the meaning of the gifts was: 'Unless you become birds, Persians, and fly up into the sky, or mice and hide you in the earth, or frogs and leap into the lakes, you will be shot by these arrows and never return home.' Thus the Persians reasoned concerning the gifts." Those modern cultural historians who may object to some of my reconstructions based on comparisons between ancient peoples and modern primitive societies cannot easily overlook the weight of such parallel usages from ancient and modern times.

3. In the library, find a scholarly journal from an academic or professional field that interests you. Describe in detail the documentation system and the format of notes and bibliography used in the journal. You may find a statement of documentation policy in the first few pages of each issue.

4. Using the MLA format presented in this book, write both note and bibliography entries for each of the following items. Also write reference list entries following the APA style.

a. A quotation from page 137 from an article in the December 1979 issue of *Scientific American,* volume 241. The article is by David Regan and is entitled "Electrical Responses Evoked from the Human Brain." The article extends from page 134 to page 146.

b. A summary from pages 10 and 11 of *Madame Bovary* by Gustave Flaubert in the translation by Francis Steegmuller, published in 1957 by Random House in New York City.

c. A paraphrase of an idea on page 123 of an article "Notes on a Conversational Practice: Formulating Place" by E. A. Schegloff. The article appears on pages 95 through 135 of *Language and Social Context,* an anthology first published in 1972 and reprinted in 1977, both times by Penguin Books of London. The editor of the anthology is Pier Paolo Giglioli.

d. A quotation from a book review of the novel *Darkness Visible* by William Golding. The review appears on page 108 of the November 5, 1979, issue of *Newsweek,* is entitled "The Inferno— Here and Now," and is by Peter S. Prescott.

Index

Chapter 3: Bertrand Russell. Copyright © 1950 by Bertrand Russell. Reprinted by permission of Simon and Schuster, Inc.   From "On Cloning a Human Being" from *The Medusa and the Snail* by Lewis Thomas. Copyright © 1974 by Lewis Thomas. Originally published in the New England Journal of Medicine. Reprinted by permission of Viking Penguin Inc.   Alexis de Tocqueville *Democracy in America,* ed. Andrew Hacker (New York: Washington Square Press, 1964), 182–83.   Selection (pp. 70–71 from *The Life Science: Current Ideas of Biology* by J. B. Medawar and J. S. Medawar. Copyright © 1977 by Peter and Jean Medawar.   From "The Declaration of Independence in American" copyright 1921 by Alfred A. Knopf, Inc. and renewed 1949 by H. L. Mencken. Reprinted from *A Mencken Chrestomathy* by H. L. Mencken, by permission of Alfred A. Knopf, Inc.   E. M. Forster, excerpt from "Culture and Freedom" in *Two Cheers for Democracy* copyright 1951 by E. M. Forster; renewed 1979 by Donald Parry. Reprinted by permission of Harcourt Brace Jovanovich, Inc. and by Edward Arnold (Publishers) Ltd., London.   Salvador E. Luria, excerpted from *Life: The Unfinished Experiment.* Copyright © 1973 Salvador E. Luria. Reprinted with the permission of Charles Scribner's Sons.

Chapter 4: Lawrence Lichty, from *The Wilson Quarterly,* Special Issue 1982. Copyright 1982 by the Woodrow Wilson International Center for Scholars.   Mort Rosenblum, specified selection (pages 93–97) from *Coups and Earthquakes: Reporting the World for America* by Mort Rosenblum. Copyright © 1979 by Mort Rosenblum.   Daniel Boorstin excerpted from *The Image: A Guide to Pseudo-Events in America.* Copyright © 1961 by Daniel J. Boorstin. (Originally published under the title "The Image or What Happened to the American Dream"). Reprinted with the permission of Atheneum Publishers.   Michael Schudson, "The Politics of Narrative Form," reprinted by permission of *Daedalus,* Journal of the American Academy of Arts and Sciences, Fall 1982, Cambridge, MA.   From *The Interpretation of Dreams* by Sigmund Freud, translated from the German and edited by James Strachey, 294–295. Published in the United States by Basic Books, Inc., Publishers, New York, by arrangement with George Allen & Unwin, Ltd, and the Hogarth Press, London. Published elsewhere by George Allen & Unwin, Ltd.   From Donald D. Trunkey, "Trauma." Copyright © 1983 by Scientific American, Inc. All rights reserved.   Ernest L. Hartmann, from *The Functions of Sleep.* Copyright © 1973 by the Yale University Press. Reprinted with permission.

Chapter 5: Excerpt from "As I Please" in *The Collected Essays, Journalism, and Letters of George Orwell,* Volume 3. Copyright © 1968 by Sonia Brownell Orwell. Reprinted by permission of Harcourt Brace Jovanovich, Inc. and the estate of the late Sonia Brownell Orwell and Martin Secker & Warburg Ltd.   Dale Carnegie, "Do This and You'll Be Welcome Anywhere" copyright © 1936 by Dale Carnegie; renewed 1964 by Donna Dale Carnegie and Dorothy Carnegie.   "Second Class Citizens" reprinted from *Psychology Today* magazine copyright © 1983 American Psychological Association.   From George Washington Plunkitt, *Plunkitt of Tammany Hall* (New York: Dutton, 1963).   Selection reprinted from *The Interpersonal Theory of Psychiatry* by Harry Stack Sullivan, M.D., by permission of W. W. Norton & Company Inc. Copyright 1953 by William Alanson White Psychiatric Foundation. Copyright renewed 1981 by William Alanson White Psychiatric Foundation. Kate Moody, copyright © 1980 by Times Books. Reprinted by permission of Times Books/The New York Times Book Co., Inc.   From *Growing Up on Television* by Kate Moody.

Chapter 6: Senator Joseph McCarthy, as quoted in *Congressional Record* 6 July 1950, p. 9715.   Ludwig Wittgenstein, preface to *Philosophical Investigations.* Used with permission of Basil Blackwell Limited, Oxford, and the author's literary executors.   From Jerome Beatty, Jr. *Our 100th Anniversary 1875–1975.* Copyright © 1975 R. J. Reynolds Industries, used by permission.   From Maurice Corina, *Trust in Tobacco: The Anglo-American Struggle for Power,* pp. 144–145. Copyright © 1975 by St. Martin's Press, Inc. Used by permission.   From *Cigarette Country* by Susan

Wagner. Copyright © 1971 by Praeger Publishers Inc. Reprinted by permission of Holt, Rinehart, and Winston, Publishers. From Charles Kellog Mann, *Tobacco: The Ants and the Elephants,* p. 30. Copyright © 1975 by Olympus Publishing Co.

Chapter 7: Two reviews from *Popular Mechanics,* June 1978, p. 62. Copyright © 1978 by the Hearst Corporation. Used by permission. From *Aroused by Books* by Anatole Broyard. Copyright © 1974 by Anatole Broyard. Reprinted by permission of Random House, Inc. Jean S. Kennedy, rev. of *The Complete Book of Bulbs,* by F. F. Rockwell and Ester Grayson. *Horticulture* LVI, no. 6 (1978), p. 14. Copyright © by Jean S. Kennedy. Used by permission. James Lewis, rev. of *Hazardous Waste in America* and *The Amicus Journal* Winter 1983. Used with permission. David Leary, rev. of *Human Nature in American Thought* from *Isis* 74, no. 271, March 1983. Used with permission. From *Kirkus Reviews,* 1 January 1980, p. 41. Copyright © 1980 by Kirkus Service, Inc. Used by permission. Rev. of *Trading with the Enemy* reprinted by permission of the American Library Association from *Choice* 20(9): 1338 (May 1983); copyright © 1983 by the American Library Association. Page 195.

Chapter 9: From Reynold M. Wik, *Henry Ford and Grass Roots America,* 165–167. Copyright © 1972 by The University of Michigan Press. Used by permission. From *Henry Ford,* by Roger Burlingame. Copyright 1954 by Roger Burlingame. Reprinted by permission of Alfred A. Knopf, Inc. From *The Legend of Henry Ford* by Keith Sward. Copyright 1948 © 1976 by Keith Sward. Reprinted by permission of Holt, Rinehart, and Winston, Publishers.

Chapter 10: Computer printout courtesy National Newspaper Index.

Chapter 12: Pat Washburn, "New York Newspapers and Robinson's First Season," from *Journalism Quarterly* 58, 1981, pp. 640–644. Used by permission. Charles Bazerman, "Time in Play and Film" from *Literature/Film Quarterly* V, 1977, pp. 333–338. Used by permission.

Chapter 13: Glenn Petersen, "Ritually Changing the Seasons" used by permission of the author. Virginia Brooks, "Sex Differences in Student Dominance Behavior in Female and Male Professors' Classrooms," from *Sex Roles,* Vol. 8, No. 7, 1982, 683–690. Used with permission. From Erving Goffman, *Relations in Public,* pp. 9–13. Copyright © 1971 by Erving Goffman, Basic Books, Inc. Publishers, New York.

Chapter 14: "The Bimodal Perception of Speech in Infancy," by P. K. Kuhl and A. N. Meltzoff, from *Science* Vol. 210, pp. 1138–1141, 10 December 1982. Used with permission. "Time Urgency Among Coronary Prone Individuals" © 1982 by the American Psychological Association. From *Journal of Abnormal Psychology* 91:3. Reprinted by permission of the publisher and author.

Chapter 15: "Some Perplexities about Time" by R. Collingwood. Reprinted courtesy of the Aristotelian Society, London.

Chapter 16: From pp. 43–44 in *Henry James — The Treacherous Years: 1895–1901* by Leon Edel (J.B. Lippincott). Copyright © 1969 by Leon Edel. Reprinted by permission of Harper & Row, Publishers, Inc.

Chapter 17: From I. J. Gelb, *A Study of Writing,* pp. 3–6. Copyright 1952 by the University of Chicago Press. All rights reserved. Used by permission.